OXFORD STREET, ACCRA

OXFORD STREET, ACCRA

City Life and the Itineraries of Transnationalism

Ato Quayson Duke University Press Durham and London 2014

Designed by Amy Ruth Buchanan
Typeset in Quadraat by
Westchester Book Group

Library of Congress Cataloging-
in-Publication Data
Quayson, Ato.
Oxford Street, Accra : city life and the
itineraries of transnationalism / Ato Quayson.
pages cm
Includes bibliographical references and index.
ISBN 978-0-8223-5733-9 (cloth : alk. paper)
ISBN 978-0-8223-5747-6 (pbk. : alk. paper)
1. Oxford Street (Accra, Ghana)
2. Accra (Ghana)—History. I. Title.
DT512.9.A3Q39 2014
966.7—dc23
2014000767

Cover art: Thomas Cockrem / Alamy

For Rosina Ayeafer—
mother, trader, storyteller (?–2006)

and Keshav, Kamau, and Kairav—
for playing with my head

CONTENTS

PREFACE ix

INTRODUCTION Urban Theory and Performative
Streetscapes 1

PART I *Horizontal Archaeologies*

1. Ga Akutso Formation and the Question of Hybridity:
    The Afro-Brazilians (Tabon) of Accra 37

2. The Spatial Fix: Colonial Administration, Disaster
    Management, and Land-Use Distribution in Early
    Twentieth-Century Accra 64

3. *Osu borla no, sardine chensii soo:* Danes, Euro-Africans,
    and the Transculturation of Osu 98

PART II *Morphologies of Everyday Life*

4. "The Beautyful Ones": Tro-tro Slogans, Cell Phone
    Advertising, and the Hallelujah Chorus 129

5. "Este loco, loco": Transnationalism and the Shaping
    of Accra's Salsa Scene 159

6. Pumping Irony: Gymming, the Kòbòlò, and the
    Cultural Economy of Free Time 183

7. The Lettered City: Literary Representations of Accra 213

CONCLUSION On Urban Free Time: Vladimir, Estragon, and Rem Koolhaas 239

APPENDIX Tro-tro Inscriptions 251

NOTES 255

REFERENCES 279

INDEX 293

PREFACE

It was a casual conversation with Jeeba in 2003 that gave birth to this book. We met as teenagers while at boarding secondary school some sixty miles outside Accra, he a class above mine and me counting him as a mentor and confidant. Leaving Ghana first to go and study abroad and then to work has not abated our friendship. Like me he was and still is an avid reader and after months without any communication we would relight our friendship simply by sharing with each other what we had been reading in the interim. Jeeba was also blessed with a highly acerbic sense of humor, the brunt of which could be directed at any subject, including himself. On this occasion I was in Accra for a few weeks visiting and, as usual, had gone to his house at the Ringway Estates not far from Oxford Street to have lunch and to shoot the breeze, one of our favorite pastimes. I left his place in the middle of the afternoon to check my e-mail at a cybercafe on Oxford Street. At that time cybercafes were only then getting in vogue, and it was not unusual for them to also double up as communication centers (or "comm" centers for short), with the requisite array of telephones, fax machines, and photocopiers in addition to the standard set of computers. This particular cybercafe was different and cultivated a more elite ethos by serving the clients coffee while they sat at the computers. I finished my business fairly quickly that afternoon, which mainly comprised clearing my in-box and replying to some pressing messages from my students and a couple of colleagues in the UK. Stepping out of the café, I took a deep breath, inhaling all the fervent smells of an Accra afternoon and declared to myself proudly: this is globalization. I rushed back to Jeeba's place in excitement to share my insight. His response was spontaneous and characteristically wry: "Ato, your problem is that you mistake Oxford Street for a street in *Romeo and Juliet*." He never explained what he meant by that remark and I never asked. We just laughed at his usual turn of wit and left it at that. But the remark haunted me: what did it mean that I was mistaking Oxford Street for a street in Shakespeare? Two things gradually crystallized in my mind as explanations: first was that I was overly romanticizing the street and what I thought to be its globalized character, and second and perhaps more unsettling was that despite growing up in Accra I knew more about Shakespeare than the city that had shaped my childhood, adolescence, and young adulthood. I was so shaken by this insight that I decided to test his hypothesis by asking casual preliminary questions about the street from friends and acquaintances. The more I asked, the more confused I became. This book is the product of that quest for understanding the meaning of Oxford Street and of Accra and my thanks go first to Jeeba for triggering the long and complicated process by which I sought to respond to his witty remark.

....

Many people have helped me on my way in the course of researching this book. They are too many to name or even remember. But of those that come to mind readily, I want to say a special thanks to Kwaku Sakyi-Addo, who first helped me articulate the concept of horizontal archaeologies in an early interview he conducted with me on the project in 2005. Kwaku was persistent over the years in reminding me about the term, and it finds its way into this book mainly due to his prompting. I should also like to thank the many marvelous research assistants I have had over the years and without whom I could not have brought this project to fruition: Barbara Archampong, Evans Mensah, Afua Prempeh, Emma Pimpong, Vera Adu, Esther de Bruijn, Jessica Cammaert, and Samuel Ntewusu. Ntewusu grew to be more than just a research assistant. In his own research on the Tudu Lorry Park in Accra and his phenomenal facility for unearthing the most arcane documents from the historical archives, he provided me with very welcome instruction on how to think like a historian. That I may have failed signally in thinking like one is no fault of his, yet without a doubt whatever comes through these pages as a historical account comes from the numerous conversations I have had with him first as a research assistant, then as a friend, and subsequently as my teacher. To Evan Snyder I want to express special gratitude for stepping in to edit and format the manuscript at the last minute before I submitted it to the press and to Antonela Arhin, Ken MacDonald, Anna Shternshis, Kevin O'Neill, Girish Daswani, and Alejandro Paz for being such great colleagues at the Centre for Diaspora and Transnational Studies. They were among my most stimulating interlocutors in Toronto at various stages in the progress of researching and writing the book. To Pekka Sinervo and Meric Gertler, successive deans of the Faculty of Arts and Sciences at the University of Toronto, warm thanks are due for the approval of generous research funding. This was in further support of a Standard Research Grant awarded to me by the Social Sciences and Humanities Research Council of Canada (SSHRC) from 2009 to 2012, without which the project would have turned out much differently.

I also want to thank Emmanuel Akyeampong, Joanna Lewis, Carina Ray, Ray Kea, Naborko Sackeyfio, Irene Odotei, John Parker, Carmela Garittano, Ananya Kabir, Lloyd Amoah, Sylvia Amoah, Ken Mills, Valentina Napolitano, Ayebia Clarke, Amarkai Amarteifio, Diana Quayson, and Tejumola Olaniyan for variously reading and commenting on versions of chapters, pointing out interesting ideas and sources, or for just tolerating me while I got incoherently excited about yet another discovery on Accra. Martina Odonkor was instrumental in putting me in touch with Jurgen Heinel, who was extraordinarily generous in sharing with me books, documents, maps, and the hundreds of pictures he had accumulated from the late 1950s to the early 2000s on the evolution of Accra. Mr. Heinel went further to welcome me into his home in Hamburg in the spring of 2012, where I spent an amazing few days listening to some of the wonderful stories he had to share about his time as a merchant's representative and later businessman in Ghana. Martina herself also turned out to have an incredible reservoir of stories about Accra's salsa and leisure scene and was kind enough to introduce me to a wide range of *salseros* and *salseras*. Without her the chapter on salsa would have been very different from what it is now.

For invitations to share my work on Accra at various forums, I wish to say special thanks to Tejumola Olaniyan (again!) at the University of Wisconsin, Madison; Percy Hintzen, then at the University of California, Berkeley; Heike Härting at the University of Montreal; and Samuel Ntewusu and Akosua Adomako at the University of Ghana. The Johannesburg Workshop in Theory and Criticism held in June 2013 provided an invaluable opportunity for me to test out my concluding chapter, and the shape that it takes comes directly from the insightful conversations I had with the participants. Achille Mbembe, Sarah Nuttal, Leigh-Ann Naidoo, and Kelly Gillespie were magnificent hosts with whom I had many lively conversations both at the JWTC forum and beyond.

To Carol Dougherty, Jane Jackson, Elena Creef, Yoon Sun Lee, and Yu Jin Ko, and all the Fellows at the Newhouse Centre a very special thanks for making my stay as the Corneille Distinguished Visiting Professor in the Humanities at Wellesley College in 2011–2012 such a memorable and productive time. Anjali, Ralf, Keshav, and Kairav deserve more than thanks for offering me a home away from home during my yearlong sabbatical in Boston.

I dedicate the book first to my mother, Rosina Ayeafer, whose numerous stories from the markets of Accra first alerted me to the treasure troves that were rumors and urban myths, and to Keshav, Kairav, and Kamau for sharing with me generously of their childhood during my sabbatical year during the course of which the large bulk of this book was written. I am very much humbled by their dedication to all aspects of the beautiful game that is soccer and from which we had some heated if inconclusive arguments about the relative strengths and weaknesses of Arsenal, Barcelona, Real Madrid, Bayern Munich, Chelsea, and Manchester United and many others. These three reminded me of one of my favorite sayings, from the book *Big Panda, Little Panda*, by Joan Stimson: "Sometimes you want to be little, even though you are big."

INTRODUCTION

Urban Theory and Performative Streetscapes

The news caused ripples on ghanaweb.com, the Ghanaian website that carries information and news on the country for both locals and those abroad. Ghanaweb posted an item from the *New York Times* listing Accra as the fourth most desirable destination out of forty-six places surveyed for 2013.[1] Accra came hard on the heels of Rio de Janeiro (who would dare compete with Rio anyway?), Marseilles, and Nicaragua, respectively. There were six accompanying pictures to the write-up on the charms of the city, two of which were taken on Oxford Street. Though brief, the write-up done by Karen Leigh was quite suggestive:

> Accra, the capital of Ghana, has welcomed business travelers for years. Now tourists are streaming in, a by-product of the fact that the country has Africa's fastest-growing economy and is also one of its safest destinations. The Mövenpick Ambassador Hotel (with poolside bar and waiters on roller skates) opened in 2011, and the Marriott Accra—the chain's first sub-Saharan offering—will feature a casino and upscale shopping when it opens in the spring. On Accra's packed beaches, you'll see everything from snake handlers to plantain peddlers. Head to the upscale neighborhood of Osu and hit the treehouse-inspired terrace at Buka for fine West African food. The best Ghanaian adventures start with a giant plate of tomato-smothered tilapia and banku—a fermented yeast paste that's tastier than it sounds—washed down with local Star beer.

What this confirms is something long known to casual observers: Accra has been a favored destination for students for well over two decades now. And over the past ten years almost every major American university has sent its students on various programs to Ghana; these include Harvard, Michigan, Rutgers, and Colorado, to name just a few. The nine-campus University

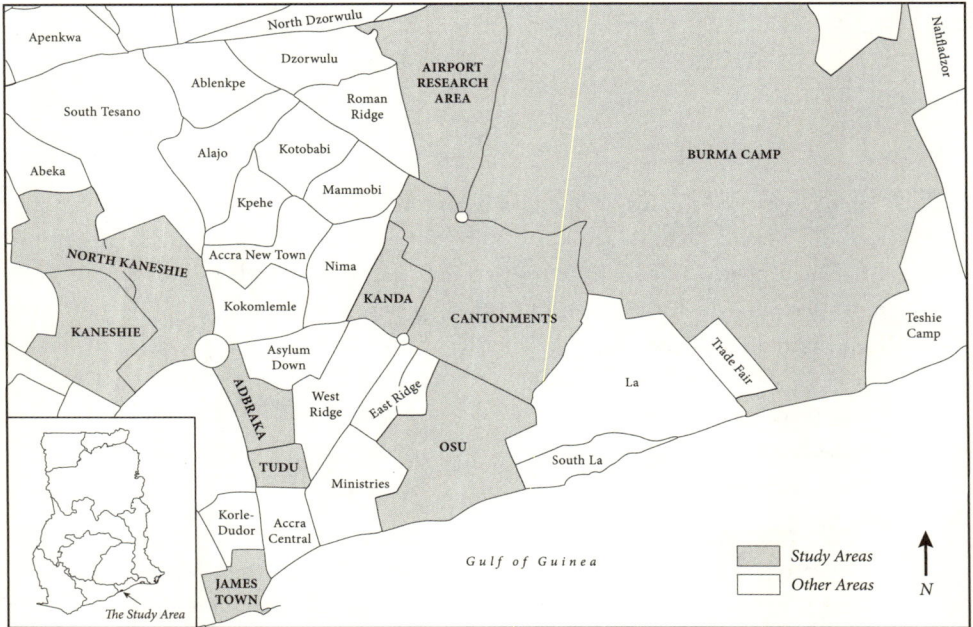

Map I.1. Map of Accra with shaded parts indicating main areas of research. Courtesy Samuel Obodai, Department of Geography, University of Ghana

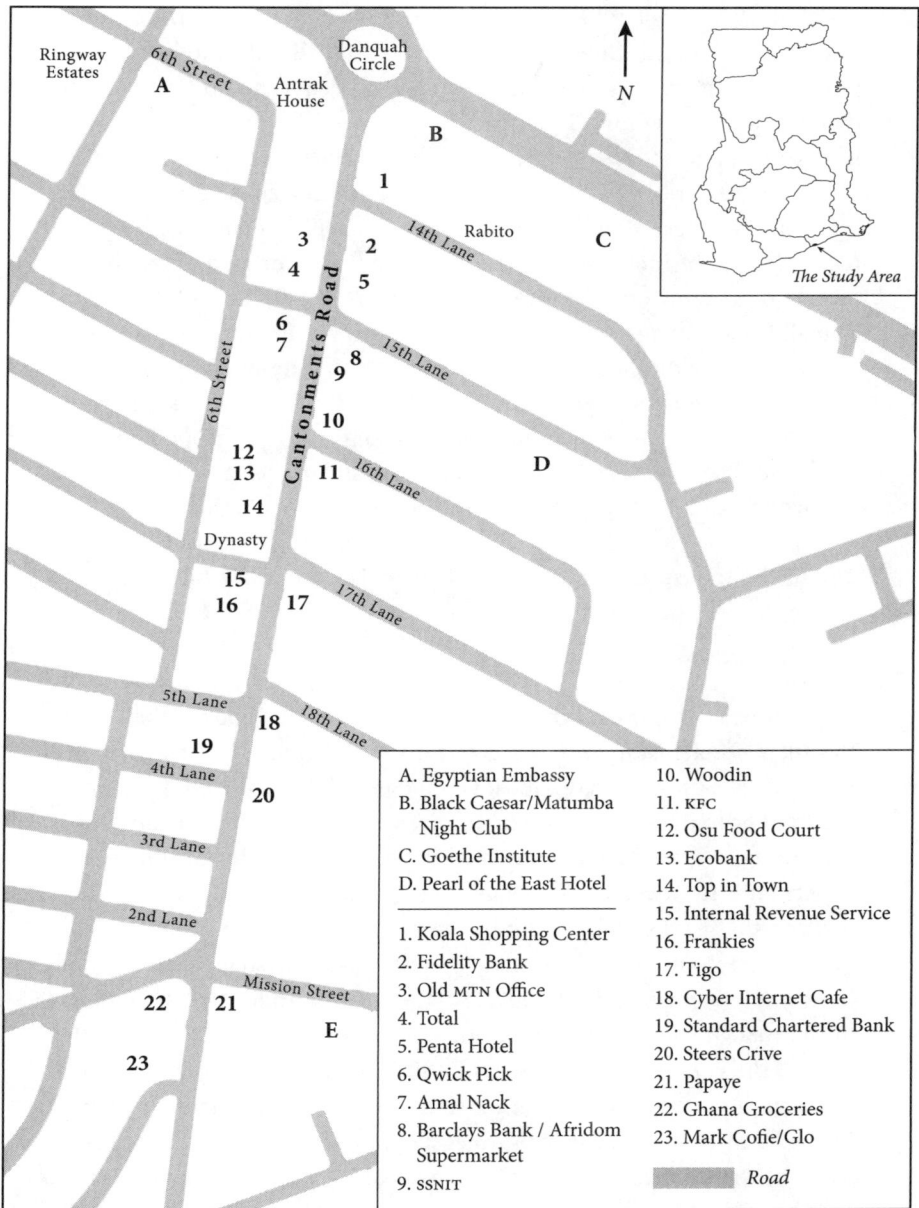

Map I.2. Cantonments Road/Oxford Street, with legend. Courtesy Samuel Obodai, Department of Geography, University of Ghana

The labels on the map are:

Ringway Estates
6th Street
Antrak House
Danquah Circle
A
B
N
The Study Area

1
14th Lane
Rabito
C
3
2
4
5
6
7
15th Lane
9 8
10
12
13
11
16th Lane
D
14
Dynasty
15
16
17
17th Lane
6th Street
Cantonments Road
5th Lane
18
18th Lane
19
4th Lane
20
3rd Lane
2nd Lane
22
21
Mission Street
E
23

A. Egyptian Embassy
B. Black Caesar/Matumba Night Club
C. Goethe Institute
D. Pearl of the East Hotel

1. Koala Shopping Center
2. Fidelity Bank
3. Old MTN Office
4. Total
5. Penta Hotel
6. Qwick Pick
7. Amal Nack
8. Barclays Bank / Afridom Supermarket
9. SSNIT

10. Woodin
11. KFC
12. Osu Food Court
13. Ecobank
14. Top in Town
15. Internal Revenue Service
16. Frankies
17. Tigo
18. Cyber Internet Cafe
19. Standard Chartered Bank
20. Steers Crive
21. Papaye
22. Ghana Groceries
23. Mark Cofie/Glo

Road

of California system has been running year-abroad programs in the country since the early 1990s while NYU has gone beyond all others to buy a large property that plays host to regular cohorts of students and professors from their campus in New York. That Accra has now been declared a favored tourist destination by the *New York Times* may be read in a variety of ways, not all of them necessarily positive. For the Accra of tourist consumption is one that may only succeed on satisfaction of the immediate demands of leisure (classy hotels, casinos, fine shopping, and the neighborhood of Osu being proffered as exemplary in this regard). Since the story of its evolution from a small fishing village through a colonial port town and into the large and bustling city we find today is very rarely told either in tourist guides or in the various government promotional documents, this means that Accra is packaged through the scaled-down impressionisms of cosmopolitan consumption. The city's history is told piecemeal, and in such a way as to make it amenable to incorporation into a series of discourses: developmentalist, Pan-Africanist, popular cultural, and now as a favored tourist destination. The retelling of Accra's story from a more expansive urban historical perspective is the object of *Oxford Street*.

....

Space provides the overall organizing principle for this book. I shall retell the urban social history of Accra from the vantage point of the singular Oxford Street, part of the city's most vibrant and globalized commercial district. I hope to trace the history of this lively commercial district and to link it to different spatial ecologies that were generated by colonial and postindependence town and urban planning for the city, alongside the transformations that have been wrought by the processes of transnationalism and globalization. The varying planning systems that have shaped the city and been amply augmented by the effects of the structural adjustment programs of the 1980s mandated by the International Monetary Fund prepared the way for the conversion of what was until the early 1990s largely a residential neighborhood into the high-intensity commercial district that we find in Oxford Street today. The high street shopping experience replicated elsewhere in the world is in this instance coupled to economic inequalities that are encoded within the very spatial arrangements of the streetscape itself. Oxford Street's variation on the high street thematic will be central to our concerns, as will the ways in which this emblematic street reveals a microcosm of larger historical and urban processes that have transformed Accra's urbanscape into the variegated and contradictory metropolis we find today.

Space, it might be said with no sense of irony, is a problem of no mean proportions. For it seems to have a brute obviousness and yet once examined defeats all efforts at simple conceptualization. And once we reflect on urban space, or any social space for that matter, we find that although space gives the impression of being a mere container, its dimensions are in fact produced by what it contains, while it also (re)configures and (re)arranges the contained elements. Thus the built environment of roads, railways, and buildings as well as the bureaucratic apparatus that brings all these elements together instigates social relationships that are in turn progressively redefined as people interact with their built environment. None of these observations are new or indeed original. For Phil Cohen, the quarrel over cities has been between "those who see the city primarily as a material infrastructure for accommodating a diversity of social functions, and those for whom it is essentially a space of representation for imagining and regulating the body politic."[2] And, as Doreen Massey and other Marxian theorists of space have taught us, the two dimensions noted by Cohen are mutually reinforcing as nodal points for understanding the manner in which space becomes both symptom and producer of social relations.[3]

When it comes to urban Africa the dual quality of urban space instigates a number of further layers of significance because of the general urgency with which questions pertaining to cities are framed. If we take African urban slums as a test case of such debates, we find that the space-as-material-infrastructure orientation undergirds an array of policy interventions launched by government agencies, urban planners, and multinational organizations.[4] This orientation is particularly evident in the array of resettlement schemes, programs for slum upgrades, or clearance or infrastructural repair that regularly get rolled out. The relationship between slums and other neighborhoods or districts in the city is couched predominantly in the discourses of public health, labor economics, and law and order. These interventions are by no means devoid of interest in the people living in the slums themselves—quite the opposite. For by targeting various dimensions of the urban spatial container, these interventions are also keen on reconfiguring the character of social relations that lie within the slum and that exist between the slum and the city in general. Such programmatic interventions define two apparently opposed attitudes, one that conceives of the African city as the case study of unmitigated crises and the other that sees it as the arena of dormant potentialities. Yet, as Ananya Roy notes in her trenchant critique of both types of policy responses, the inherent contradiction lies in seeing slums as essentially located at a spatial remove from what is assumed to be normative urban relations, rather than seeing slum inhabitation as a form of urban informality and directly constitutive of urbanism as such.[5] Garth Myers, AbdouMaliq Simone, Achille Mbembe, Sarah Nuttall, Filip De Boeck, Margaret Plissart, and Roy herself represent a new breed of Africanist urban scholarship that has not only adopted a bottom-up approach to discussions of Third World cities but adroitly combines this with creative interdisciplinary perspectives.[6]

Notwithstanding the innovative insights evident in the new urban scholarship on Africa, the bottom-up approach is itself not devoid of problems. The problems involve, first, the discursive creation of a "top" consisting of planners, governmental agencies, and international organizations that is then set against a "bottom" of ordinary people. The binary opposition between bottom and top suggests an understandable and in fact necessary critical discourse, but it also generates the necessity of keeping this template intact, which in turn leads to a number of distortions and skewed conceptualizations. The second problem, which follows directly from the first, comes from the procedures by which urban theorists extract observations from the materials at their disposal. Of the theorists just mentioned, Simone seems to me to be at once the most suggestive and yet, by the same token, also the most elusive. He has the telling advantage of not only having worked and lived in many of the cities he writes about (Jakarta, Dakar, Douala, Johannesburg, New York, etc.) but also of being a magnificent storyteller and thus able to extract great nuance and significance from ordinary incidents and encounters. First in *For the City Yet to Come* (2004) and more recently in *City Life from Jakarta to Dakar* (2009), he lays out a highly stimulating mode for interpreting cities in the developing world. In *City Life* he proffers the concept of "cityness" to account for the various ways in which cities are inhabited by different people and, perhaps more important, the ways in which cities provide opportunities for experiencing relationships of all kinds, many of which are not anticipated either by city dwellers themselves or by the regulatory mechanisms of urban-planning institutions. This concept echoes somewhat Doreen Massey's idea that chance encounters are intrinsic to spatiality. As she puts it, it is "in happenstance juxtaposition, in the unforeseen tearing apart, in the internal irruption, in the impossibility of closure, in the finding of yourself next door to alterity, in precisely that possibility of being surprised . . . that the chance of space is to be found" (2005, 8, 116).

Additionally for Simone, the creative surprise of urban inhabitation derives first and foremost from the peripheries, both in terms of urban spatial peripheries (such as slums) but also in terms of the elusive subalternity inherent to spaces that intermesh modes of formality and informality, sometimes at different times of day (such as in the magnificent example he gives of the activities of trade, organization, and even prayer in Lagos's Oju-Elegba neighborhood in the nighttime). In his account peripheralness is celebrated at various levels as the defining characteristic of cityness. However, to conceptually ground this assertion Simone is obliged to typify the managerial class of town planners as somehow either utterly counter to subaltern sensibility or perhaps even actively working toward placing constraints upon it. Thus he is able to assert:

> Cityness refers to the city as a thing in the making. No matter how hard analysts and policymakers try, practices of inhabiting the city are so diverse and change so quickly that they cannot easily be channeled into clearly defined uses of space and resources or patterns of social interchange. (2009, 3)
>
> . . . .
>
> We can then pay attention to how best to calibrate relations among people, places, institutions, responsibilities, economic activities, and social functions through more proficient forms and practices of urban governance. These calibrations are structured according to law, policy, and specific ideas about norms, efficiency, and justice. But they are also subject to relations of power. Here, specific individuals and institutions use the uncertainties incumbent in urban life and the need of most residents to have a sense of order as occasions to accumulate the material and symbolic resources that are used to exercise authority over how relations are made. (2009, 6)

The first quotation implies that the diversity and rapid change of urban inhabitation are such as to continually defeat the objectives of urban planners to regulate or direct them, while the second calls both for prolific forms of urban governance yet suggests that urban governance harbors a dirty secret of power and hegemony, but here denominated in their avatars of material distribution of resources and social management. Simone inadvertently conveys the sense of a historical hypostasis, setting up an opposition between the people and those that seem to want to have the better of them. Since he does not historicize the emergence of cityness and its variant transformations, it seems that for Simone the periphery is both elevated beyond temporality and yet also firmly entrenched within it, for otherwise how would we be able to imagine a different future for the urban dispossessed?

One central weakness of Simone's mode of argumentation in general is that while his anecdotes are rich in insights, he does not provide enough examples to ground the highly suggestive theorizations. The lack of specificity and the fine distinctions that one hopes to have been established in the comparative framing of African and Southeast Asian cities means we sometimes strive in vain to align his conceptualizations to particular configurations in the two regions. Thus, while his general propositions might, for example, be alluring to anyone who has worked on African cities and been frustrated at the gross insensitivities and frank crassness behind many urban-planning policies, his overall process of argumentation obscures the relations of complicity and overlap between top and bottom that have constituted the African city. This contradiction becomes especially evident when we extend our view of the African city to include the colonial period. As we shall see with respect to Accra, while it is an incontrovertible fact that the British colonial authorities established spatial patterns for the city that were predominantly to serve their own interests, the intra- and interethnic relations among Ga indigenes of the city and their out-of-town counterparts from other parts of the country meant that contests over who owned the city were regularly defined along lines of autochthony, primogeniture, and first arrival, thus producing various hierarchical relations that were in turn exploited by the colonial administration. For Accra top and bottom, core and periphery occupied elusive locations when it came to struggles over urban space. Pointing out the complex nature of local hierarchies does not obviate the criticisms we might make of colonialism; but it also suggests that the problems inherent to African cities come from much more complex historical sources.

A particular difficulty that I felt while researching this book was the lack of good quality information on Accra; this difficulty seems to apply in the case of most cities in sub-Saharan Africa, excluding perhaps South Africa. A passage from Amma Darko's *Faceless* (which I will discuss extensively in chapter 7) provides an unerring picture of what it takes to research the city:

> A lady journalist friend of mine was looking for information about the evolution of an Accra area to its present state. She thought it should be available at the Greater Accra Regional office. It wasn't. She was referred to the National Archives. There, she was given a little insight and was sent off to the Accra Metropolitan Assembly. They in turn referred her to their

Sub Metro office. She was told there that in fact that information was not properly documented. However, one of their employees was very knowledgeable about it and could provide it orally. Unfortunately though, he was indisposed. Could she come back when the employee was well? No, she told them. She needed the information right away. So she was advised to try the Department of Town and Country Planning. She did. And was told she could get that information only at either the Accra Metropolitan Assembly or the Regional office. She saved the energy she would have used to explain to them that she had already been to those two offices. Instead she wailed for help into the passing winds. Someone out there heard her cry and sent her packing to an informal but very reliable source; two old ladies living at British Accra. They proved to be a fine pair of human libraries. (Darko 2003, 104–105)

Whereas Darko's journalist arrives at the crucial informal oral sources for the history of the city only at the very end of her labyrinthine quest, this is in fact a research resource that urban scholars of Africa are obliged to acknowledge and incorporate from the beginning. And the path of frustration often rewards a painstaking ethnographic sensibility, which also means that serendipity is as integral to research on the African city as lengthy hours in the archives. I began research for *Oxford Street* in 2003. Over the past decade this has involved administering over 250 questionnaires; conducting dozens of interviews with city planners, shop owners, wayside hawkers, members of neighborhood exercise gyms and keep-fit clubs, salseros and salseras, artists, photographers, TV and radio presenters; as well as interrogating friends, family, and even startled pedestrians about their impressions of the city. The research has also involved poring through thousands of pages of archival documents from the Public Records Office and the British Library in London and from Ghana's National Archives holdings in Accra, Kumasi, Cape Coast, and Tamale. Over four thousand photographs of the city taken each summer since 2003, two short films of Oxford Street that I commissioned in 2006 and 2010, and the rushes for two full seasons of the TV soap *Oxford Street* that ran on GTV and TV3 in 2010 and 2011 have provided a wealth of still and moving images of the changing landscapes of the city. And yet, even after all these efforts and resources there are still many questions that remain unanswered for me as a scholar of the city.[7] Hence even though many of my observations come from years of both oral and archival research, there are still large segments that have had to be filled in through creative speculation. This means that *Oxford Street* is proffered as a fertile, if somewhat provisional starting point for further work on the city, rather than as a comprehensive statement about its past, present, and possible futures.

Improvisational Characteristics of an Urban Fragment

We are now obliged to walk the walk, in a manner of speaking, and take a stroll down Oxford Street. The name Oxford Street is partly an improvisation and chimerical projection of popular desire, for it is not the real name of the street that will be of concern to us in this study. It does not appear on any official maps of Accra. The source of the moniker is somewhat obscure, but seems to have been popularized after the return to the country of exiled Ghanaians from various parts of the world, but especially from London following the end of military rule and the restoration of multiparty democracy in 1992. As we shall see at various points in Oxford Street, the interest of returning political exiles turns out to have been symptomatic of the larger interests of global capital as well, since this strip of the much longer Cantonments Road had all the situational advantages that made of it a highly sought-after commercial corridor. Oxford Street is the roughly mile and a half of Cantonments Road that stretches between Mark Cofie to the south to Danquah Circle to the north. Cantonments Road itself extends from the Osu RE area and, merging with 2nd Circular Road, joins Airport Road to form a crucial south-north axis connecting RE, Labone, and Cantonments, all of which are among the most prized areas in the city that since the colonial period have been the favored residential neighborhoods of the ruling elites and their satellites. A few miles to the east and west of Cantonments Road are other prestigious neighborhoods such as Ringway Estates, Ridge, and Kanda and Nyaniba Estates, all of which provide a steady stream of well-heeled shoppers to the street. Significant also in the evolution and continuing vitality of its commercial character is its relative proximity to government buildings such as the State House, the Kwame Nkrumah Conference Centre, the Accra Sports Stadium, and the Ministries, all roughly within two miles of Oxford Street. Completed in 1924, the area popularly known as the Ministries contains the headquarters of all government departments. Combined with the upwardly mobile neighborhoods, the street is thus fed day and night by governmental and residential tributaries from every direction. This is what lends Oxford Street the buzz of a twenty-four-hour hub of commercial and leisure activity despite the fact that it is not actually the most densely populated commercial part of town. As we shall come to see later, this distinction is still reserved for Makola Market and the Central Business District, some three miles to the

I.1. Street sign with image of Jennifer Lopez. Photo by author.

west of Oxford Street. The farther south one goes along Cantonments Road and its connecting streets, the closer one gets to the sea and, more important, to Christiansborg Castle, the seat of government since 1877.

On entering Oxford Street from the north end (that is, from Danquah Circle; see map I.1 and map I.2), one is struck by how crowded it looks, with both vehicles and people, many large commercial buildings, and a proliferation of large-size billboards advertising everything from cell phone company products (MTN: "Everywhere You Go"; TIGO: "Express Yourself") to the services of the United Emirates Airlines; from Nescafé to sanitary pads; and from the *Nigerian Ovation* magazine to DStv with the face of Jennifer Lopez staring coyly from the billboard. To enter the street is also to be confronted by a range of features that are recognizable from high streets elsewhere in the world and yet are marked here by a mix of decidedly local characteristics. Your regular banks sit cheek by jowl alongside vendors of soccer paraphernalia, which proliferate exponentially during the years in which Ghana participates in international soccer tournaments such as the World Cup or the African Cup of Nations competition. Papaye, the local fast-food giant, has to contend with the vendor promising the exact same chicken-and-fried-rice-with-Coke combo right across the street from it, with the added enticement of a ghetto blaster with full-on Bob Marley music to accompany your food, while Woodin (retailer of beautiful print cloths) contends with "already-made" (i.e., pre-sewn) variants of dresses and shirts made from the same print cloths but available for much cheaper off the street vendors. Electronic-goods stores abound, as do jewelry shops, along with the offices of all the major cell phone companies such as Airtel, MTN, Glo, and Tigo. Koala, a grocery store to rival Trader Joe's, Sainsbury's, or Loblaws, is also on Oxford Street, while the huge edifice to American fast-food retailing that is KFC opened in September 2011 to add a further transnational dimension to the food offerings on the street. Several large Chinese and other high-end restaurants, Internet cafés, hotels, bed-and-breakfasts, forex bureaus, and a large and luscious Italian-themed ice cream parlor make of this commercial stretch a visitor's dream and the local dispossessed's mouthwatering nightmare.[8] On adjoining streets and byways off Oxford Street and within a roughly five-hundred-meter radius are various embassies and high commissions, the Goethe Cultural Institute, and Ryan's, reputed to be the best Irish pub outside Dublin, along with several other such watering holes and dance venues. And since at least the summer of 2006 a mega-size television screen has been permanently mounted in front of the Osu Food Court, streaming live TV advertisements and reality shows such as *Big Brother Africa* on a twenty-four-hour continuous loop.

Any temptation to see Oxford Street as a postmodern transnational commercial boulevard is, however, quickly to be tempered by the many signs of cultural phenomena that reach back several generations and some of which may be seen replicated in varying forms here as well as in different parts of the city and indeed in other urban areas across the country at large: the young man selling fresh coconuts whose skill for discerning the tenderness or hardness of the inside of the fruit before deftly splitting off the crown with his cutlass seems purely esoteric; the woman who sells ripe plantains roasted over a slow charcoal fire under a tree on the lively curbside corner (for good strategic reasons trees and curbside corners feature prominently in the life cycle of roasted plantains); the female hawkers nonchalantly walk-

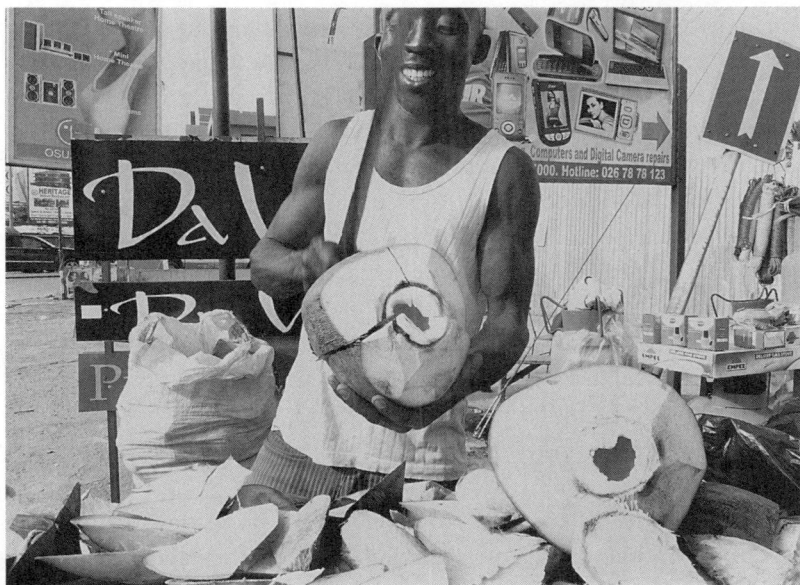

I.2. Ryan's, Osu. Photo by author.
I.3. Coconut seller on Oxford Street. Photo by author.

ing along with their wares balanced on their heads but without the prop of hands and selling things as varied as ice-cold water, or oranges, or roasted peanuts, or even charcoal, smoked fish, onions, chilies, and cassava and plantain for the evening's fufu. One or two of these women may even have a young child strapped to their back. These variant features bring the mix of businesses and vendors on the street much closer to commercial districts in other parts of the city such as Makola, Kaneshie Market, Dansoman High Street, or Spintex Road, all of which are veritable beehives of commercial activity with their own distinctive characteristics.

Apart from its name and the many businesses to be found along the street, however, the most visible yet unassuming dimension of the peculiar character of Oxford Street is actually to be experienced beneath one's feet, that is, upon the sidewalk itself. On December 18, 1926, Walter Benjamin writes in his *Moscow Diary*: "It has been observed that pedestrians [in Moscow] walk in 'zigzags.' This is simply on account of the overcrowding of the narrow sidewalks; nowhere else except here and there in Naples do you find sidewalks this narrow. This gives Moscow a provincial air, or rather the character of an improvised metropolis that has fallen into place overnight" (Benjamin [1986] 2002, 31). Even though Oxford Street cannot be said to have materialized overnight from the sky, it is true that here, too, one is forced to walk in zigzags. But this is not merely due to the narrowness of the sidewalk. For the Oxford Street sidewalk is marked first and foremost by its almost determined evanescence as a sidewalk (i.e., it looks anything but a sidewalk), and the fact that the distinction between it and the tarmac roadway itself is practically obliterated. One reason why the sidewalk does not look or feel like one is that as Oxford Street evolved into the high-energy commercial street that it is today, the sidewalk progressively became not the broad strip specifically designed for pedestrians to traverse but merely the stripped-down extension of the interior of the many commercial enterprises along the street.

Thus the sidewalk in front of various businesses on Oxford Street is taken over by them, either for customer parking extending from demarcated parking areas (in front of Frankie's or Ecobank, for example), or simply for the sprawl onto the sidewalk of manufactured goods, such as in the case of the many electronic, hardware, and bicycle stores along both sides of the street. The colonization of the sidewalk by commerce from shops and stores is augmented by the presence of vendors of various kinds, both itinerant and stationary.

I.4. TIGO, Oxford Street. Photo by author.

I.5. Parking in front of Barclays Bank, Oxford Street. Photo by author.

The items that vendors peddle vary: secondhand clothes, bags and shoes (popularly known as *obroni wa wu*, or "the white man is dead"); fruits of all vintage, but with fresh mango, papaya, and pineapple to be peeled, sliced, or diced up on the spot; Coca-Cola, Sprite, and Fanta in blue ice buckets; red snapper caught fresh from the sea that is sold by women at the seashore but along Oxford Street is mongered by young men with connections to fishing communities. Pushcarts with various goods abound, and there are also vendors of newly manufactured products covering everything from dog chains and flashlights to soccer balls, shoe polish, toothpicks, vibrators, and *Time* magazine.

Cars and pedestrians mix freely on the roadway itself. Even though the sidewalk is demarcated from the tarred roadway by the notorious and practically ubiquitous open-sewage gutter, the sidewalk and the road remain at an uneven height (i.e., while the sidewalk is supposed to be raised some four or five inches above the roadway it is actually for long stretches at par with it on both sides of the street). To walk along Oxford Street is also to be constantly invited to pause and look at things: not in the manner by which shop windows in commercial boulevards elsewhere pose various enticements for the pedestrian to stop, take a quick cosmetic look at their reflection in the glass, and perhaps enter the store (the window displays performing the function of whetting your desire and inducing a crossing of the boundary between inside and outside), but rather by the constant barrage of vendors of all manner of goods vying to make a sale. The invitations to treat, to use a well-known phrase in commercial law, are only an irritation if one is actually in a hurry to get to a fixed destination. If not, the invitations to treat proffered by vendors on Oxford Street may open up into varied kinds of culturally saturated modes of haggling and bargaining, with jokes, teasing, and overall good humor thrown in for good measure. There is a distinctly carnivalesque quality to this aspect of the street. But this also means that the character of walking on Oxford Street and the human interactions one has on it are very different from that of commercial streets elsewhere, in London, or Singapore, or Johannesburg, to cite but three contrasting examples.

Since, as we have seen, much of the length of the sidewalks on both sides of the street has been taken over by businesses and vendors, and cars have no monopoly over the roadway, the experience of walking along Oxford Street involves a lot of zigzagging, moving off and onto the sidewalk or roadway with the negotiation of one's peregrinations amid various kinds of vehicles, vendors, goods, and pedestrians as convenience and inclination dictate. The walk on Oxford Street, as in many parts of Accra, is thus an object of improvisation. (I have also spent many fine hours watching how people walk on the street: the gentle swagger led by the left shoulder slightly tilting the body to one side, the constant "flexing" with cell phones, and the bemusement and otherwise irritated hurrying-to-get-somewhere-yet-being-constantly-interrupted quality of walking. With the proliferation of MP3 players, iPods, and their attendant earplugs, there is also a dimension of distractedness that is introduced into people's gait. Yet oddly enough, listening to something else while walking on the street is not very common; the street demands attention in a way that does not allow zoning out of its ambient sounds. Oxford Street proffers a form of sensorial totality that is only unpleasant if you go against the flow of its multimodal sensory offerings.) If there is a performative dimension to the street it is not to be mistaken for the performativity of occasional theatrical and political events, such as the annual December carnival, or the spontaneous outpourings of jubilation whenever Ghana makes strides in the international soccer tournaments it has had the unalloyed ecstasy to participate in. Rather, the character of walking on the street that has just been described exposes itself to the possibility of spontaneous "events" that themselves follow sets of performative scripts and reveal what we shall come to see as certain important spatial logics.

The messy interaction of pedestrians with other pedestrians, with pushcarts, with itinerant hawkers on the sidewalks, and with vehicles on the roadway means that misunderstandings regularly break out as to the proper courtesies of street use. These are not reducible to the ordinary road rage variety of misunderstandings. Insults may be quickly traded between pedestrian and pedestrian, pedestrian and hawker, pedestrian and motorist, or between one motorist and another. However, the traded insults turn out to be an important aspect of the intersection of spatiality and spectatoriality endemic to Accra's street life, such that the ultimate fact of seeing and being seen translates everything in the heated altercation into the display of the mastery of unstated yet critical cultural codes of rhetoric and delivery. Reference to various parts of the human anatomy and its effusions proliferate in such exchanges, but the hyperinflation of the body is not the real point of the scatological insults. What is crucial is to produce a memorable twist on a known theme or themes both to show superiority over your opponent and to raise a laugh from casual observers who will quickly have gathered to enjoy a spot of spontaneous street theatre. Rhetorical mastery may involve the clever deployment of local language proverbs, but not exclusively.

My favorite of the many I have witnessed? A taxi driver is speeding toward a zebra crossing and has to apply his brakes reluctantly, with tires screeching to let a bunch of pedestrians go across. They turn around and rain all manner of insults on him as they do so, to which he lustily retorts in Twi: "Hwe nyen ho tan tan bi, a se ngyamoa atɔ gya mu" (Look at all you nasty people, like a bunch of cats that have fallen into a fire!). To which there is general laughter, followed by more insults hurled at the fast-receding exhaust fumes of the cab. And yet the effectiveness of the driver's insult and its memorable quality derive not so much from the mention of cats as to the domestic setting signaled by the reference to fire, something that would immediately invoke a traditional kitchen very well known to most denizens of Accra. Cats in a traditional kitchen evoke all kinds of chaotic scenarios, including the potential for loud din and total confusion in the tipping over of pots and pans, and perhaps of even the meal being cooked on the charcoal fire. The entire insult therefore combines implicit references to dishevelment, to chaos, and to improper and unpredictable behavior within a domestic setting, which then acts as a correlative of the confusion of the pedestrians who, in the driver's opinion, do not even know how to negotiate the city's streets. And this despite the fact that it is he who is patently in the wrong for rushing to whiz past the zebra crossing before the pedestrians could successfully navigate it. The implication from the driver's insult then is that despite all appearances to the contrary, the zebra crossing does not in and of itself encompass the full protocols of how to cross a busy Accra street.

A similar observation can be made for motor vehicles negotiating Accra's increasingly dense and frustrating traffic. For example, here the rules for cutting in front of another driver are highly complicated, but generally the object of tacit agreement by most drivers. The first principle when doing something you shouldn't do is to absolutely avoid eye contact, and the second is to demonstrate determined intent, that is to say, to move your vehicle as if not afraid of hitting the other vehicle or being hit by it. Waving a quick thank-you after the maneuver must be rigorously observed, otherwise insults or road rage may quickly ensue. Taxi and tro-tro drivers are experts at this, and one is quickly enjoined to learn from them if one wants to survive the hectic density of Accra's traffic.

If the anecdote of the taxi driver's insult gives the impression that those behind the wheels of motor vehicles are somehow at an advantage when it comes to such confrontations, this is quickly dispelled by other stories in which it is the pedestrian that has the last word. In one such instance, a lumbering and clearly much-exhausted market woman makes her way slowly down from the back of a wooden tro-tro (a popular passenger lorry, and the subject of chapter 4). The tro-tro driver honks his horn impatiently and begins to rain insults on her. Her response, in hoarse yet pinpoint Ga: "Okyε some, Adwoa Atta" (Your father's vagina, Adwoa Atta!), to which the dumb-struck driver mumbles some incoherencies and promptly takes off. Loud laughter and wagging fingers follow him in his embarrassed exit from the scene, gearbox cranking and a splutter of protest emanating from the lorry's startled engine. "Your mother's vagina!" with the upraised right thumb pointing toward the object of your derision and deliberately wiggled up and down against the clenched fingers is one of the most common and ready insults in Accra. The insult may be translated into something like "your mother's vagina birthed you for nothing, you useless person." It is not uncommon to hear even a mother hurling this insult loudly at her own children, in which case the implication is that she has wasted her time giving birth to them. The twist in the woman's hurled insult at the tro-tro driver turns first on suggesting that his father was not a "proper man" (he had a vagina instead of a penis) and second, that the driver should be embarrassed to have been born as only half a woman. Adwoa is the name for a girl born on Monday, while Atta refers to a twin, thus the reference to "Adwoa Atta" comically insinuates that the driver is somehow incomplete. The gender twists to the insult were not lost upon the listeners, because it also carried the suggestion that the driver was ultimately an anomaly, having been birthed by a man who was really a woman, and he himself appearing as nothing but half of a real woman. These compounded significations are then to be taken into account for the tro-tro driver's monstrously rude behavior toward her, a proper, full-bodied, and uncompromising market woman.

....

In the definition of spatial practice that Henri Lefebvre proffers in *The Production of Space* (1992), the concept is both empirically observable and coincident with space as structured and regimented. For Lefebvre, the reproduction of social relations is central to spatial practice. As he notes: "The spatial practice of a society secretes that society's space; it *propounds* and *presupposes* it in a dialectical interaction; it produces it slowly as surely as it *masters* and *appropriates* it, i.e., through the network of roads, motorways and the politics of air transport" (1992, 38; italics added). The various verbs used in this formulation attribute to spatial practice a form of active agency, and Lefebvre adds that the *form* of space approximates to the moment of communication, and thus to the realm of the perceived. A number of implications may be extrapolated from Lefebvre's comments: the first is that space as a concept acts upon space as it is experienced in the form of social relations. The dialectic of concept and social relations aligns Lefebvre's notion of space to that of other Marxists such as Doreen Massey and David Harvey, but with the distinction that Lefebvre goes on to set up a triangular relationship between spatial practice, representational space, and represented space, such that each concept is automatically entailed in the others in complex and often elusive ways.[9] An added implication of Lefebvre's definition of spatial practice is that individual spaces are the localized instantiations of a larger spatial logic inherent to a given society. We must gloss this to mean that the dialectical interaction between concept and articulation must also have a specific cultural and historical character to it, thus enabling us to perceive subtle or epochal shifts in spatial practice as being correlated to an entire range of changes within a given society. Additionally, it may be interpreted to mean that even if the concept of space in a given society is historical it also veers toward hegemony, that is, that it procures acquiescence in social arrangements that are not always necessarily in the interests of those who ordinarily traverse space, but rather of those who want to naturalize a particular hierarchy of social relationships in each given epoch. Hegel is suggested in the link Lefebvre makes between a hegemonic spatial logic and specific spaces as instantiations of that logic. But, as in the case of Simone that we saw earlier, Lefebvre does not fill out in detail what he means by the hegemony of spatial practice, leaving us to take it in different directions. The implication of social struggle built into his idea is only sporadically worked out by Lefebvre, but must be borne in mind in any deployment of the concept of spatial practice. Following on the implications of the historicity of spatial practice we noted earlier, we find concomitantly that space itself does not remain static but that it is also progressively transformed, first by the communicative character of the local instantiations of spatial practice, and second by the alterations in the overall technology of human interactions enabled by changes in the network of roads, motorways, and other means for the traversal of geographic space. We will have to add to Lefebvre's technologies of interaction the social media that have also come to impact upon how people interpret themselves and their relations to others in an era of social networking. As Jenna Burrell (2012) has shown, in Ghana the inherently interpretative flexibility of the Internet has allowed it to materialize a space for self making that involves both licit and illicit uses as well as an investment of the symbolic register of enchantment commonly associated with Christianity.

However, it is what Lefebvre writes about spatial practice as an approximation of the moment of communication that strikes a special chord with respect to the performative and highly eventful character of Oxford Street.

The question to ask is, how do we define the moment of communication out of which we might extrapolate the spatial practice(s) of a place like Oxford Street? Such a moment of communication is to be taken in the form of a multilayered expressive fragment that is to be assumed to encapsulate a larger social totality. But our interpretation of the expressive fragment must be conducted carefully. The fact that unlike other streets in Accra, Oxford Street is lined on both sides by a phalanx of billboard advertisements large and small means that it can be creatively seen as at once a demarcated spatial theatre yet one that is also extraordinarily permeable in terms of the intersections of variant dramaturgies. At the highest register of articulation, then, all of Oxford Street may be taken as a geographically demarcated expressive fragment constituted by a number of common and distinct spatial and discursive features, some of which are nodal expressive fragments in and of themselves. To look at the evanescent sidewalk is to see a different vector of interpretative possibilities from what is implied in looking at the shopping to be had on the street, for instance. The two are not mutually exclusive, yet each starting point produces different emphases, the first a signal of urban planning crisis and the second a signifier of local entrepreneurial drive. With the proliferation of languages (Ga, Twi, pidgin, English, etc.) and discourses (those of billboard advertising, tro-tro inscriptions, etc.), our interpretation of such an expressive fragment may be made exclusively on the basis of sociolinguistic and discursive considerations, something that we shall indeed attempt in chapter 4. However, the expressivity of the fragment must not be limited solely to language and discourse but ultimately charged to the nature and variety of interpersonal interactions on the street. The interpersonal interactions manifest different dimensions of economy, culture, and society and their transformations through time. Language is thus only the entry point into a broader structure of multilayered levels and relations. It is out of the interactive multidimensionality of all such levels that we gain a sense of the spatial practice(s) to be seen on Oxford Street. The two anecdotes encountered earlier, far from connoting a breakdown of communication, rather divulge the character of spatial practice precisely manifested as a flashpoint of rhetorical intensity. In other words, such rhetorical flashpoints, coded at the simplest level as debates about the civilities of road use, are actually the points at which spatial practices reveal themselves.

Thus if we return to our two anecdotes, we find that the altercations were also simultaneously the attribution of social consensus upon the human interaction on the street. The idea of social consensus does not imply any direct notion of agreement but rather the recognizability of the interaction as being part of a normative social domain, that is to say, of the terms by which a moment on the street might be recognized as the product of specific sociocultural norms. But the sociocultural norms in this instance also instantiate a peculiarly spatial dimension, since it is the quarrel over the use of space (road use) that triggers the angry rhetorical exchanges in the primary instance. The normative social domain in the taxi-driver anecdote is generated specifically from the tacit understanding of the rules that govern the negotiation of zebra crossings and their distortion in the domain of usage, either by pedestrians or drivers. The taxi driver challenges the hegemony of the spatial practice signaled by the zebra crossing in his rude attempt to prevent the pedestrians from crossing safely and in the insult he delivers. For he is effectively suggesting that the formal protocols of a zebra crossing (what come together to constitute its *langue*, to take a leaf from structuralism) are not limited to or in this instance even coincident with the individual instantiations of such usage (the pedestrians' or taxi driver's *parole*), both of which of course are governed by the force of law and can trigger certain sanctions if contravened. Rather, we are encouraged to conclude from the rhetorical implications of the insult he delivers that the hegemonic and law-bound spatial practice in this instance also intersects with specifically cultural rules that include the terms of urban performativity, the main characteristic of which is the fact of seeing and being seen by a potential audience on the street. In other words, in this instance the discursive register of the formal rules of zebra crossings is intersected by a different kind of register, whose protocols are those of a local urban performativity. Despite the appearance of being ad hoc, however, the protocols of urban performativity that irrupt in the quarrel between the taxi driver and the pedestrians are also the articulation of a spatial practice yet whose terms seem more fluid and negotiable because of their invocation of traditional rhetorical codes.

Thus we see two distinct forms of spatial practice intersecting in the taxi-driver anecdote: first is the universal rule-bound nature of how to negotiate a zebra crossing and second are the rules of participation in a colorful and culturally saturated altercation on the streets of Accra. Both categories of spatial practice interact regularly with each other on the streets but with the second actively and regularly distorting the protocols of the first at eventful conjunctures. Far from signaling the collapse of communication, the altercations signify the precise moments at which contradictory spatial practices are given articulation, and hence affirmed as both pertinent to the negotiation of space in Accra. (As an aside, the rhetorical devices that challenge the standard understandings of road usage are not limited to flashpoints of altercation; they are also commonly found in light banter between drivers, or even in tro-tro slogans. Thus "Zebra Crossing" may be found as a slogan on a tro-tro to remind road users of its potential assimilation into the expressive discourses and compositions of tro-tro sloganeering). With the anecdote of the lady and the tro-tro driver, on the other hand, a different set of spatial practices come into confrontation. At issue in that instance are not the protocols of road use, but rather those of the chivalrous relation between male and female, but here obscured in its articulation as the hierarchical relation between a tro-tro driver (exclusively male) and his female passenger. The driver's rudeness may have been due to the authority assumed by controling the steering wheel of an automobile, an instrument of evident social power in the African urban domain. As we shall see in chapter 4, a passenger lorry that ferries customers between various destinations has been an instrument of great cultural prestige since at least the end of World War II, when the British administration introduced Bedford vehicles into the colony for the conveyance of both passengers and freight. What the woman does, then, is to completely invert all the available hierarchies that might be presumed to govern the relationship between driver and passenger and that have come to obscure the more foundational one between male and female. For the ultimate point of her insult is that the driver is ignorant of how to treat a woman on the streets of Accra. And if he thought that the mere fact of being a man gave him some sort of authority over her, she also whisks that away by letting him know that his father was not a proper man, and that he himself cannot even aspire to be a full woman. While what I have just described might be taken to confirm spatial practice in Lefebvre's sense of the term, we can at the same time assert that his concept does not quite exhaust the communicative complexity of human interactions to be perceived on a place like Oxford Street, or indeed on similar streets in many parts of Africa. And yet what we have just discussed must not be seen as somehow providing the template of a demotic critique of hegemonic spatial practice, since the rhetorical irruptions are hardly if ever rationalized by anyone as direct challenges to such a hegemony. Rather it is precisely in the untheorized practices of everyday life (to recall de Certeau) that the challenge inheres. For no law or set of rules laid down by urban planners can legislate away the possibility of altercations on Accra's streets. And once such altercations break out they automatically trigger a particular performative logic that at once acknowledges the assumed acceptable protocols of road use while also undermining them through their incorporation into culturally coded rhetorical contests about what constitutes urban knowledge. I do not intend here to glorify haphazard and improper road use or to praise the culture of impunity and rudeness that may often be seen on display on the streets of the city, but rather, through the analysis of the apparently banal form of urban altercation, to clarify the significance of attending to such banalities as a means of understanding the status of spatial practice(s) in the context of Oxford Street and of Accra in general.

The Impact of Commercial Morphology on the Interactions on Oxford Street

The focal point of formal commercial activity on Oxford Street derives from the discursive authority attributed to the price tag. This is relevant to understanding what happens inside of the commercial enterprises on the street and helps to distinguish explicit norms of shopping behavior. As a general rule, the price tag performs the function of foreclosing the types of interactions between vendor and client to be seen outside on the street itself. If the shopping behavior outside is governed by modes of haggling and improvisation, what occurs inside the formal context of banks, restaurants, jewelry stores, and cell phone companies on Oxford Street is marked by what we may consign to formalized economic predication. Predication here bears the echo of one of its grammatical functions, namely, the quality of asserting or basing a statement upon a categorical foundation. The condition of formalized economic predication is grounded fundamentally on a tacit understanding of a particular logic that banishes chance, improvisation, or surprise from the shopping experience. This is because in formal commercial contexts the terms of the transaction are preset by the price tag. On Oxford Street the price tag signifies an implicit separation of economic practice from the kind of cultural logics that apply, say, in the anecdote of the taxi driver. Thus, whereas the purchase of fresh fish, or a soccer shirt, or a bunch of bananas off the street may be subject to forms of haggling that invoke sophisticated cultural repertoires, the transactions inside of a bank, jewelry store, or grocery shop, where everything bears a price tag (or in a restaurant, where the menu performs the same function), tend to produce an absolute predictability of roles that is diametrically opposed to what we find outside. This does not necessarily mean that economic transactions on the street do not follow a rational economic logic, but that that logic is so saturated by cultural forms of interaction that the cultural logic takes the place of the economic logic and converts all forms of economic decision making into a dimension of cultural competence. A good illustration of the culture-as-economy nexus is to be discerned in the arrangements for procuring credit from food and alcohol vendors on Oxford Street and in the city in general. These have been practiced for generations.

Studies show that an average of 32 percent of an Accra urban household's budget is spent on prepared food bought from vendors on Accra's streets, with the figure rising to 40 percent for poorer families.[10] Much of the money spent is a mixture of direct payments and purchases on credit, with credit purchases being the preferred method in many instances. Food vendors and their clients often strike up varying relationships of trust grounded in an understanding of specifically cultural codes of conduct. The codes stipulate that the customer is not solely an object of economic negotiation but rather a total complex of cultural dispositions, some of which are directly pertinent to their being economic subjects in the first place (i.e., customers and clients). The arrangement for getting credit from food vendors turns on the management of intricate cultural codes for engendering and maintaining trust between vendor and buyer. Thus, for example, a roadside *kenkey* seller may have a long list of clients who buy her food on credit, and she will have to balance the purchases on credit from those based on cash in order to see her business succeed. The management of the kenkey turns out to be crucial for maintaining business longevity. Since there is no direct "collateral" to be placed by the buyer for the continuing extension of credit by the food vendor, what is given in exchange are stories of personal exigencies of various levels of intractability. These stories, often not devoid of self-deprecating humor and even sarcasm, then become a reservoir of disciplinary instruments in the hands of the food vendor. A. B. Crentsil's famous hit from 1985, "Akpeteshie Seller Give Me Quarter," captures this arrangement perfectly. The central premise of the song is the credit arrangement that pertains between the *akpeteshie* seller and a hapless alcoholic who comes to her with sad stories about his salary not carrying him till the end of the month and the untold difficulties he encounters in paying his children's school fees. These stories are lodged with her as a means of extracting more drink on credit. The song's refrain—"*Akpeteshie* seller give me quarter [of a beer-size bottle], I go pay you tomorrow aaa-yay"—still remains commonplace in Ghanaian popular culture to this day. The stories that a hapless husband or wife lodges with the food seller may in given circumstances be readily put about by the food seller to create general humiliation for the debtor and as a dire warning to others that might be contemplating similar default. Even though it is not unknown for this to happen, the social embarrassment is so great that it is extremely rare that a buyer willfully fails to meet his or her debt obligations to a food or alcohol vendor. They would rather do a vanishing act until such time as they are able to clear their debts. And it is not unknown for road-side food vendors to suddenly recall an incident of failed payments after a long hiatus on seeing a client that owes them money. The extent and reach of such vendors' memories and the range of information they are able to master without apparent recourse to any documentation is truly phenomenal. The relationship between food vendors and clients described here is not exclusive to Oxford Street; everywhere in Ghana's towns and cities this relationship is completely commonplace. But the most noteworthy aspect of these interactions is that here predicative economic logic has been displaced or at least converted into an essential dimension of cultural logic. The normative rules that govern such interactions and credit arrangements are not reducible to pure economic categories but have to be understood as part of large and complex forms for establishing trusting relations that may originally have been instigated by cold predicative economic transactions. This is so because to build trust the customer has to be sure to make cash payments for several purchases before the credit arrangements are permitted. In other words the predicative economic logic is necessary for first "introducing" customer to vendor as viable economic subjects. It is only once that is established that the new cultural register of borrowing is allowed to kick in. And even when the customer's fortunes change and they revert back to the predicative economic logic, the banter and camaraderie that are necessary ingredients of the cultural register may still be maintained. As noted earlier the predicative economic logic of the price tag or menu clearly obliterates such culturally nuanced possibilities inside the shops, restaurants, and other enterprises on Oxford Street in which they feature.

In each instance of formality or informality, distinct spatial practices come to bear upon the social relation implied in the commercial transaction. This seems so obvious to most people as to pass without notice. The differences between inside and outside, formal and informal, are tacitly understood to the point where few make the mistake of transferring the modalities of one domain into that of the other. Since Oxford Street is shaped by a heavy concentration of outfits governed by forms of economic predication existing side by side with the plethora of opportunities for improvisation, the dialectical interaction between formalism and improvisation comes to express a particular spatial configuration that serves to distinguish this particular street from other commercial districts in Accra. Purely on the basis of a crude count of enterprises on this street we are able to assert that the mix between the formal and informal leans in favor of the formal, giving Oxford

Street the semblance of a largely Westernized high street. This is despite the fact that it is mainly associated with fast food and leisure activities in the popular imagination, rather than the clothes and shoe stores that are definitive of high streets in the West. Only foreigners or wealthy out-of-towners would shop for clothes or shoes from Oxford Street. Most ordinary people would likely go to Makola Market to satisfy such shopping needs.

Makola is also a high-intensity commercial district that shares many of the features of Oxford Street we have encountered, including the character of improvisation and of performative irruptions, except that at Makola price tags do not appear in any of the many manufactured-goods stores that populate the market at every turn. Furthermore, as a market Makola requires one to traverse the maze of alleyways that define it, an experience quite different from that of walking on Oxford Street. At Makola one is allowed to haggle down the price of any of the goods on display, whether inside the small stores that populate the market and its local environment or at the multitude of vendors that peddle similar goods to those in the stores. (In fact at Makola it ~Makola~ is common practice for store owners to give some of their goods to itinerant vendors to sell outside on the streets. This hardly ever happens on Oxford Street, partly because of the different and more expensive character of goods sold in the shops there, and partly because price tags command no status on the outside). The lack of price tags at Makola comes from its peculiar and colorful history. The market was first founded by the colonial government on the site of an open-air cattle grazing field in what was then the outskirts of Ga Mashie. Upon being built up from 1924 as the largest walled fresh food market in the growing town, shops and stalls erupted around it to make it the commercial nerve center of the Central Business District. By the time of the decolonization struggles of the 1940s and 1950s, Makola was considered the seat of women's political organization, with Kwame Nkrumah drawing strong and effective support from the market women. Given that the original cattle herders formed a tightly knit community in what became a densely populated and culturally hybrid environment made up of varying waves of northern migrants and Yoruba traders from Nigeria, and waves of Hausa speakers from the Northern Territories, many of whom did not have the benefits of the colonial education system, the character of Makola was never allowed to be completely divested of its strong informality. This persisted even after its destruction in 1979 by the Rawlings regime, when the fresh-food market was evacuated, bombed, and later turned into a car park. Its immediate environment was surrendered exclusively to commercial enterprises and shops. Fresh food had been concentrated in Makola No. 2, built in the 1950s to absorb the spillover from the original Makola and that by the 1970s had also become a bustling food market in its own right. No. 2 was not touched by Rawlings, and by the late 1980s the lively commercial activities that remained in that commercial district got centered at No. 2 and gradually helped to reenliven the entire Makola area and the Central Business District in general.

At Makola the distinction between informal commercial transactions on the street and the formalized routines that occur inside the shops and stores is completely blurred, whereas on Oxford Street the formal and informal remain sharply distinct. In the manufactured-goods shops on Oxford Street all of the merchandise carries a price tag; this is definitely not the case with the shops at Makola, where the prices of goods on display have to be ascertained orally from whoever (often women) keeps the shop. This provides ample opportunity for haggling, with all the consequent cultural rhetorical fluencies that are called into play. On the other hand, and in contrast to both Oxford Street and Makola, at the Accra Mall all shops and enterprises are governed by the exclusive principle of formalized economic predication (i.e., there is no room whatsoever for carnivalesque improvisation in the commercial transaction). Everything in every store, bookshop, or even food joint carries a price tag, with restaurants guaranteeing that there will be no improvisation by recourse to the expedient device of the printed menu, sometimes boldly displayed on the wall. This is no doubt a function of the fact that the mall is a completely self-enclosed shopping arcade, with the roof obliterating even the view of the sky above it. Modest in size though it is, the Accra Mall is a direct mimesis of the shopping experience of such malls elsewhere in the world, where the price performs the same function of obliterating improvisation and the carnivalesque.

On Rhythmanalysis: Time, Space, and the Thematics of an Urban Key

Taking his cue from music, Henri Lefebvre suggests in Rhythmanalysis (2004) that space and time share some fundamental rhythmic features in common. This goes beyond the standard idea of space being shaped from distinct temporalities in the way it is traversed. As he notes, music is produced from a configuration of reiterations (i.e., beats of different timbres, stresses, and durations), sequences (long-short followed by short-long or any combination of the previous two), and the spaces and pauses between them, again of different lengths. Spacing opens music up to measure(ment) and it is the finely tuned measures of music that allow us to differentiate that from simple noise. Once we grant that musicality derives from measures, and that musical measures depend upon both cyclicality and linearity, the analogy with space as read through the common ground of musical analogy becomes complete. As he notes: "Time and space, the cyclical and the linear, exert a reciprocal action: they measure themselves against one another; each one makes itself and is made a measuring-measure; everything is cyclical repetition through linear repetitions. A dialectical relation (unity in opposition) thus acquires meaning and import, which is to say, generality. One reaches, by this road as by others, the depth of the dialectic" (9).

Lefebvre's conceptualization of space/time does not answer all the questions that might be posed to it. For example, how is space cyclical in the way we experience it if we traverse it in predictably straight lines, as in the daily repeated commute between home and work? And how do the reiterations of key features of geographic space such as trees, electric pylons, or even the horizon seen from different directions interpose themselves on our experience of the measurability of space thus differentiating such measures from those of music?

As is quickly evident the Lefebvre of *Rhythmanalysis* is quite different from the one of *The Production of Space*. Even though rhythmanalysis is ultimately also about understanding space as a product of social relations, as a method it suggests applications beyond the social. When Lefebvre lays out the outline of spatialized temporalities on the analogy with music, he is also admitting into view the question of perception and its modulation. For the musical analogy may also be taken as a statement on the structure of human perception in which the hearing of music is produced out of not just the reception of ordered sounds, but the commingling of those sounds into a matrix infused by memory, anticipation, and emotion. In other words, the measure of music is also a metronome of our emotional responses to it, and that is what allows it to be pleasant or unpleasant to the listener. Space, on the other hand, is populated both by objects, whether these objects be trees, pylons, and so forth, and the more labile and ephemeral human social interactions that also come to fundamentally define our experience of it. Thus there is a physical-cum-social interactional materiality to space that distinguishes it from the sonic (materialities?) of music. This requires that the rhythmanalytical logic and history of space be established differently from those of music. What I take from Lefebvre for the story of Accra I hope to provide in *Oxford Street* is that my account is as much subjective, personal, modular, and rhythmic as it is grounded in detailed observations of history and social relations. But the fact that it is subjective does not mean that it is private; quite the opposite. What I have sought to show in this introductory chapter and will hope to reiterate incrementally in subsequent ones, is that urban space has an inherently rhythmic quality that can only be ascertained from modulating our perspectives along diverse vectors of interpretation, sometimes sequentially, but often also regulated by different forms of simultaneity.

Several spatial precepts thus inform *Oxford Street* part I, under the general rubric of "Horizontal Archaeologies," takes for inspiration a central premise of the discipline of archaeology regarding the relations between parts and wholes unearthed by excavation and that have to be painstakingly pieced together by the archaeological interpreter of the past.[11] This takes Lefebvre's rhythmanalysis in the direction of understanding the relationship between spatial dimensions (both material and sociological) and the totality of which they are a part not by establishing modes of measurement beforehand but by systematically oscillating between such vectors. When the archaeologist picks up a shard from what might be a vase or other object, the principal approach to the shard is that it must somehow connect to something else larger than itself. The pressure of its pastness, long or short, is a primary portal of signification. This is so even if the larger vase of which it is a part has not been fully assembled (or may never be, for that matter). Furthermore, the relationship is between not just shard and vase, but the shard and the larger cultural system of which it is assumed to be an aspect. Thus there is a multilayered conceptual operation taking place in the mind of the archaeologist that proceeds by taking the shard as the nodal point not only of a material culture but also of a semiotic system that has to be aggregated from different elements. If the initial trigger for my exploration of Oxford Street was the impulse to read the street in the guise of a Benjaminian flâneur as well as through the deployment of a Lefebvrian rhythmanalysis, these were quickly subsumed under the more urgent charge of grasping the details of the street as a means of understanding the totality of Accra's urban form in general. The details that one sees on Oxford Street all help us to understand the larger framework that is Accra's urbanscape, yet each detail provides a different aspect or route to that framework. In the context of *Oxford Street*, I couple the notion of horizontality to that of archaeology to highlight the fact that every phenomenon to be perceived in Accra today, whether economic, cultural, or sociological, is (a) connected to other phenomena that may not appear in the first instance to be immediately related to it, and (b) has to be historicized both with respect to the specific phenomenon in question and in terms of the sociocultural relations of which it is an expressive fragment. Thus, my mode of contextualization is to situate apparently isolated phenomena within a larger relational framework, the ultimate objective of which is to draw out the mediated relations between different aspects of a potential totality. To establish the relations among what are apparently discrete elements on the street, each element will be seen in terms of multi-spatial and multi-scalar modes of articulation.[12] While the principle of a horizontal archaeology will be illustrated in a variety of ways in part I, the most sustained attempt to engage with this principle will be specifically provided in chapter 4 "'The Beautyful Ones': Tro-tro Slogans, Cell Phone Advertising, and the Hallelujah Chorus," where I focus on the veritable zodiac of tro-tro slogans and inscriptions that proliferate on Accra's streets. A connection will be made, on the one hand, between these slogans and the scripts of large-scale billboard advertising on Oxford Street and, on the other, to the popular songs, television programs, and other media that help to sustain this kind of urban street wisdom as part of the discursive ensemble of relays between tradition and modernity, and locality and transnationalism. The location of chapter 4 in part II, "Morphologies of Everyday Life," is meant to act as a conceptual bridge between the strictly geographical concerns of the first part of Oxford Street and the more ethnographic emphases of the second.

Hence the chapters in part I will focus primarily on urban spatial evolution, with the accretions of districts and neighborhoods from the historic Ga Mashie area from the middle to the late nineteenth century onward being at the core of our considerations throughout. However, an additional and quite crucial spatial precept that will also cumulatively inform the chapters in part I takes all neighborhoods and districts as the spatial aggregations of social forces. It is these aggregations that have come to determine the dimensions of cityness in Accra today. To think of spatial aggregations of social forces requires us to interpret the dynamics of urban settlement from a different perspective than that of demography. For social forces are not amenable to brute enumeration; they must be understood as processes of both aggregation and fissure. While it is self-evident that Ga Mashie is largely a Ga ethnic enclave, that is not as significant an observation as the fact that there has been a steady differentiation between this enclave and the other groups that have progressively accrued to Old Accra and the Central Business District. To indicate the complex and differential character of aggregations and their connection to ethnicity and hybrid identities, I shall contrast Ga Mashie and Osu in chapters 1 and 3, respectively. The contrast is by way of exploring the status of two transnational and hybrid groups that have been central to overall Ga identity formation. These are the Tabon of Ga Mashie, and the Danish Euro-Africans (mulattoes) of Osu, both of whom have had a significant, if until now largely ignored, impact on Accra's social character. An ethno-political nomenclature drawn from Ga sociopolitical realities— *akutso* (quarter), *mantse* (chief), and *asafo* (socio-military group)—will be read in both instances to explore how these two hybrid groups *became* Ga over a period of more than two hundred years, but without completely shedding their cultural hybridity. And in the process of their *becoming* Ga they also illustrate the different rhythms and temporalities by which Accra's urban space may be further understood. The intervening chapter 2, on the other hand, attends to the colonial administrative function and its effect on the conversion of land in Accra from agrarian to urban usages.

Part II, under the rubric of "Morphologies of Everyday Life," focuses predominantly on urban representations, with a decidedly ethnographic methodological orientation to the question of space making. As already noted, the ubiquitous and colorful tro-tro inscriptions will be the subject of chapter 4. In chapters 5 and 6 the social rhythms of the particularized spaces of the salsa dance floor and the gym will be used to highlight how the youth perform their inhabitation of urban space in contemporary Accra. Such urban spaces are inherently intersectional and open to the shaping dynamics of larger transnational processes that impinge upon them. Chapter 7 transfers the template of analysis into the literary domain, with the source of spatial examples being drawn mainly from the work of Amma Darko and Kofi Awoonor, but with wide-ranging references to other representations of Accra by Ayi Kwei Armah, Kojo Laing, and Martin Egblewogbe, among others. In this chapter my interest is in connecting spatial traversal (i.e., the ways in which characters literally walk or otherwise traverse the city) and the larger issue of sentimental education. For, as we shall see, the traversal from one spatial location to another, completely different location, is often a way of demarcating the terms of an existential crisis for the protagonist.

Two central questions additionally ebb and flow throughout *Oxford Street*: first, how do we speak of urban space in an African city when that space is overdetermined by seemingly contradictory spatial logics? And second, what are the mechanisms by which global capitalism and its transnational cognates produce a mimetic universalism of urban forms while engendering a split from the recognition of the inequalities brought on by this mode of universalism? Each issue requires careful detailing and interrogation. While the wide-ranging literature on globalization will be touched upon at various points, the concept is not going to be taken either as the demon of regress or the archangel of progress, but rather as the conduit for the production of a variety of contradictions that are seen to be manifest at the economic, cultural, and social levels and that raise implications for thinking about the urban space of Accra in a complex and nuanced way beyond its immediate designation as the capital city of Ghana. In the concluding chapter, I propose to situate Oxford Street and Accra securely within the discourse of urban studies of the developing world more generally. Here the question is whether, following Jean and John Comaroff's *Theory from the South, Cultural Anthropology* (2010) and Rem Koolhaas's disquisitions on African cities, we can argue that places like Accra hold portents about the "city yet to come," to echo the title of AbdouMaliq Simone's book.[13]

My retelling of Accra through Oxford Street has been historically conventional in a number of respects while also wedding the account to a more idiosyncratic description. History has been present throughout in two interrelated ways. The retelling of the life of the city provided in this study has been a historical account tracing it from the arrival of the Gas from Ayawaso in the mid-seventeenth century through to the city's variegated expansion in the twentieth and twenty-first centuries. This largely chronological account has been anchored in a series of significant dates: 1680 (Akwamu defeat of the Gas), 1722 (the Danish school at Christiansborg), 1836 (the arrival of Afro-Brazilians), 1877 (Accra declared capital of the Gold Coast Colony), 1908 (outbreak of bubonic plague), 1939 (devastating earthquake), 1957 (Independence), 1979 (the bombing of Makola), 1992 (the Fourth Republic), among various others. The gallery of dates however provides only an ambiguous history, for much of the story here will also be relayed in terms of small-scale histories of say the Brazilians of Otublohum, the Danish-Africans of Osu, and of the tro-tro inscriptions, salsa, and gymming that I shall detail in different chapters. The variant temporalities of these microcosms do not run counter to the trajectory of the larger history but are what give it weft and form. The overarching narrative of a sequential history has thus only been made manifest via the retellings of nodal anecdotes that themselves represent an overlay of different temporalities and are meant to be cyclical in terms of the specifically human-interest dimensions that they repeatedly invoke as a central if concealed aspect of the largely chronological history of the city.

This, then, is a modest paean to the city I acknowledge as mine, but which I also recognize as the product of the past, as well as of the social, cultural, economic, and transnational changes that impact upon it. Accra's transformation reminds me forcefully of the many parts of myself that have been lodged there, here, and elsewhere, but which come together in the retelling of this great African cosmopolis.

PART I
HORIZONTAL ARCHAEOLOGIES

CHAPTER 1

Ga Akutso Formation and the Question of Hybridity:
The Afro-Brazilians (Tabon) of Accra

At one of the top private schools in Accra a conversation takes place between two fourteen-year-old girls. Ama is the older of two daughters and her mother is an Ashanti cloth trader at Makola. They live in the posh McCarthy Hill neighborhood right on the outskirts of Accra. Her friend Sara, an only child whose parents are both prominent professionals, lives in the Airport Residential Area. She is trying to persuade the increasingly skeptical Ama that she is a Tabon and not just a Ga and, moreover, a descendant of one of the earliest Tabon families that arrived in Accra in the nineteenth century. She cites a long list of prominent Ghanaians of Tabon stock: Miguel Augustus Riberio, she notes proudly, was Ghana's first ambassador to Washington and Dr. Aruna Morton was President Kwame Nkrumah's first private physician, while Azumah Nelson, the finest boxer Ghana has ever known, was also a Tabon. When she gets to Justice Georgina Theodora Wood, the country's first female chief justice, Ama can hide her surprise no longer. "Georgina Wood! A Tabon?" Ama interjects, the list of prominent Ashantis she was rehearsing in her mind as a riposte suddenly seeming somewhat paltry in comparison. "Well, she probably didn't know either," ventured her friend kindly. "But as for me, I am a Tabon and I want you always to remember that. Always."[1] The fact that Sara, after over 150 years of the Tabon's coming to settle in Accra and their adoption of the customs, language, and culture of the Ga people, can still assert a strong Tabon identity ahead of her identification as a Ga should not really come as a surprise. Rather, this conversation raises the larger question of cultural hybridity and the processes by which the Tabon progressively *became* Ga and yet managed to retain a persistent sense of their Afro-Brazilian identity. Clearly, the designation of Tabon is not just one imposed upon them by those with whom they came to interact, but is also a self-declared mode of identification that has persisted from their first arrival in the nineteenth century to this day.

There are no secure figures for the demographic changes that took place in nineteenth-century Ga Mashie until the first colonial census of 1891. Even then demography was reduced to questions of gender ratios, the population flows from different parts of the colony, the tribal provenance of residents, and, finally, the racial composition of the town. The last census element just listed was a key means of monitoring the needs of the European population in relation to those of other nonnatives such as the Lebanese, whose numbers came to increase steadily in the course of the twentieth century. Rather than being the banal articulation of a demographic detail, the Tabon allow us also to raise the question of the differences between multiethnicity and multiculturalism. We shall see how the census elements of tribes and races help in the consolidation of multiethnicity during the period of colonialism but frustrate the grounds for the articulation of multiculturalism then and afterward. In the overall processes by which the Tabon were transformed from being Portuguese-speaking Afro-Brazilians to being counted as "native" Ga, we see the tensions between ethnicity, multiculturalism, and hybridity, and the implications that these raise for understanding the cultural constitution not only of Accra but of Ghana in general. To understand these processes and questions, however, we are obliged to take a detour into the overall history of Ga Mashie akutso formation from the seventeenth century onward and how the Tabon came to be inserted into this process on their arrival from Bahia in Brazil.

Accra: A Potted Historical Sketch

Oral tradition suggests that the Gas arrived in Accra at different stages from about the thirteenth century, with the most popular account asserting that they appeared like a mass of ants from the eastern horizon, likely from the western part of today's Nigeria. The ant image accounts for the Akan name Nkrang (ants) by which they are referred to to this day. However, by the early seventeenth century, the Gas were already a well-organized group, with a discernible sociopolitical structure and six settlement townships or *man* (pl. *manjii*) along the coastline that included Ga Mashie, Osu, La, Teshie, Nungua, and Tema. In this period the capital of the Ga polity was situated at Ayawaso, some eleven miles inland from the coast. The Abonse Market at Ayawaso was a major hub for the exchange of goods between the coastal peoples and those of the hinterland. European goods such as cloth, basins, knives, guns, and rum were exchanged for gold and slaves at the market. In addition to the imported commodities, products such as salt, fish, and cattle were sold by the Ga in exchange for crops from the fertile inland regions. The Abonse Market was so well organized that it had its own trade minister who regulated prices and levied taxes on commercial transactions.[2]

While there had always been traffic between the inland Akan tribes and the Europeans on the coast, Ga mastery of European trade languages made them indispensable middlemen and interpreters for all Akwamu, Akyem, and Ashanti traders. Things were to change dramatically from the 1640s when the Gas attempted to institute a monopoly on trade with the Europeans, insisting that all commercial exchanges be concentrated at the Abonse Market at Ayawaso and restricting coastal access to traders from the hinterland Akan groups. This state of affairs was to trigger major conflicts, culminating in wars with the powerful military kingdom of Akwamu from 1677, which comprehensively defeated the Gas in 1680. The Ga kingdom at Ayawaso was utterly decimated and their king Okai Koi decapitated. Akwamu was to exercise sovereignty over the Gas until 1730, when they were in their turn defeated by a joint army comprising Ga, Akyem, and Akwapim soldiers with the active support of the Europeans on the coast. Other oral traditions suggest that Ga society also underwent a period of rule by priests. However, Ga social evolution and the fact that they had to contend with other warlike ethnic groups meant that by the end of the seventeenth century they had adopted asafo military organization from their Akan neighbors. The Gas had also progressively severed priesthood from chiefly rule and consolidated the institution of chieftaincy as the main instrument of political organization, while also assimilating minimal sacred roles of priesthood to that of the chief.[3] One of the main effects of the destruction of the Ayawaso kingdom, their enforced migration to the coast, and the Ga adoption of Akan military forms was the fissuring and interethnic hybridity that came to define Ga identity, especially in the formation of the *akutsei* (sing. akutso) under the shadows of the different European forts and castles on the coast.[4] By the nineteenth century the overlap and later competition between chiefly and priestly roles came to also manifest itself in arguments about primogeniture among the various traditional elders and their more Westernized cultural elites who had taken sides in pursuit of their own modernizing agendas. With Accra's rapid urbanization in the first part of the twentieth century, arguments about primogeniture became central for adjudicating land ownership, who had natural claims to the land and who could claim ownership only as a stranger, thus suggesting contradictory yet profound *spatial* implications drawn from the oral traditions. The spatial implications of native versus stranger derived ultimately from the nature of Indirect Rule, but was shown most forcefully in the distinction between traditional Ga areas and the various zongos (stranger quarters) into which migrants from the north were encouraged to settle. We shall learn more about the zongos in chapter 6.

It is to the observations of travelers to the coast from the nineteenth century, however, that we ought to turn for a sense of the character of the town's early settlement patterns. The description that Henry Morton Stanley provides of Accra's coastline in 1874 has been much cited by historians of the city and provides a good starting point for tracing a number of details about its early spatial form. We are obliged to quote the relevant passage at some length:

> At seven o'clock I was awakened by a hideous din of human voices jabbering alongside the ship in their surf-boats and unintelligible jargon of words such as no Christian like myself could stand without nerves getting unstrung. I therefore looked upon what was called Accra with a sullen face and in no amiable frame of mind.
>
> The scene ashore was that of a straight beach backed by a mud terrace, which stretched to the right and left and rear of Accra for many miles singularly open and clear as seen from shipboard. Accra itself straggled for nearly a mile on the edge of a terrace overlooking the beach, many pretentious houses, whitewashed, attracting attention from their prominence above the clay-brown huts amongst them. Almost to the extreme left was the Commandant's house; its wide verandah promised coolness, and the wide space around it informed you that at one time or another some occupant of it had been assiduous to procure unpolluted air. Away to the extreme right was another large house with wide verandahs, and abundant grounds about it. This was the Basle Mission House, occupied by a singular community of religious Swiss and Germans, who have banded together for the sensible purpose of teaching the natives and making money by them from honest trade in palm oil and gold dust. In the very centre of the town was the port and lighthouse of Accra. Between these houses the body of the town of native and European buildings jammed itself. Some three miles to the east of the Basle Mission is the village of Christiansborg, a picturesque mass of whitewashed buildings consisting of a ruined castle, a ruined martello tower, and another large establishment of the enterprising Basle Mission.[5]

Stanley's reference to the "mud terrace, which stretched to the right and left and rear of Accra for many miles singularly open and clear as seen from shipboard" is suggestive of an attempt at enframing the description, almost as if describing a picture. The word "terrace" usually denotes a level paved area or platform next to a building or a patio or veranda, but another meaning also refers to the slope of ground that stretches to a body of water, be this a lake, a river, or the sea. Thus to state that the mud terrace stretched to the right, left, and rear for many miles and not just in front of the town leading toward the sea produces a picture frame for the description that unfolds within it.[6] The contrast between mud, with its suggestions of potential for disorderly dissolution and even disease, and bush, with its implication of land that has not yet been claimed for settlement and cultivation, is a telling semiotic dyad that becomes a recurrent thematic in debates on Accra's urban planning well into the colonial period. While the blatantly racist attitude toward the local population expressed by Stanley was by no means to continue in such an explicit form into the later workings of the colonial administration proper, the essential coupling of the civilizing impulse with that of nausea for local life was to be restated in a variety of formal and informal contexts, but most significantly to promote sanitation and decongestion policies in much of the colonial period and also to justify the racial segregation of European housing that was to have a major impact on the nature of the town's morphology and expansion.

Strictly speaking, however, the value of Stanley's remarks comes from the settlement topography he provides us of the town. As he rightly goes on to point out later in the description, the Accra township of 1874 was divided into three distinct European spheres of influence. While the Portuguese had arrived at Elmina as early as 1471 and were the dominant traders all along the coast for the next 150 years and thus had a telling impact on all coastal societies, as we noted earlier it was the mid-seventeenth-century wars with hinterland groups that saw the Ga social polity decisively fissuring and reconstituted under the aegis of different European spheres of influence. The Dutch had built Fort Crèvecoeur in 1649 (later renamed Ussher Fort) at Usshertown, also known as Kinka, a cannon's shot away from James Fort which was itself put up by the English in 1672 in what was later to become Jamestown but is also called by its alternative local name of Nleshie. The Danes, on the other hand, established themselves much farther eastward at Christiansborg Castle, itself taken over from the Swedes and completed in 1659 at Osu, where three and a half centuries later Oxford Street was to flourish. The conjuncture of the dates of the establishment of European merchant presence on the coast with the escalation of conflicts between the Gas and their neighbors at midcentury is not entirely accidental, as it has been shown that the European presence heightened the need for military protection of hinterland trade routes to guarantee the continuing flow of goods from the Europeans into the hinterland and vice versa. By the end of the seventeenth century, the slave trade had instituted a comprehensive transformation of coastal states, converting war into a concomitant and necessary aspect of the slave trade itself. The Europeans were also obligingly to supply guns and ammunitions to the Gas in exchange for favors of land, privileged access to hinterland markets, and expansion of the slave trade.[7]

Despite the detail of his account, Stanley's description of the morphology of the town in 1874 was already being swept into the dustbin of history even as he was penning it. The Anglo-Danish Treaty of 1850 and the Anglo-Dutch Treaty of 1874 ensured that the entire Gold Coast was finally taken over by the British, with all the forts and castles on the coastline passing over to them. The incorporation of the Northern Territories as a protectorate in 1898, the annexation of Ashanti in 1901, and the ceding to Britain of part of the mandated territory of Togoland (previously run by Germany) by the League of Nations in 1922 was to set up the essential geographical boundaries of what was later to become independent Ghana. More important, the unification of the British administration under the new capital of Accra in 1877 coupled with the progressive pacification and incorporation of the other territories set up a dynamic relationship between the growing township and its various labor and economic hinterlands, thus also ultimately altering the evolution of the town for good.

While Ga allegiance was for a long time to remain splintered along the European spheres of influence even after the forts and castles were all incorporated into the singular British scheme from the mid-nineteenth century, it is the Ga system of divisional akutsei (quarters) that was to feed into political conflicts with the British colonial administration, and from the early twentieth century into the character of Accra's spatial expansion. Each of the six Ga townships is divided into different akutsei or quarters with the Ga Mashie township being constituted by seven akutsei, namely, Abola, Gbese, Asere, and Otublohum located in Kinka/Usshertown, with Akanmaji, Sempe, and Alata to be found at Nleshie/Jamestown. If the formation of the Ga Mashie akutsei in the seventeenth century was influenced primarily by factors of kinship localization and the occupational specializations of fishing, fish processing, salt making, and trade, by the end of the nineteenth century the akutsei were more significant as self-interested collective political agents in their interactions with the colonial administration as well as within the context of inter-akutso rivalries.

Ga Mashie political organization was generally decentralized and, as co-lonial rule got consolidated, exposed a number of crucial stress points. For complex reasons of historical priority, the Ga Mantse (chief) was normally nominated from among the leading families of the Gbese and Asere akut-sei, Gbese itself having originally split off from Asere.[8] Each akutso has its own divisional chief or headman, whose interests have historically not al-ways coincided either with those of the Ga Mantse or with other divisional chiefs. Furthermore, the power of the akutso mantse was countered by that ascribed to *oblempon* (rich man) stools, normally established by successful merchants commanding the allegiance of a large number of commoners and slaves. With the invigoration of the asafo as organized channels of youth dissent from the 1920s, a challenge was also to be felt from commoners, with the number of calls for chiefly destoolment multiplying severalfold between 1920 and 1950.[9] Ga chiefly authority was to be fundamentally desta-bilized by colonial policies that, while attempting to codify a coherent sense of what passed for customary law, also progressively undermined the Ga chiefs' power to exercise authority over their own subjects. At a formal level the process of colonial intervention into Ga chiefly structures was articu-lated through various instruments such as the Town Councils Ordinance of 1894, the Public Lands Ordinance of 1876, the Native Jurisdiction Ordinance of 1910, the Municipal Corporations Ordinance of 1924, and the Native Ad-ministration Ordinance of 1927. These and various other ordinances, poli-cies, and laws sought to institute governance procedures for the town that ultimately came to pitch the chiefs against their Western-educated elites on the one hand and against the colonial authorities on the other. Stranger groups provided a further overlay of complications to any idea of a uniform Ga Mashie identity, as the example of the Tabon exemplifies.

The Tabon of Accra

The sociocultural mixtures central to Ga akutso formation in the seven-teenth century have been noted by various scholars, but never specifically with respect to the significance of these fissures and hybridities for the town's spatial expansion beyond the core Ga Mashie area.[10] Hybrid akutso formation was evident in several akutsei, but of special interest to us here is that of the Alata and Otublohum quarters. When the British came to build their fort on the Accra coast in the 1670s, they brought with them slaves from Allada, also known as the Slave Coast, in modern-day Benin.[11] Fishermen from Morée, a town close to Cape Coast, augmented this slave labor pool.

The Allada slaves and the Morée fishermen subsequently settled close to the fort and constituted themselves into the Alata quarter of Jamestown. With regard to the Otubluhom akutso, John Parker provides a lively description that takes account of the complex layering of conflicting social, political, and economic interests:

> The Otublohum *akutso* originated as a branch of an Akwamu lineage descended from Otu, the first Akwamu governor of Accra. Like Wetse Kojo [chief of the Alata quarter] Otu began his career as a "company slave," having been pawned by his Akwamu family to the Dutch at Fort Crèvecoeur. The Dutch subsequently made him their chief broker (*makelaar*) and, following the consolidation of Akwamu power on the coast in 1681, he was appointed as the representative of the Akwamu king in Accra. His son Amu, however, played a key role in the revolt against the Akwamuhene in 1730, enabling the Otublohum *akutso* to consolidate a position of influence in Kinka after the overthrow of Akwamu overrule. As in other quarters, the balance of political power within Otublohum remained highly fluid. By the late 1820s, the Dutch *makelaar* and most powerful figure in the *akutso* was not the established *mantse*, but rather one Kwaku Ankra. Accra's leading slave trader until his death in 1840, Ankra founded an *oblempon*, or "rich man's" stool, which remained a source of alternative authority within Otublohum throughout our period. His clout was demonstrated in 1836 when a party of ex-slaves deported from Bahia in Brazil landed in Accra. The returnees, most of whom were Muslims originally from the Sudanic savanna, were incorporated into Otublohum under the personal patronage of *makelaar* Ankra. The insertion of the "Brazilian" or "Tabon" community represented a significant modification to Accra's increasingly diverse town quarters. Within a few years of their arrival a number of Tabons had emerged as wealthy entrepreneurs, having forged commercial links with fellow returnees in the ports of the Slave Coast.[12]

The rise of an ex-slave to a position of great power and influence, the fragmentation of Akwamu suzerain authority brought about by descendants of those originally sent as resident ambassadors of their king after the Ga defeat, and the split in effective political power signaled on the one hand by a self-made merchant-cum-cultural broker (*makelaar*) and on the other by the divisional or town mantse may all be considered pertinent to understanding the dynamics of akutso political and social functions. But it is the reception of the Tabon that provides a crucial dimension of Ga ethno-cultural hybridity that was later to have a significant impact on urban formation.

Parker's remark that many of the Brazilian returnees were Muslims originally from the Sudanic savannah requires some qualification. While many Hausas and Fulanis found themselves as slaves in Bahia, the heavy preponderance of Yorubas, also referred to in Brazil by the umbrella term of Nagôs, means that the returnees were as likely to have come from Yoruba stock as from elsewhere. The two ethnic categories are not, however, mutually exclusive for understanding the provenance of the Afro-Brazilian returnees. The bulk of slavery in that period came from today's Benin/Nigeria region of West Africa and may be accounted for with reference to the expansionist jihads undertaken by Uthman Dan Fodio from 1804 to 1815. These jihads were to trigger crises in Yorubaland itself, especially in the rebellion and subsequent wars that were launched by the Are-Ona Kakanfo Afonja from the military encampment of Ilorin in northern Oyo from 1817 to 1824. In the early nineteenth century, Ilorin was predominantly Yoruba but with a heavy Hausa-Fulani presence, and Afonja's troops were composed of Muslim slaves skilled in horse riding.[13] The combination of Uthman Dan Fodio's jihads (which were key to the formation of what was later to become the powerful Sokoto caliphate) and Afonja's wars (which helped to consolidate the Emirate of Illorin) was to lead to an upsurge of Yoruba and Muslim captives (often one and the same due to widespread conversion of the Yoruba) who ended up being sold in the slave port of the kingdom of Dahomey (Benin), itself populated by the Anago, also a Yoruba-speaking people. Thus when scholars such as Pierre Verges, J. Lorand Matory, and João José Reis point out that many of the Muslims of nineteenth-century Bahia were Nagôs, we must understand this as suggesting a complicated history of provenance from that region of West Africa.[14]

The Yoruba connection is not inconsequential for our study of Accra, for it also allows us to conceptually join the Tabon of Otublohum to the people of Alata, at least in terms of their partially shared Yoruba provenance. Today the terms Alata (derived from Allada) and Anago (derived from the Yoruba group originally located on the present-day Benin/Nigeria border) are both used by Ghanaians to designate anyone from Nigeria, whether of Yoruba provenance or otherwise.[15] While it might be too far a stretch to suggest that the Yoruba presence on the Accra coast in the seventeenth century could be aligned to the vibrant commercial networks they were to establish in the Gold Coast in later periods, it is still important to note that Yorubas had a major impact on Accra's urban formation well into the twentieth century. Both Makola Market and Tudu Lorry Park stand as testaments to Yoruba trading influence on the city. Furthermore, the highly controversial Aliens

Compliance Order of 1969 during Busia's regime had as much to do with stemming the undoubted influence of Yoruba traders in the country as with protecting local industries from foreign ownership and intervention. The effect of the order was to drive thousands of Yoruba traders away from Ghana back to their own country, something that was to be reciprocated to great cost in the expulsions of Ghanaians from Nigeria in 1982. However, by the early twentieth century the Yoruba community in Gold Coast/Ghana was not composed only of traders but also of other professionals that came to actively contribute to the country's political and social life. The Akiwumi family offers an illustrative example of this professional group. S. O. Akiwumi was born to a royal family in Lagos in 1858. After working for two years in the Public Works Department as a shopkeeper in his early twenties, he decided to set himself up as a general merchant in Accra from 1887. He became a highly successful cocoa merchant and led an active life in the social circles of the time; in 1917–1918 he took over chairmanship of what was later to become the Accra Tennis Club, in succession to Sir Hugh Clifford, then governor of the colony. S. O. Akiwumi also acted as vice president of the Red Cross League, donating £150 of his own funds to the organization when it was first established. He sent eight of his twelve children to boarding schools in England, with one of them, Alfred Molade Akiwumi, furnishing an even more remarkable contribution to Ghana's social and political life. Born in Nigeria in 1891, but coming to settle in the Gold Coast with his father as a child, Molade Akiwumi went on to read law at Cambridge University, marry Helen Kabuki Ocansey from a prominent Ga family, and rise to become justice of the Supreme Court and later second speaker of Ghana's National Assembly from February 1958 to June 1960. The rise of a man of Yoruba and Nigerian origins to such national heights in his adopted country is hard to conceive of in today's Ghana (or the reverse in Nigeria), where the discourse of postindependence nationalism has also narrowed the sense of Pan-African interchange that defined the colonial and early postcolonial periods.[16]

Parker's reference to the early Tabon's forging of commercial links with fellow returnees on the Slave Coast is also significant for understanding the transnational networks that they came to cultivate. As J. Lorand Matory has pointed out, as many as eight thousand manumitted slaves from Bahia returned to West Africa from 1822 to 1899, with many of these settling in colonial Lagos. Among the reasons for the resettlement of returnee Afro-Brazilians in Lagos was the active British interest in freeing slaves who had been ensnared in the residual slave trade after its abolition in 1807.[17] Since British West Africa in the nineteenth century included several other territories in the region, Lagos must not be taken as an isolated focus of British antislavery or indeed resettlement efforts.[18] The administrative connections between Sierra Leone, the Gold Coast, and Lagos were to prove highly significant for the dynamic settlement patterns of returnee stranger groups from the New World to West Africa in the period, raising significant implications about hybridity and intercultural exchange beyond the Bahia-Lagos nexus Matory traces in his excellent study. Indeed, as we shall see presently, the returnee Afro-Brazilians to Accra in the nineteenth century knew of their people in Lagos and Porto Novo and actively sought to establish commercial and cultural networks with them.

Strictly speaking, however, the Tabon arrived in Accra in three different stages between 1829 and 1836, with the arrivals of 1836 constituting the largest group and the ones that were to have the greatest impact among their hosts. The name Tabon derives from the form of greeting they exchanged among themselves and with their hosts ("como esta?"; "esta bom"). The numbers attributed to the group from 1836 vary, but scholars are generally agreed that they were in the region of two hundred persons and represented at least seven separate family groups. Given that the Malê (Muslim) slave rebellion had taken place in Bahia in 1835, and that the returnees constituted distinct family groups, it has been surmised that at least some if not all the Tabon of 1836 may have been deportees from that rebellion.[19] This accounts for Parker's remark about their largely Muslim heritage. It has also been noted by scholars of the Tabon that it is they who introduced Islam to the Accra coast and that this was originally concentrated at Otublohum, where they had originally settled. The group arriving in 1836 was led by Nii Azumah Nelson I and included the Vialla (Viera), Manuel, Gomez, Peregrino, Mahama Nassu (or Nassau), and Zuzer families.[20] Other Tabon names common in today's Accra and traceable to later arrivals are Ribiero, Morton, Olympio, Nelson, Da Costa, Da Rocha, Fiscian, Maslieno, and Da Silva. The warm reception extended to the Afro-Brazilians by the Dutch makelaar Kwaku Ankra ensured that the Tabon were quickly extended special Dutch protection on their arrival. They were given large tracts of land at present-day Asylum Down, Adabraka/Kokomlemle, and North Ridge not long after their arrival, on which they cultivated various vegetable crops including tomatoes, potatoes, and okra, along with the staple cassava. This continued until the early part of the twentieth century, when intense urban pressures forced the conversion of these lands from agrarian to urban uses.[21] The conversion of lands generated a number of significant tensions within the Tabon community and between them and their Ga hosts, as we shall come to see more fully in the next chapter. As in the case of other large-scale farming enterprises such as those of the Danes in the same period, the Tabon depended heavily on local slave labor for their agricultural efforts. Yet they were also notorious as transatlantic slave merchants, an irony that has as yet not been satisfactorily explained in the existing literature. In the illegal slave trade that continued after abolition in 1807, there were several well-known Brazilian (Portuguese) traders such as the Baëtas and the Olympios, who established long-running trading dynasties among the Ewe in the east of today's Ghana and within the same nexus as the erstwhile Slave Coast in Dahomey that had flourished from the late seventeenth century. The trading networks of the Baëtas and the Olympios encompassed the extensive Afro-Brazilian communities spread across West Africa, with Kwaku Ankra and the Tabon actively taking part in this general trading nexus.[22] Having left the continent originally as Africans, the returnees came back to West Africa as Portuguese-speaking Brazilians with multiple identities and sentiments. Pragmatism as much as the quest for survival was to see them forge a multitiered hybrid identity that aligned them, on the one hand, to Portuguese-speaking trading networks that extended across the region and that extended back as far as Brazil, and on the other to their host communities in Lagos, Porto Novo, and Accra.[23]

The building of Brazil House by Mama Nassu shortly after the Tabon's arrival in 1836 must also be taken as a manifest signifier of their spatial integration into local commercial and cultural networks, for it quickly became the center of their social and cultural life. Fully restored as a UNESCO Heritage site in 2005, Brazil House, located on Brazil Lane between Ussher Fort and James Fort, directly overlooks the old harbor. As Mae-Ling Lokko points out in her architectural study of Brazil House, it was no accident that most of the houses built in that area had their backyards overlooking the Jamestown Harbor and their front verandas directly opening onto the busy Brazil Lane. Brazil Lane was a short distance from what was later to develop into the busy High Street.[24] Their location right on the harbor, the spatial gateway to the township that came to be progressively connected to the rest of the colony by a network of railways and roads by the end of the nineteenth century, gave the Tabon many situational advantages and helped them consolidate their commercial networks from very early in their sojourn. Also, given the mixed land-use dimensions of the areas close to the harbor, which comprised a mixture of large offices-cum-warehouses and residential units for both European merchants and the local population, Brazil Lane quickly became a prized community location for trade, and later for the provision of accom-

1.1. Brazil House, Jamestown. Photo by author.

modations and warehousing facilities to the many European entrepreneurs that dominated large-scale businesses in Accra in the period.

The changes in the occupational character of Brazil House from 1874 until the middle of the twentieth century also speak to the social and economic transformations of the entire area and of the Afro-Brazilians' place in it. The land and property values of the coastal strip that included Brazil House, Brazil Lane, and the areas close to the Ussher and James Forts increased exponentially as the twentieth century wore on, such that by mid-century many of the more prosperous Tabon had leased their properties to European businesses for use as offices and warehouses and had moved out to live on their lands at Adabraka, Kokomlemle, and elsewhere. In 1874 the original structure of Brazil House was torn down and rebuilt by Kofi Acquah, the eldest grandchild of Mama Nassu, who had trained as a chef in Warri, the bustling trade port in today's western Nigeria.[25] Acquah renamed the refurbished property Warri House in commemoration of his successful sojourn abroad and converted parts of the house into warehouses for rent to European businesses. This state of affairs was to remain in place until the 1940s, when on the departure of the last European tenants of Brazil House

Acquah's younger sister, Adelaide Apponsah, moved in with her family to establish a highly successful fishing enterprise.[26] Scissors House, another landmark Tabon building at Otublohum, was built by Aruna Nelson in 1854 and remained the center of Tabon tailor craft until it was destroyed by a fire in 1977. To this day one of the most highly regarded tailors in Accra is Dan Morton, a direct descendant of the Mortons from the first generation of Tabons. As Mae-Ling notes, the early Brazilian houses at Ga Mashie were built of stone, with a design generally reminiscent of the two-story buildings of Bahia. This fact requires us to revise Stanley's account of Accra (1874), in which, as we might recall, all the whitewashed and grander buildings were on his assumption owned either by Europeans or the Basel Mission.

In 1860 a shop for blacksmiths was opened at Christiansborg by the Basel Missionary Trading Company, where students were taught to make wheels and produce barrels and carts for exporters of palm oil, palm kernels, coffee, and later cocoa.[27] It would not be hyperbolic to assert, however, that it was the Tabon that first introduced such skills with a specifically urban inflection into the general local economy. When they first arrived, the Tabon were already well skilled at shoemaking, carpentry, metal forging, architecture, and tailoring; they were also highly experienced farmers, skilled in irrigation techniques and in the location and digging of wells.[28] This confirms the observation proffered by Reis about the sophisticated occupational characteristics of the African slaves that filled the streets of Salvador in Bahia. As he notes, they "worked in the open air as artisans, washerwomen, tailors, street vendors, water bearers, barbers, musicians, artists, masons, carpenters, stevedores, and sedan chair porters."[29] The digging of wells and the availability of good drinking water was especially useful to their Ga hosts, as potable water was not to be generally available until the 1920s with the opening of the Weija Waterworks, and even then after serious disagreements about water rates between the Ga chiefs and the colonial administration.[30]

If the Ga of nineteenth-century Accra were focused predominantly on the occupational specializations of fishing, fish processing, salt making, and trade, the Tabon came to contribute early forms of urban livelihood diversification that were later to strongly resonate with the large numbers of migrants to arrive from other parts of the colony and West Africa. Unlike company artisanal slaves (cooks, carpenters, blacksmiths, etc.) who worked in the European forts and castles from the seventeenth century and whose allegiance was primarily to their masters, or the converts to early Christianity who fell under the aegis of the Basel Missionaries, the Tabon had allegiance only to themselves as a distinct sociocultural group forging a place within a new urban environment.[31] Their urban skills set must then be interpreted as a crucial element of urban exchange value, tied neither to the residual slave economy of the European forts and castles nor to the normative religious implications of the Christian missions. Their early access to tracts of land both close to the Jamestown Harbor and farther inland also meant that they were quickly to occupy the upper entrepreneurial echelons of society, since they not only owned significant means of agricultural production but also had the requisite skills to establish highly valued craft industries such as tailoring and blacksmithing. The Tabon possessed skills that became increasingly significant for negotiating urban life and, given the circumstances under which they first arrived, implied a significant resource for their integration into the Ga society. By the 1930s the burgeoning town was to be defined very much along the lines of urban skills represented by the Tabon, with the opportunities for working in the expanding colonial civil service, in the labor and building industries, and in commerce fully altering the nature of urban assimilation of variant migrants to the town. Gradually, success in the town was no longer linked to the goodwill of either the European trading enterprises or to the indigenous Gas as collective owners of the lands where migrants sojourned. Furthermore, with greater urbanization Accra was to become more and more dependent on agricultural produce from outlying areas, also shifting the nature of the networks that were to feed the town. While early Tabon agricultural enterprise played a central part in the feeding of Accra, later migrant groups also came to make a decisive contribution. At Tudu the community of Muslim merchants drawn from Yoruba, Hausa, and the Northern Territories contributed cattle, milk products, shea butter, kola, and other important items to the diversification of Accra's diet.[32] But even in the diversification of urban diets the Tabon seem to have led the way.

If the Tabon make salient a number of features that were later to be woven into Accra's urban fabric, there still remains the question of how they came to be so well received in the first place within a Ga community that was culturally and linguistically different from what they had experienced in Brazil. On closer examination the intelligibility question turns out to be less intractable than might first be supposed. Portuguese traders had dominated commercial exchanges in West Africa from as early as 1471 and despite the fact that the Dutch and then the British had effectively displaced Portugal as a trading force by the 1650s, Portuguese pidgin remained the preferred trade lingua franca all across the West African coast well into the nineteenth century.[33] In other words, when the Tabon arrived, they shared a partially comprehensible language that had originally been seeded in the region by the Portuguese over nearly two centuries. Alcione Amos and Ebenezer Ayesu also point out that Kwaku Ankra had a son named Antonio and a nephew called Pedro and from this fact speculate that he and other family members may have had contact with Brazilian women some time before the arrival of the cohort from 1936.[34] The explanation that seems more likely, and that Amos and Ayesu refer to only tangentially, is that occupying the coveted position of makelaar and being the largest slave trader in the period, Kwaku Ankra saw the Tabon as providing a golden opportunity for expanding his commercial networks. Aided by the common use of the Portuguese trade pidgin, by the mid-nineteenth century these networks involved trade across the Afro-Brazilian returnee communities in Lagos, Porto Novo, Ouidah, and Accra, and perhaps more important, between West Africa and the New World. Matory points out that "there were dozens of ships and hundreds of free Africans travelling from Lagos to Bahia or through Bahia to Rio or Pernambuco between 1855 and 1898" and that a transnational identity configuration and commercial endeavor existed among these groups long before transnationalism and globalization became the catchwords that they are today.[35] Ankra was himself to recruit the Tabon as slave traders; but the more important point is that as the makelaar he must have seen in them the opportunity for establishing trade networks well beyond his usual circuits. The Tabon then represent complex and layered dimensions of recursive African diasporas, cultural hybridity, urban skill sets, and the necessary assimilation of stranger groups in the spatial formation of Accra.

On Becoming Ga: Multiethnic Polities, Multiculturalism, and Hybridity

And now to return to the questions that we started with. How do we understand the conversion of the Tabon into a Ga group that nonetheless continues to assert its Brazilian heritage? What is the morphology and shape of its hybridity? And how do these relate to the presence or absence of multiculturalism in the cultural formation of Accra? Despite the many confluences of cuisines, languages, and cultural styles that have shaped Africa from the period of Arab and European contact stretching for several centuries, the term "hybridity" is not one commonly used to describe societies on the continent by African studies scholars. Even in Paul Zeleza's fine two-volume collection of essays *The Study of Africa* (2005 and 2007), the word "hybridity" and its cognates from postcolonial studies such as "creolization" and "transculturation" do not appear even once in any of the thirty-six chapters. This is a peculiar absence, especially when we consider that various regions of the continent have had large-scale interracial and intercultural mixings that were intensified during the period of colonialism from the mid-nineteenth century onward. Whether in West Africa, East Africa, or South Africa, the contribution of Syro-Lebanese, South Asians, and even Jews to the character of these regions is utterly inescapable.[36] This is not to say that scholars of East Africa and South Africa have not attended to the contributions of South Asians, but that the critical idiom has somehow managed to sidestep central insights about hybridity and transculturation that have been common to postcolonial studies. The only exception to this general rule in African studies is Mauritius, where the realities of Indian Ocean cultural exchanges have been amplified for the local cultural landscape to the degree that it is impossible to speak about the culture of the island without proper reference to the discourse on hybridity.[37] Moreover, Mauritius lends itself to comparisons with Trinidad, Barbados, and Guyana, all places in the Caribbean that have had similar demographic and cultural intermixing.

But what might be the reason for this general reluctance to deploy insights on hybridity in African studies? This may be assigned to two reasons, both of which apply firmly to Accra, and indeed to much of sub-Saharan Africa. The first is that while there is much evidence of cosmopolitanism all across the continent (think of Johannesburg, Nairobi, Lagos, or Accra), Africa is still largely multiethnic rather than multicultural. To understand the difference between the two we are obliged to go back to the discourse of Indirect Rule. No one has done more to clarify the racial character of colonial governmentality than Mahmood Mamdani, and it is to his *Define and Rule: Native as Political Identity* we now have to turn for guidance:

> First, the census divided the population into two kinds of groups; some were tagged as races and others as tribes. When a census-taker entered your name, it was either as member of a race or as member of a tribe. What determined whether you belonged to a race or a tribe? The distinction was not between colonizer and colonized, but between native and non-native. *Non-natives* were tagged as races, whereas natives were said to belong to *tribes*. *Races* were said to comprise all those officially categorized as not indigenous to Africa, whether they were indisputably foreign (European, Asians) or whether their foreignness was the result of an official designation (Arabs, Colored, Tutsi). *Tribes*, in contrast, were all those defined as indigenous in origin. Rather than highlight the distinction between colonizers and colonized, the race-tribe distinction cut through

a single category—colonized—by politically distinguishing those indigenous from those foreign. When the state officially distinguished nonindigenous races from indigenous tribes, it paid heed to one single characteristic, *origin*, and totally disregarded subsequent developments, including, *residence*. By obscuring an entire history of migrations, the state portrayed the native as the product of geography rather than history. (2012, 46–47; italics in original)

The consequence of indirect rule was to install origin as the dominant mode of understanding native populations and to render migration an anomaly. It was not uncommon to find migrants from the Northern Territories referred to as "aliens" in the colonial record. This was completely in keeping with the idea that only those historically settled in a particular area could claim rights to origin and therefore land. Not only that, as Mamdani continued to show, the privileging of tribes as the primary conduits of political comprehension also produced monotribal administrations "overseeing a triple tribal monopoly—over land, governance, and dispute settlement" and thus also institutionalizing tribal discrimination (52). Given that the Tabon were not quite a race in the nomenclature of the British administration, they were assimilated in the census of 1891 and those that followed into the Ga as part of that tribal category, thus officially ethnicizing them in the process. A similar fate was to befall the mixed-race progeny of the Danish-Africans of Osu, and in fact all Euro-Africans along the coastal regions. In all the censuses they were counted as part of the dominant ethnic groups among whom they resided, again ensuring that an ethnic category would predominate over other salient identity markers that might be called forth.

Following from the political genealogy of ethnicity and tribes from the period of Indirect Rule, we can assert that the difference between multiethnicity and multiculturalism is that while forms of exchange and mixing constitute both, it is only multiculturalism that is undergirded by a set of policies that explicitly acknowledge cultural difference as requiring protections in the process of nation-state formation. From the colonial period even while acknowledging the presence of other races such as Arabs and other Europeans, colonial policy restricted race privilege exclusively to the British. This did not constitute multiculturalism but rather racial segregation, something that strongly marked the social character of places such as Cape Town and Nairobi until the postcolonial period in the 1990s and 1960s, respectively, but also of Accra up to the 1930s. (The different rates of the dismantling of racial segregation in these places has to do with the stark differences between settler colonialism in the first two cities and administrative colonialism in the third, something that goes beyond the ken of this study but which we ought to note in passing.) The postcolonial regimes of Africa and elsewhere adopted the ethnic policies developed under Indirect Rule but failed to critique the racial policies that were their concomitant, thus privileging tribes over races even in the constitution of municipal governance. To this day the mayor of Accra is routinely drawn from among the Ga despite the blatant fact that Gas form less than 15 percent of Accra's population, down from 60 percent at independence in 1957. At heart multiculturalism turns on forms of structural functionalism; in other words, multiculturalism comprises the socioeconomic and cultural status of distinct cultures that constitute the larger polity. While what goes under the aegis of multicultural policies are the creation of twentieth-century liberal democracies, the character of multicultural accommodations may be traced much further back, with the best examples being provided by the historical instance of the Jews.

Thus John Armstrong argues in a much-cited essay in Jewish and diaspora studies for understanding the structural relationships between proletarian and mobilized diasporas and their lands of sojourn. Focusing on the dynamic interactions of different ethnic groups within multiethnic polities from the sixteenth to the twentieth centuries, he outlines the degree to which mobilized diasporas illustrate certain crucial features of boundary maintenance and the significance of these for their multiethnic societies of sojourn. These features include the versatile multilingual and mercantile skills of the Jewish mobilized diasporas in various historical epochs, a strong internal cultural elite that pursue the task of mobilizing their co-ethnics, and finally, a strong foundational myth that acts as both lubricant and glue to the work of cultural identification within the community. While many of these features are shared with other ethnic diasporas such as the Chinese in Southeast Asia or the Indians in East Africa and the Caribbean for example, in the case of Jews the foundational myth is of both an ethnic and religious provenance, with the religious disposition providing the essential form for articulating ethnic identity. Drawing on assumptions from exchange theory, Armstrong goes on to argue that while the myth of the Jewish homeland remained important, the true function of the ethnic myth was to influence the two central boundary-maintaining mechanisms of communications specialization and role specialization, both of which turned out to be crucial to the community's participation in the hegemonic ethno-polities in which they found themselves (Armstrong 1976, 394–396). This is not to say that mobilized diasporas are not fragile; in the end, as he persuasively argues, their viability and longevity ultimately depend on their use-value to the dominant elites of the places of sojourn. With changing political conditions their status changed rapidly, as can be shown for the condition of Jews in czarist Russia in the late nineteenth century, for example.

More recently, E. Natalie Rothman's *Brokering Empire: Trans-Imperial Subjects between Venice and Istanbul* (2011) illustrates a similarly variegated picture of multiculturalism. The book is set mainly in the Venice of the 1550s–1670s and focuses on the cultural mediation performed by various actors, including the famed dragomans (translators), Venetian commercial brokers, traders, converts, and a host of other personages. *Brokering Empire* is literally teeming with cultural ethnicities and social functions: Jews, Armenians, Ottoman ambassadors, and Arabs, along with a plethora of Venetian commercial and political elites. As Rothman adroitly shows, the composite households of commercial brokers acted as switchboards of interchange between "locals" and "foreigners" and thus provided a theatre for the ongoing recalibration of these two categories, and for the insertion of the various ethnicities into the complex multicultural mix that was Venice. The attraction of both Armstrong's and Rothman's accounts is in what they suggest about the accommodation and/or protections that were provided for certain ethnicities because of the functional roles they offered to their multiethnic cultural environments. We should note that the process of establishing accommodations within a multiethnic environment is as much dialectical as it is pragmatic, emanating from both sides of hegemonic elite and mobilized diaspora perspectives. The mechanisms for achieving accommodation do not always come naturally and may sometimes have to be procured through political struggle.

Will Kymlicka's highly insightful *Multicultural Odysseys* (2007) provides a handy entry into how to frame the distinctions between multiculturalism and multiethnicity that we might handily transpose into an African context. As a general rule that he suggests applies to a range of Western liberal democracies, multiculturalism involves targeted policies toward three different collectivities: autochthonous groups (such as the Aborigines of Australia and Canada), substate actors (such as the Quebecois in Canada or the Basque separatists in Spain), and immigrants. The composite of all the targeted policies is what constitutes a multicultural environment and not just the usages of one sociocultural and ethnic group. Furthermore, there is a sliding scale of application of multicultural policies that allows us to see some countries as more multicultural (Canada, the United States) than others (Germany, Sweden). African examples suggest a resistance to multicultural accommodations rather than an odyssey toward it (to appropriate Kymlicka's title). At different points in the history of Nigeria, for example, the strong substate claims made first in relation to the Igbos and Biafra (1967–1970) and, more recently, with respect to resource rights for the Ogoni peoples in the delta region of the country (1990s to the present day) that might have been addressed through multicultural policies were placed within a schematic ethnic framework and seen as direct threats to the coherence of the nation-state. It did not help that in both instances the requests for accommodation were couched in the discourse of resource distribution, thus at once exposing the inherently skewed relationship between the bureaucratic center and its regional peripheries. To compound matters even further, the unwritten contract of Nigerian politics is that the three dominant ethnic groups of the Yorubas, the Hausas, and the Igbos must take turns at holding the presidency, thus installing an essential *ethnic* principle at the very heart of governmental rationality. This ethnic principle derives directly from the logic that informed Indirect Rule, installing settlement and origin and completely ignoring the historically mixed character of Yorubas, Hausas, and Igbos that has obtained since before the arrival of British colonialism. The ethnic principle is accepted by the political elites of the three Nigerian groups without question, thus consolidating the sense of privilege and excluding the smaller ethnic groups from power despite the problems that the arrangement has historically posed for the process of democracy in the country.

From yet another angle, the policies of Africanization that unfolded after independence in East Africa, while designed to rectify the perceived injustices of the colonial system, were ultimately instruments for the disavowal of multiculturalism, the effect of which was to lead to the disenfranchisement of the Indians of East Africa and their dispersal in the late 1970s to different parts of the world in the phenomenon that Parminder Bhachu has described as "twice migration" (1985). And in Ghana, the disavowal of multiculturalism was played out first in the legal debates in the 1960s as to whether the Lebanese were entitled to full citizenship in the country as well as with the dramatic consequences of the Aliens Compliance Order of 1969, whose effect was a form of ethnic *and* racial purification in the name of economic protectionism.[38]

There are countless examples across the continent showing that Africa has been shaped as much by migrants as by indigenous peoples, and yet migrants have been viewed mainly under the rubrics of security and/or law and order, or in relation to pressure on resources. In a word, through the lens of xenophobia. Hence in South Africa migrants from other parts of sub-Saharan Africa are designated by the title of *makwerekwere*, a term that is glossed by the South African blogger Khanya as follows:

> As far as I know it is a piece of interlinguistic slang. It is modified according to the language of the speaker. A Zulu-speaker might say *amakwerekwere*, a Sotho-speaker might say *makwerekwere* and an English-speaker might drop the prefix altogether and say *kwerekwere*.
>
> I haven't seen a convincing account of its origin. One suggestion was that it was like the Greek *varvari*, from which the English word "barbarian" comes (and the name Barbara). It has been suggested that *varvari* represents the strange sounds of foreign languages to Greeks. The Dutch called the people they found in the Western Cape *Hottentoten* for a similar reason—it was how they described the languages with click consonants that the local people spoke. So, it is said, *kwerekwere* represents the sounds of a foreign language.
>
> If that is so, it may have originated in Zulu, where the "r" sound is foreign, and "ɪ" is used instead. My own speculation (and it is nothing more that speculation) is that it may be derived from *kwelakwela*, an old slang word for a Black Maria (which is an even older slang term for a police van that carries arrested persons to the police station or jail). *Kwelakwela* is derived from the Zulu word *khwela*, meaning "climb," and policemen used to say to people they had arrested (usually for infringing the pass laws) "Kwelakwela," meaning "Get in! Get in!" Bus conductors also used to say it to passengers if the bus was running late, urging people to hurry up and board the bus. Perhaps *kwerekwere* has developed from that usage signifying illegal aliens being rounded up and arrested before being deported.[39]

Whether in South Africa, Nigeria, Libya, Ivory Coast, or the Democratic Republic of Congo (to take instances where the question of migrants has often led to political and social turmoil), migrants have never been placed under the rubric of multiculturalism despite the extensive history of migrant sojourns in different parts of Africa. They are all firmly ethnicized and subject to various forms of exclusion.

At heart then, multiculturalism in our own era ultimately depends on policies that acknowledge the aggregation of significant cultural, social, and economic forces as manifested within different ethno-cultural segments of the population. These forces are often accounted for in terms of certain correlatives (language skills, whether individual or multilingual; niche economic know-how; dress and dietary codes; religion and overall cultural orientations, etc.) that are then taken as bearing either straightforward economic or indeed normative value for the negotiation of cultural identities within the multiethnic context. Multicultural accommodations are then devised either through informal cultural practices or, as has been more typical in the twentieth and twenty-first centuries, through targeted laws that protect the character of specific ethno-cultural identities. Thus, while almost every society known to human history may be said to fall under the rubric of Armstrong's multiethnic polities, not all such polities have been multicultural. Multiethnicity lies in the domain of everyday life but almost never in that of specific policy accommodations, while the history of multiculturalism everywhere suggests that it is the product of policy as well as everyday practice, with policy taking precedence in *shaping* everyday attitudes to the multiethnic dynamic. Multiculturalism may thus be said to represent a different politics of recognition from that of multiethnicity, and this in turn impacts differently upon how cultural differences are articulated and situated as part of an overall semiotic of identity.[40]

In Ghana the realities of multiethnicity were first shaped by colonial policy, for British Indirect Rule, as we have already noted, was designed to install so-called customary laws as a key aspect of colonial governmentality at various levels. This provided a fillip for the instrumentalization of ethnicity, something that continued into the postindependence period. As we shall see with respect to conflicts over Ga lands in the next chapter, their cultural elites were keen to prove that they had authentic ethnic genealogies that formed a reservoir for the making of value claims about land ownership and its potential alienation. The nature of these ethnic genealogies became the subject of intense conflicts as the lands in Accra became progressively converted from largely agrarian to predominantly urban usages. Ethnicity also gained further salience in the constitution of the rights of chieftaincies, for chiefs are considered to be the primordial personifications of ethnicity. Over time while ethnicity was to become the primary modality of political identification, it still failed to produce concomitant protections at the level of the overall constitution of the multiethnic polity that might help to convert ethnicity into a systematic multiculturalism in the terms laid out by Kymlicka and others.

Of course, a quick riposte to the claims I am making here about the differences between ethnicity and multiculturalism is that multiculturalism is ultimately about the negotiation of race relations and that since Africa has no races, this cannot be a problem. Such a riposte deftly avoids the impact of other races in the shaping of the continent. But the point of such a riposte is that in Africa it is ethnicity and not race that is the primary vehicle for the articulation of identity. Irrespective of where it is to be found, race is always converted into a mode of ethnicity: the many terms used to designate Europeans on the continent, such as *mzungu* (East Africa), *oyinbo* (Nigeria), *toubab* (Senegal), and *obroni* (Ghana), can be read as ethnic markers masquerading as racial designations because they allow all white people, irrespective of their provenance, to be treated as if they were of the same ethnicity and thus utterly predictable in their responses to various conditions. It is also instructive that such terms are equally applied to locals, either due to their education, as a term of endearment, or to indicate a special relationship. To be called an obroni in Ghana is to have the ethnic attributes of obronis, rather than any indication of being pigmentally Caucasian as such. This is an implication that is often missed by African-American visitors to the country, who are sometimes deeply offended when they think they are being referred to as white people.[41]

Conclusion: The Tabon as Ga

With these in mind, we are able to conclude that the Tabon were not only assimilated to the Ga, but that their assimilation proceeded on the basis that they had been converted into an *ethnicity*, the terms of which were partly shaped by their adoption of Ga ways, and partly by the processes enjoined by colonial rule. What we described as the Tabon's heritage from Bahia must also be understood as formed recursively by the African retentions in the New World that were constantly augmented by cultural flows from Africa itself and then subsequently returned to Africa. As Richard Price and Sidney Mintz (1976) and Matory (2005) have instructed us, the New World was a crucible for the formation of creolized cultures that were at various times augmented by freshly arriving Africans, and, perhaps more important, returned back to Africa in a lively transnational cultural exchange that made Africa coeval with the New World and not just a fossilized ahistorical motherland. Whether with the much celebrated religions of Santería and Candomblé, or with the cuisines, hairstyles, and dress codes that are commonly shared between West Africa and the New World, cultural interchange must be understood as having been standardized by the nineteenth century. While the first cohort of Afro-Brazilian returnees to West Africa included people of first-generation slave descent, the point is not so much to establish that they had returned "home" to their original cultures. Rather, "home" and its cultures were co-constituted by the recursive relays of cultural details that played out between the West African subregion and Bahia, such that it was very difficult by the mid-nineteenth century to speak of any straightforward origins of, for example, the culinary habits they brought back with them. More important than any notion of return was the process of progressive ethnicization that the Tabon were inserted into and which converted them into Gas.

The process of *becoming* ethnic involved in the first instance adapting to aspects of Ga political and ritual practice. As we noted earlier, while the Ga Mantse is normally selected from either the Gbese or Asere quarters (considered the oldest of the akutsei), the choice of the Tabon Mantse involved the nomination of a leader by the heads of all the original seven Tabon families. The Tabon have followed this more democratic principle to this day, and yet have also absorbed large portions of Ga chiefly ritual attributes, including their chiefly regalia and their installation rites. The Tabon also actively participate in the Homowo festival and also practice male circumcision, two key signifiers of being Ga for males. By the beginning of the twentieth century, the Tabon Mantse had succeeded in being elevated to the seat of *benkumhene* of the Ga Mantse, in other words, the wise counselor that sits to the left of the principal chiefly overlord.[42] The designations of *nifa* (right) and *benkum* (left) are also military designations and imply that in times of war the relevant chief will provide soldiers for the right or left flank. The ascension of the Tabon Mantse to the position of benkumhene was no ordinary feat of assimilation to Ga political order. The early twentieth century was to see the eruption of internecine conflicts within the Tabon community as to whether the Tabon Mantse was comparable to an indigenous Ga chief and thus had the same rights of dispensing lands as their hosts.[43] Thus his elevation to Mantse and then benkumhene later became a matter of internal political contestation as the democratic principle of communal election run directly counter to the hegemonic principle of premogeniture that was taken to rationalize Ga chiefly succession, with all the implications that this raised for how much right the Tabon Mantse had to dispose of the lands that the community had been given on their first arrival.

At the same time the process of becoming Ga did not completely obliterate certain features brought from Bahia that incorporated into Ga ritual to make the Tabon variants of Ga ritual that were essentially ciphers of cultural memory. With respect to the Homowo festival, the ritual celebrations see the Ga Mantse sprinkling *kpoikpoi* (ground and slightly fermented maize mixed with palm oil) for the benefit of the ancestors, while the Tabon for their part sprinkle *akara/koose*, *waakye*, *massa*, *pinkaso*, and a variety of special foods of presumed Bahian genealogy. Yet each of the foods just mentioned in fact has a mixed West African and New World provenance, with a suggestive Muslim marking for akara/koose (black-eyed beans ground, seasoned with chili, then fried; this food being common to Muslim communities in both Nigeria and Ghana); and waakye (rice and beans, varieties of which are found both in Brazil and the Caribbean, as well as among Ghanaian Muslim communities in the north of the country). Also significant for ritual hybridities are Tabon *outdooring* (child naming) and marriage ceremonies, where despite close similarity between theirs and those of their host community, the copious chewing of kola nut suggests a clear reference to everday practices within Muslim communities, even if now this is expressed by the Tabon in an exclusively ritual form.[44]

Perhaps the one element that was to ensure their ultimate ethnicization is that the Tabon never managed to retain a grasp of the Portuguese language. Their small overall numbers, the pressure of conversion of a large part of their number to the dominant religion of Christianity, and the fact that they were among the first to take to Western-style education meant that within two short generations they had all but lost their mastery of the Portuguese language, except in the residual and largely denigrated form of the Pidgin that was later on to mark youth culture in the country. The loss of Portuguese did not, however, prevent them from retaining their Afro-Brazilian names, something which they use to this day as a means of signaling their special genealogy and retaining a continuing sense of viability as a community. It is for this that Sara, the insistent Tabon teenager with whom we opened this chapter, was able to reel off a series of high-achieving Tabon names as a means of telling her Ashanti friend that she too was "somebody," as we say in Ghana. If we learn anything from the Tabon for our understanding of Accra, it is that they represent a mode of cultural hybridity that is easy to bypass due to their degree of apparent ethnic assimilation into Ga culture. But the example of the Tabon also teaches us that despite being no more than a group of returnee Africans from the faraway lands of enslavement, the process of settling into their new "homeland" was far from straightforward. It involved a long process of ethnicization that helps to distinguish them from other stranger groups that came to settle in West Africa. Strictly as part of a future research agenda, it would be instructive, for example, to compare the Afro-Brazilians of West Africa to the African-American returnees to Liberia of the nineteenth century or the black Nova Scotians of Sierra Leone of the late eighteenth and early nineteenth centuries, all of whom seem to have been assimilated to their local African backgrounds and yet retain significant signifiers of their diasporic provenance. Each instance raises significant questions about ethnicity, multiculturalism, and hybridity, and the processes by which a stranger group *becomes* African.

CHAPTER 2

The Spatial Fix: Colonial Administration,
Disaster Management, and Land-Use Distribution
in Early Twentieth-Century Accra

To shift from the hybrid formation of Ga akutsei and their assimilation of
stranger groups such as the Tabon that we encountered in the previous
chapter to the domain of town planning is to move from the description
of sociocultural space making and on to the layered and sometimes contradictory processes that undergirded colonial town planning from the end
of the nineteenth century. More important, it is to confront the fact that as
Accra expanded outward from the core Ga Mashie area the neighborhoods
and districts that were added to it came to define an aggregation of differential social ecologies located in space. What I name as aggregation invokes
to a certain degree David Harvey's concept of the spatial fix.[1] In Harvey's account the spatial fix is composed of two interlinked dimensions. The first,
pertaining to the resolution of the perennial crises of capitalism, involves
the incorporation of peripheral productive zones into the capitalist economy, either in the form of a ready reservoir of surplus labor, or as markets for
expansion from metropolitan centers. This point is a conventional explanation for the political economy of empire and colonialism, whose effect
at the global level was the progressive transformation of different regions of
the world into economic peripheries of Europe and at the more local level
the conversion of rural areas into subservient hinterlands of urban economies.[2] The subservience of rural hinterlands to urban networks, which was
set in the colonial period and continued in the postindependence phase, explains in great part the structural and endemic nature of African rural-urban
drift to this day. The second aspect of the spatial fix relates to the material
fixing of infrastructure that facilitates capitalism's overall transactional processes. This infrastructure includes roads and highways, airports, harbors,
railway lines, and even the knowledge economy represented by schools and
universities. Furthermore, as A. D. King (1976) and others have shown, the

colonial spatial fix also implicated the particular configuration of colonially dominated townships, with the attendant separation of core and peripheral commercial districts, the segregation of residential neighborhoods, and the disposition of recreational spaces subserving the spatial interests of colonial powers.[3] The more integrated the spatial nexus of the colonial template, the lower and more efficient the transaction costs for its control and extraction of resources from their colonies.

While the idea of the colonial spatial nexus is definitely pertinent to explaining the commercial layout of Accra's Central Business District (CBD), the aggregation of social ecologies as an essential aspect of the city's overall evolution must be seen as the combined effects of demography, interethnic relations, and race (with reference specifically to the siting of European-only areas). Furthermore, the term "ecologies" is supposed to highlight the relationship between the built environment and natural habitat, such that different areas demonstrate different ratios between population densities, the character of the built environment, and nature. These provide key aspects for understanding the configuration of the city from its core areas and the logics of its expansion outward as the twentieth century progressed. If we consider the accretion of neighborhoods to have proceeded radially from the Ga Mashie area outward from the end of the nineteenth century to roughly the late 1950s, we see that the spatial accretions also defined a series of differentiations along a native (Ga)/foreigner (northerner) axis as well as along the axis of spatially distributed socio-ecological distinctions. This is not to say that the Ga Mashie area was ever exclusively a Ga enclave; indeed, the establishment of Salaga Market within the area in 1874 was to ensure that northern migrant market vendors were a necessary aspect of Ga Mashie's social character. And yet it was only with the establishment of the separate zongos (Hausa: stranger quarters) at Tudu from 1915 and at Nima from the 1950s that such migrants became a distinguishable entity from their Ga hosts. Furthermore, a distinctive social ecology was also defined along the axis of native/European areas. This subtended the native/immigrant axis and yet is strictly speaking distinguishable from it. Thus the area lying roughly between Ga Mashie and Osu to its east, and variously encompassing Adabraka, Ridge, and Cantonments, all of which had been established by the 1920s and 1930s, reveals colonialism's spatial imprint most clearly. By the 1950s the city had physically expanded to also include the largely Akan migrant community at Kaneshie and the exclusively northern migrant community at Nima that helped to fundamentally alter the hitherto Ga residential character of the town in earlier periods. Read in another way, we see that by 1957 the overall effect of the city's spatial configuration was the visible production of a heartland corridor of privileged neighborhoods to which were appended poorer districts in different spatial and social relationships to this heartland. While today the ruling sociocultural elites and their local and transnational satellites may be found all over the city, it is also true that historically these have tended to concentrate along the privileged residential corridor spatially defined by Ridge, Osu RE, Kanda, Cantonments, and Airport, with the postindependence neighborhoods of Labone and Nyaniba Estates contiguously completing the privileged spatial corridor. The contrast with the mixed-migrant and much poorer neighborhoods of Tudu and Nima that also lie at different points within this corridor only serves to highlight the contrast between power and penury that is made evident when we see the city from the perspective of the aggregation of differential ecologies grounded in space. To put it in the starkest terms, Tudu and Nima are slum districts with heavy population densities, a low level of amenities, and little correlation between built environment and nature, while the erstwhile European neighborhoods of Ridge and its cognates have a more complementary social ecology in the terms we described earlier.

If up to the 1950s the colonial administration was driven primarily by the impulse toward facilitating European commercial and residential dominance of core areas, some aspects of town planning were also unfurled in a largely ad hoc fashion and in direct response to the three major disease epidemics that hit the town in the early part of the twentieth century and the big earthquake of 1939 that forced a major spatial rethinking of the city. Other fundamental impulses that affected urban spatial diversification emerged from contests about land tenure between various Ga and non-Ga cultural constituencies that were worked out outside the direct purview of the colonial administration's commercial and residential interests. As we shall see later in the chapter, the specific debates that emerged in the long-running Kokomolemle Lands Case in the 1940s and 1950s turned on contradictory interpretations of the roles of various Ga cultural actors and their nonlocal migrant interlocutors as to their relative rights to lands in Accra. Subsequently, the postindependence government of Kwame Nkrumah was to take up the colonial blueprint of town planning almost wholesale, only adding a strong nationalist emphasis of monuments and other development projects to reflect new priorities. However, speaking strictly in terms of Accra's spatial morphology and the largely centralized yet incoherent town planning impulses that have governed the city's evolution from independence onward, it is hard to argue against the view that the city suffered a decades-long planning stagnation until after the implementation of the IMF-instigated policies of the mid to late 1980s. These policies were aimed primarily at liberalizing the Ghanaian economy and opening it up to market forces, yet the most visible impact of the policies was the degree to which they instituted a decisive spatial imprint for the forces of globalization. This is best exemplified by the formation of Oxford Street itself. As Richard Grant and Jan Nijman (2002) show in their comparative paper on Accra's and Mumbai's corporate geography, one of the best ways to understand today's imprint of globalization on cities in the developing world is to take a strictly historical view of urban spatial formation and to compare the current phase of globalization to the earlier ones of the colonial and early postindependence periods. Thus, rather than seeing any of the aforementioned phases separately, we must see them as overlapping and mutually reinforcing in the shaping of Accra. It is this essential multiaxial perspective to urban space that I hope to keep in view as I outline different layers and complexities to the evolution of the city. To understand the city as a whole we are obliged to keep shifting our analysis to encompass the moving pieces of a geographic jigsaw puzzle, which, depending on which way we turn, divulges slightly different perspectives on urban space. This method of interpreting Accra is much like what Chinua Achebe recommends in *Arrow of God*: if the world is like a mask dancing, you cannot see it by standing still (1964, 46).

Spatial Diversification I: Sanitation, Disease Control,
and Disaster Management

By 1903 Accra stretched for three miles along the coastline from the Korle Lagoon in the west to Christiansborg Castle in the east, with the settlement of Labadi falling well outside the town's boundaries and lying much farther to the east of the core areas.[4] In these early stages, Accra included only the townships of Jamestown, Usshertown, the newly developed European estate of Victoriaborg, and Osu, which had evolved quietly from the seventeenth century under the shadow of Christiansborg Castle. While the evolution of Victoriaborg, Ridge, and the other low-density, high-cost neighborhoods were driven purely by the colonial administrative and residential functions, the disease epidemics of 1908 (bubonic plague), 1911 (yellow fever), and 1918 (influenza) were to introduce new factors into the dynamics of town planning, with each epidemic leading to frantic efforts to decongest the core Ga Mashie area. The bubonic plague of 1908 was especially significant in this regard and was to affect mainly the Nleshie/Jamestown area, with several recorded deaths between the first reported cases in August 1907 and May 1908.[5] Desperate measures were required to contain the situation and the Colonial Office dispatched Sir W. J. R. Simpson to the colony. Simpson had already established his credentials fighting a bubonic plague epidemic in Calcutta in 1896, with his *Treatise on Plague* (1905) quickly becoming a comprehensive classic on the question.[6] His invitation to manage the colonial administration's response to the epidemic set the precedent for the transfer of best practices relating to disease- and disaster-management protocols from other areas of empire to the local context, with systematic cross-referencing to analogous colonial situations becoming most explicit in colonial correspondence on Accra following the earthquake of 1939.

While colonial officials had had a number of meetings with the Ga chiefs to agree on crisis measures, the arrival of Simpson brought with it a new note of urgency for all parties involved. Simpson's preferred method was the segregation and quarantine of infected or suspected individuals and, more controversially from the perspective of the residents in affected areas, the complete destruction of houses marked as harboring the offending mice. A cordon was also thrown around the town, with everyone required to carry a stamped document showing clearance to travel outside its boundaries. The enforced quarantines was first applied following the bubonic plague and then again during the yellow fever epidemic of three years later. The first quarantine led directly to the founding of Korle Gonno in 1908, about a mile across the narrow isthmus west of Jamestown, and Adabraka, some four miles to the northeast of the coastal area. Korle Gonno was originally an isolation camp of temporary wooden houses for the relatives and associates of those who had died in the Alata quarter of Jamestown during the plague. It remained a largely makeshift settlement until the highly energetic Kojo Ababio, the Alata Mantse, who had strenuously organized his people in the early stages of the crisis, put forward a formal request to the colonial administration to convert the temporary camp site into a more permanent settlement. With the building of the Korle Bu Hospital in 1923, Korle Gonno was further transformed into a labor-resource neighborhood to service the new medical establishment, with low-cost houses for workers laid out in close proximity to the hospital itself. However, the mainly European doctors and medical administration officers in the period were conversely assigned houses in the newly developed Europeans-only neighborhood of Ridge.

Adabraka, also started in 1908, was not properly developed until after the yellow fever epidemic of 1911. It was planned originally as a way of relieving pressure off the central coastal district during the two epidemics, but in the event became attractive to the Ga educated elite, who moved there out of the Ga Mashie area to establish the first African middle-class neighborhood in Accra. The Ga elites were persuaded of the prospects of the new township by the colonial government's introduction of a hire-purchase scheme, by which the Ga could borrow money from the government to build their houses and pay these back over a period of time, depending on the size of the loan and the rates of repayment. The grant of financial facilities from the colonial treasury for establishing the two emerging neighborhoods did not escape the vagaries of inter-akutso rivalries, for the land at Korle Gonno was owned by the Alata stool and that at Adabraka by the Sempe stool. As Jonathan Roberts (2003) points out in his fine discussion of the bubonic plague and its immediate aftermath, heated arguments about the Korle Gonno settlement exposed the sharp fissures and even the threat of violence between the people of Alata, universally considered to have arrived at Accra only from the 1670s, and those from Sempe and Asere, traditionally considered as among the founding Ga akutsei that had arrived on the Ga-Adangme plains as early as the 1300s.[7] It was pressure from the Sempe stool that led the colonial administration to introduce the loan scheme for Adabraka. The chief of Asere on the other hand was to petition the colonial government in 1920 for an extension of the same financial arrangements as had been given for the earlier settlements. He sought a similar scheme for establishing a new township at Kaneshie, some eight miles to the northwest of Ga Mashie and at that time mainly a farming community.[8] The Asere chief was explicit in citing the cases of Korle Gonno and Adabraka in his request, suggesting that perhaps some favoritism may have been at play in the funding of the earlier settlements.

The development of Kaneshie was however to wait for another nineteen years, delayed by the colonial administration for a variety of reasons. The lengthy debate between the Asere Mantse, the colonial administration, and a number of other interested individuals such as John Bannerman is detailed in dozens of letters that were exchanged between the various parties until the earthquake that hit Accra in June 1939.[9] With the passage of the Lands Acquisition Ordinance in 1940, the colonial administration was able to gain control of a large tract of land at Kaneshie upon which to develop the second African middle-class residential district in the growing town, this time planned as a series of low-cost estate houses on a rent-and-purchase loan scheme reminiscent of the Adabraka model. Kaneshie was a much bigger residential development project than Adabraka and also incorporated a larger variety of ethnic groups beyond the Ga. The Kaneshie tract of land procured by the colonial administration stretches from today's Obetsebi-Lamptey Circle, on the right side of the Winneba Road, down to the First Light neighborhood at Mataheko, and extends northward from this east-west axis to incorporate the Awudome Estates down to the Awudome Cemetery alongside the Ring Road. Having been established in the 1940s and originally earmarked for junior to midlevel civil servants, by the 1970s Kaneshie was teeming with lawyers, students, and members of the professional middle classes who came to offer robust resistance to General Acheampong's military junta of 1972–1978.[10] A similar grouping of oppositional middle-class activists was also to develop at Dansoman Estates, the sprawling neighborhood originally planned by the Kwame Nkrumah government but only coming to fruition in the early 1970s.

Thus we see that not only did the disaster-management procedures lead to the expansion of Accra in a variety of directions, they also seeded the aggregation of certain social forces that were located in space, a point we will spend more time elaborating later in the chapter in an extension of the concept of social ecologies. The preliminary triggers of disease epidemics and disaster management also revealed two distinct principles of town planning during the period. On the one hand, the colonial administration's town planning appeared to proceed reactively in response to such crises and not as part of a clearly integrated urban development plan. And yet, on the other, a semblance of overall planning was to be discerned when these reactive developments were contrasted to the housing provided for Europeans in the areas of Victoriaborg, Ridge, and Cantonments in the same extended thirty- to forty-year period. While Korle Gonno, Kaneshie, and later Mamprobi and Chorkor (the last developed especially in response to the arrival of American troops during World War II) were planned primarily as small-size, low-cost houses typically with toilet and bathing facilities situated outside of the individual units, those at the largely European-only areas were planned as low-density high-cost houses on much larger plots of land. The European areas had a completely different social ecology and were much better integrated into their natural environments. The contradiction between reactive and planned urban development was to be properly confronted only after the end of World War II, when a variety of factors including the clamor for decolonization led to a more integrated vision of urban planning. However, as we shall see shortly, it is the logic of the areas originally laid out for European habitation that ultimately provided the modernist assumptions undergirding the planning document of B. A. W. Trevallion and Alan Hood that was commissioned by the colonial administration toward the end of its tenure and a few years before full decolonization in 1957.

Spatial Diversification II: European Commercial Function

THE EUROPEAN COMMERCIAL FUNCTION

The Europeanization of Accra's commercial and residential districts had an effect on urban form quite distinct from anything that emerged out of the disease- and disaster-management dynamic. The partial Europeanization processes proceeded in tandem with the geographical configurations that emerged from the earlier axes we described, yet must be discussed separately before being brought back together for an overall spatial overview of the evolution of the city.

One of the main spatial correlatives of the impact of European influence on the city can be readily seen in the official toponyms that mark Accra both along its coastal neighborhoods and further inland. Thus a drive from Ga Mashie eastward along High Street toward Osu and its proximate environs reveals a number of toponyms memorializing prominent personages of the colonial period. And so we find: Granville Avenue, Lutterodt Street, Baden Powell Memorial Hall, Selwyn Market Street, Knutsford Avenue, Guggisberg Avenue, Derby Avenue, Thorpe Road, Barnes Road, Bannerman Road, Reverend Richter Street, Lokko Road, Kimberly Avenue, Liberia Road, Carl Reindorf Street, Troas Crescent, Joel Sonne Street, and many others. Derby, Thorpe, Selwyn, and Kimberly are to be found in other parts of the British Empire, while Troas takes its inspiration from Paul's Second Epistle to the Corinthians. Robert Baden-Powell was the famous British founder of the Boy Scouts, a branch of which was formed in Ghana in 1912, while Guggisberg (Gordon) refers to the highly respected Canadian governor who oversaw many development projects for the city from 1919 to 1926. Names such as Bannerman, Richter, Lokko, Lutterodt, and Sonne do double service, referring on the one hand to various British, Dutch, and Danish governors of the forts and castle but also signaling the place of their highly influential mixed-race offspring from the liaisons they had with African women on the coast. Several local and African patriots were also to be commemorated with street and place names after independence, among them Wetse Kojo, J. B. Danquah, Kwame Nkrumah, and Kojo Thompson, with the street names for Gamal Abdul Nasser, Jawaharal Nehru, Thomas Sankara, and Olusegun Obasanjo also signaling Ghana's pan-Africanist credentials.

The latticework of European-inspired toponyms was further augmented in the colonial period by two more substantial correlatives of European influence, the first being the stratification of businesses and thus of spatial arrangements in the Ga Mashie area and the districts abutting it and the second tied to the early residential segregation that was established from the 1890s as part of the administrative function and consolidation of colonial rule. By 1900 colonial policy was to ensure that commerce on the Gold Coast was dominated mainly by European merchant houses, several of which were attracted to the colony precisely because of the security provided by such policy. As Richard Brand points out, the spatial configuration of Accra's CBD by the 1920s directly proves the thesis of European commercial privilege in the political economy of colonialism. Of the thirty-seven European-owned businesses in the CBD, one was very large-scale (i.e., with over one hundred employees), thirty-one were large-scale (employing fifty to one hundred), four were medium-scale (employing fifteen to forty-nine), with just one being small-scale (employing fewer than fifteen people). Conversely, of the twenty-one African-owned businesses he lists, just five were large-scale, with eight medium-scale and eight small-scale.[11] The European domination of the CBD was to continue well into the postindependence period, with the central areas finally reverting to African-controlled businesses only after Busia's infamous Aliens Compliance Order of 1969.[12]

The harbor at Jamestown also provides a useful focal point for understanding the town's spatial economy during the period. Even though the breakwater at Jamestown was not constructed until 1906, by 1884 the port was already one of the busiest in the entire Gold Coast Colony. K. B. Dickson describes the harbor this way:

> The port of Accra was a busy one: gold dust, ivory, palm oil, maize, cattle, and other miscellaneous products arrived in a steady stream. Gold came no doubt from Akim and Ashanti; palm oil from the Akwapim Mountains and their foothills and from Krobo, where the oil palm tree had been systematically cultivated for many years. Maize was cultivated in the Accra Plains, where herds of cattle were also reared. The cattle were shipped from the port not to Europe, but to other European forts on the coast. Also, small quantities of coffee and cotton were apparently exported now and then. Outside of Cape Coast and Elmina the greatest number of European merchants resided at Accra, not to mention the large number of African merchants who also lived there. Some of these merchants, like those at Cape Coast, had invested large sums of

money in huge stone houses, of which there were no fewer than eight in the town. For the reasons outlined, to which must be added the important fact that Accra was the terminus of one of the principal trade routes between the coast and Ashanti, the town ranked as a major port, although landings at Dutch and Danish sections of the town could be dangerous.[13]

He goes on to note that by 1911 the most valuable export from Accra and other ports along the coast was cocoa, which had outstripped the value of rubber, palm oil, gold, kola nuts, timber, and ivory, all of which had generally come into ascendance after the demise of slavery.[14] We should pause for a moment to visualize the bustling scene that marked the Jamestown Harbor by the first half of the twentieth century. From the earliest period of European contact and well into the introduction of steamships in the 1850s, all ships had to lay anchor some three to four miles off the coast. Canoes then brought the goods in from the outlying ships to the landing shore and transferred whatever shipments there were from the coast back onto the ships. Imports in the early part of the twentieth century included all manner of manufactured goods, with the canoes carrying everything from textiles, whisky, bicycles, and motorcycles to entire pianos and other such bulky goods. Motor vehicles were brought in pieces and reassembled by John Holt Bartholomew and Company on Station Road. Come the 1950s the scene laid out on the beach will have been an extraordinarily lively one, with European merchant representatives, insurers, small-scale buyers, and customs officers performing their several assigned roles amid the teeming African boat crews and their variant cargos.[15]

The commercial activities around the harbor were to ensure that the Jamestown area retained all the characteristics of a lively commercial hub until 1962, when all transshipment activities were transferred to the newly opened and much larger Tema Harbor, eighteen miles to the east of Accra. From a strictly spatial standpoint, Ga Mashie was nothing but a warehouse township, with the landscape dominated by large commercial warehouses owned by the likes of the British Elder Dempster Lines and G. B. Ollivant, the Anglo-Greek Paterson Zochonis (PZ), the Greek-Cypriot AG Leventis, the French Compagnie Française de l'Afrique Occidentale (CFAO), the Swiss United Trading Company (UTC), not to speak of African merchants such as E. A. Manyo Plange, T. P. Allotey, S. O. Akiwumi, and A. J. Ocansey, all of whom had businesses in the CBD at varying distances from the harbor.[16] Signs of the many warehouses can still be found in the area.

2.1. Elder Dempster Lines, Jamestown, 1959. Photo by Jurgen Heinel.

The European domination of the Ga Mashie area and its adjoining CBD must, however, not obscure the complexly stratified pools of labor that serviced these districts, but which in the early part of the twentieth century turned mainly on the presence of migrants from the Northern Territories. Whereas Gas could be relied upon to act as laborers and porters in the immediate environs of the Jamestown Harbor, the colonial administration's expanding infrastructural projects had begun to place real pressure on labor supplies. The overall attachment of Gas to the fishing industry meant that there was a frequent shortage of cheap labor to service the harbor, the CBD, and the colonial administration and even to act as porters carrying goods to and from the harbor. As we have already noted, Salaga Market was founded in 1874 in the Ga Mashie area. The significance of the date of its founding, however, is that it marks the defeat of the mighty Ashanti kingdom in the Anglo-Ashanti War that was concluded in the same year. Salaga Market was aimed at directly subverting Ashanti control of the kola trade from the north.[17] With the opening of Salaga Market, the colonial administration provided a

2.2. Canoes off-loading goods at Jamestown. Photo by Jurgen Heinel.

2.3. Old Paterson Zochonis Warehouse, Jamestown.

specific incentive for northern migrant traders to bring their goods directly to Accra from the hinterland and to explore shipping opportunities to Lagos and other ports. But the opening of Salaga Market also provided an opportunity for the establishment of a small northern migrant settlement first at Ga Mashie itself and subsequently spreading into the area of what was later to become Makola, about a mile from the Jamestown Harbor. Ultimately, however, the significance of Salaga Market is that it links to the larger picture of the place of non-Ga migrant workers in the evolution of the city. Thus with a broader historical sweep than I can provide here, Samuel Ntewusu outlines how slaves from the north had always been used to perform key economic functions in the town.[18] In the period of the slave trade itself Grushie slaves were used in Accra for the cultivation of crops and also as porters by long-distance traders and farmers. With slave abolition and the shift in the economy to cash crop production, northerners were subsequently deployed for the cultivation of palm oil by both Ga and Euro-African businessmen. After the Anglo-Ashanti War and toward the end of the nineteenth century, periodic conflagrations between the historically militaristic Gonja and their neighbors also led to more northern arrivals into the city.

With the cocoa boom from the 1900s, the need for porters increased the value of northerners in Accra's economy, and many of these came to further augment the essentially northern character of the Makola area, as witnessed by street names such as Cow Lane and Zongo Lane.[19] The building of Makola in 1924 had already signaled a shift in the commercial nerve center of the town, with Makola now placed at the core of the CBD. By the 1910s, as Ntewusu goes on to show, Tudu had also evolved with the blessing of the colonial administration as a specific northern settlement enclave to the north of the CBD. Tudu was to supply a steady stream of laborers for the construction industry, as members of the fledgling police and army (of which more in chapter 6), and as porters to facilitate the transportation of increasingly large volumes of commercial goods across the city. The Tudu Lorry Park, which was opened in 1936, was designated as the station for clearing goods into the city from the Takoradi Harbor, itself opened in 1928 in the west of the colony. The opening of the Tudu Lorry Park immediately converted the area into a lively commercial hub right at the edge of the CBD and led to a further expansion of the commercial center, which had shifted over the previous three decades from the Jamestown Harbor to incorporate Makola in the 1920s and Tudu in the 1930s. With the opening of the Tudu Lorry Park, Kibi Road (to be renamed in 1982 as Kojo Thompson Road, but before that also known as Boundary Road) became the main tributary connecting Accra to the food basket of the eastern provinces of Kyebi, Aburi, and Prapram. The increased traffic on Kibi Road also came to attract Lebanese businesses, which by the early 1930s had transformed the space between Tudu and Adabraka into a lively commercial corridor that was integrated into the CBD.

The important thing to note, however, is that the presence of northerners in the city and their decisive contributions to the commercial character of Accra meant that by midcentury the city was no longer a purely Ga entity, despite the conclusion that might be drawn from colonial administration documents. The correspondence shows a decisive bias toward servicing Ga ethnic interests. Even after the 1939 earthquake the debates between the municipal authorities and the colonial administration about the town's rehabilitation referred to northern migrants as an essentially anomalous group. Indeed, this is the impression conveyed in a letter of October 13, 1939, from Arnold Hodson, governor of the Gold Coast, to Sir Malcolm MacDonald, the colonial secretary in London: "Arising out of the provision of housing for the permanent inhabitants of Accra rendered homeless by the earthquake, it has also been necessary to take into account the requirements of the considerable floating *alien population* which is always present and which provides most of the supply of unskilled labor. To this class the purchase of a house offers no attraction, even if it were financially possible, and the only method of providing for their accommodation is by the construction of quarters which can be hired out at a fixed rent" (italics added).[20]

We should recall quickly from the previous chapter Mahmood Mamdani's discussion of the structural differences in the relations established by colonialism between "native" and "migrants," with the former enjoying all the rights over land and its distribution. Hodson's suggestion was to build compound houses for this "alien population" (read northerners) for rent at Sabon Zongo, another northern enclave that evolved in the 1910s but was located about six miles to the northwest of the city core. There is no evidence that the compound houses for northern migrant workers were ever put up following the earthquake, the emphasis rather being on the new township at Kaneshie. By midcentury there is no doubting the fact that northern migrants provided a very crucial reservoir of cheap labor for the colonial administration. More important, partly by the pressure of their own enterprise and necessity, and partly due to ad hoc and specific colonial administrative planning, the northern migrant workers had been assigned to particular spatial locations within the evolving townscape. This spatial aggregation of cheap labor, especially from the North but also increasingly from other rural parts of the country, was with time scaled up to define the essential geographical configuration of the entire city, providing us with the key terms by which the privileged and poor areas might be integrated into an analytical whole. As Richard Brand notes: "Migration status and its spatial manifestations are powerful dimensions of differentiation within Accra. Migrant destination nodes are themselves highly differentiated, and there is also differentiation between elite migrant tracts and most central city indigenous tracts. However, migrant status is not independent of overall socioeconomic status" (1972, 197). This is something we will have cause to return to in our discussion of the largely ethnic character of the gyms in the White Chapel neighborhood of Madina in chapter 6.

THE EUROPEAN ADMINISTRATIVE
AND RESIDENTIAL FUNCTIONS

The bustling picture we invoked earlier of the Jamestown Harbor and its immediate environs has to be placed in the context of the congestion and poor conditions of the Ga Mashie area itself. The area's congestion was to remain a perennial theme in town-planning debates. According to the Census Committee Report of 1891: "In Accra [i.e., Ga Mashie] . . . the houses are built in very close proximity to each other, and are most defectively constructed from a hygienic point of view and are also overcrowded so that it is difficult to understand why the vitality of the people has not been more seriously affected by the continuous inhalation of impure air, especially during the night hours" (12). We should recall in passing Henry Stanley Morton's description of the Accra township of 1874 we encountered in the previous chapter, where he observes at one point: "Almost to the extreme left was the Commandant's house; its wide verandah promised coolness, and the wide space around it informed you that at one time or another some occupant of it had been assiduous to procure unpolluted air." The quest for what was considered unpolluted air by Europeans was clearly one that had been going on for some time. At any rate in 1901 Governor Nathan was to state his express wish to remove all Europeans from the Ga settlement, noting that the Africans did not seem to be much concerned with improving their sanitary situation.[21] The census of 1891 showed Accra's population to be 19,999, with 541 of these being Europeans. These census figures did not take account of the many mixed-race offspring of European men and African women that had become a significant feature of coastal societies during the course of the previous three centuries and which, by the start of the twentieth, formed a significant part of Accra's social milieu. As previously noted, some of these mixed-race offspring came to be commemorated in the street names and toponyms that festoon Accra. The absence of any reference to mixed-race progeny in the census of 1891 mirrors the residential segregation that was eventually to take root in pursuit of the administrative function.[22] While it was not uncommon during the phase of European merchant capitalism for European merchants to either live among the native population in rented accommodation or above their own commercial emporiums close to the harbor, this situation was to change dramatically from the 1890s, when the consolidation of administrative colonialism was to inaugurate the start of racially segregated areas as an essential aspect of colonial governmentality.[23]

Invoking health concerns again, the colonial administration decided to build specially segregated housing for European civil servants and merchants in Victoriaborg in 1898, roughly two miles east of Jamestown. By 1924 the Ministries, as the area of government departments adjoining Victoriaborg came to be known, had been completed. Fresh complements of much larger low-density, high-cost houses for European civil servants were to follow Victoriaborg at Ridge from 1916 and Ringway Estates in the 1920s to complement the Ministries. Housing developments for Europeans and senior civil servants later came to incorporate Cantonments from the 1920s and then the Airport Residential Area two decades later. Cantonments had evolved originally in 1893 as a settlement of demobilized northern soldiers from wars with the interior Ashanti kingdom, but by the 1940s the settlement had been encircled by more salubrious residential developments. Airport Residential Area was initially developed during World War II to house the large numbers of personnel of the Pan American World Airways system who were active in the delivery of support services for air force units. The buildings at Victoriaborg, Ridge, and Ringway Estates were to establish the overall tone for all the houses that were designed for European residents and their satellites. Built on sizable plots of land, each unit had an added servants' quarters, with the general area graced by all the attractive amenities of parks, a club house (today's Accra Tennis Club), a race course, polo grounds, playing fields, and the leafy prospect of trees and cultivated gardens. Water, electricity, and access to all significant road networks to and from the area of government offices (Ministries), the major banks (High Street), and the CBD (Makola) were all incorporated into the planning of these European neighborhoods. Victoriaborg and Ridge in particular were also to mark the explicit European preference for residential racial segregation.[24] Until the start of World War II and only ceasing after intense pressure from an organization called the Aboriginal Protection Society in London, Africans, whether of the incipient professional class or otherwise, were debarred from moving into Victoriaborg and Ridge.[25] The originally European enclaves remained exclusive well into the 1940s as much due to the prohibitive costs of housing in those areas as to the direct policies of exclusion (which were discontinued before the end of the war anyway). Citing Dudley Seers and C. R. Ross's "Report on the Financial and Physical Problems of Development in the Gold Coast" of 1952, Richard Brand points out that the prohibitive cost of housing at the Airport Residential Area ensured that no Africans were able to live there, at least not until well after the war. The large bungalows to be found at the Airport Residential Area cost between £8,000 and £10,000, whereas African housing for a laborer consisting of a separate kitchen, veranda, and bathroom cost £391, or "about 1/25 of the mean cost of a house in the Airport Residential Area." The low-cost housing planned for areas such as Korle Gonno, Mamprobi/ Chorkor, and Kaneshie (after the earthquake) was conceived of differently. When contemplating the layout of houses to be built up at Kaneshie, colonial administrators initially stated that these should have compound kitchens shared by several units at once. The idea was ultimately abandoned, on the reasoning that such an arrangement might provide grounds for unnecessary conflict among women in the households. Governor Arnold Hodson put it in a letter to the colonial secretary thus: "The specification mentions communal kitchens. The consequent saving is undeniable, but the arrangement is one that has proved intensely unpopular in various parts of the world. Family quarrels resulting from a combined kitchen will render life so trying, that the tenants will move rather than endure them. A separate lean-to building of iron for each house can be easily and cheaply built, for it need not be large, and the resultant contentment of the housewife will assuredly justify any slight extra cost."[26]

The domestic gender hierarchies felt to obtain in native households as revealed in this extract are stated as an intuitive fact rather than argued out. Hodson also implies a different conception of labor, since he assumes that men would be working outside the home, perhaps for the expanding colonial administration itself, while women were likely to stay at home to look after the kids. This scenario was blatantly false, since all studies have shown that women have always worked outside the home in both formal and informal sectors to help sustain their families even from as far back as the precolonial era.[27] Even though Hodson does not specify which other parts of the world have kitchen arrangements that are thought to cause confusion, the correspondence from the local administration and the Colonial Office in London regarding what should be done following the earthquake was filled with references to other places such as Japan, the Gambia, Trinidad, Tapia in the West Indies, as well as, remarkably, Slough Trading Estate in Berkshire, to the west of London, which at one point was proffered by the Colonial Secretary as a good potential model for Accra.[28] Yet these references all had the implicit assumption of class stratification, tellingly revealed in the reference to the Slough Trading Estate, which soon after being built in 1920 attracted the derision of commentators as being a brute concrete jungle and devoid of any aesthetic value whatsoever.

As colonial government intervention in the housing market was consistently geared toward the replication of colonial hierarchies, the spatial economy of privilege should not appear entirely surprising. Wordsworth Odame Larbi has noted that the Accra Racecourse provided a buffer between the European Ridge Residential Area and Old Osu to its east. To the west of Ridge, on the other hand, "the land stretching north from Accra Polytechnic to the Holy Spirit Cathedral covering an area of 20.84 hectares was acquired for a building-free zone."[29] The spatial seclusion of Ridge was aided by the geographical feature of a huge ravine that extended roughly from today's Electricity Corporation at Makola and zigzagged uninterrupted northward and ended at the western edge of the current Ridge Hospital, thus providing a natural geographical barrier between Ridge and the other African neighborhoods to the west of the ravine, Tudu and Adabraka. The ravine was progressively filled throughout the colonial period and well into independence such that by the 1970s it was no longer visible, except for a telltale and inexplicable hole in the ground next to the northwest side of the Ridge Hospital, which was used to gather rainwater until the 1980s.[30]

The road that runs south to north dividing Adabraka from Ridge was called Boundary Road until 1982, when it was changed to Kojo Thompson Road by the Rawlings regime in commemoration of one of the most prominent Ga lawyer nationalists of the colonial period.[31] The only other high-class, low-density neighborhood to be found in Accra by 1957 was Tesano, some ten miles to the northwest between central Accra and Legon. Tesano was conceived of primarily as an automobile commuter suburb not different from such suburbs in much of Europe. It was built in the 1950s to accommodate the growing teaching staff at Achimota School and the new University of Ghana campus at Legon, both of which were heavily expatriate at the time. It bears repeating that to this day all the areas that were first built to house European merchants and civil servants retain the character of high-status neighborhoods and the preferred locations for the political and business elites and their various local and transnational satellites. And from a real estate perspective the Victoriaborg/Ridge to Cantonments Road/Airport Residential Area corridor is today among the highest priced and policed in town. The assured security of this corridor is guaranteed given that both the police headquarters and Burma Camp (the erstwhile demobilized soldier's settlement from the nineteenth century and for decades the headquarters of the army) are located along the same spatial corridor. Some of the most expensive gated enclaves have been built in this general area, giving further credence to the fact that the coupling of high securitization to these developments has more to do with the declaration of a cosmopolitan lifestyle—one of whose marks is the display of the wherewithal to assuage middle-class anxieties—than any real concerns with security as such.[32] All these flow from the nature of the colonial administrative and residential functions that came to have an overdetermining impact for the differential social ecologies of the growing city.

Urban-Planning Rationalization and Its Pitfalls: The Trevallion and Hood Plan

It was only at the end of World War II that the four axes of epidemic/disaster management control and the colonial commercial, administrative, and residential functions were brought together and rationalized as elements of a unified urban-planning ideology. Thus in 1945 the colonial administration enacted the Gold Coast Town and Country Ordinance, which was to take a "broader view of planning . . . orderly and progressive development of land, town and other areas, whether urban or rural to preserve and improve the amenities thereof and other matters connected therewith."[33] In 1954 the colonial administration commissioned a major urban-planning document for the town. The full report of *Accra: A Plan for the Town* was finally submitted to the newly independent government in 1958. It was a substantial revision of a plan originally put forward by city planner Maxwell Fry in 1944, which had itself formed a major plank of the earlier ordinance. *A Plan for the Town* was put together by a team led by B. A. W. Trevallion and Alan G. Hood, with an introduction by the Honorable A. E. Inkumsah, minister of Housing, and a foreword by Kwame Nkrumah, the prime minister himself, signaling how seriously the new government at least received the document. The Trevallion and Hood Plan, coming hard on the heels of an earlier one undertaken by Ione Acquah from 1953 to 1956, is remarkable for outlining in meticulous detail the already-existing ordering of the town and for envisioning the precise spatial arrangements that might guarantee its future as a growing and modern city. Much unlike Acquah's document, the Trevallion and Hood Plan contains dozens of maps that help elaborate a broadly modernist aesthetic vision. They consider Accra a modern city that must be comprehended through the discourses of modernity that were dominant in Europe at the time. The notion of Accra as a modern city comparable to others in Europe and in the wider empire had already crept into colonial government correspondence during the lengthy debates that took place around the reorganization of the city following the earthquake in 1939. The colonial administration took natural disaster as an opportunity to seriously consider a complete refashioning of the city, an aspiration that was, however, followed only piecemeal due to financial and other constraints.[34] But there is ample evidence in colonial office records and in the Trevallion and Hood Plan that the question was taken very seriously.

Chapter 3 of the Trevallion and Hood document, simply titled "Open Space," is highly instructive with regard to the new design template that was being considered. Starting with an inventory of open and built spaces in the town and accompanying these with several detailed maps, the authors draw a distinction between "green wedges," envisaged as the corridors of open space between existing residential areas, and the residential areas themselves. This marks out their views as dramatically different from Ione Acquah's, which for all its mass of data did not demonstrate a properly relational spatial sense of the city. Trevallion and Hood note in "Open Space" that the most attractive gardens in the center of Accra lie on Crown lands, with the most important being those "surrounding the Supreme Court and the war memorial, the grounds of the Ministerial buildings on Rowe Road, and the Cathedral gardens," with "smaller ornamental gardens on the traffic islands and adjoining some of the more recent buildings such as the Ghana Bank and the Industrial Development Corporation Building" (1958, 23). These gardens were carefully tended, watered, and manicured. The two planners proceed to argue for the desirable features of an open-space system, which would essentially integrate opportunities for relaxation and recreation into built residential environments as aspects of unified residential districts properly integrated with their natural environments. Furthermore, they go on to point out that an open-space system has been proved "to be extremely beneficial to the micro-climate of a town. In the absence of open spaces the average air temperature can be expected to rise progressively with the growth of the town and with the accompanying restriction in air movement the climate of the town would be adversely affected" (1958, 23). The crucial consideration with respect to the open-space system, they go on to note, is that all unused corridors that already existed at the time between the different neighborhoods can be converted into recreational use and not allowed to slide into unplanned development, of which there was already-worrying evidence in the period they were writing about. When we see how much research has subsequently been done on the correlation between lack of greenery and the fluctuation of temperatures in built-up urban environments all over the world, Trevallion and Hood must definitely be considered ahead of their time in thinking about what would be required for the sustainable future for an African city such as Accra. More important, even though they did not express their views directly in the idiom of social ecologies that I outlined earlier in this chapter, their views provide ample substance for linking population to built and natural environments. In laying out their logic for green spaces for the city, Trevallion and Hood also invoke famous green landmarks in London. They specifically mention Regent's Park, St. James's Park, Hyde Park, and Green Park, stating that these are "not only well known to Londoners but are so famous that people who have never visited London or even Britain have heard of these parks as being a feature of the London scene" (1958, 24). The idea that these parks have attained an iconic status is also significant, for in their planning document Trevallion and Hood were clearly projecting a possible analogous iconicity for Accra. The preface to the Plan, written by one "W. H. B." already intimates this sensibility, stating: "The City already has the basic physical form of a good town, and no one can deny the appeal of palm trees, colourful vegetation, white sand, and the roar of the Atlantic surf." That this description is akin to what might be found in a tourist brochure extolling the exotic virtues of a seaside location is not to be dwelt upon here; rather, the insistence on the trope of a potential postcard iconicity should be noted as being echoed by Trevallion and Hood in their planning document itself. Though there was nothing comparable to Regent's Park and such other London landmarks in Accra at the time, they actually hit upon an idea that was quite daring in its spatial assumptions. Trevallion and Hood suggest that apart from "very limited sections the whole of the area on the seaward side of the coastal road comprising the Old Winneba Road, High Street, 28th February Road and Ada Road stretching from Manprobi [sic] in the west to Labadi in the east should remain virtually as open space and that the only development which should be allowed in the area should be that connected with its use for recreation and relaxation" (1958, 27). The claim for making this nearly five-kilometer stretch of Accra's coastal strip into a vital and protected green space was essentially an extrapolation from what had already become an integral aspect of the

European-only neighborhoods that we encountered earlier, which as early as the 1930s had a racecourse, a tennis club, and fine and leafy gardens as part of the overall colonial administration's sanctioned plan for the areas.

Trevallion and Hood's fine suggestions were regrettably not taken up by the postindependence government, Nkrumah's focus being more on prestige symbolic projects such as the State House and various landmark monuments. But there was another and perhaps more practical reason why the suggestion for converting the coastal strip into a protected green zone was not taken up by the new administration. The sea that laps Accra's coastline has for centuries been a source of fishing livelihood and sustenance for the communities that live along it. Thus Trevallion and Hood's admirable open-system concept, while readily applicable to the more inland lying areas of the town, clearly ignores the culturally saturated character of the coastal strip directly abutting the ocean itself. This in its turn indicates one of the fundamental problems for Accra's urban planning that has persisted to this day, namely, that the coastal strip all across the Gulf of Guinea has as yet not been fully evacuated of its cultural signification. The cultural signification produces a residual resistance to change and transformation, something that can be witnessed by the difficulties that all governments have had with attempts at rehabilitating the Jamestown area close to the disused harbor. That area has not only been shaped by its long economic relationship to the sea, it also happens to be what Nat Amarteifio, onetime mayor of Accra, has described as "the most ritually saturated part of the Ga landscape."[35] Until the early twentieth century, the Ga practice of burying their dead inside the home attracted the persistent attention of the colonial administration, with frequent skirmishes marking the enforced move to burials at the Osu cemetery, when it was opened in 1888. The practice of burying an elder inside their home ensured that such a burial place became the center of the *weku shia* (extended family house) which all members of the *weku* were obliged to return to on ritual occasions. As Parker (2000a) notes, it was the patterns of conversion to Christianity that came to reshape Ga attitudes to death and burial. But these took a very long time to change, and definitely not securely until the 1920s.[36] If Trevallion and Hood's suggestions for transforming Accra's coastal strip into a Western-style promenade were doomed to failure because of the ritual saturation of those areas, the larger question that this dimension of their plan raises is whether it is possible to think through urban modernization alongside the preservation of ritual and traditional attitudes to space or whether, alternatively, the struggle between the two is one of such epistemic non-commensurability that its resolution can only be secured in the name of one or the other but never both simultaneously. And this despite the fact that all commentators take "tradition" as inherently in flux and constantly in the process of (re)making. As we shall see shortly with regard to the famous Kokomlemle Consolidated Lands Case, the conversion of land from agrarian to urban usages was judicially adjudicated primarily with recourse to oral traditions that not only sought to provide a saturated cultural logic for understanding land tenure and its distribution but, more important, expressed a strict hierarchizing impulse in relation to which all the key social actors in Accra had to be positioned, whether these were Ga akutsei claiming primogeniture, the Tabon who found their hitherto uncontested lands the subject of intense controversy, northern migrants who developed various settlements as footholds for carving a presence in Accra, or, in the final instance, the colonial government itself.

The second point to be taken from the Trevallion and Hood document is the degree to which the authors drew their planning justifications from an implicit rationalization of what already existed. In other words, most of their suggestions depended on ignoring the contradictory and often fraught historical processes that had *produced* Accra's urban features in the form in which they saw them in the first place. Rather, their suggestions sought to project the process of urban formation as the *posterior effect* of central planning, rather than the dialectical product of the messy mixings of planned and unplanned processes. The messy processes of urban formation bequeathed to town planners and governments alike a particular spatial problematic. For in reality the pursuit of different town-planning policies from the early colonial period generated a mode of multi-synchronicity in the terms first suggested by Fredric Jameson. As he puts it, multi-sychnchronicity is "the coexistence of various synchronic systems or modes of production, each with its own dynamic, or time scheme" (1981, 97). The "or" between synchronic systems and modes of production in this formulation is a telling sign of ambivalence on Jameson's part, since the two terms are clearly not equivalent. If we focus on the multiple social, cultural, economic, and psychic sedimentations that colonial and postcolonial urban-planning phases have produced for the city, we find that the concept of multi-synchronicity names the character of a persistent spatial problematic for Accra. The urban-planning phases for the city may productively be read as physical, in terms of the urban fabric of roads, buildings, public parks, and so forth, as well as cultural, emotional, and affective, in terms of how people have reacted to the often contradictory unfolding of the urban form. Thus we see that each aspect of Accra's urban landscape was not simply superseded by subsequent forms. Rather, such aspects and phases were only partially assimilated to a coherent urban structure, such that the response to these partial assimilations may be seen in variant attempts to "privatize" the city by its denizens, in the sense of converting different dimensions of the public urban fabric into private or familial uses. As we shall come to see in part III, this conversion takes place at a number of levels and incorporates discursive and symbolic as well as material (re) appropriations of the form of the city. The discursive messiness and unpredictability of this process is something that the Trevallion and Hood plan and others like it have not been able to acknowledge, much less plan for.

Spatial Diversification III: The Cultural Politics of Land Tenure and Acquisition and the Kokomlemle Consolidated Lands Case

If colonial intervention in the housing market led to the production of differential socio-spatial ecologies for Accra, this must also be considered against the backdrop of land-use conversion from agrarian to urban usages. Land-use conversion has in its turn to be understood in the light of the politics of land acquisition and tenure, what Kathryn Firmin-Sellers (1996) describes as the distributional conflicts pertaining to land rights. While these conflicts were focalized around various town council, taxation, and native administration ordinances, the most pressing questions they raised were those concerning land tenure and land rights among the Ga themselves. The effect of the progressive yet incoherent layering of British principles of private land ownership over collective understandings of land tenure and alienation led to reconfigurations of power relations among the Ga chiefs, their Western-educated elites, and the colonial government, with serious controversies generating the first ethnopolitical parties. Since what passed for customary law was far from homogeneous or indeed straightforward, the attempts of chiefs to establish claims to absolute political authority in their interactions with the colonial administration triggered serious challenges from their secular elites and urban youth.[37]

The question of colonial governmentality has to be understood at multiple intersecting levels. At the highest level was the colonial state, which, via broad mechanisms under the general rubric of Indirect Rule, sought to govern through native institutions. But this disposition was itself to cause severe disjunctures within the governance mechanisms themselves, partly because, as Firmin-Sellers notes, the colonial state was wary of deploying its considerable institutional apparatus to intervene on the side of different social actors when it came to controversial customary interpretations of land acquisition and tenure.[38] A brief account of the mechanism of land ownership among the Ga serves to illustrate the complex nature of the questions that their land-tenure system was to pose to the colonial government. For the Ga land was held in collective trust on behalf of the lineage (the we, or family/lineage). The management and allocation of lineage land were (and still are) under the regulation of the lineage's principal members, the family head elected from among the elders of the lineage acting in the role of a *primus inter pares*. Each member of a lineage can claim rights of usufruct over some portion of lineage land, and on the death of a person who is unproductive the land and any improvements on it are ordinarily considered to revert to the collective lineage. In certain instances, however, a family member may claim family land as private property that they can then alienate by lease or sale to others. The lines of conflict between the contradictory principles of collective land ownership and those of private property were incrementally exacerbated during Accra's long process of urbanization. As the twentieth century wore on, the colonial administration's interventions in the purchase of lands for development projects (housing, roads, waterworks, etc.) led to the emergence of various actors who sought to capitalize on the compensation that the state offered for such lands. At the same time, the restructurings of chieftaincy under the rubric of Indirect Rule were also to impact upon the dramatis personae that were to play in the theatre of land-tenure controversies.

It was the Native Jurisdiction Ordinance of 1878 that had transformed the loose military federation of Ga townships (the manjii) into a rigid hierarchy. The Jurisdiction Ordinance split the Ga townships into Ga Mashie (Jamestown and Usshertown) and the leeward Ga (Osu, Labadi, Nungua, Teshie, and Tema). Furthermore, it elevated the Ga Mantse into the position of paramount chief and thus the representative and spokesman for all Gas. This meant that he had the sole authority to represent all the townships at the various forums at which chiefs from across the colony were required to make legislative representations. The immediate effect of the Jurisdiction Ordinance was first to introduce a hierarchy among the various Ga townships that had not existed before then, and more significant for the impact it had on future intra-Ga controversies, to place the Ga Mantse above all other chiefs, whether within Ga Mashie itself or among the various Ga townships. The elevation of the Ga Mantse to the position of ascendancy immediately focused various Ga social actors' minds on processes of legitimation, including the issue of his selection and deposition, matters that have continued to generate a great deal of enthusiasm and boisterousness within the Ga social polity to the present day. Another effect of the ordinance and others that followed it was to foster the invention of tradition, which in relation to land also meant the invention of a mechanism by which different social actors might control the distribution of land rights. While Firmin-Sellers provides a fascinating account of the politics of invented traditions that arose around land tenure by paying specific attention to the assertions of private rights instigated by Dr. Charles Reindorf and the Onomrorkor We family group, her account removes from view the interplay of migrant and stranger-group interests that served to further complicate the debates during the colonial period. The Kokomlemle Consolidated Lands Case (1940–1951), within which Reindorf and his family were one set of actors, provides a useful template for examining how multiple traditions were rehearsed from both nativist (Ga) and nonnativist (stranger-group) positions. Even more important, it also reveals the acute schisms among the large Ga Mashie land-owning families and between them and those at Osu township which under the regulations stipulated in the ordinance would fall under the superior suzerainty of the Ga Mantse. The Osu cultural actors' invocations of oral traditions supporting their claims to Accra lands were often at variance with those put forward by the Ga Mashie akutsei.

The Public Lands Ordinance of 1876, enacted to ease the colonial government's acquisition of land for development purposes, was augmented in 1896 by a Town Council Ordinance that stipulated a town council with powers to deal with environmental sanitation, the maintenance of buildings, and the planning and layout of streets for securing public health and proper urban development. Toward the end of the nineteenth century these administrative arrangements only served to formalize the processes of land acquisition for the colonial government without successfully rationalizing land-tenure procedures under customary law. As the twentieth century wore on and lands in Accra skyrocketed in price, further pressures were placed on the traditional mechanisms for the procurement and alienation of land. A plot of land at Adabraka had sold at £418 an acre in 1947, with a resale value of £1,500 an acre by 1951. The commercial value of land all along Station Road, which itself emerges from the General Post Office and goes alongside Makola and up through the Kantamanto railway terminus at Tudu, sold for £6,000 per acre in 1949 but by the mid-1950s the same tract of land could go for as much as a whopping £30,000 per acre. Similarly, at Korle Gonno there was a value increase of 50 percent per acre between 1947 and 1953.[39] The rising land prices in the central areas and the increase in the urban population began to exert development pressure on the areas that lay on the immediate outskirts of the central districts. By the early 1930s, the immediate outskirts of the Ga Mashie/CBD area included the now fully developed African middle-class neighborhood of Adabraka along with parts of Kokomlemle in one unbroken residential/commercial nexus linking the CBD to proximate residential hinterlands. Nima, which lies alongside Kokomlemle to the northeast, was initially settled by Alhaji Amadu Futa (Mallam Futa) in 1931. Alhaji Futa was a wealthy northern migrant and owner of large herds of cattle who had first settled at Zongo Lane near Makola. But his move to Nima was quickly to convert the settlement into one of the preferred entry points for northern migrants into the city. Mallam Futa was joined at Nima by other northern migrants reluctant to pay the high rents exacted by landlords at Tudu, the CBD, and those areas close to Ga Mashie. In the 1930s the early settlement at Nima had none of the benefits of colonial government planning and the settlers were left to develop it as they chose. After World War II more land there was given out by the colonial administration to demobilized northern soldiers from the West African Frontier Force, such that by 1950 Nima was the largest unplanned slum district in all of Accra, a distinction it retains to this day.

What came to be referred to as the Kokomlemle (or Akwandor) Consolidated Lands Case touched upon various adjacent districts, including Kokomlemle itself, Nima, Mamobi, Kanda, and Lagos Town (now Accra New Town). Kokomlemle is bounded to the northeast by Nima, to the north by Accra New Town, and to the south by Asylum Down. In addition to these districts, the areas under dispute in the case included Kpehe and Mamobi. Kanda, to the west of Nima, was also significant as the target of colonial government land acquisition for the development of further housing for civil servants. It was in fact the colonial government's acquisition of land at Kanda in 1931 and the process of identifying whom compensation was to be paid to that triggered the entire gamut of disputes about who had rights to the lands in these areas. In 1936 the Survey Department set about extensively surveying Kokomlemle with the view to planning drainage lines and extending electricity to the area to encourage private housing development. Apart from Kokomlemle and Asylum Down, which both developed as private African middle-class suburbs, and Kanda, another of the well-planned cluster of government estates originally set up for civil servants, the rest of the aforementioned areas in the lands case are generally characterized by a dense long-distance northern migrant demographic. They are poorly planned and with only intermittent access to social amenities such as potable water and electricity.[40]

The areas that were clustered under the Kokomlemle Consolidated Lands Case all lay some five miles north of the CBD and across from the Ring Road, a road that acts as an extended distributive boundary to the CBD and an artery linking the city's core to various outlying neighborhoods. Ring Road links to the current Cantonments Road toward the east, which in the colonial period was the only road that led outward to Ada, Dodowa, and the food- and cocoa-producing sectors of the eastern regions. The Ring Road was also reached directly from the CBD by Station Road (now Kwame Nkrumah Avenue) and Kibi Road (formerly Boundary Road, but now Kojo Thompson Road). Going westward the Ring Road traverses Awudome and Kaneshie, extending through the Winneba Road to Weija, Winneba itself, Cape Coast (erstwhile seat of the colonial administration until 1877), Takoradi, and all the western regions of the country. As noted earlier, Takoradi Harbor had been completed in 1928 and served to open up a significant dimension of the transshipment of exogenous manufactured goods for distribution to Accra and other parts of the country. With the development of Adabraka and Asylum Down as viable neighborhoods for housing the African middle classes and the interest shown by the colonial government in developing Kanda and Kokomlemle, all the lands in the areas under dispute were suddenly inserted into the intensified spatial economy that had already led to rising costs of land elsewhere in the town. Given the fact also that the Ring Road provided a crucial connection between the CBD and various parts of the country, it is not entirely surprising that the Kokomlemle lands situated along it became of such great speculative interest.

Several stools, families, and individuals representing variant social constituencies were drawn into the Kokomlemle Lands Case, among them the Ga, Gbese, and Korle stools (acting as a single collective unit); the Osu stool; the Odotsio Odoi Kwao family of Christiansborg; the Tabon, represented by their chief Nii Azumah Nelson III; Mallam Futa and the Nima community; and the prominent Euro-African Reindorf, Lutterodt, and Bannerman families.[41] Twenty-five claimants prayed for declaration of their title to lands in a case that ran in the court system from 1940 to 1951, when judgment was finally handed down. The judgment and proceedings report to the case runs to 150 pages. And yet the names of the various protagonists to the case are not as important as the different and often sharply contradictory principles of land acquisition and tenure that they argued for. With specific reference to the Kokomlemle portions of the disputed lands, Justice J. Jackson noted that as of 1938, when he first made a preliminary survey of the areas, much of what he saw was exclusively used for farming, with cultivated crops including cassava and groundnuts and only a few farm buildings dotting the landscape. However, by 1943, "whilst these actions have been lying dormant in the Court, [the land has] developed into what I would style a good middle-class residential area."[42]

For heuristic purposes I will divide the twenty-five litigating parties into four categories: (1) Ga collective groups such as stools and lineages that evoked customary law and practice as a means of staking their claims to the lands; (2) Ga and Osu families that staked their claims by virtue either of outright purchase, land-for-debt agreements, or long residency on the relevant lands; (3) migrant groups that insisted they had participated in outright sale/purchase transactions; and finally (4) the colonial government. The colonial government was not actually a respondent or participant in the Kokomlemle Lands Case and only featured in the overall background to the controversies unfolding because of the issue of who might gain compensation for lands procured by the government under its various ordinances. As we have noted already, it was this that instigated a jostling for position regarding who had the right to alienate land in the first place. The colonial administration thus retains an interest for us primarily through its interventions in the land market and the triggers that such interventions provided for the exacerbation of arguments regarding land ownership.

Of the claims articulated by the four provisional categories just outlined by far the most complicated were those put forward by the Ga, Gbese, and Korle stools. The reason for their collective positioning was not hard to fathom once we pay attention to the oral traditions they put forward to rationalize their claims. In the interest of sifting between hoary legend and brute fact, Justice Jackson attempted to distinguish between stories that suggested that the Gas had emerged from the sea—"a belief that rocks now in the sea are fossilized remains of some who failed to get across"—and what he considered to be the more "historical" accounts. What the judge considered to have been a historical account went this way:

> The earliest historical knowledge of the Gas or certainly the Gbese section of the Gas, is that they inhabited a place called Ayawaso, about 12 miles [sic] north of Accra. Among the Gbese people was a family called Onormroko and the tradition is that they were hunters and that during their travels they discovered the Korle Lagoon, which runs into the sea just west of James Town.
>
> There they are said to have found two large pots containing some beads, named "Korle," which they took home with them to their hunting camp. There a woman named Dede is said to have become inspired by the spirit of the Lagoon and what is now known as the Korle Fetish then came

into being, and the lands all around were placed under the protection of the priestess (Wulomo) of that juju and from that day to this has been known as Korle Wulomo.

In those ancient days the Priest was regarded as the owner of all of the lands around, and which are now known as Accra and which include the lands now in dispute.

. . .

In the ancient days quite clearly the family known as Onormroko or Korle would be regarded as the unit which owned the lands, with the Fetish priest as its spiritual protector.[43]

The story as told to the judge about Gbese primogeniture among the Gas has been seriously questioned by Ga scholars, due mainly to the fact that Gbese was historically part of the Asere quarter and only broke away from them on the destruction of the Ayawaso kingdom in 1680. According to Irene Odotei, the two original Ga akutsei are Asere and Sempe (the two together forming the famed Ga nyo Krong or "pure Ga" of popular parlance). All the other akutsei were either splinters from these two quarters (for example, Akanmaji was a political breakaway faction from Gbese) or, as in the cases of Alata and Otublohum, evolved directly out of stranger groups on the arrival of the Gas fleeing from Ayawaso to the coast and shaped either by the long encounter with the Europeans, or interactions with hinterland Akan ethnic groups such as the Akwamus.[44]

The point of the story as recounted by the learned judge must then not be seen to reside in its veracity or falsehood (though that was definitely paramount in his own mind in coming to a judgment on the claims before him) but rather in the processes of hierarchization implied first in the theme of transition from nomadism to sedentarism, and, more significant, in the legitimation mechanism implied by the invocation of a deity, here embodied in the person of the Korle *wulomo* (fetish priest). The question of a guardian deity is no ordinary one; Ga scholars have noted that in fact for the people of Ga Mashie the ultimate owners of all lands are the gods that inhabit the three main bodies of water with which the Gas are associated, namely Korle, Sakumo, and Nai.[45] The judge went on to summarize six principles regarding land tenure, ownership, and alienation among the Ga:

1. A member of a Stool may farm where he wishes upon stool land which is unoccupied without first obtaining any formal leave or permission;

2. Casual farming for a season or two, which is later abandoned, creates no interest in land;

3. Sustained occupation coupled with the erection of buildings in furtherance of such occupation by farming creates a hereditable interest in land or even continuous farming alone provided it be sufficiently localized;

4. Upon the death of the founder of such farms and buildings the land then acquires the character of family property;

5. Land not built upon but farmed by the successor in title of the founder of such farm also in similar circumstances becomes clothed with the character of "family lands" whilst so farmed;

6. Land unoccupied by buildings or farms may be allotted by the Head or Caretaker of the Stool to other members of the Stool either by way of gift or license.[46]

Each of the six principles listed above sheds light on different dimensions of the acquisition of agrarian lands and their conversion from stool to family lands and then as alienable property. Most of the judge's focus is on the proof of effective occupancy which, as we can see from points 3–5, turned on claims of settlement and long-term cultivation. In further glossing the six points, the judge also clarifies that collectively owned lands cannot be alienated except in case of a debt for which land might be exchanged as a mode of defraying such debt. And even here permission has to be sought from all members of the stool or family who might have vested interest in the said land. Though left largely unacknowledged in the judge's disquisition, present in the background of the various points he outlined was also the barely articulated protagonist of the private individual, in this case denominated as the "head" of the family, through whom by virtue of long residence or cultivation a piece of agrarian land came to be privately "owned" by a family. Long-term cultivation of a piece of land by the head of a family empowers him (or her) to place the land within the domain of vested family interest, that is, in the domain of private property. Even though the judge was at pains throughout the proceedings to insist on the essentially collective ownership character of the lands in dispute, in reality as soon as it was granted that stool or lineage lands cultivated without permission of the stool or lineage could be bequeathed to an individual's family rather than being restored back to the stool, the mediating protagonist of the private individual (family head) begins to gain salience and ascendancy within the domain of land transactions. In the Kokomlemle Lands Case the shape of that individual did not seem to as yet have the character that was later to be associated with corporations or indeed of the singular individual divested from all collective appendages, familial, lineage, or otherwise. Justice Jackson expresses surprise that the most striking feature of all the cases brought before him lay in the "clandestine" nature of the transactions, namely, that the alienation of either stool or family lands had been done without express consultation with other members of the stools or families in question.[47] But what he sees as lying in the domain of secrecy may also be read as the rise of the private individual working in his own self-interest as opposed to that of the collective. It is the enterprising private individual working in the interest of him/herself and of his/her own family, as opposed to in the service of a collectivity represented by a lineage or stool, that emerges as the ghost in the machine and the one whom all the litigating parties were ultimately wrestling with.

The claims put by Odoi Kwao and the Tabon lay at the intersection of all the vectors we have encountered so far: Ga/Osu, stool/lineage/family, collective/individual. The structural significance of the Ga, Gbese, and Korle claims to primogeniture over all of Accra lands is illustrated in the story that was put to the court regarding Osu stool lands. From their own account, the people of Osu had come to the coast from Osudoku in the latter part of the seventeenth century, settling first around Legon and subsequently moving farther southward until they arrived at their current location at Osu, where they settled on the land with the permission of the Gbese stool. Even though the Osus admitted that they had originally been granted farming lands by the Ga stool in all the locations they had traversed, three hundred years to the middle of the twentieth century, their having settled on these lands were taken by them to have transformed them incontrovertibly into Osu lands, that is to say, theirs without the need of recourse to the Gbese stool. More curiously, the litigants from Osu made no reference whatsoever to the old legend of their fleeing from Osudoku in 1620s because of a quarrel over precious beads, and that when they arrived at their present location they were granted lands by the chief of the La people and not the Gbese as they had put forward in this claim. This second and more popularly known account did not seem salient to the claims being made in the Kokomlemle Lands Case, but we shall return to the implications of this second story more fully in chapter 3. In this court case it was the issue of the boundaries between Ga Mashie and Osu lands that was at issue. Furthermore, the issue of boundaries became even more salient because of the claims being made by the Odotsio Kwao Odoi family, an important scion of the Osus, but who had as a family unit farmed lands that included Nima for over at least a century prior to the lands case. Their rights gained through long settlement and cultivation is what allowed them to sell a large tract of land to Mallam Futa for the founding of Nima village in 1931. Mallam Futa had been dutifully paying regular annual fees to the Odotsio Kwao Odoi family until both the Gbese and Osu stools raised questions in separate court cases regarding ownership of that particular tract of land. While Mallam Futa had documents that were legally binding and admissible in evidence, the case of the Kwao Odoi family's claim to the land was settled strictly on the basis of the oral traditions that proved that they had been resident cultivators of the land in question for at least a century prior to its sale to Mallam Futa.[48] If the Osus' oral traditions of their settlement and cultivation of the lands illustrated the general principles of their conversion from nomadism to sedentarism, the Kwao Odoi family's story illustrated the simultaneous cultural and economic significance of separating individual family interests from those of a collective, in this case of the people of Osu. By virtue of the principle of long-standing land cultivation and therefore effective occupancy, the Kwao Odoi family could assert ownership of the Nima lands and thus their right to sell it to whomever they chose and without reference to the interests of the Osu stool in general. As the judge was at pains to point out, vested family interests did not justify outright alienation or sale of a piece of land except in the case of a family debt for which a piece of land could be exchanged in clearance of such debt. In such cases, however, both stool lands and family lands were interpreted as collective properties and according to customary law cited by the judge could not be alienated except with the full and express agreement of all members of the collective stool or family. Clearly, in the case in question, the leader of the Kwao Odoi family had proceeded to sell the land (a) not for defraying a debt accruing to the family, and (b) without recourse to the knowledge or agreement of other family members. The fact that the Kwao Odoi family, through their family head, had sold the Nima land not due to any debts also showed that they were exercising their agency as a collective urban landlord and not in the form of a lineage governed by the customary traditions of land tenure. The family was thus taking full advantage of the rise in land values in Accra.

The contradiction between collective and individual alienation of land must ultimately be read as the struggle between agrarian and urban land uses within a geographical domain that was being subjected to concentrated and severe forces of urbanization. For in rural agrarian usages there is no question of the outright alienation of land since the land is the object of cultivation of family groups for long periods, sometimes for decades at a time. Furthermore, wherever large tracts of agrarian lands are available, and without the intervention of modern agricultural methods of cultivation, the farming methods that are deployed tend to be inherently nomadic, with farmers practicing a form of shifting cultivation in which a patch of land is farmed for several years until it is completely exhausted, upon which it is left fallow for another few years while the farmer moves on to another patch of land. The rationale and practice of shifting cultivation also means that the specific boundaries between agrarian lands are hardly ever observed, if they are recognized at all. Conversely, urban land usage is grounded on an essentially sedentary logic, in which the person or community on the land seeks to establish a sense of permanence rooted in space. This is often marked by the siting of buildings upon the land, in line with the logic of the spatial fix that converts geographical space into a transactional commodity. While commutes may be undertaken to farm or herd animals elsewhere, the erection of permanent buildings is meant to indicate a sense of longevity, sedentarism, and, I would add, ultimate commodifiability. It is the sense of permanence conveyed by buildings that naturalizes the aura of land commodification in the urban sphere and at the same time invokes the boundary markings that are rarely observed in largely rural agrarian contexts. It is the spatial fixing of buildings that translates the immediacy of private ownership, whether in fact the building and the land on which it is sited is owned by an individual or a collective. The more permanent and diverse the structures erected upon the land, the more commodifiable the land comes to be. Thus Justice Jackson's observation that the Kokomlemle lands had altered between 1938 to 1943 from a place where vegetable crops were cultivated to "a good middle-class residential area" could only have been made with reference to the permanence and diversity of the built structures that he found on them. We see then that in the late colonial period and amid Accra's steadily urbanizing vista, the distinctions that were customarily drawn between nonalienable collectively owned lands and the domain of private property had become blurred by the pressures placed on land conversion from agrarian to urban usages.

If Accra's evolution has depended on various functions—commercial, administrative, residential, and ethno-political—these now define a space of contradiction as well as opportunity, of local dynamics as well as global processes, and of a spatial logic that can only be understood by way of historicizing all the dimensions of its transformation from the small fishing village that it was in the mid-1600s to the buzzing city that it is today.

CHAPTER 3

Osu borla no, sardine chensii soo: Danes,
Euro-Africans, and the Transculturation of Osu

The history of Osu spells a complex interaction between Denmark and the local population that spanned nearly two hundred years from the mid-seventeenth to the mid-nineteenth centuries, when the interaction was discontinued upon the purchase of Christiansborg Castle by the British in 1850. A form of disjointed social incrementalism may be shown to have defined Osu during the period, yet the overall upshot of this process was the production of a particular sociocultural and spatial dynamic that in its turn has helped to generate and sustain a phenomenon such as Oxford Street. The concept of disjointed social incrementalism echoes the interpretation of political process and decision making proffered by William Bacchus in which he argues that decisions are often made not by unitary actors but by several actors and political agents who pursue their objectives inconsistently and with respect to various contradictory conceptions of national (read also ethno-cultural) organizational and personal goals. His phrase seems to me highly appropriate for describing decisive moments in the relations between the Danes and the people of Osu, as well as for grasping the mechanisms by which the township evolved in the long period under discussion.[1] The onset of formal colonialism, the choice of Christiansborg Castle and Accra as the seat of government in 1877, and the attenuation of the position of Euro-African merchant princes that had developed through relations between Europeans and Africans on the coast were to mark sharp changes in the fortunes of Osu's social and political landscape, but these proved necessary to its reconstitution as a commercial district whose fortunes have turned out to be quite distinctive from those of English and Dutch Accra. In drawing on the extensive work that has already been done on European trade relations with various towns in the Gold Coast and on the specific economic, cultural, and social events that have helped to shape Osu RE and Oxford Street in the twenty-first century, in this chapter my ultimate objective is to revisit current definitions of transnationalism to account for the variegated and insistently hybrid aspects of Osu's history.

The saying in the first part of the title to this chapter, which roughly translates as "at the Osu garbage dump all you find are sardine cans," is used by Gas from other parts of Accra to insinuate that the people of Osu have historically been overly eager to absorb European influences. At one level, however, the absorption of European influences by the Osus cannot be said to have been unusual from what occurred in other coastal areas with a European presence such as Elmina, Cape Coast, and indeed Dutch and English Accra.[2] And yet at the same time, Osu was qualitatively different from these other townships for a variety of reasons. Following the building of the Danish Christiansborg Fort (later Castle) at Osu in 1661, what was then a small settlement went through significant transformations in culture, labor practices, lifestyles, and, most importantly, in the class and social hierarchies that came to be marked increasingly by race and skin color.[3] Among the telling effects of the building of the fort at Osu was that the sparsely inhabited area close to the fort became attractive to migrants fleeing from conflicts from the hinterland. The area also became a significant trade hub for the same reason. Like all the areas that developed around the European trading establishments on the coast, Osu became the external core for the extraction of surplus from the hinterland for the benefit of commercial companies in Europe. And by the start of the eighteenth century, Osu had become fully incorporated into the transatlantic slave trade as a minor outpost of the trade and within a hundred years had given rise to an influential Euro-African community whose roots could be traced back to the inception of trade relations between the Danes and the people of the settlement. In the 1720s, and with the active instigation of the Europeans, already-existing political conflicts were exacerbated between the coastal peoples and the Akans of the hinterland, leading to further population dispersal to the coast and demographic and sociopolitical changes for the people at Osu.[4]

Historically what seems to have contributed most to Osu's distinctiveness among other coastal settlements similar to it was the establishment of a school for mulatto children at Christiansborg Fort in 1722, which was to have a major influence on the ideological and cultural reproduction of a hybrid Euro-African consciousness. The Euro-African consciousness was to remain spatially integrated into Osu society long after the departure of the Danes and the consolidation of colonial rule in the late nineteenth century. The better-known school in the history of the Gold Coast/Ghana was also famously started for mulatto children by Philip Quaque (1741–1816) at Cape Castle in 1766, four decades after the Danish school had been established at Christiansborg. Furthermore, unlike Ga Mashie, Osu did not have a viable harbor, which also meant that its spatial evolution was not tied to the economic vagaries of one. The geographical character of Ga Mashie evolved alongside the terms dictated by this crucial economic and commercial nexus, thus by the start of the twentieth century Jamestown and its surrounding areas could be described essentially as a conurbation of warehouses integrated into the densely congested population. The social character of the area was firmly shaped by the services that emerged in support of the harbor and its lively warehouse trade, such as porterage, insurance brokerage, bulk breakdown and transshipment, surf boat operations, and so forth. After the opening of the much larger deepwater harbor at Tema in 1962, Jamestown was to suffer progressive malaise, desuetude, and decay. Not having a harbor or even a proper landing point meant that Osu's spatial morphology was not afflicted by the same vicissitudes as that of Jamestown and Ga Mashie. It was thus free to develop in a completely different direction. All these factors had a telling impact on the society and culture at Osu.

As already noted, by the late eighteenth century Danish company officials and free traders had built several stone houses to accommodate themselves and their families in various parts of the township. The houses of some renowned Euro-African families may be found in the neighborhoods of Amangfong (on today's Castle Drive, within easy reach of the castle) and at Kuku Hill and Salem (further inland and a short distance from today's Oxford Street). These families include the Richters, Wulffs, Bannermans, Bergessens, Lutterodts, Clelands, Lokkos, Reinholdts, Holmeses, Hesses, Hansens, Brocks, Engmanns, Quists, and various others.[5] Osu Salem is also significant for introducing a form of spatial differentiation tied specifically to Christianity. Salem village was originally conceived of in the 1830s as the Basel Christian "quarter" of Osu. As Urilke Sill notes in a comparative study of the Salems at Osu and Akuapem, these were "conceptualized as comprising the mission house, church and school, as well as the compounds of the Christians" (2010, 195). Even though the reality of its interactions with the rest of the township was far from simple, Salem was perceived by most Africans as constituting a separate and exclusive community enforcing a strict distinction between itself and the already-existing culture and society that the Christians had come to encounter. That notwithstanding, the Osu Salem school opened in 1843 for all Africans and adopted instruction in English in contrast to the Danish of the Christiansborg Fort school, which now lists among its alumni some of the most accomplished Ghanaian professionals, many of whom are of mixed-race heritage.[6]

Like those at Ga Mashie, the akutsei at Osu were formed from a variety of sources, including older Ga-Adangme settlers from the 1600s (Aneho), slaves brought in by the Portuguese in the 1640s to help build their trading lodge (Osu Alata), Akwamu and Ashanti traders who came to settle on the coast after the wars of 1677–1680 (Ashinte Blohum), and in the aftermath of a major battle between Dutch and Danish Accra in the 1730s, what came to constitute the Osu royal family akutso (Kinkawe).[7] While all these akutsei currently show signs of dilapidation, the same cannot be said for the Salem and Kuku Hill districts. By the onset of formal colonialism in the 1850s, the Salem and Kuku Hill districts could be seen as lying on the outskirts of the already-existing township that had been made up of the four akutsei lying closer to the fort. Thus with their large European-style stone houses, Salem and Kuku Hill represented not just a decisive expansion away from the fort, but the spatialized identification of hybrid Euro-African identities that had evolved differently from the lineages of the akutsei while still overlapping with them. Given that the earliest converts to Christianity at Osu were also the mulatto children who had attended the fort school since the 1720s, the arrival of the Basel Mission and its procurement of lands in the Salem and Kuku Hill areas for the construction of a pietist community also meant that Christianity was to be cross-articulated with race and class at both places, their communities bearing the early marks of Westernization and an incipient cosmopolitan modernity.

The vicinity of Salem and Kuku Hill, favored locations for the homes of Euro-Africans and their families, became the first installment of what was later to be joined to other parts of Accra as the preferred zones for housing the ruling elites and their satellites (see chapter 2). A century later in the 1940s, Osu acquired the epithet of RE, a name extrapolated from the vicinity around the old American embassy where British Royal Engineers had been camped in tents during World War II. The colonial administration's direct investment in the low-cost housing at Osu RE following the earthquake of 1939 was to have a further impact on the spatial configuration that was later to produce Oxford Street. The low-cost housing served to diversify the class characteristics of the area, so that by the 1990s there existed a dense rental hinterland abutting yet also concealed by the economic vitality of Oxford Street itself. Prior to that, Osu RE was universally acknowledged to be the nightlife capital of Accra, with clubs such as Black Caesar's, Mama Muchi, Cave Du Roy, Number One, and Keteke (to name but a handful from the period) catering to the leisure tastes of the elites and their well-connected cohorts. Beer, live music, and prostitutes have been central to the character of the area since then. The fact that Oxford Street was part of the longer Cantonments Road, which traverses some of the most high-end neighborhoods in the city, was also a boon to the vitality of the street. The bombing of Makola by the Rawlings regime in 1979 and the structural adjustment programs of the mid to late 1980s were to trigger the flight of capital and commercial vitality away from the CBD, with the Oxford Street area being the key beneficiary of this event in the decades that followed.

The Early Settlement at Osu: Politics, Culture, and Economy

Any attempt to reconstruct early life at Osu must start from the oral traditions of its first settlement. The area was originally populated sometime in the 1620s by Ga-Adangme-speaking peoples that had brokered the trade between the inland Akan groups and the Europeans on the coast.[8] However, oral tradition also has it that by the middle of the seventeenth century a cohesive sociopolitical group of families fled a conflict over some precious beads at Osudoku in the Shai Hills and came to settle at the present-day Osu. It was this group that gave the town its name—Osu—in commemoration of their original homeland. The refugees from Osudoku were led by Noete Doku, a renowned wulomo of the Nadu shrine, who helped to get them the hospitality of the people of the neighboring Labadi as well as of the already-existing groups of Ga-Adangme settlers. Some scholars have suggested that by 1698 Noete Doku was already well known to the Danish factors at Christiansborg and that he had by then become the lumo or king of all the Osus. He was also a highly respected caboceer. The role of caboceer was a combination of trade captain, political leader (often but not always a chiefly role), and diplomat and frequently involved liaising between the Europeans on the coast and Akan traders from the hinterland. It was also not unknown for a caboceer to have a large retinue of followers, and sometimes even an army. The Danish records show that caboceers drew a regular monthly stipend, along with being showered by gifts and other favors by the Danes. A caboceer was, however, not tied to any single European trading company, and it was not unknown for his allegiance to be actively sought by more than one set of Europeans on the coast.[9]

A good instance of shifting allegiances and the political nature of the caboceer's role is to be seen in the case of Okaija (sometimes also spelled Okaidja by historians, but Okanie in the Danish records), who was originally from Kinka in Dutch Accra, but after a major misunderstanding over a debt moved with his entire retinue of family and followers to Osu. The Danish records state that his arrival at Osu would considerably expand the town "for the force he has brought with him from the Dutch town is more than 200 guns as well as a large following of family and friends and others which he has everywhere here at the Coast."[10] The Danes justify extending their hospitality to him because other people on the coast had sworn to "die with him" if there was any attempt to arrest Okaija and send him back to the Dutch. Clearly, caboceer Okaija was a very influential man.[11] The events surrounding Okaija occurred between 1736 and 1738, and even though the Danes extended him hospitality and protection, they were also anxious not to provoke the Dutch, who historically seemed to have had superior firepower and the reputation for fomenting trouble for them anytime the opportunity presented itself, not only at Osu but also at Ningo, Ada, and Keta, where the Danes had strong trading interests.[12] The combination of Noete Doku's political leadership of the Osus, his status as powerful wulomo, and his role as caboceer not only made him a formidable ally, but also indicates the multiple functions that came together to define the nexus of wider social relationships and hierarchies over which the caboceer presided. Whether the spiritual, economic, and political/diplomatic functions just enumerated for Noete Doku were articulated separately or collectively in the personal biographies of particular individuals, these have to be seen within the larger framework of the socioeconomic shifts that were taking place in the Gold Coast from the sixteenth to the nineteenth centuries.

As noted in chapter 1, by 1680 the Akwamus had decimated the powerful centralized Ga state at Ayawaso, scattered its people to the coastal districts of Ga Mashie, and reduced them to tribute-paying vassals of the Akwamuhene. Osu was to suffer a similar status of vassalage until the final overthrow of the Akwamus by a combined army of Gas from Ga Mashie, Osus, and Akyems in 1730, amply supported by all three European merchant groups on the coast. Akwamu vassalage was, however, quickly succeeded by Akyem overlordship, which in its turn was followed hard upon by Ashanti control over large swathes of the coastal populations across the Gold Coast, from the 1740s onward. Critical to understanding the series of Akan dominations of the Accra coast, however, is what Ray Kea adroitly describes as the shift in the overall cultural economy of the seventeenth and eighteenth centuries that redefined the relations between urban settlements and trade networks in the Gold Coast in general. This shift was one from the accumulation of capital drawing upon the gold trade and relying primarily on profits from caravan-based trade and exchange networks to that of accumulation tied to political-military projects and the extraction of tribute and other levies from conquered populations. As Kea notes: "Persons of means were able to participate fully in an extensive commodity exchange network and to generate important levels and concentrations of market activity" (1982, 289). In both phases "networks of capital accumulation were embedded in and subordinated to networks of power" (Kea 1986, 11).[13] Significantly, however, the political-military processes of capital accumulation coincided with the Atlantic slave trade and were intensified by it. What Kea points out as commodity exchange networks and concentrations of market activity had a number of interrelated dimensions to them. In the first place, the Atlantic slave trade was to make locally available a whole range of new commodities, such as *salampores* (woven cotton stripe cloth from India), all kinds of East Indian silk and half-silk cloths, tallow, pewter basins, beads, guns and gunpowder, English stoneware from Staffordshire, coffee cups and platters of Chinese vintage, along with brandy, sugar, tobacco, and various other goods whose procurement was for a long time reserved for the rich and powerful.[14] The new European goods that were put into circulation also went through significant supply-and-demand cycles as the merchant companies on the coast tried to satisfy the specific demands of their African clients while also inducing new tastes and consumption patterns.

In the context of the overall political economy of the coastal settlements, markets have to be understood as complex networks both for satisfying the new consumption patterns in European goods and for managing the alterations in agricultural production that came to service the urban settlements nucleated (the word is Kea's) by the trade networks that had been generated by the European presence on the coast. The term "market" must also not be misunderstood as coinciding exclusively with specific spatial locations, even though some of these (such as the periodic markets at Osu, at the fort, and on the slave ships) were signally important in establishing different patron/client and credit relationships across a wide array of social platforms. The market also covered an entire range of monetization processes, dominated at the higher levels of trade by gold. By the eighteenth century, gold was conventionally used for the payment of bulky or more expensive commodities such as slaves, elephant tusks, and various other prized commodities from the hinterland, while cowrie shells, reputedly introduced by the Dutch from India, came to be deployed for daily purchases and smaller payments. By the middle of the eighteenth century, the scarcity of surface gold had led to its shortage and provided an impetus to mining in place of alluvial sifting. The relative depletion in the availability of gold also coincided with the slave trade and was triggered by the proliferation of wars in the hinterland that did damage to gold production while augmenting the trade in slaves.[15] Gold was progressively replaced by coins toward the end of the nineteenth century when the increasing size of the colonial bureaucracy and the volume of new trade led to the establishment of banks that in their turn ultimately led to the precious metal's complete demonetization. The fate of gold in the history of the Gold Coast must also be interpreted in relation to the shifting power relations between Africans and Europeans, and indeed to the demise of accumulation through military projects that Kea alludes to. Since control of the gold trade was also fundamental to the rise of Ashanti power, its progressive demonetization under colonial rule was also a sign of the demise of Ashanti authority in the Gold Coast. The final plank of colonial administrative overlordship of the colony was intimately tied to the processes by which the precious commodity ceased circulating in common usage and instead was progressively replaced by the system of British seigniorage, which of course meant significant profits for the colonial administration and the European banks, at the expense of their African trading counterparts.[16] But prior to that it was of primary concern to the individual European merchant operations on the coast. Gold's acquisition, its storage and transportation, and what goods it might be exchanged for in the local economy feature prominently and almost obsessively in all the correspondence from the Danish factors at Christiansborg to their Guinea and India Company directors in Copenhagen. In fact, there was hardly a letter leaving Christiansborg to Europe that did not itemize the gold stock at the fort and did not express concern about how it might be dispatched to arrive safely in Denmark. This continued until the Danes finally departed from the coast in 1850.

While the new commodities and consumption patterns gave rise to influential political and commercial elites, the social life at Osu was not limited to the lives of the powerful. As Per Hernæs (1996) has noted, within a few decades of the arrival of the Europeans, the fort and the entire township at Osu had evolved into a single commercial unit where members of both became tightly integrated via familial, social, and economic networks. The social life of the township was tied to the economic rhythms implicit in its status as a minor outpost of the transatlantic slave trade. Thus by the 1730s, the increase in the number of company slaves and the lack of space inside of

Christiansborg itself meant that they were required to live in the township and to commute to work at the fort on a daily basis. These slaves may have found accommodation in the Alata akutso, which was originally started as a community of ex-slaves brought in by the Portuguese from the Allada slave coast of Dahomey in 1649 to help build their trading lodge before it changed hands in quick succession first to the Swedes and then to the Danes. As in the case of the building of James Fort, the ex-slaves of the Alata akutso were also augmented by Fanti fishermen from Morée, who acted as *remidors*, or rowers of the canoes that were used to ferry slaves and goods to and from the ships that dropped anchor some three miles off the coast.

(Two unrecognized monuments to slavery that can be found at Osu today are Tolo Mɔn (pronounced to rhyme with "kong"),[17] originally the house of Heinrich Richter, the famous mulatto merchant prince and one of the wealthiest traders in the Gold Coast in the late eighteenth century and first part of the nineteenth.[18] It is commonly believed that an underground tunnel extended from inside Tolo Mɔn through to the Christiansborg Castle, and that this was used for captives to pass through on their way to the slave ships. The tunnel is said to have been blocked in the 1980s by Rawlings's regime due to security fears.[19] But the significance of Tolo Mɔn lies in its name. Tolo is a Ga corruption of the word "Tolon," the name of a town close to Yendi. Yendi was itself a major slave market in the eighteenth and early nineteenth centuries, and the people of Tolon were part of the Dagomba military establishment and thus had various connections to slavery, either by becoming slave captives themselves or capturing others to form part of the annual tributes that the Dagombas were forced to pay to the Ashanti kingdom in the eighteenth century. The word mɔn simply means "prison." In Ga parlance, when one is imprisoned it is referred to as: "Awo le mɔn" (he/she has been put in prison) or "Awo le tsu min" (he/she has been detained in a room). Thus Tolo Mɔn was the prison for slaves that had been captured in the wars up north. The rooms where the slaves were kept in the courtyard of the house, along with a stone stairway that originally led into the main building (now demolished) is still pointed out by people who live there today. The second unsung memorial to slavery at Osu is the tamarind-tree avenue that was planted by Danes after the abolition of slavery to demarcate the route from the castle to their plantation and holiday homes at the foot of the Akwapim hills. The remnants of the tamarind-tree avenue, originally planted by freed slaves, are still visible in some parts of Osu today, with the last row of trees to be found still standing at the end of the line in Siseme village, some nine miles inland north of Osu and close to today's Abokobi.)

The periodic docking of ships off the coast of the township in the period under discussion also represented the arrival of sailors and other transient visitors whose requirements of food, drink, and the satisfaction of sexual appetites were met by the people at Osu. In a somewhat censorious note born no doubt from his strongly Christian disposition, Nii-Adziri Wellington describes the social scene in his fictionalized historical account of Osu in this way:

> The poisonous atmosphere inside Christiansborg manifested itself at Danish-Osu in various ways as both the growing number of young mulattoes, together with their local clansmen and women imitated the loose life of sin and debauchery that went on behind the high walls of Christiansborg. Such corrupted and corroding ways of life in Danish-Osu were at times taken to extremes when slave-ships arrived in the roads on the coast. According to the Stones [the metaphorical sources of Wellington's fictionalized history], in addition to their cargo of goods for exchange, these ships sometimes brought along short-term visitors—sailors, merchants and adventurers dispirited and emotionally dissipated through long and dangerous sea voyages, who were looking for avenues on land to release their tensions and trials. These visitors found their way into town through the gates of Christiansborg and added their influence to the Danish-Osu social world, roaming about in the community, drinking, pursuing hedonistic pleasures and gratifying their lusts. (2011, 56–57)[20]

The motif of mimicry that Wellington introduces here is one that we will come to see in a different and more significant cultural context later in our discussion. There is, however, also no doubt that life for company employees inside Christiansborg was brutal and depressing, with ample evidence from the historical sources suggesting rampant alcoholism, quarreling, pettiness, and outright madness. In one well-documented example, Wulff Josef Wulff was passed over for promotion at the fort several times in what was a blatant example of entrenched Danish anti-Semitism. This prompted him to finally leave the fort and build a house in the Amangfong neighborhood not far from it. He married Sara Malm, a mulatto woman, and had three children with her. Their descendants still live in the house at Amangfong, where his remains were buried upon his death in 1842.[21] It was also not uncommon for company workers to be indebted to market women in the township for food and drink, and auction lists from the sale of items on the death of Danish company employees at Christiansborg indicate frequent debts that had to be cleared against the auctioned goods.[22]

The ships arriving on the coast also offered different kinds of opportunities for traders at Osu. Company ships had set limitations on whom they could trade with, which means all goods that were brought on the ships had to be exchanged for gold by company factors at the fort itself. However, the same rules did not apply to interlopers (private vessels, often Portuguese but also sometimes Dutch) that were free to trade with anyone with the means to do so.[23] Even though the more powerful caboceers were known to trade with such interloper vessels, the era of the slave trade and the risks involved for any black person meant that most African traders conducted their commercial exchanges away from the ships and on shore.[24] The important thing to note, however, is that the commercial opportunities presented by interloper vessels meant that African traders were not dependent exclusively on the company factors at Christiansborg. This flexibility impacted on how, on the one hand, African coastal merchants accessed the new commodities that were being made available through the European presence and, on the other, how they came to negotiate their relationships with their Akan counterparts from the hinterland, who were until the period of vassalage completely dependent on them for gaining access to European goods on the coast. Several references in the Danish records suggest that the interloper vessels were considered a major interference to the regulation of the types of commodities that were to be made available on the coast and to their overall circulation. There were often urgent requests to the company directors in Copenhagen to send out ships laden with specifically named goods to facilitate further trade relations between the Danes at Christiansborg, their trading caboceers, and other people on the coast, as well as to give them a stronger hand in the intense inter-European rivalries that frequently flared up with the Dutch and the English. Market processes thus represented a complex array of economic as well as social relationships, all of which came to impact upon the later sociocultural character of Osu.

The Christiansborg School and the Growth of a Euro-African Community

In *Kokó's Daughters* (2008) Pernille Ipsen persuasively demonstrates how the interracial marriages contracted between Danish men and African women at Osu serve as a useful barometer for understanding the changing social, economic, and cultural relationships that were established between the township and fort communities. As a general rule, and across the various European trading groups on the coast, it was mainly men that were sent out to the merchant establishments in West Africa. Most came young and un-married, and even if they had been married in Europe bringing one's wife along was strongly discouraged, both by company policy and from the many travel narratives and stories that circulated in Europe about the brutal condi-tions that obtained on the coast. Life expectancy among them was extremely short, and it was not unknown for new arrivals to die of dysentery, malaria, and other diseases within a year of arrival. Morbid thoughts of death, home-sickness, and an overall confusion about the culture of the fort and of the African settlement that they came to encounter quickly led to disorientation and despondency for the fresh arrivals. For most European men, as Ipsen shows, marriage was an absolute necessity, with mid- to senior-level person-nel such as governors, assistants, barber-surgeons, and soldiers opting to contract marriages as soon as possible upon arrival.[25] The marriages went under the general rubric of *cassare*, the Portuguese word for marriage, but were contracted according to Ga customs, and upon the payment of the stip-ulated dowry to the family of the woman, she continued to reside among her people but took regular trips to visit her husband at the fort. The marriage arrangements were bound by mores that the Danes fully complied with, and it is only with the rise of the power of chaplains at Christiansborg from the 1720s and their insistence on Christian edict that recognition of such mar-riages was even questioned.[26]

Among traditional Gas male children live with their mothers in a wom-en's-only household until age ten or eleven and thereafter move to be with their father in a men's-only household after that while girls, on the other hand, remain within the women's household throughout their life.[27] Since surrogate parents are readily available within this family structure, the na-ture of the gender-split household arrangements has the advantage of pro-viding a mechanism for absorbing fatherless or motherless children. In the period under discussion, Ga household arrangements also made it easier for a family to accept a daughter's marriage to what was essentially a foreigner, whether this was to a member of the uncircumcised Akan tribes (male cir-cumcision being central to Ga identity) or, as became increasingly com-mon, to Europeans from the fort. Danish husbands were thus conveniently integrated into Ga familial networks without necessarily being physically incorporated into their household arrangements. The system just described is still pertinent to Gas who live in the more traditional areas of Nleshie, Kinka, Osu, Labadi, Teshie, Nungua, and Tema in today's Accra, except that this has been variously altered by Christianity, Westernization, and the com-ing to dominance of the idea of the nuclear family unit among the educated elite. At any rate, as we have already noted, by the end of the eighteenth century several Danish merchants and company men had built stone houses in the Osu township and proceeded to live in a nuclear family structure surrounded by wife and children.

It has to be remembered that not all mulatto children at Osu were from formal marriages between European men and local women. Many were from concubinage arrangements between fort workers or private traders and local women; some derived from the sexual relations between European itinerant sailors and locals, while a number also issued from the rape of female slaves shackled in the fort for export. All these meant, however, that by the end of the eighteenth century a lively Euro-African community had evolved and become progressively consolidated at Osu. This community provided a significant cohort of marriageable women for Danish employees at Christiansborg, and in the case of boys, a steady stream of soldiers to work there. As we shall see presently, while Euro-African identity was heavily shaped by the social morphology of race that developed on the trails of the Atlantic slave trade, it was also significantly influenced by the resolutely Christian education provided by the school for mulatto children that was opened inside the fort. Even though the school was originally started by Chaplain Thomas Steenhild in 1722, it was the energetic Chaplain Elias Svane who was to outline the rationale for its continuation and expansion in the service of the offspring of Danish men and their African mothers. Among other things Svane found it reprehensible that the children were allowed to stay in the township with their "heathen mothers, who teach them only how to speak Negroish—a confused and difficult language which hardly any Christian has yet properly mastered—as well as diverse sorts of superstition and ungodliness, so that they have even, like the Black children, borne some of it about them—indeed what is even worse—and have been capable of sacrificing to the fetishes of the heathens" (Justesen 2005, 303). He insists that the language he calls Negroish was surely "the root and birth of all evil and the greatest obstacle to all that is good and godly" (Justesen 2005, 303–304). Earlier in his letter, Svane had suggested that Danish men be encouraged to bring their wives along with them, hoping that by

> sewing and washing for the Whites at these three adjacent forts [they] could regularly earn not a little. And then they could teach these girls of ours to do the same, by which means these too could in future earn their bread in an honest manner, and [by] other housework that is suitable for the female sex, and thus be freed from idleness and aimlessness,

which have taken hold here among the heathens, in particular among the women, whose only work is to shred millie, bake bread and make Negro food; other good work even the ablest cannot do with their hands. For the most part, the rest of the others are almost common whores and concubines. (Justesen 2005, 302–303)

As can readily be seen, for Elias Svane the heathenism of black life was self-evident in the general idleness that he thought endemic, and with specific regard to native women, the ever-present threat of sexual immorality. Svane's opinions were thus couched within the terms of a salvational discourse.[28] Salvation was to be achieved not just through religious conversion but also by way of the specific disciplinary regimes of work, schooling, and the education of bodily demeanor and habits. To Svane, then, it was imperative that the children's Danish fathers take greater responsibility for their upbringing and induct them into their own more civilized European culture. There is little evidence in the records of the period, however, to show that the Danish employees at the fort had any particular disposition toward the education of their mulatto offspring. That was to come several decades later. Thus at this stage in the late 1720s Svane's call for greater Danish paternal responsibility acted mainly as a device of suasion to help guarantee company funding for upkeep of the school. The ideal scenario to his mind was for the children not to return to their mothers in the township at all, but to be permanently boarded inside the fort and to take instruction from the chaplain and his appointed assistants. What the children's mothers and their families would have made of this proposal was not something that he cared to reflect upon. However, the significance of Svane's letter, and indeed of the educational goals established for the school, was that it expressed in quite explicit terms the parameters of ideological conditioning by which the mulatto children at Osu would become progressively acculturated into European forms of civility.[29] Apart from being given a Christian education (this was literally the case, as their education was mainly reading the Bible and preparing for baptism), they were to be weaned off their African eating habits, taught European table manners, and educated into the roles of European domesticity.

The inherently ideological/pedagogical inflection of Svane's disquisition must also be set against the material conditions within which the school had to function. As a mark of these material conditions, Svane's reference to the stench that permeated the schoolroom from the slave pens just below it in the fort's courtyard proves instructive: "In the school the schoolmaster can hardly apply himself with as great industry to the children as he should, for in the school *casse* [i.e., room], which is small and one of the lowest and worst, it is not only very close, because of the presence of so many children and no sensation of airiness and wind; it also has a very foul smell, if I dare speak so, because of the gutters and the uncleanliness of the slaves" (Justesen 2005, 308).[30]

If the concern expressed here about the small size of the schoolroom is of a practical nature, it must also be read as pertaining to the disgust and revulsion that Svane holds in relation to the slaves themselves. Given that he has already been at pains to set up a distinction between the mulatto children and the presumed heathenish ways of their black relations in the township, we should not doubt that this revulsion must have constituted a means by which, as a chaplain and teacher, he mediated the responses of his pupils to the direct facts of slavery that were laid out before their very eyes. This insinuated a racial hierarchy as a key dimension of their subject formation.

Notwithstanding the fact that until well into the nineteenth century all mulatto children at Osu were sent by their mothers to attend the fort school and thus to be taught in Danish, in the event Svane's plans for downgrading "Negroish" did not prove to be successful for several more decades after his letter.[31] For many years after the school's establishment, the children did not understand the language of instruction and surrendered to learning things by rote with only minimal comprehension. This was to change only toward the end of the eighteenth century, with the new Basel Mission School set up in 1843 providing an exclusive English-language option and thus challenge. Following further interventions by later chaplains and governors at the fort, the curriculum was gradually augmented to allow for the systematic training of mulatto girls in sewing, embroidery, cooking, and the finer arts of European domestic science, thus making them even more highly prized as wives for the Europeans. The boys, as mentioned earlier, were mainly conscripted as soldiers to work at the fort. Many of the mulatto girls subsequently came to occupy highly significant positions in the credit and trade relations between the Danes and their African counterparts. Ipsen cites the fascinating example of the mulatress Lene Kühberg, whose husband Frantz Joachim Kühberg on his death in 1769 left her a stone house at Osu. Lene was culturally Euro-African and, like other women at Osu who had married Danish men before her, she "dressed, cooked, spoke and lived in ways that were affected by the long history of the Europeans on the coast" (Ipsen 2008, 163). Furthermore, Lene's daughter Anna Barbara was to marry Johan Emmanuel Richter, a Danish private merchant and later governor, with whom she lived in another stone house in the Kuku Hill area of Osu. J. E. Richter sent his son Heinrich to study in

England. Heinrich returned to become a formidable merchant prince and one of the wealthiest and most illustrious traders of his generation between 1810, when he was twenty-five years old, and his death in 1849.[32]

Another important instrument of ideological subject formation for the mulatto children at Osu was the *fattige mulattebørns kass*, or Mulatto Children's Fund. The central principle of the fund, established during Chaplain Svane's tenure at Christiansborg, was to require all Danish members of the fort community to make an obligatory monthly contribution to a common welfare reserve out of which a stipend could be paid to their wives and, in the case of untimely death or their departure back to Europe, for the upkeep of their mulatto children. Some Osu women had also insisted that they would only send their children to the fort school if the company paid for their food during the day. As Ipsen notes, by the 1740s Chaplain Edvard Hagerup had appointed a "*spisse-moder*," or eating mother, that is, a cook that was paid by the company to prepare food for the schoolchildren. Hagerup also divided the children into three categories: "1. Those who had both father and mother on the coast, who should be supported fully by their parents, 2. Those living under 'medium' conditions, whom the church would clothe but whose parents were also asked to support them, and 3. Those who were *nødlidende* (destitute), who received food, clothes and monthly payments from the *fattige mulattebørns kasse*" (Ipsen 2008, 138). This welfare system seems to have been exclusive to the Danish fort and does not appear to have been replicated for the Dutch and the English establishments on the Gold Coast. At any rate what amounted to a European educational and cultural episteme was simultaneously undergirded by an economic welfare mechanism for the support of mulatto children and their mothers. It would not be hyperbolic to suggest then that the combination of Christian ideology and educational curriculum at the fort school, the not-so-subtle distinctions that were deployed for distinguishing the mulatto children from their black families in the township, the direct evidence of what happened to the enslaved bodies that the children saw at the fort, and the hierarchical nature of authority exercised by Danish men that they bore witness to on a daily basis must have generated a privileged, if also fraught, sense of identity for the mulatto children at Osu. As we shall see later, the sense of privilege that the Danish-Africans enjoyed was to continue until the institution of formal colonialism under the British in the 1880s, when a virulent racism was to undermine any sense of cosmopolitan entitlement that their mixed-race heritage and European education might have given them.

Ipsen goes on to suggest that by the start of the nineteenth century there must have been about one hundred Euro-African families at Osu but that they were too few to form a distinct social class, in comparison, say, to the larger group of interracially mixed families to be found in Whydah farther down the coast in today's Benin (Ipsen 2008, 176). There are grounds for disagreeing with Ipsen's conclusion that the Euro-African families at Osu did not form a distinct social class. Apart from what we have already noted regarding the effects that going to the fort school had on mulatto children, Ipsen herself points out that the transatlantic slave trade had introduced a significant policing of racial boundaries that doubled as a protection against enslavement. The boundary was not merely one between black and white, but between free and unfree. Even if most enslaved people were captured in the course of wars in the hinterland that was not the only route by which one could fall into slavery. Pawning for debt, either of one's own self or of members of one's family, was common in the period, with failure to clear the debt often ending up in sale to the slave ship. More pernicious was the practice of *panyarring*, in which a debtor's property or persons in their family or retinue could be seized and held in debt bondage but with the full risk of being sold to clear such debt.[33] In all such instances the only protection was to have strong family ties, something that must be understood along a spectrum of efficacy as an insurance against enslavement. At the lowest extreme was the slave captured in war a long distance from the coast. Such captivity marked the dissolution of all family ties and the denuding of the slave as social being, what Orlando Patterson (1982) has famously described as a form of "social death."

While the historical records show that some people in the coastal settlements that were inadvertently sold into slavery were freed on the strong protestations of their powerful families, this was not a privilege that could be enjoyed by the slave captured in war. The pawned laborer or the one that had been panyarred by someone else in abeyance of a debt also ran the great risk of being sold outright. However, in such a scenario the credit system could be modulated through familial intervention, since it was possible for a pawned or panyarred person to have his or her debts paid off and thus for him or her to enjoy a measure of freedom. This did indeed happen from time to time but was not so common. At the highest end of the spectrum of the relation between slavery and freedom must be placed the Euro-African families and their offspring. Their mulatto race differentiated them on sight as free peoples. More important, the fact that as persons they had strong relationships to the fort community, either through marriage, trading relations, attendance at the school, or working there as domestic servants or soldiers also meant that the mulattoes were effectively extracted from the inhumane credit networks that distorted the relation between free and slave. Notwithstanding any ambivalence that may have attended black people on the coast whose status roles, whether of caboceer, market trader, or artisan, might change suddenly and expose them to the real and ever-present threat of temporary or permanent enslavement, this did not impact upon members of the Euro-African community, who by the end of the eighteenth century had become acculturated in dress, food habits, and domestic arrangements and thus were seen as part of an extended yet firm nexus subtending the culture of the Europeans in the fort itself. This accords with the overall state of affairs pertaining to other Euro-African communities in West Africa in the long interactions with Europeans. To put it another way, during the period of transatlantic slavery the mulatto on the Gold Coast effectively short-circuited the process by which a body could be consciously or inadvertently converted into the body of a slave on sight and thus interpreted as always potentially unfree.[34] As George E. Brooks shows in his *Euro-Africans in Western Africa* (2003), if the status of mixed-race groups such as the Luso-Africans of Senegambia, the Anglo-Africans of Sierra Leone, and the Danish-, Anglo-, and Dutch-Africans of the Gold Coast occupied an uncertain social status at the start of trade relations with Europeans in the fifteenth century, by the end of the eighteenth their status as privileged cultural and economic brokers was firmly and incontrovertibly established. The status and influence of Euro-African identity was normally procured through women, who in several instances Brooks discusses became highly influential commercial and power brokers. As he also notes, the expansion of slave-trading networks had a telling effect on African societies in general, with the question of color becoming prominent as a means of demarcating privilege and exclusivity among all communities that had Euro-African enclaves, especially in moments of social conflict. And slavery was the major engine of dramatic upheavals, conflicts, and social change in all the societies that were touched by its processes.

British Colonialism and the Reconstitution of Racial Privilege

To understand the impact that British colonialism had on the social configuration of Osu we are obliged to scale up the discussion of the lives of mulattoes in the township and read it alongside that of the changing status of Euro-Africans all across the Gold Coast during the course of the nineteenth century. For the institution of formal colonialism under British rule was to fundamentally alter the terms of the racial hierarchies that had obtained in the colony in general. As has already been noted, Britain bought

Christiansborg from the Danes in 1850; by 1872 it had acquired all the European forts, lodges, and castles on the coast. More important, commerce on the Gold Coast went through several transitions from the abolition of slavery in 1807. Susan Kaplow (1977) conveniently breaks the period down into three phases, namely: (1) the phase of European capitalism's creation of an African merchant group as economic and political intermediaries, 1808–1852; (2) the growth in the strength of European capitalism and the progressive weakening of the economic and political positions of African merchants, 1852–1880; and (3) European monopoly capitalism's steady destruction of the African merchants and the completion of their political ouster, 1880–1900.[35] The control that various European chartered companies had had on the coast went into abeyance immediately after Britain's acquisition of the forts and castles on the coast, partly due to the ensuing uncertainty of the business environment and partly due to the fact that Victorian Britain was at midcentury not clear on how far to extend its political control beyond the original British establishments at Cape Coast, Elmina, and Accra. The abolition of slavery had led to a shift in the local economy toward cash crop production, with the demand for lubricant in Europe during the Industrial Revolution stimulating the local production and trade of palm nut and its derivatives. Furthermore, the more enterprising African merchants in Kaplow's first period came to benefit from favorable credit arrangements from consignment houses in Europe that maintained major operations on the coast, such as Forster and Smith, F and A Swanzy, and Hutton and Company. African merchants received manufactured goods on credit from the major European establishments and often made repayments in agricultural produce such as palm oil.

Yet the honeymoon for African merchants was not to last indefinitely. First, from the 1850s more and more preferential credit arrangements were extended to the larger European firms on the coast to the increasing detriment of African businesses. By the 1880s cases tried in court showed that African merchants had been paying between 25 percent and 75 percent more on similar goods than their European counterparts.[36] While the introduction of the steamship in the 1820s had allowed for faster, year-round travel and had also introduced the carriage of smaller product consignments that opened up a fresh niche for African merchants, the decision in 1894 by steam-line owners in London, Manchester, and Liverpool to form the West African Shipping Confederation imposed higher freight rates on trade to and from the region. Several bankruptcies ensued, with some African merchants swinging from large wealth to complete penury in the space of just two decades.[37] At the political level, the 1880s also saw the introduction of more explicit instruments for the consolidation of British colonial rule, whose underlying economic principle at the end of the nineteenth century was the consolidation of commerce in the hands of Europeans. As Kaplow notes, "Racism grew increasingly virulent as an ideological component of imperialism" (1977, 328), which of course also translated into fewer opportunities either for African entry into or advancement within the burgeoning colonial civil service.[38] Colonialism ultimately meant a fundamental, even if initially subtle, conversion of what had been the relations of dependency and accommodation that had defined the commercial interactions between Europeans and local groups since the fifteenth century to one of domination without accountability by the end of the nineteenth.

Business, politics, and government had been firm bedfellows throughout the period of European merchant relations on the coast, but colonialism was to fundamentally alter the terrain in which these three elements continued to interact. In 1821 an act of Parliament abolished the Company of Merchants Trading to Africa and transferred all its property (i.e., the various English forts and castles on the coast) to the Crown. In 1828 the British government transferred control of all its interests in the Gold Coast to a committee of London merchants, who were to elect a council and its president to run affairs at Cape Coast and Accra. These councils were the first edition of what later evolved to become the Legislative and Executive Councils under the British Indirect Rule system. Thus in 1850 Queen Victoria issued a charter to the forts and settlements on the Gold Coast providing for a governor and Legislative Council to govern all the said settlements and properties. And in 1858 a Municipal Corporations Ordinance established the terms for municipal authorities with the power to assess house taxes in all the British areas. But it was in 1854 that the British first attempted a direct introduction of a poll tax for the areas under its administrative control. These efforts met with vehement opposition from all sides, and at Osu people were mobilized to try and take over Christiansborg Castle, by that time the seat of administrative authority in Accra. Several areas of the township were flattened by the British bombardment of the coastline that quickly ensued.[39] The Basel Mission had to relocate from Salem to Abokobi, several miles north of Accra, and only returned to Osu in 1857. Apart from the signal of forceful intent, however, the bombardment was also a sign of the fundamental shift in relations between the new colonial authority and the local peoples, something that would necessitate a radical reinterpretation of the roles of all involved, but especially that of the Euro-Africans. Whereas under Danish protection the Euro-Africans at Osu had enjoyed a measure of privileged access to the fort (now castle) and indeed to the trading networks that the Danes had evolved all along the coast in the nearly two hundred years of their presence there, now it was quite clear that this privilege was no longer to be taken for granted. As Susan Kaplow also notes, during the course of the nineteenth century, any aspirations that the "race of native capitalists" and their Western-educated children in the Gold Coast had of being the "natural heirs" to British [read European] authority was fundamentally dented. This applied even more harshly to the Euro-Africans at Osu, who quickly saw their status fall behind their counterparts at Nleshie and Kinka, historically and spatially much closer to British interests in Accra.

Colonialism was also to frown upon interracial marriages, thus also attempting to reconfigure the private sphere of sex and social reproduction in addition to the ongoing spatial reorganization of commercial hierarchies in Accra we noted in the previous chapter. In 1907 Governor John Rodger issued a local circular completely prohibiting sexual relations between British colonial officers and African women. This was confirmed in 1909 with the issuing of an anti-concubinage circular by Lord Crewe, Secretary of State for the Colonies, to all of Britain's African, Pacific, and Asian territories. Allegations of concubinage between European officers and African women in the Gold Coast peaked after the release of the two circulars, with investigations into these continuing throughout the second decade of the twentieth century.[40] Even though the prohibition was limited only to European officers in the colonial civil service and thus had no effect on European merchants and those who worked for them, for the sake of stricter policing of racial boundaries and hierarchies the anti-concubinage circulars were part of the overall colonial scheme to reverse acceptance of the centuries-old practice of interracial marriages and sexual relations. If we recall also that the professional African classes were expressly debarred from residence in the European-only areas of Victoriaborg and Ridge up to the 1930s, we see then that social distinctions between Europeans and Africans were being solidified at all levels of interaction.

*Pen Pictures and Euro-Africans: From Trade
to the Professions and Politics*

These several factors were to trigger the migration of the Gold Coast elite from trade and commerce into the professions. Even though Africans, especially from chiefly backgrounds, had gained ground in education by the mid-nineteenth century, it is still the case that Euro-Africans on the coast had had a long lead in that sphere. We get a sense of the demographic characteristics of the educated elites in the Gold Coast from Charles Francis Hutchison's superb *Pen-Pictures of Modern Africans and African Celebrities,* first published in the late 1920s and reissued with a new and elaborate introduction and notes by Michel R. Doortmont in 2005. Hutchison's book is invaluable for understanding social life on the Gold Coast in the late nineteenth and early twentieth centuries. The pen-pictures genre was a popular kind of Who's Who of the period, and in Hutchison's case included not only biographical sketches but also fulsome praises of the personages' various achievements. Doortmont comments on the fact that Hutchison seems to have been obsessed with "whiteness," for in various instances he praises the inner whiteness of the personages he is presenting, while at others he draws attention to their skin color. The theme of whiteness is sometimes even taken to farcical levels, as Doortmont goes on to note. However, there is good reason for Hutchison's deployment of a discourse of whiteness. For one thing he himself was descended from Euro-African stock, with his grandfather, William Hutchison (d. 1834), having been a British official and merchant at Cape Coast. What becomes quickly evident on reading the portraits themselves is that a large number of them were men of Euro-African background. There were very few portraits of women. Of the 162 entries in *Pen-Pictures,* at least 70 were of direct Euro-African descent. This is sometimes ascertainable just by looking at their last names (names such as Bannerman, Quist, Van Hein, Holm, Scheck, etc. are easy giveaways). Several others without European names also had at least one Euro-African parent; this was the case with the well-known nationalist Kobina Sekyi, whose mother was Wilhelmina Pietersen, of Dutch descent, and also of George Ekem Ferguson, the famous cartographer who died in colonial service up in the Northern Territories. Ferguson's mother was Emelia Neizer, scion of a very prominent and wealthy Afro-Dutch family at Cape Coast.

What is perhaps most significant about the pen pictures, however, is the range of educational achievement of the majority of the personages that Hutchison lists. Two families, one Euro-African and one largely African, provide a good sense of the nature of educational pursuits of these early elites. These are the Bannerman and Quartey-Papafio families, respectively. I use the term "largely" African with respect to the Quartey-Papafio family partly because even though they were from a traditional and well-known Ga family, in at least the instance of Emmanuel Quartey-Papafio, marriage was contracted to a Euro-African woman. He married Anna van der Puije, "a member of the powerful Accra-Elmina Van der Puije (Vanderpuye) clan" (Doortmont

2005, 347). To quote Doortmont further on the Quartey-Papafios: "The Quartey-Papafio family was one of the leading families of Accra in the nineteenth and early twentieth centuries. The first three men described here [i.e., in the relevant pen-picture entries] are brothers and sons of Akwashotse Chief William Quartey-Papafio, alias Nii Kwatei-Kojo, alias 'Old Papafio,' head of the Kpapatsewe lineage of the Asere quarter of Dutch Accra in the 1880s . . . and Momo Omedru, a wealthy businesswoman from Gbese (Dutch Accra). The family name comes from the Ga 'Kwatei Kpakpa-fio,' whereby kpakpo stands for good, brave, virtuous" (Doortmont 2005, 347).

Emmanuel Quartey-Papafio (1857–1928) was listed as a merchant and agriculturalist while Benjamin William Quartey-Papafio (1859–1924) went to Fourah Bay College in Freetown, Sierra Leone, and was awarded a BA from the University of Durham in England before proceeding to a medical degree in Edinburgh. He became a medical officer in Gold Coast government service from 1888 to 1905, member of the Accra Town Council from 1909 to 1912, and unofficial member of the Legislative Council from 1919 to 1924. Arthur Boi Quartey-Papafio (1869–1927) was educated at the Wesleyan High School in Accra, then Fourah Bay College before going on to study law at Christ's College in Cambridge. He was called to Lincoln's Inn in 1897 and returned to Accra to start private practice and to write several scholarly articles on Ga customary law and Accra history, becoming editor of the Gold Coast Advocate newspaper, member of the Accra Town Council from 1905 to 1909, as well as founding member and joint treasurer of the National Congress of British West Africa (NCBWA). E. W. Quartey-Papafio (1882–1928) and Hugh Quartey-Papafio (1890–1928) also had similar educational backgrounds and both became prominent Accra lawyers and active public figures (Hutchison/ Doortmont 2005).

The Bannermans, on the other hand, were a very well-known mulatto merchant and political family at both Cape Coast and Accra. Charles Edward Woolhouse Bannerman (1884–1943) was educated at the Roman Catholic school in Cape Coast, read law at the Middle Temple in London, and was called to the bar in 1913. He entered into private practice, became a magistrate of the Supreme Court of the Gold Coast, and was awarded an OBE in 1942. His father, the Honorable Samuel Bannerman, JP, became district commissioner, government auditor, comptroller of customs and government treasures as well as a member of the Executive and Legislative Councils. However, C. E. W. Bannerman's great-grandfather was the Euro-African James Bannerman (1790–1858), who was himself a well-known merchant prince, and was educated in Cape Coast, then in England as a lawyer. James

Bannerman is credited to have aided with the introduction of the Legislative Council in 1850 and became an unofficial member of the body from 1850 to 1856 and lieutenant governor of Cape Coast Castle from 1850 to 1851. He was married to Princess Yeboah, daughter of Osei Tutu Kwadwo, also known as Osei Bonsu, who was king of Asante from 1800 to 1823 (Hutchison/Doortmont 2005, 114–119).

Beyond the dazzling education, business, and personal achievements of the personages just mentioned, which seems to have been the standard for most of the personages described in Hutchison's book, three things stand out. The first, as I have already noted, is the number of them who were of Euro-African descent or married to or in other ways affiliated to Euro-African families. This was so common as to appear a central aspect of elite formation in the period. The second pertains to how many of the emerging educated elites combined the role of merchants with other kinds of professional activities in the colonial civil service. In fact, the closer we come to the twentieth century, the more likely the educated elite were to seek positions in the civil service, rather than in business. David Kimble provides further guidance on the educational and political activities of the Westernized elites on the Gold Coast from 1850 to 1928. Even though he correctly insists on referring to everyone as African, almost all the people Kimble discusses in his chapter on the subject are actually Euro-African. These include the various Bannermans just mentioned, along with Joseph Smith, Henry Barnes, and James Hanson, among various others. According to Kimble, by 1788 "there had been fifty mulatto and African children from the Windward and the Gold Coast being educated in Liverpool alone" (1963, 64fn8). His account also shows that even though the inception of colonial rule attempted to be color-blind in terms of the opportunities and openings provided to Africans, on the arrival in 1857 of Sir Benjamin Pine as governor an openly racist tone was to become dominant. The racism continued progressively into the twentieth century, as we have already noted from Kaplow, and was a source of great friction between the colonial administration and their Western-educated African counterparts. This brings us to the third conclusion to be drawn from Hutchison's pen pictures, namely, the number of Euro-Africans that joined the ranks of proto-nationalists in the late nineteenth and early twentieth centuries.

One of the sources of severe tension in the period was the cleavage that soon became evident between the chiefs and the educated elites, something that was especially pronounced in the politics of Accra between the 1920s and 1950s. For the Gold Coast in general, the Aborigines Rights Protection Society (ARPS) had been formed jointly by both chiefs and educated elites on the passage of the Lands Bill in 1897, while the NCBWA was set up in 1920 largely by educated elites to air their grievances regarding the inequities of the Indirect Rule system. It did not take long for the NCBWA to see itself pitched directly against the chiefs.[41] Instructively, however, almost all the cofounders of the NCBWA were of Euro-African stock, and included Thomas Hutton-Mills, its first president,[42] J. E. Casely-Hayford, the first vice president,[43] along with F. V. Nanka-Bruce,[44] A. B. Quartey-Papafio,[45] H. Van Hien,[46] Kobina Sekyi,[47] A. Sawyer,[48] and Edward Francis Small. Except for Edward Francis Small, whose background cannot be ascertained conclusively, the cofounders were all of Euro-African descent. The predominance of Euro-Africans in the rank of early proto-nationalists did not stop at the inception of political groupings such as the NCBWA but also extended into the founding of various newspapers, which were soon to become vociferous critics of the colonial regime.[49]

It is interesting to note that the long list of Euro-Africans that we have just enumerated gives very few clues about the contributions of Danish-Africans from Osu. Nor does Hutchison's very useful compilation shed light on this anomaly, since the only Osu personage he mentions is Emmanuel Charles Quist (Hutchison/Doortmont 2005, 359–361). To complicate matters further, John Parker's highly informative *Making the Town* (2000b) barely mentions any Osu personages. The paucity of references to the contribution of Osu Euro-Africans to the political and social life of the Gold Coast in the late nineteenth and early twentieth centuries raises a number of questions. If they were, like the other Euro-Africans along the coast, as highly educated and also increasingly invested in the professions, why is it that they are not mentioned in any of the main sources of the history of the period? This question may be answered from a spatial viewpoint. Osu was of course geographically separated from Dutch and British Accra, both of which by the end of the nineteenth century had fused into a single township. On the assumption of full-scale colonialism, Osu was progressively to recede from the colonial record, for as we can glean from the primary sources predominantly drawn upon for Parker's book, the social politics of Ga Mashie in the making of the town ultimately came to heavily inflect the colonial archive itself. This is definitely the impression one gets from trawling through the materials on Gold Coast/Ghana in the National Archives at Kew Gardens in London. During the early period of colonialism from the 1850s to the 1880s, the main way in which any person or group entered the colonial record was either through petitions for one thing or another to the colonial administration or some form of contestation against the imposition of various colonial ordinances. From the 1890s entrance into the colonial record was to come predominantly through the framework of municipal and town planning, as well as with respect to the progressively complex constitution and tasks of the Legislative Council. If the primary drivers of town planning into the 1930s were disease and disaster management and the spatial fixing of European commercial and administrative functions, then the reference point of these was Ga Mashie and its immediate environs. The expansion of Accra into Victoriaborg and Ridge that we noted in chapter 2 must be understood as being *away* from Ga Mashie rather than *toward* Osu. In terms of town planning, Osu enters the colonial record only sporadically and mainly in relation to various requests for housing at the Ringway Estates and adjacent areas that were regularly made to the colonial governor's office. Osu, referred to in official documents mainly through the name Christiansborg, enters into the framework of colonial town planning in its own right and not as a surrogate for civil servant housing only after the earthquake of 1939, when a low-cost estate was put up in the area between today's Barclays bank and the offices of TIGO stretching eastward to the very edge of Nyaniba Estates. The area where these houses were located was originally referred to as "Ngãnor" (bush) by residents of the vicinity, indicating that it was an uninhabited and overgrown area before the colonial administration's show of interest.

Even if Hutchison's pen pictures furnish scanty evidence of Osu elites' contribution to the social and political milieu of late nineteenth- and early twentieth-century Accra, this must not prevent us from striving to identify other sources for completing the frame. The Osu elites' lack of prominence in the political arena does not allow us to conclude that they lacked in any achievement, either in business, in the colonial service, or in politics. A partial corrective to the picture is provided in Wellington's chapter titled "Sung and Unsung Heroes," where he provides an extensive list with complementary descriptions of the achievements of Euro-Africans at Osu (2011). Included in his list are Ernest Richter (b. 1922), an international diplomat, and Philip Christian Richter (b. 1903), reverend minister of the Presbyterian Church of Ghana and later professor at the Kwame Nkrumah University of Science and Technology. And we are informed that in 1826 Frederick Noi Dowuona was selected by the Danes to be educated in Europe and returned to become a prominent chief and cultural broker among his people. We also learn of Reverend Carl Christian Reindorf (1824–1917), the renowned historian whose *History of the Gold Coast and Asante* (1895) is a standard reference text for the history Accra. Sir Charles Emmanuel Quist (1880–1959), who was listed in Hutchison's pen pictures was speaker of the National Assembly between 1951 and 1957; Theodore Taylor (1888–1968), enstooled as Nii Kwabena Bonne III, was a very important figure in the decolonization struggles of the 1940s. These are just a few of the many profiles of Euro-African descendants at Osu that Wellington provides us with. And many of them were Euro-Africans.[50]

To return to the Osu township then, by the 1920s the dominance of education as a means toward self-advancement had firmly replaced that of trade, such that Osu, especially in the Kuku Hill and Salem neighborhoods, had acquired the reputation of being among the most educated in Accra. While it is not possible to establish a direct correlation between the presence of a highly educated cohort of Euro-Africans in the area and the character of economic vitality that we see at Osu and Oxford Street today, we would not be going astray in asserting that its long historical relationship to the Danish community at Christiansborg was to play to its advantage in the overall commercial evolution of the area. The fact that Osu fell within the nexus of high-end and aspirational neighborhoods traversed by Cantonments Road (which, as we saw in previous chapters, is an urban corridor servicing some of the districts that have traditionally housed the ruling elites and their satellites) means that Osu has always been the spatial conduit for transnational circulations. As previously noted, that Osu did not have a port like the one at Jamestown not only insulated it from the economic vagaries of a port economy but also ensured that it did not develop initially as a warehouse township, as Ga Mashie had. Not being as densely populated, it provided a fine prospect for the building of larger accommodations, another thing that distinguishes it from Ga Mashie. At Ga Mashie the entire settlement was historically governed by its relationship to the sea and the many occupations that this produced, but again this was not the case for Osu. More important, Osu has always attracted a diverse and racially variegated population. Thus by the 1960s it had come to attract a heavy concentration of Lebanese residents who moved into the area in increasing numbers as the originally Lebanese areas around Tudu became more and more congested. As Ntewusu (2011) shows, the Lebanese had dominated the Tudu business district from the early 1930s, but by the late 1960s had decided to set up their homes elsewhere. Osu, clean, culturally and racially diverse, upwardly mobile, and about fifteen minutes' drive from Tudu, became a much sought-after neighborhood and definitely cheaper than the erstwhile European-only neighborhoods of Ridge and Cantonments, now given over to African government officials and senior civil servants. Today the Maronite Temple at Osu that stands opposite Trust Hospital is testament to the presence of the Lebanese. There were also several Lebanese-run businesses in the past that have left their imprint on the area, especially in the memory of older residents. Businesses such as Cedar House (now Koala, currently also run by a Lebanese-Ghanaian), Papaye, and Frankie's (again both owned by Lebanese-Ghanaians), as well as Osu Food Court (a franchise of INNSCOR, the fast food, retail, and manufacturing multinational giant based in Zimbabwe but run in Ghana by a Lebanese consortium), all provide testament of the strong Lebanese presence at Osu.[51] Tracing the vitality of today's Oxford Street to the long history of Danish-African relations by no means gives us an untrammeled view of history, but rather to suggest that what we now see as the heady transnationalism and globalization of this buzzing business district has long and variegated roots and is not just the magical product of the late twentieth century.

PART II
MORPHOLOGIES
OF EVERYDAY LIFE

CHAPTER 4

"The Beautyful Ones": Tro-tro Slogans, Cell Phone
Advertising, and the Hallelujah Chorus

If the street in contemporary urban studies is conventionally seen as the
locus for the transfer of representations and cultural practices, the domain
of a peculiar geographical and cultural imaginary, and the site for the colli-
sion of architectural forms, these perspectives are grounded on the implicit
assumption that its boundaries feed into hinterlands of both social and political relations. But what happens when we stop seeing streets as geographical locations and rather interpret them as lively expressive archives of urban
realities? And what if, in focusing on an African street such as Oxford Street,
this archive is interpreted not as static, but as providing a transcript of dynamic discourse ecologies, at once historical yet also bearing the sense of
the vital immediacy of oral cultures?[1] Whereas the standard postmodernist
view that contemporary urban desires and aspirations are merely refractions
of images produced by the media is easily illustrated, this truism assumes
too narrow a focus on the relationship between technology, images, and
the formation of urban identities. For the real task in grasping the character
of the archive that is Oxford Street lies instead in demonstrating that the
link between technology, representation, and desire is mediated through
variegated discursive environments, some of which have nothing to do with
technology. Often these pertain to the interactions between apparently evanescent local traditions that coalesce into inventively syncretic new wholes
and the spectral globalized processes that materialize in commodities and
their attendant imagescapes. The discourse ecologies on Oxford Street and
streets like it in Accra are the result of variously interconnected and complex
elements bringing together writing, images, and soundscapes in a relationship quite different from what might be gleaned from social media networks like Facebook, YouTube, or Instagram. The citational networks and
practices that undergird these discourse ecologies have to be understood as

strenuously local as well as remotely global, to echo the title of Charles Piot's book (1999).

To elaborate our understanding of Oxford Street as an archive requires us to attend to the veritable galaxy of mottoes and slogans on lorries, cars, pushcarts, and other surfaces that are frequently to be encountered upon it. Such mobile slogans are a distinctive feature of Accra and of many African urban environments. The central mark of these mottoes and slogans is an elusively inventive and improvisational character that installs writing ambiguously between literacy and orality. Thus the urban scriptural economy is often shaped around items that draw *simultaneously* from repertoires of both orality and literacy. This is evident from sources as diverse as funerary and obituary notices; popular performance and literary texts that draw on oral discursive traditions; concert party and film posters; and the sayings, slogans, and inscriptions on walls, print cloths, canoes, lorries, cars, and other surfaces across the urban landscape.[2] Each of these items extends from a domain of oral performativity and reaches into the domain of writing, such that the process of reading them requires an innovative understanding of their mixed genres and the orality/literacy spectrum from which they draw their meaning(s). And yet the archive that is Oxford Street encompasses more than just mottoes and slogans. It also encompasses a plethora of billboards advertising all manner of products from coffee to sanitary pads, from fast food to cell phones. Through a reading of cell phone advertising on Oxford Street from 2005 to 2010, I shall draw some conclusions on how multinational company advertising deploys transnational imagescapes to reconfigure local processes of meaning making and their attempts at converting locality into an instantiation of the transnational and vice versa. To justify bringing the two domains of vehicular slogans and billboard product advertising together as dual aspects of the street's archive requires us to place them both against the background of wider discourse ecologies of which they are but symptoms and articulations.

Primarily the two dimensions of inscription on the street—vehicular slogans and cell phone advertising—come together as rich urban transcripts that define an arc of enchantment.[3] Proceeding from the bottom up, we shall see how enchantment is articulated first as a dimension of a syncretic social imaginary, second as an extension of the message and ethos of prosperity pronounced by Accra's mega churches over the last forty years, and third as a mediation of shifting transnational and local cultural identities. Thus Oxford Street is to be taken as an analogue of wider urban discursive processes that go well beyond the discrete elements to be found upon its surface.

The history of motorized transport in Accra reflects the production and circulation of a demotic expressive form. The introduction of motor vehicles into the country from the early part of the twentieth century was to radically alter the social landscape, with the development of new entrepreneurial and technical skills and the establishment of petrol stations, automotive workshops, and new companies of various sizes collectively creating a special social status for the motor vehicle. In addition, motorized transport also generated new forms of political mobilization and impacted upon the expansion and consolidation of the bureaucratic state apparatus (see Gewald et. al, 2009).

After World War I, Ghana was flooded with cheap but highly economical American Ford lorries. However, the introduction of Ford vehicles coincided with increasingly tense competition between British and American firms for dominance of the rapidly expanding global market, with Africa being a major factor in their calculations.[4] It is with the end of World War II and the introduction of Bedford lorries by the British into Ghana and the rest of their West African colonies that a decisive shift began to take place in the cultural symbolism of the motorized vehicle. By the late 1950s, the motor vehicle had already become a key emblem of modernization and was featured in one way or another in newspaper advertising campaigns to publicize items as varied as shoes, vodka, toothpaste, bicycles, and airline travel. Moving on in life was connected to all these products, but overdetermining every element of progressive modernity was access to or ownership of good motorized transport.[5]

After World War II, the British imported the chassis of Bedford lorries, which were then customized locally for carrying either passengers or freight. This often entailed raising a wooden frame up on the lorry chassis. As a means of decorating the wooden bodies of the first imported Bedford trucks that came to be called "mammy lorries," their enterprising owners began to paint them with motifs from folk narratives and to festoon them with language, in effect making the lorries billboards expressing the complex cultural significations that had existed within the domain of traditional popular culture for generations before. The painting of folktale motifs such as mermaids and *sasabonsam* (folktale devil) was gradually replaced by the late 1970s predominantly with writing (see figure 4.1). The sayings to be found on the bodies of the lorries were eclectic and of variant inspiration, but their legacy was to proliferate sometimes cryptic and often wry observations as a permanent visible feature of the urbanscape, whether this was

4.1. Tro-tro slogan. Courtesy Ghana Information Services Department.

through the mobile surfaces provided by the lorries or, as became increasingly common, transferred to other surfaces such as makeshift sign-writing billboards and graffiti inscribed on barber shops, hairdressing salons, local chop bars, and even on people's houses. Christianity was also to magnify the process of urban inscription by providing an endless source of inspiration from sacred scripture and, with Islam, ensured that the character of such urban inscription was never to remain entirely secular. All this produced a fascinating discourse ecology.

On Oxford Street and other commercial districts in Accra, messages and images of a transnational provenance jostle with traditional mottoes, sayings, slogans, and proverbs inscribed on all available surfaces. Writing, in its full assemblage of calligraphic features, inflections, and expressive forms, is the primary modality in which this discourse ecology of popular lore is expressed, with images sometimes providing a dialectical addendum that both affirms indigenous sensibilities while disclosing their inescapable syncretism. And yet the signifying surface on which this writing is undertaken is not to be mistaken for the depthless surface that postmodernists have adumbrated as part of the condition of late capitalism. Rather, the superficial markings of this local discourse ecology are often the foreground of intricate imaginary hinterlands that are cast in relations of historical light, ambiguity, and shade. The relation between these surfaces/foregrounds and the multiple backgrounds that they conceal is often defined by an oscillation between telescoped personal narratives and veiled social commentary. The articulation of the personal with a cognizance of social and sometimes political vectors, as we shall see, has altered steadily in the course of the last forty years, with a progressive shift from slogans and mottoes of a largely secular kind to ones of a predominantly Christian religious orientation.

As a general rule, however, all writing surfaces are appropriated as part of a cultural procedure for displaying distinctive experiences as object lessons to serendipitous and not-so-casual observers. Thus "Observers are Worried. Why?" inscribed on a house or lorry is a nose-thumbing gesture at people who might be questioning the source of the wealth that was used to build said house or purchase said lorry. Other slogans of variant vintage solemnly declare: "I No Be Like You," "Mama Chocolate," "A Short Man Is Not a Boy" (which has subtle sexual innuendoes), "Belly Never Know Vacation," "You Too Can Try" (a subtle challenge/insult translated from local languages), "Envy Never Lights a Fire," "Still, It Makes Me Laugh," "And Jesus Wept," "Enye Easy" (It Is Not Easy), "Insha'Allahu," "Gold Never Rust," "Mammy Watta," "Fear Man and Take Snake," "Kwaku Ananse" (the last three all inspired by folktales), and simply "Auntie Akos," as tribute to the person that helped procure the vehicle. The slogans and inscriptions are also oftentimes translations of globalized signifiers onto the local cultural scene. Thus "Nike," with a barely recognizable swoosh beside it on the back of a passenger lorry signals the global reach of the sportswear company. A barbershop display depicting haircuts of Barack Obama alongside Mike Tyson suggests that they both pack a mean punch while also enticing customers for a similarly "powerful" haircut. Images of Kofi Annan, erstwhile President Rawlings, and Princess Diana may also be placed together on the same sign-art poster to suggest that they were all three "of the people, by the people, and for the people," problematic as this might seem to ignorant skeptics. Fascinatingly, both sets of images might also double as artwork on passenger lorries, with appropriate inscriptions "for the road," as it were. Read correctly, then, each signifying surface defines a dramatic scene, where the writing plus any added images are the nodal points of much wider discursive propositions. They all in their own distinctive ways invite viewer participation in the improvised scene laid out, whether the scene is exclusively written or a combination of writing and images.[6] The participation indexed by these slogans, sayings, and mottoes differs markedly from that implied in the inscriptions and images to be found on the advertising billboards of multinational corporations. With respect to TIGO cell phone adverts on Oxford Street and those of other multinational corporations like it, such advertising depends for its efficacy on bypassing the contexts of local cultural mediation. Multinational billboard adverts route their invitations to consumption via a transnational circuitry of images and expressive styles that often require that the local is made to invoke translocal realities and vice versa in a restless relay of significations. Their only point of convergence with the lorry slogans and mottoes on the street, as we shall come to see, is ultimately the invitation to enchanted self making.

Crucially, the scriptural surfaces of urban inscription divide into two seemingly distinct yet mutually reinforcing categories: the stationary and the mobile. Under the stationary may be classed official road signs and toponyms, the designations of buildings, and advertising billboards of government and large corporations (Ministry of Health, Coca-Cola, Barclays, MTN, etc.). We may provisionally include in this stationary class smaller signs that advertise a range of goods, services, and even prohibitions in all manner of languages and grammatical facility ("Shoes Are Repairing Here," to herald the presence of a cobbler down the road; or "Urinating Here Is Strictly Not Aloud," on a wall to ward off potential miscreants). The smaller signs to be found on the street bridge the divide between the grand semiotic of transnational or governmental discourses and the more syncretistic cultural sensibilities that are normally encapsulated in mobile slogans and signs. The mobile category of course encompasses the motor vehicles we have alluded to, but we must also include in this category inscriptions on head pans that are borne by a variety of vendors as well as those on other forms of porterage. The fresh coconut seller's pushcart in figure 4.2 lays claim to rightful occupancy of the road by way of a mock registration plate "BL—11," while the drawings of coconut trees on the tire flaps metonymically invoke the beaches from which the fresh coconuts are plucked. And the motto "Save Me 'O' God" quickly aligns it with religious sentiments to be seen on many transport vehicles all across the city. As a general rule, writings on mobile surfaces tend to be either fragments of longer proverbs, transpositions from indigenous languages and sacred texts, or expressions of personal aspirations. Collectively, all inscriptions of local popular vintage found on either stationary or mobile surfaces function as the foreground of orientations toward a world

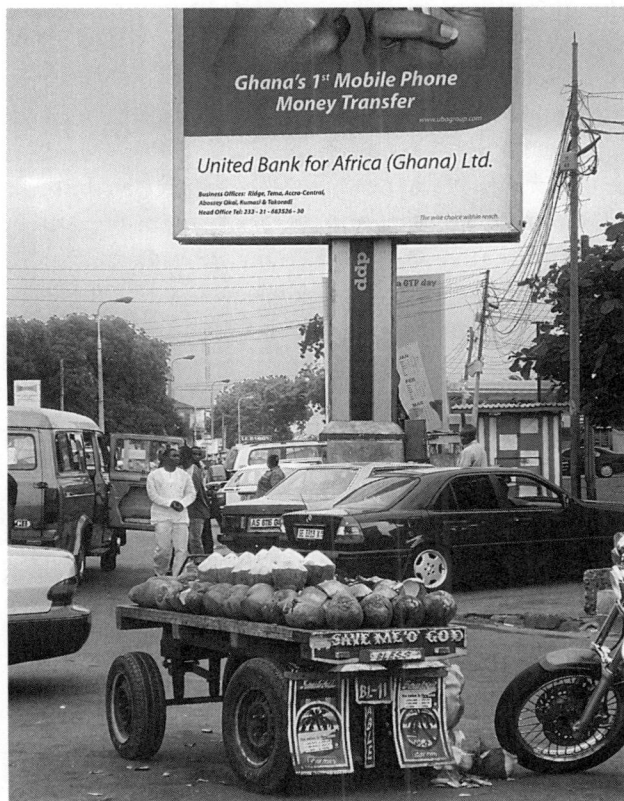

4.2. Coconut seller pushcart on Oxford Street. Photo by author.

perceived to be in a state of flux. They provide a collective transcript of responses to social transition, to which we shall return later in the chapter.

Discursive Ensembles and the Dialogics of Entextualization

Many of the slogans and mottoes on tro-tros and other vehicles point to forms of discursive multi-modality. If they happen to celebrate functions considered central to urban life, they are also highly likely to have been circulated across several popular genres and platforms. Thus urban functions that have acquired iconic status and are celebrated as tro-tro inscriptions such as "Taxi Driver," "Akpeteshie Seller" (seller of a strong locally brewed alcoholic beverage), "Maame Dokono" (kenkey seller), or "Ashawo" (prostitute) may also be found in popular songs, as names of kiosks and small-scale businesses, or simply as scrawled graffiti on the walls of buildings. They may also serve as the nicknames of easily recognizable television characters while doing service across all the suggested platforms. They display and celebrate the social variety of life, whether urban or otherwise.

Instructively, of all the explanations that have been proffered on the social variety of tro-tro slogans none is more instructive than the one provided by the famous Ghanaian folklore musician Nana Kwame Ampadu, in his song titled "Driverfo" (Drivers) in 1985. Here Nana Ampadu describes the social life of drivers, their often fraught and wily dealings with law enforcement agencies, and the camaraderie and fellow feeling they express toward one another on the roads and lorry parks across the country. It is, however, the extensive list Ampadu lays out of such slogans that is of direct interest for our discussion here. He divides the inscriptions into those on old cars and those on new, the terms "old" and "new" not being a function of age, but as Sjaak Van der Geest points out, of ownership. It is not uncommon for such lorries to change ownership several times during their lifespan, with subsequent owners keen to impose their own interpretative slogans on newly procured vehicles (Van der Geest 2009, 272–273). And so, Ampadu sings:

> The following are inscriptions on new tro-tros:
> Cool and Collected, Lover Boy,
> Envy No Man, Pɛ Wo Dɛi (Look for your own),
> Aho Ya (Skin Pain), Eyɛ Wo Ya (It pains you),
> Ɔtan Nni Aduru (Hatred has no medicine),
> Yaa Baby, Still, Good Boy,
> Ɔdo Ye Wu (Love like death),
> Sweet Jesus, Jah Bless,
> Rastaman, Honest Labor,
> Anyway, I Shall Return, Roadmaster,
> Girl Bi Nti (Because of a girl),
> Sea Never Dry, Abele (Corn),
> Akwei Allah (Allah exists),
> Ele Mawu Si (It is in the hands of God),
> Lɔlɔnyo (Love is good), Kamfo Yehowa (Praise God),
> Two Friends, Fa Yɔnko Pa (Make good friends),
> Agya Pa Yɛ (A supportive father is a good thing),
> Ase Pa Yɛ (A supportive in-law is a good thing),
> God is King, Halleluyah.[7]

The song continues with a further lengthy list of slogans to be found on old vehicles. The central point of the lists is not so much their detailing of the variety of slogans to be found on vehicles as the fact that the song creates a veritable archive of such slogans. The entire song is in Twi, but its archiving function dutifully captures expressions in a variety of languages, in both English and local languages (predominantly Twi, but also Ga, Ewe, and Hausa). Thus all the slogans, including the English ones, are effectively presented in discursive quotation marks within the Akan-language lyrics in which the song is performed. The social materiality of Nana Ampadu's "Driverfo" derives from the fact that it places within the domain of oral discourse (song) slogans that are in many instances themselves transposed from other non-written contexts of communication before being set down in scriptural form. In its quotationality the song rewrites the slogans, but in such a way as to entextualize them for both contemplation and mnemonics. The song becomes a script of scripts, self-consciously displaying the practice of entextualization on an orality/literacy continuum that is commonly activated in the social life of urban Africans.

It is to Karin Barber that I am indebted for the concept of entextualization. She offers it as a way of describing the links between texts, persons, and publics in various contexts. Entextualization highlights the process by which a given instance of discourse is rendered as text, and thus ultimately detachable from its immediate context of primary articulation. Extrapolating from earlier anthropological studies, Barber explains: "Discourse is the unremarked and unrepeated flow of utterances in which most human activities are bathed. Text is created when instances in discourse, by being rendered detachable from their immediate context of emission, are made available for repetition or re-creation in other contexts. In other words, there are stretches of discourse which can be reproduced and transmitted over time and space. . . . Proverbs are a classic case of entextualization: succinct, patterned and pithy, available by definition for application to multiple alternative contexts, they are made to be quoted" (Barber 2007, 22).

In Barber's account the term "discourse" implies orality, and entextualization invokes both oral and non-oral forms of transfer. Entextualization incorporates a wide range of devices, but in the African urban context may be understood specifically in relation to the varied sociological, linguistic, and cultural mediations that define life at the intersection of oral and written repertoires. The mediations that define urban Africa have not oscillated only between indigenous languages and the various European tongues introduced into the continent, but also across indigenous registers themselves, as can be glimpsed from Ampadu's song.

Ampadu is also famous among Ghanaians for his clever use of folklore for subtly veiled forms of social critique. The well-known tro-tro inscription "Ebi Ti Yie" (Some Sit/Are Sitting Well) is also to be found as the name of small goods stores, barber shops, and even simply scrawled on the wall of a public latrine. It was made famous by a song of the same title recorded by Ampadu and the African Brothers Band in 1968. This was two years after the overthrow of Kwame Nkrumah and the ascension to power of a new brand of Western-trained politicians. The new politicians were perceived by the general population as not only elitist and out of touch but also corrupt. "Ebi Ti Yie" tells the story of all the animals being called to a big town hall meeting to discuss the fate of the jungle. The duiker (a type of small antelope) has the distinct misfortune of being seated right in front of the lion, who lays his right paw gently on the duiker's shoulder. When the gathering is asked if they have anything to say, the duiker pipes up suddenly to speak, but on feeling the mild pressure of the lion's paw upon his shoulder, morosely declares: "Some are sitting well, but others are not sitting well at all" (Ebi ti yie, na ebi nti yie koraa). The subtle twist in Ampadu's song sparkles from the fact that the word for "to sit" in Akan is also a homonym for "to live," so that the duiker's complaint was quickly interpreted by listeners for what it really was: a gentle yet pointed criticism of the beneficiaries of the political upheavals that had followed Kwame Nkrumah's overthrow, and who were busily amassing wealth and living a comfortable life at the expense of the ordinary Ghanaian.

Ampadu's is not the only song whose lyrics have been given a satirical twist and subsequently been recycled through different genres of popular culture. Another dramatic expression of the same process is to be seen in the reaction to Sidney's hiplife song "Scenti No" (2004). The song goes through a series of scenarios in which a sudden stench emanates from an unexpected source, such as, for example, from the socks of an MP when he takes off his shoes on arriving home from work. With 2004 being an election year in Ghana, the song was immediately interpreted as a critique of the culture of corruption in the country at the time. The extraordinary popularity of the song led the then New Patriotic Party (NPP) government to contact Sidney to ask if it could obtain the copyright to the song so as to convert it into a party slogan for the upcoming elections. Sidney rightly refused this strange offer and his popularity increased exponentially in consequence.[8] Like "Ebi Ti Yie," "Scenti No" has been entextualized as part of the discourse ecology of slogans and is no longer tied exclusively to the song that originally gave birth to it.

Van der Geest is generally correct in suggesting that the driver has rapidly attained to the position of culture hero in the Ghanaian context (2009, 266). He is also insightful in observing that the inscriptions on cars and lorries are part of a larger nexus of decorative impulses that span a broad range of expressive sites. However, like most scholars who have paid attention to such popular inscriptions, Van der Geest falls under the lure of attempting to categorize them. This is completely understandable: the scintillating zodiac of inscriptions incites a typologizing and ordering impulse that though seemingly inescapable, proves in every instance ultimately futile.[9] The reason for the futility is quite simple: the slogans and inscriptions cover every imaginable vector of urban and social life, from the paranoia regarding witchcraft and the evil eye, to wry social observations on gender wars, family conflicts, political chicanery, the celebration of the lives of drivers and motor vehicles, and even to meta-critical pronouncements on the act of writing itself. Everything that touches on the life of Africans as they make their way through change, transformation, and transition is amenable to the process of entextualization in the form of a slogan or saying. Irrespective of what proverbial and sociological verities the slogans encapsulate, they have to be seen as providing a collective transcript of transition. This is the latent langue out of which the parole of the urban scriptural economy emanates.

Following Van der Geest, we are also obliged to distinguish between modes of transportation on which these slogans and mottoes appear and the many other cultural objects that also inspire entextualization. The distinction is between items that enable the mass movement of people and goods (such as canoes and lorries as seen in figures 4.3 and 4.4) and material objects that are incorporated into the overall semiotic of ritual functions (asafo flags, funeral *adinkra* cloths, gold weights, etc.). All these sites are noted by Van der Geest but not differentiated according to their significance for the overall scriptural economy of the inscriptions. By facilitating the physical transition of persons or goods from one place to another, canoes and motor vehicles bear entextualized inscriptions, some of which are displaced from ritual functions into modes of secular expression. Contrastively, on asafo flags or funeral adinkra cloths such inscriptions retain the aura of their originally ritual functions. Canoes and motor vehicles also spatialize and accrue to themselves *the idea of mobility and transition as such,* thus providing an essential surface for the projection of the social imaginary of change and transition that moves away from exclusive ritual functions. Furthermore, the

4.3. Tudu Lorry Park. Photo by author.
4.4. MTN-themed fishing boat, Jamestown. Photo by author.

vehicular projection of a popular social imaginary of transition incorporates an entire galaxy of dramatis personae that includes vehicle owners and their drivers, their creditors and benefactors, and the sign artists primarily responsible for customizing the vehicles through their design and words. The dramatis personae collectively imply the desire to "get somewhere" both in the banal sense of physical mobility and of getting on in life. This is quite different from what pertains to asafo flags and funeral adinkra cloths, which as a rule foreclose the possibility of variational playfulness and institute a recognizable ritual order at the foreground of representation.[10] The choice of the term "dramatis personae" I am using here is not idle. For the lorry slogans are, in the words of George H. Lewis, "reminders of the individuality of the new African, as well as [of the] symbols that unite driver, passengers and street viewers within an African cultural context" (1998, 166). As we have seen from Ampadu's song, lorry slogans also entextualize the movement of transition between multi-nodal points of discursive significance, including local and translocal languages, orality and literacy, tradition and modernity, and the exchanges between different popular media that are shared by everyone that traverses the city's streets.

Deterritorialization and the Vehicular Nomos

In discussing the writings of Kafka, Deleuze and Guattari elaborate a four-part linguistic model to explain the language registers out of which deterritorialization is produced: "Vernacular, mythic, or territorial language, used in rural communities or rural in its origins; vehicular, urban, governmental, even worldwide language, a language of businesses, commercial exchange, bureaucratic transmission, and so on, a language of the first sort of deterritorialization; referential language, language of sense and of culture, entailing a cultural reterritorialization; mythic language, on the horizon of cultures, caught up [sic] a spiritual or religious reterritorialization. The spatiotemporal categories of these languages differ sharply: vernacular language is *here*; vehicular language is *everywhere*; referential language is *over there*; mythic language is *beyond*" (1975, 23; italics in original).

Vehicular language is *everywhere*. Deleuze and Guattari's definition of deterritorialization itself is notoriously elusive. It seems to imply first that the writer of minority literature alienates the dominant language from within its own discourse, either by intensifying its metaphorical registers or by paring language down to its barest expressive minimum (Joyce and Beckett exemplify the two poles for them, though one might proffer Wole Soyinka and J. M. Coetzee from a postcolonial African perspective). And yet it is from the spatial implications of deterritorialization and the implicit contrast between ideas of stasis and mobility in their definition of language functions that we glean something applicable to the condition of the lorry slogans in Accra. Deleuze and Guattari's four-part model suggests that language registers originate out of specific spatiotemporal relations: while mythic language is situated at a communal and presumably more homogeneous organic level, vehicular language is contrastively seen as facilitating spatial transpositions and the heterogeneities that lie beyond a rural or pastoral structure of feeling. What Deleuze and Guattari emphasize in their description of vehicular language is its simultaneously mobile and mobilizing qualities, in other words, its urban yet focalizing dimensions. While their model assumes that the vehicular register best encapsulates the rhetoric of bureaucratic rationality and potentially creates the nomos of the public sphere, we might suggest that in Africa it is lorry slogans and inscriptions that exemplify not just the vehicular register but an integration of all the other levels of the the tetralinguistic model. Lorry slogans utterly disavow the exclusive bureaucratic rationality of Deleuze and Guattari's model while dialogically integrating the four registers the philosophers enumerate in a configuration that appears to territorialize and deterritorialize at the same time. This is not done sequentially or indeed hierarchically, but by means of what Esther de Bruijn describes as "semiotic stacking." Drawing on the linguistic work on Akan and other West African languages by William E. Welmers, she explains how "this loading of metaphors functions according to the practice of semiotic stacking that is prominent in Ghanaian oral and visual culture, and that finds its parallel in the Niger-Congo linguistic practices of adverbial and adjectival reduplication for the purposes of intensification." De Bruijn is writing in the context of the sensational character of Ghanaian market literature, where devices of reduplication operate at different levels drawn from popular culture to ensure the memorability of the text. The examples she goes on to relay range from phonemic reduplication to structural repetitions at the level of well-known tropes from oral literature that the market literature transfers into its domain.[11]

In terms of tro-tro slogans and inscriptions, the feature of semiotic stacking draws for its efficacy partly on a mode of palimpsestic layering in which the layering is not to "paper over" previous discursive traces but to render the relationship between the traces inherently mobile and nonhierarchical. Thus it is a futile exercise to try and determine the precise etymology or first expression of a tro-tro slogan, whether this is traced to a local language proverb, a song or media program, or just as a part of urban knowledge that comes to circulate without apparent source or ultimate direction. Secondly, the stacking or layering also depends on the oscillation among different and often distinct languages and registers (e.g., from English to Akan and Ewe and back again, as we saw in Ampadu's "Driverfo"). In Africa the vehicular register, in terms strictly of being borne across on vehicles, is thus attuned to the social imaginary of a public sphere that is at once collective yet owned by no one in particular: "All the World Is a Stage," as one lorry slogan puts it. While being transposed from Shakespeare's *As You Like It*, in the local context this slogan acquires a distinctive inflection. The lorries on which this motto appeared used to travel between Nsawam and Accra in the late 1980s and early 1990s, ferrying people and goods through towns in the Eastern Region and into the national capital. All eight of the vehicles on which the same slogan appeared were owned by the same lorry owner at Nsawam, and the slogan was considered both his signature and his nickname. It was not unusual for him to be hailed on the streets of both Nsawam and Accra simply as "All the World" to which he would reply in a mixture of Akan and English, "Eye Stage" (is a stage). Once when I asked him where he got this fine Shakespearean insight from he replied, not without a knowing twinkle in his eye: "In this world things are changing all the time, and that is all we need to worry about." All the world *may be* a stage, but for him the emphasis was not on our entrances and exits but on the transitionality against which we have to shape our lives.[12] Ayi Kwei Armah's *The Beautyful Ones Are Not Yet Born* (1968) also provides us with a fascinating angle to the transitionality to which tro-tro slogans bear witness. The title of his novel is taken from a tro-tro slogan inscription from the 1960s, and the novel itself tells of the existential alienation of "the Man," who works at the railway station in Takoradi and struggles to understand the corruption that surrounds him in the newly independent Ghana. But the point of Armah's title lies in the wry recognition that the ones that might bear the burden of the hopes of the new nation—the Beautiful Ones—are not yet here and may never actually materialize because of the endemic conditions of corruption that have undermined the potential for any form of idealism in the young country. Here the sense of transition carries the twinge of mourning for what is both lost and has not yet been born. "All the World Is a Stage" and other vehicular slogans like it capture the transitionality of social life in their dazzling variety and thus contribute to the ways in which the public sphere is experienced.

The vehicular slogans and mottoes also focalize several layered backgrounds against a foreground that is produced as an invitation to interpretation. This is also part of the slogans' semiotic stacking. The invitation is proffered unobtrusively, in the sense that you are not obliged to pause in whatever it is you are doing to give the motto or slogan any special attention. The real force of the invitation comes from the citational density of the slogan (the fact that it may have traveled across various popular cultural platforms before becoming a slogan) as well as from the subtle rhetorical twists embedded in it. The rhetorical twists that are intricately tied to a slogan's citational density act as a guarantee of its mnemonic efficacy precisely because it reminds you of the many other different sites upon which you may have encountered the same slogan or variants of it. At the same time, as we shall see in chapter 6, the inscriptions come to provide a ready gallery of ethical perspectives that can be adopted as propositions for the prosecution of different kinds of argument. In this they share an ethos with proverbs and wise sayings but not because of their pithiness but because of their process of entextualization. In point of fact, a tro-tro slogan does not need to be pithy to be memorable. Quite the opposite. All that is required is that it be recognized as part of a larger citational nexus in which writing has been installed in the ambiguous space between literacy and orality. The fact that slogans are already entextualized as *vehicular* means that they are also embedded within the highly sophisticated practice of quotation that marks all local-language rhetorical forms in Ghana. Slogans thus become a reservoir of popular wisdom, ready to be taken up or disavowed as context requires and without any deference to strict doxological authority.

To go a step further, we need to note that especially within the urban environment in which these slogans are expressed what would be deployed in monolingual local-language discourse as an ordinary proverb to spice up an argument or as a piece of admonition or advice is here automatically converted into the modality of multilingual code-switching, another dimension of the semiotic stacking that defines these slogans. Code-switching between English, Ga, Pidgin, Twi, Hausa, Ewe, and the various other languages to be found in Accra is completely normal and cuts across all social classes. Yet, unlike in other multilingual environments elsewhere, the code-switching is often undertaken in order to incorporate a piece of wisdom or some other gnomic observation from one language tradition into another, much in the way that Ampadu's "Driverfo" illustrates for us by entextualizing various language proverbs into the Twi of his own song. The reading of such urban scripts then takes place in the intermeshed vitality of lived experience, with other dimensions of such existence impinging upon their interpretation both at the level of immediate encounter (i.e., as one sees the lorry whizzing past or is about to board it) and, more important, from the variable practices of everyday life. In this respect the fit between the slogans as a form of *work* (the creative discourse of which they are an expression) and *world* (lived experience) lies in the dialectical relation between sociocultural signification and the multilingual lifeworlds that take shape within an African urban setting. The most important thing to remember is that no one can claim efficacious copyright to what is essentially a collective cultural phenomenon, thus making it practically impossible for the slogans to be regulated or put under the impress of any singular authority, whether this be the government, a particular ethnic group, or indeed a multinational corporation. The multi-nodal, multilingual, and variously inspired scriptural economy of tro-tros becomes an inherent aspect of the urban landscape and makes the slogans clearly available to all. This means that the drift between the vernacular, the vehicular, the referential, and the mythic languages spoken of by Deleuze and Guattari becomes a naturalized aspect of the public sphere of discourse without any threat of its appropriation or domination by any person or group of persons, much less by the bureaucratic rationality of the state apparatus itself.

TIGO Cell Phone Adverts: The Transnational, Delocalized

To lift our gaze upward from the pedestrians, lorries, cars, and mess of activities that take place at street level on Oxford Street is to encounter another kind of scene that appears at first sight to occupy an entirely different expressive universe. Large- and medium-size billboards advertise everything including cosmetics, computer colleges, foreign magazines, airlines, fizzy drinks, restaurants, sanitary pads, and coffee in an idiom that appears utterly distant from the vehicular slogans we have encountered so far. Cell phone outdoor adverts are expressive of an especially Janus-faced function: located firmly on the streets of Accra they incorporate imagescapes that appear more insistently transnational than local. They also appear to want to abjure or short-circuit the local cultural semiotic processes we have identified with the vehicular altogether. This is not to suggest any simple dichotomy between the local and the transnational but rather to distinguish the imaginary that these adverts tap into from those of tro-tro inscriptions. For cell phone advertising is not designed to produce a reservoir of entextualized motifs drawn from the multi-modality of Ghanaian popular culture but rather to distill material cosmopolitan desire whose referents lie as much elsewhere as they do in the contexts of local consumption. The adverts for cell phone companies such as MTN, OneTouch/Vodafone, Zain/Airtel, TIGO, and more recently Glo are particularly noticeable on Oxford Street because of the grand size of their billboards and their strategic clustering on prominent corners and intersections all along it. The advertising campaign for TIGO has perhaps been the most fascinating for the complex ways in which the company has sought to delocalize the local and to convert it into an instantiation of the trans-local. My observations here will be specifically focused on TIGO's outdoor advertising campaign of 2006–2008, although it can readily be shown that their subsequent campaigns and indeed TV advertising reprise the same ideals, if in a somewhat attenuated form, from what I shall argue is their classic and original mode.

TIGO is a subsidiary of Millicom International Cellular SA. According to Millicom's website, TIGO's parent company originated in 1979 as part of a phone company in Sweden during the early days of the cellular industry. In 1982 Millicom, along with others in the industry, came together to form a conglomerate that later evolved into Vodafone. It is not clear what the relationship between Millicom and Vodafone currently is, at least not in Ghana, where TIGO and Vodafone seem to have distinct operations. TIGO arrived in Ghana in 2005 and is one of thirteen Millicom subsidiaries operating across Central and South America, Africa, and Asia. With a subscriber base of 3,757,977 as of September 2012, TIGO is the third largest cell phone company in the country, with 15 percent of the market share after MTN (45 percent) and Vodafone (formerly OneTouch, 20 percent).[13] To put these figures in proper perspective it has to be recalled that the current population of Ghana is estimated at twenty-five million. With an overall cell phone subscriber base of 24,884,195, it is considered one of the fastest growing cell phone markets in Africa. Other companies that operate in the country apart from the big three include Kasapa, Glo, Airtel (formerly Zain), and Expresso.[14] Each cell phone company devises a distinguishing thematic to mark itself off from its competitors. Thus whereas OneTouch, originally a government-owned company, modeled itself between 2005 and 2007 on a thematic of familial harmony (figure 4.5), MTN focused on the theme of fun-filled youth activity (figure 4.6) and the inherent attractiveness of "going somewhere" in contrast to that of "standing still" (figure 4.7).

In its 2006–2008 campaign, TIGO struck a more distinctive cosmopolitan and transnational tone. This was well captured in its billboards, but in ways that were more subtle than straightforward. The pictures in figure 4.8 and figure 4.9 were taken in the summer of 2006, at the height of the soccer World Cup held in Germany for which Ghana had for the first time qualified. Both giant billboards were on either side of the same tall pillar at the entry into Oxford Street from Danquah Circle. The site of the billboards was highly suggestive, as they practically announced a significant aspect of the cosmopolitan character of the street itself. And yet the first thing to note about the billboards is how cosmopolitan the models in the pictures are compared to those on the MTN and OneTouch billboards located further down the street. Prominent in contrast to the models used on the other cell phone billboards is the light hue of the models in the TIGO adverts, which

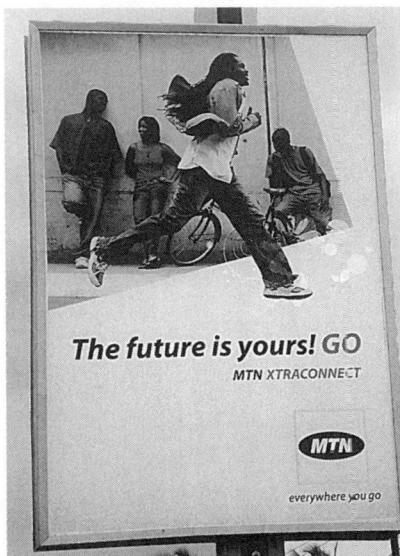

4.5. OneTouch billboard, Oxford Street.
Photo by author.
4.6–4.7. MTN billboards, Oxford Street.
Photo by author.

suggests mixed-race origins. The models also wear well-known fashion labels, quite distinctive from that of the singing girls in the MTN advert in figure 4.6. The cosmopolitanism of TIGO's models is for example suggested by the young woman in the yellow Calvin Klein T-shirt in figure 4.9. Another TIGO billboard not featured here has a young man in a green Abercrombie and Fitch T-shirt at the foreground of the frame. Significantly, both male and

4.8–4.9. TIGO billboards, Oxford Street. Photo by author.

female models sport either dreadlocks or some form of highly expressive hairdo, such as that of the young woman in the foreground of figure 4.8. The overall impression conveyed by their skin hue, their fashion sense, and their gestures and demeanor is that these are black youth well versed in the urban youth chic to be found in every large metropolis in the world today, from New York to London to Milan to Johannesburg to Sydney to Amsterdam to Toronto. Furthermore, this urban youth chic is not exclusive to black youth in these cosmopolitan contexts.

An initial suspicion that the TIGO billboards were self-consciously projecting transnational imagescapes was later borne out by my discovery that Creative Eye, the firm in charge of TIGO's outdoor advertising, had a brief completely different from those of any cell phone company operating in the country in that period. Creative Eye was founded in Dar es Salaam toward the end of 2005 and had been specifically charged by TIGO with creating images of Pan-African black youth for its outdoor advertising.[15] Similar billboard adverts to those in Accra were also run in Tanzania in the same phase.[16] The idea of Pan-Africanism being deployed here seems to have no relationship whatsoever to the ideals first espoused by Kwame Nkrumah, Gamal Abdel Nasser, Julius Nyerere, and other charismatic African statesmen of the 1960s. Rather, it pertains to an image of black youth that allows it to be assimilated to various categories of fashion that are (a) not readily localizable, and (b) not limited to an exclusively black ethnic identity. The delocalized content of the images may have had something to do with the cultural roots of Creative Eye itself, for Dar es Salaam and East Africa in general are well noted for their multicultural mix, having been home to an active South Asian community from the 1880s and prior to that various waves of Islamic Arab and Persian trading influences from the fourteenth century onward. Swahili, the lingua franca of the region, is a hybrid mix of Arabic, Persian, and local words and has a long and distinguished literary tradition. Furthermore, it turns out that though Creative Eye developed the Pan-Africanist concept for the billboards, the task of assembling the images into the generic format we see on the billboards was outsourced to a firm in Bangalore. That the people at Creative Eye would choose such a place-less image of African youth makes perfect sense in view of the fact that their understanding of what constitutes an "African" is subject to the highly hybridized and diasporic context of East Africa itself. Given the waves of mass migrations from outside the continent that have defined sub-Saharan Africa since at least the sixteenth century, is it any surprise that the referents of African identity are being subjected to creative transposition and play? This is apposite when, in envisioning Africa, we think not only of the well-known and explicit cultural hybridities of East Africa, South Africa, and Madagascar, but of the vast populations of diasporic Africans scattered all over the world, the ranks of which are filled by people who can no longer be identified with any unproblematized black Africanness, whatever blackness is taken to signify in different cultural discourses today.[17]

A Caribbean flavoring is also evident in the transnational image of black youth on the TIGO billboards. This is registered especially by the coconut trees and clear blue skies that seem to enframe or envelope the images. In figure 4.8 the all-glass exterior of the building in the picture reflects the clear bright blue of the sky above. More pertinently, the blue skies and palm trees framing the models serve as metonymic insinuations of the sun-soaked beaches normally associated with such images. Given that in Ghana much of the seafront is liable to be used as God-given latrines than anything else, the invocation of a blue-sky-and-coconut-tree motif points somewhat away from a Ghanaian or indeed West African evocation and toward the semiotic of Caribbean leisure landscapes that have traditionally played in the global imagination as the natural site for such beaches. Thus in the structured space of the TIGO adverts, space has been converted into a form of merchandise, invoking a spatial ideal that is already associated with another well-known location of leisure and consumption. Even more, the evocation of the Caribbean also situates the images within another intersecting grid of blackness, one associated with the black diaspora of the New World. Whether these light-toned models are descendants of the black folk transported across the seas through the dastardly memorial of slavery or have been born from the more recent processes of postcolonial diasporization and interracial mixing is somewhat beside the point. It is the simultaneity of identities—African/Caribbean/Euro-African, and so forth—coupled with the invitation to local TIGO product consumers to imagine themselves within the imagescapes proffered by the billboards that is the central performative effect sought by the billboards.

In contrast to the OneTouch and MTN billboards we have seen, the images of the TIGO adverts put ethnic African blackness in question by eliding it into images of racial hybridity. The semiotic efficacy of the TIGO adverts must be taken as operating on multiple levels at once, and it starts from the direct invitation to consume cell phone products, which is no different from any other invitation to consumption proffered by the many multinational companies that have their advertisements on Oxford Street, such as Coca-Cola or Barclays or Nescafé or KFC. The difference in the TIGO adverts lies in the fact that the invitation is proffered through a particular image of blackness that is severed from any locality and thus made transnational (in the sense of crossing bordered nationalities). In TIGO's discourse hybrid blackness, ethnicity, and urban youth chic are just a few of the commodifiable elements of their image making. These are situated alongside those of Caribbean leisure landscapes and of vague diasporic longings. Whether we follow a theoretical route mapped out by the famous Anglo-Ghanaian philosopher Kwame Anthony Appiah (1992, 2006) or by the equally well-known Afro-Canadian writer Lawrence Hill (2001, 2007), the modalities of what constitutes an African or indeed black identity are increasingly being put under scrutiny. It would be too much to say that the TIGO adverts are fully conscious of such debates, but there is no doubt that in their image making they have opted for a version of Africanness that cannot be easily assimilable to a normative ethnic blackness, however we decide to define this term.

"No Time to Die": TIGO, Tro-tro Slogans,
and the Discourse of Enchantment

If by a routing of semiotically hybrid images of black youth the TIGO adverts seem to bypass the local cultural mediation that sustains the vehicular and other inscriptions that crisscross the urban landscape, they also dialectically meet these writings on the terrain of a shared discourse of enchantment. The enchantment we speak of here is not what might be attributed to magic or witchcraft, a social detail that some commentators on contemporary African cities assume to be endemic to their urban form.[18] The terrain of enchantment is rather to be discerned in the message of self making and prosperity that has undergirded the rise of new evangelical mega churches in Accra, and additionally, in the phenomenal rise of Oxford Street itself alongside such churches, with Oxford Street coming to figure as the place where enchantment is materialized in the form of the commercial boulevard. Even though I gave the impression that the tro-tro slogans were largely secular, what I declined to point out is that the ratio between social and religious commentary marked in vehicle slogans has shifted steadily over the past forty-odd years in favor of the religious. This has not been entirely accidental. In Kojo Gyinaye Kyei and Hannah Schreckenbach's *No Time to Die* (1975), a collection of poems using inscriptions and slogans on Ghana's passenger lorries for inspiration, we find that only 17 of the 141 they collect for their book have a religious inspiration. The vast bulk of their slogans were in English, with just ten in local languages. In contrast, of the 246 such sayings collected on my behalf over a four-day period in Accra in October 2007, 133 had a direct reference to God, Jesus, or some other religious theme.[19] This represents over 50 percent of my collected sample. The main difference between the current range of vehicular inscriptions on the streets of Accra and the ones captured by Kyei and Schreckenbach is that whereas theirs detailed in the main a veritable galaxy of secular and traditional aspirations and desires, the current Christian-inspired inscriptions act predominantly as forms of religious testimony. This is not to say that religious testimony was not to be found in earlier incarnations of the slogans. Now, however, they have become explicitly religious by way of entextualizing less and less from traditional oral discourses and predominantly from the Bible, with slogans from the Quran in a small minority. These religious slogans are proffered as succinct reminders of God's activity on earth and what relationship the owners or drivers of the vehicles have with Him. Thus the colorful inventiveness of the Kyei and Schreckenbach collection increasingly makes way for a set of inscriptions of a straightforwardly religious kind: "Inshallah," "Yesu Mmo" (Congratulations, Jesus), "God Is Great," "My Savior Lives," "Hallelujah!" or some such saying adapted from scripture, whether in English or an indigenous language. And yet the force and efficacy of religious sentiment writ large upon these surfaces can only be properly understood when read alongside the ideology of enchantment that has conclusively permeated the social imaginary of urban dwelling as a whole, sometimes displacing the traditional cultural semiotic but oftentimes just coopting it as a form of like articulation. The process of this cooptation has long historical roots that we cannot delve into here, but suffice it to note that since the arrival of missionary Christianity in the eighteenth century it has involved a systematic form of translation of the ethical values inherent to traditional religious cultures into the now hegemonic idiom of Christianity.[20] While this cooptation always suffers different forms of elision back into traditional cultural forms, it has been insistent over the past at least two hundred years and become stronger with the rise to dominance of a Christian and Westernized educated elite.

Rather than seeing the increasingly religious character of vehicular writings as somehow counterpoised to those on the large multinational billboards, we must interpret them as the dialectical articulation of a discourse of enchantment. Both vehicular slogans and billboard adverts overlap in the attribution of prosperity to personal choice and, more important, to the possibility of self making as an attribute of transnationalism, whether this is manifest as a feature of Christianity or of global capitalist consumption. More significant, I want to insist on seeing Oxford Street as the *expressive spatial analogue* of the discourse of enchantment that has swept Ghana since the IMF-inspired neo-liberal reforms of the late 1980s. As the commercial boulevard upon which both types of discourses find a peculiar saturation (witness the coconut seller's pushcart in figure 4.2), it provides the perfect window for seeing the display of the discourse of enchantment at various intersecting and mutually reinforcing levels. To perceive the coincidence of enchanted discourse with the spatial form of this street requires as much conceptual as historical understanding. The task now is to grasp history in terms of its multi-synchronicity, as Fredric Jameson reminds us.

The decision to conceptually group together the invitations of the TIGO adverts on Oxford Street with the increasingly Christianized mobile inscriptions on the tro-tros and to the prosperity gospel of mega churches in Accra serves to highlight the fact that far from them all being on different sides of a field of aspirations (the first side loudly declaiming the pleasures of capitalist consumption and the other two calling reverence and gratitude to God; mammon versus deus), these three elements collectively define complementary dimensions of what the Comaroffs have described as millennial capitalism: "a capitalism that presents itself as a gospel of salvation; a capitalism that, if rightly harnessed, is invested with the capacity wholly to transform the universe of the marginalized and disempowered" (Comaroff and Comaroff

2000, 292). For the Comarroffs millennial capitalism is marked by the ever-increasing relevance of consumption and speculation over and above the verities of production. With respect to Oxford Street, these complementary dimensions are to be seen operating via different yet intersecting categories: the commercial boulevard as the space for the traversal of variant cosmopolitan shopping experiences; the billboard adverts that convert transnational imagescapes of ethnic identity into instruments for the promotion of products and services at a localized level; the vehicular and other mobile inscriptions that display a syncretic zodiac of variant sentiment, yet now leaning heavily toward a Christian ethos; and finally, the mega churches themselves, which though not directly present on the street have had a significant impact on the overall contemporary social imaginary of self making at least since the mid-1980s. That these categories appear distinct—geographical space, advertising space, vehicular space, and religious space—must not obscure the necessity of reading them collectively as aspects of the same discourse of enchantment.

If the discourse of enchantment is most heartily encapsulated in the prosperity message of today's mega churches, the source of it lies in the dire economic realities of the 1980s. It is not insignificant that the emergence of Accra's mega churches coincided with the "pamscadization" of the country at large. This word is ludically derived from the acronym for the IMF's Program of Action to Mitigate the Social Cost of Adjustment, or PAMSCAD, and registers the laugh-to-prevent-yourself-from-crying thematic that was a marked Ghanaian response to the vicissitudes of the period. The effects that PAMSCAD was meant to address became endemic from the moment Rawlings introduced the IMF-inspired Economic Recovery Program (ERP) in 1983. Inflation peaked at 123 percent by the mid-1980s, and women, the rural poor, and jobless workers were rendered the worst victims of the economic upheavals that followed. This vulnerable economic demographic rarely benefited from the skills training and material support that was introduced as part of PAMSCAD programs for cushioning them. As Agnes Apusigah (2004) notes, the "stress on job creation, above all else, was indicative of its [PAMSCAD's] neo-liberal roots and emphasis on efficiency. Ignoring the deficiencies of the reforms in the ways that they contributed to the heightening of vulnerability and intensification of exclusion, the plan found an 'easy way out' through compensatory programs that provided a quick fix, not sustained relief." Given that the cedi also rapidly depreciated relative to the dollar (from 2.75 cedis to the dollar in 1983 down to 9,000 cedis to the dollar in 2003) and that the economy was heavily dependent on imports, the situation in the country was desperate by any standard of assessment.[21] It is from this environment that the mega churches in Accra emerged, with the founding of Nicholas Duncan-Williams's Christian Action Faith Ministries (CAFM) 1979, Mensa Otabil's International Central Gospel Church (ICGC) in 1984, Charles Agyin Asare's World Miracle Bible Church in 1987, Dag Heward-Mills's Lighthouse Cathedral in 1991, and Salifu Amoako's Resurrection Power Evangelistic Ministry in 1990. These churches, especially the first two, have been extraordinarily successful, with hundreds of branches across Ghana and elsewhere in the diaspora. The International Central Gospel Church has gone on to establish a highly successful university, with Mensa Otabil consolidating the reputation of being as much a thinker, social critic, and teacher as he is a man of God.[22]

Not coincidentally, Oxford Street also began to take its current form from the early 1990s following the government's decision to loosen foreign exchange controls in the last quarter of 1989. The immediate impact of this IMF-instigated policy was the rise of forex bureaus all across the city. But the more decisive effect for our understanding of Oxford Street was the appearance of several high-end shops, restaurants, and banks that appeared to mushroom out of nowhere along the Cantonments Road corridor. As we have noted in previous chapters, this corridor had historically serviced the high-end neighborhoods favored by the ruling elites and their satellites since the colonial period. Most of the landmark businesses on Oxford Street date from the late 1980s and early 1990s: Quik Pik (a major grocery store), 1988; Tip Top Chinese Restaurant, 1992; the Trust Hospital (a hospital set up by the Social Insurance Trust), 1993; Barclays bank, 1994; National Investment Bank, 1994; Papaye (the locally famous fast-food restaurant that we have already encountered), 1995; Frankie's (another famous fast-food restaurant, with a bakery and ice cream parlor), 1997; Kwatsons (a large electronic-goods store), 1997; Standard Chartered Bank, 1997; Osu Food Court, 2001; Agricultural Development Bank, 2001; Ecobank, 2005; MTN, 2005; AMAL Bank, 2008; and Fidelity Bank, 2009. This is only a selection of the most well-known places on the street. With the speed at which Oxford Street developed to rival Makola Market and the Central Business District, which themselves had evolved slowly from the middle of the twentieth century, it is not hyperbolic to suggest that this street is the explicit materialization of the dream of prosperity invoked in the prayers of the evangelical churches themselves. Not just that, as we have already noted, the prosperity message of these mega churches has also come to permeate the very structure of feeling that had hitherto dominated tro-tro inscriptions of previous decades.

Paul Gifford gives a detailed description of the prosperity thinking that is expressed at Sunday service, prayer meetings, and Bible classes in such churches. In one instance among several others he reports, a priest asks congregants to visualize making out a huge check to themselves which they will then pray to come to fruition in the real world (Gifford 2004, 49–52). Even more significant, as Ruth Marshall (2009) shows for Nigeria, prosperity churches also put into circulation elaborate displays of Americanized accents along with globalized models of wealth and success that are meant to register to congregants their access to a global repertoire of self-fashioning made available via the ideology of prosperity preached incessantly at church. On this account we might even venture to formulate a slogan that can serve Oxford Street, the multinational adverts to be found on it, and the mega churches themselves, and that may one day conceivably find itself inscribed boldly on a tro-tro: "Shopping Is Believing!" For the proof of belief and good standing with God is ultimately the ability to put oneself on display through the weekly rituals of testimony that are commonly found in the churches. Such displays themselves become invitations to treat, proffered to nonbelievers and believers alike so that they may intensify their church-related activities (and financial contributions, which a cynic might say often turn out to be the real measure of participation). Both Oxford Street and the mega churches share a disposition toward spectacularity, or of the delight in seeing and being seen, even if for different reasons as we noted in the introduction. (With respect to the rhetoric of insults that sometimes erupts in quarrels on the street, it is also not unusual for such quarrels to descend into religious invocations and curses from either or both sides, often a certain sign of escalation. In such instances the invocation of a religious discourse lifts the altercation into a register of moral superiority, rather leaving it at the level of cultural know-how.) Thus if the emergence of the mega evangelical churches and of Oxford Street is not to be taken as mere coincidence, it is because they were both mutually overdetermined by the processes unleashed by the IMF-inspired policies of the 1980s.

To read all the categories that we have encountered so far (street, slogans, adverts, and churches) dialectically as dimensions of a discourse of enchantment, we are obliged to read them beyond their discrete autonomous domains. This requires a form of defamiliarization, since their historical significance can no longer be read separately; rather they must be seen as inextricable dimensions of the same multi-synchronous whole. In other words, and in the spirit of horizontal archaeologies we elaborated in the introduction, we must now read all the elements as part of interconnected discourse ensembles, all of which, despite appearances to the contrary, intersect as an aspect of the larger integrated history of a discourse of enchantment tied firmly to self making. The discourse of enchantment shared by all these vectors is intensified and rendered a *historical necessity* by the terrible effects of IMF policies, articulated in a fragmentary fashion by forms of invitation to transnational self making on the street and in a more coherent manner in the prosperity discourse of the mega churches. Thus street, cell adverts, urban slogans, and prosperity churches have to be read in terms of mutually imbricated social processes that exist in Accra and Ghana today.

Faith in TIGO

If there were any lingering doubts about the vital proximity of the cell phone company's invitation to self making and that suggested by Accra's evangelical churches, this is thoroughly dispelled by TIGO's campaign in November 2008 that explicitly linked their products to the discourse of prosperity. Hitherto the message of prosperity had been exclusively associated with the churches, but of course it is no surprise that the two domains perceived a shared interest. Thus, from TIGO's campaign website:

> Nothing is beyond your reach
>
> Put SOUL into your life, passion into your LOVE and RELAX with our tips from our new, exciting Be Alive service. We strengthen your FAITH, help you get RICH, mend your broken HEART and bring you inner PEACE when you subscribe to Be Alive.
>
> Keywords:
>
> Relax. Bible. Faith. Peace. Soul. Love. Vital. Family. Rich. Happy. Heart. Cheer.

The message is further expanded by clicking on the introductory page:

> With TIGO'S BE ALIVE promotion, you stand the chance of winning CASH prizes, IPods and Cell Phones! Just Send any of the keywords job, rich or excel to TIGO short code 444. You will receive a daily inspirational message on the keyword to enhance either your chances of getting a JOB, how to save and get RICH or how to EXCEL in life! Each text received is 10p.
>
> The more inspirational messages you receive the greater your chances of winning US$400, IPods and cell phones in weekly draws! Your name

would [sic] be drawn and you will be contacted by a phone call to collect your prize at the TIGO Head Office. This is the only location your prize can be claimed. Win prizes whilst possibly winning some great prizes! [sic] TIGO! EXPRESS YOURSELF . . . .

This promotion will end on the 28th of November 2008. To DEACTIVATE or UNSUBSCRIBE send STOP XXXX (the service you subscribed for) to 444 i.e: Send STOP JOB to 444[23]

The key element to this promotion is that you only get a chance to be entered in the raffle upon accepting a certain number of inspirational messages. But to get the inspirational messages, you have to text the relevant keywords to TIGO for which you will part with ten Ghana pesewas a pop.[24] And since the magical numerical threshold of inspirational religious messages is to be determined by the cell phone company without consulting its consumers, the direct material benefits of prosperity ultimately accrue to the company itself. An endless loop is created whose main elements are dreams of prosperity, desire for self making, faith, clever commercial product advertising, and the continual deferral of the customer's satisfaction to an ever-receding horizon ("if it is true that another customer has been successful on this faith-based raffle [from the urban rumors that generally circulate about these things], then how about me?"). Thus commerce is dressed in the garments of faith; the laborer's appetite works for him and hunger drives him on firmly into the bosom of the capitalist circuit.

The question of individual agency may be raised to counter what has appeared in this analysis as an ultimately skeptical view of the relationship between the discourse of enchantment and the consciousness of the ordinary Ghanaian. Yet any attempt to romanticize the possibilities of a countervailing individual self-consciousness in their interface with such a discourse would be ignoring a rather rude fact of present-day urban life in Accra, namely, that there is as yet no serious evaluation or critique of such a discourse. Sure enough there have been voices raised against the cell phone companies, but these have mainly been to complain about the lack of efficiency in the delivery of their products. They take much money but deliver only poor and fitful services in return, is the common complaint. If what we have discussed so far is of any value for understanding the archival status of the street, it lies in unsettling the banal and commonsensical ways in which the discourse ecologies on Oxford Street and others like it may be understood, and in seeing them as intricately connected to other domains of cultural and religious life that may at first appear utterly distinct and autonomous. My objective here has been to read the street as an archive of lively discursive interactions, at the level of detail, concept, and historicity. To close then, let's turn to an Akan vehicle slogan in praise of eternal vigilance: "Wan hwe no yei a, wo ho no yie" (If You Don't Look Well, You Will Not See Well).

CHAPTER 5

"Este loco, loco": Transnationalism and the Shaping of Accra's Salsa Scene

Two aspects of youth culture in today's Accra—salsa and gymming—provide the focus for this and the next chapter. The social dimensions of salsa dancing and gymming however raise separate if related notions about beauty, cosmopolitan identities, and the overall participation in a global cultural economy of bodily, cultural, and aesthetic practices. The rationale for participating in either scene is determined in large measure by interpretations of the status of free time and its relationship to leisure. While there are no barriers to participation in either scene, the nature of the choices that are entailed in being a salsero imply a different time and financial commitment from that of gymming, such that the two scenes come to divide roughly along class lines. As a rule all serious gymmers seek to alter or improve their economic situation; they gym because they want to get better work than whatever they might be doing in the present. Unless they want to be instructors, salseros rarely participate in the salsa scene because they think that salsa will have an impact on their economic situation. Thus gymming is more directly tied to immediate economic considerations than salsa. The two scenes also divide roughly along gender lines. Salsa dancing in Accra, as in other cities across the world, is a scene in which women outnumber men, and sometimes by a substantial margin. The gymming scene we will be looking at in the next chapter is on the other hand heavily oriented toward men. Even though there are definite overlaps and interchange between the two scenes, as a rule the more extreme gymmers, that is, the bodybuilders among them, perform specific functions for the salsa scene, the most obvious of which is to act as bouncers at salsa-related events. On the other hand, since regular salsa dancing is thought to satisfy the need for exercise, very few salseros are involved in the gymming scene. Finally, the multi-scalar dimensions of both salsa and gymming scenes in Accra will be contrasted as a means of understanding their different intersections with transnational leisure cultures.

Salsa Mania at the Coconut Grove

The scene that balmy Wednesday at Coconut Grove was eye-popping! I had been invited by Vera Adu to get there by 8:00 PM so I could get a sense of the salsa to be had at this popular spot. Vera had been my research assistant for the previous five years and was a true and inventive urban girl: every year without fail she came up with a new idea for reinventing herself. At one time she was fascinated by beauty shoots and took herself to a studio to have black-and-white pictures taken of her. They turned out gorgeous and ended up on her Facebook page "liked" by many. The general idea was to circulate her portfolio to a few of the city's modeling agencies to see if she could get a slot on one of the many billboards advertising a wide variety of products (see chapter 4). Rumor had it, she said earnestly, that some girls who were "into fashion" had got themselves some very big contracts. She even claimed to know a girl displayed on one of the computer-school billboards she pointed out to me. (It turned out on further questioning that she did not know the girl personally but had heard about her from a friend who said she went to school with her. This is itself a telling feature of how urban legends circulate in Accra.) Another year Vera was all for acting in the made-in-Ghana movies and television soaps that seemed to proliferate cultural icons endlessly. She even went a step further and took a course in film production at the National Art Film and Television Institute (NAFTI). A couple of walk-on roles in a TV soap opera and one in a movie ensued, but nothing major. She also knew everything about Facebook beach parties and where the best Internet scammers operated from. Out of sheer curiosity, she had hung out for some weeks at one of their lairs and had picked up quite a bit of information on the nature of their operations and the stories they traded with the outside world and among themselves. One characteristic that always worked to Vera's advantage was that despite being in her midtwenties she had the face and build of someone much younger. She also had a disarmingly innocent demeanor that encouraged people, especially young men, to imagine immediately on meeting her that they were dealing with their younger sister. This younger-sister syndrome meant that people readily divulged all kinds of incredible secrets to her. Vera inspired a lot of trust and was absolutely invaluable as a research assistant, interlocutor, and friend. Early in 2012 Vera called me up with a completely different venture she had got herself into: this time she had become a fashion designer and had already opened her own fashion label—Adu Amani Klodin. She specializes in handbags and shoes with Ghanaian kente or adinkra cloth finishing, something that seems to have caught on wildly after she put up images of her work on Facebook.[1] Evidence of the popularity of her clothing line was that she was featured in TV programs and was also nominated for a Young Entrepreneurs Award by the National Youth Achievers Awards Committee in 2012. That she did not win was no disappointment to her. Just the further opportunity for networking seems to have been enough reward. For now.

The salsa idea was originally mine. I had phoned Vera about six weeks before my arrival in June 2009 to tell her the next phase of our research was going to be on salsa and that she should scout around to find out the main salsa instructors in the city that we might interview together. The result of my casual prompting was that by the time I arrived Vera had taken salsa lessons, visited by turns all the main five or six salsa places in town, and already made friends with DJs, salsa instructors, and a good number of salseros and salseras! The visit to Coconut Grove was but the first of several she took me on across town that year, but it was this first place that remains ingrained in my mind, and for very good reason, as it turned out later. The scene that met me when I arrived that night was one to scramble the senses. Some sign as to what was to come was already hinted at in the number of cars that were parked in front of the hotel and the many people who were milling around the place. It was upon walking through the gates, however, that the extraordinary scale and energy of the scene made itself manifest. There were more people milling around inside the gates, some close to a kebab seller who took orders in rapid succession while managing to turn out chicken or beef or sausage kebab freshly barbecued on the blazing charcoal grill he had set up on a strategic spot under the eaves of one of the buildings. The aroma of the special spice he sprinkled on the kebabs wafted enticingly in every direction. Some ten or so feet away from him and all around a twenty-by-ten-foot swimming pool the mother of all salsa parties was taking place.[2] By 9:00 PM there must have been at least two thousand people around the pool dancing heartily to salsa, merengue, zouk, and bachata music. A young man shadow danced with an imaginary sweetheart in his arms not far from the kebab seller. He performed exquisitely, gazing steadfastly into her eyes and even remembering to bow lightly and blow a kiss to his invisible lady at the end of the track that was playing. He had been waiting for his kebab order! Behind the mass of dancers around the pool, and toward the back wall that also acted as a stage where the DJ had his equipment, groups of dancers were going through routine dance steps. This turned out on inspection to be a dance class and was run from 7:00 PM to 8:00 PM every Wednesday before the real party began. But the class did not necessarily stop completely: some people continued practicing their steps in small groups even after the real evening had started. Classes were divided into beginner, intermediate, and advanced, but it did not take long to notice that it was only the beginners that concentrated on what the instructors were belting out during the class period against the loud and milling music. The intermediate and advanced groups regularly drifted off to join the larger dance crowd or mingle with the beginners and kept giving unsolicited advice on how to step, hold, twirl, and cha-cha. There was more spontaneous shadow dancing here, too, but this time for the keen eyes of the eager learners. Part of the attraction of the Coconut Grove scene is that inexperienced pundits are encouraged to take classes for free and then to participate in the dance proper but only as they grow in confidence. Migrations between the class area and the dance floor went on for much of the evening. The entire atmosphere was light, easygoing, and carefree.

The ratio of women to men was at least four to one. The crowd itself was made up of a variety of people, predominantly young (roughly between eighteen and twenty-five), but with quite a generous sprinkling of older people, some portly enough to suggest that they were not there necessarily to dance but just to enjoy the scene. As we shall come to see later, the presence of non-dancing observers at salsa events all across town indicates a significant change in the salsa scene that has become particularly marked since 2005. Coconut Grove also presented a lively and thoroughly multicultural scene: there were lots of American exchange students from the University of Ghana, a half hour's drive away to the north, along with a good sprinkling of South Asians and quite a few mixed-race youth. People changed dance partners regularly throughout the night. A Mexican man (I was firmly informed by Vera) threw an impromptu demonstration of how to do things properly and with his Ghanaian counterpart went into a vigorous routine, rapidly resetting his fedora hat at various rakish angles and allowing his partner a good measure of freestyling. The attention suddenly given to this couple was by the next track quickly usurped by two pairs of young Ghanaian dancers nearby, who switched partners with dizzying speed as they danced in what was evidently a well-rehearsed set of routines. The older people on the dance floor seemed mainly to be multiracial couples; several of them were exclusively European. Many of the older people also sat at tables around one side of the pool, drinking beer and just enjoying the amazing scene unfolding before them.

While the dancers that caught the eye were clearly well versed in the techniques of salsa dancing, the scene at Coconut Grove was definitely not geared exclusively toward the salsa aficionado. This emerged most strongly from the number of "lineups" that were regularly used to interlace the salsa, merengue, bachata, and zouk music segments. The lineups were carefully choreographed collective group dances in which everyone followed the lead provided by a group of instructors who were stationed in front of the dancers all around the poolside. Lineups were extremely popular, since on cue most of the people who had been sitting or just milling around climbed up to the pool and began following the choreographed sequences. Some of the lineup music was clearly well known and in such instances the instructors were barely needed. More interestingly, the lineup dances were not all set to salsa music. While the Spanish Latin dance duo Los del Río's "Macarena" was a predictable favorite, there was also a good dose of calypso, soca, and Ghanaian music that served the purpose of the lineups. One of the more surprisingly popular tunes in the summer of 2009 was the Australian Vanessa Amorosi's "Absolutely Everybody," whose refrain was repeated with gusto by salseros and may have been second in popularity only to the "Macarena."

When I returned in the summer of 2011 the old lineups had been supplemented with what was inventively called "Azonto Salsa," which was a new urban music and dance craze that had caught on among the youth. Popular hiplife artist Sarkodie's "U Go Kill Me O" was one of the repeatedly played lineup songs during this period, but the Azonto dance genre has now been fully established as a recognizable global brand among Ghanaians everywhere.[3] Amid the choreographed moves, the lineups also provided ample opportunity for freestyling. I spotted a couple of girls seriously whining Jamaican dancehall style. Both freestyling and whining were in evidence among the good salsa dancers, too, with the best of them clearly incorporating a number of African dance moves and gestures while keeping to the basic salsa steps. The objective of the lineups was to get everyone to join in the dancing. In this they were wildly successful.

To my further amazement I came to learn that all the excitement of that Wednesday night and of all other Wednesday nights at Coconut Grove was actually the subject of a special salsa program called Salsa Mania, broadcast by CitiFM on 97.3 from 7:00 PM to 8:30 PM to coincide with the Coconut Grove bash. On being set up in 2004, CitiFM decided to adopt salsa as a means of carving a special market segment different from JoyFM, whose well-established urban listenership they had very little hope of winning. This is how *Salsa Mania* is described on the CitiFM website:

> "Salsa Mania" is a dance and entertainment event organized by Citi 97.3 FM at the Coconut Grove Regency Hotel every Wednesday from 7 pm to 10 pm.
>
> The event brings together salsa music lovers and dancers of all ages, business executives and members of the general public to dance, relax, network amongst themselves and release the stress of the week.
>
> "Salsa Mania" attracts hundreds of people including members of the international community, diplomats and tourists.
>
> It also airs live on Citi 97.3 FM every Wednesday between 7 to 8:30 pm.[4]

As we shall come to see later, what CitiFM highlights regarding "members of the international community, diplomats and tourists," and the opportunities for networking that the Coconut Grove event offers is more than just a publicity stunt. Forms of transnational networking have been central to the salsa scene since it burst upon Accra's cultural map in the late 1990s.

At various points the evening's DJ interrupted the music to provide directions to radio listeners who might be heading that way. The CitiFM salsa show had been airing since December 2004, and everyone I spoke to agreed that it was this that had given salsa in Accra such a remarkable boost. But it was precisely this business model of marketing salsa that was threatening to hijack and indeed unrecognizably transform its more amateur and largely ad hoc community roots. That was the view of the salsa aficionados, most of whom had been dancing salsa from the late 1990s and regarded themselves as a community of like-minded people. Several of these early salseros and salseras had become instructors; they had put on major salsa shows for corporate consumption at annual events and the like and had also traveled across the country and abroad to introduce salsa elsewhere or to participate in salsa programs and related activities. Nigeria was a prime destination for instructors and salseros alike, as was London and other parts of Europe.[5] One Italian salsera I met at Coconut Grove said she had first been introduced to salsa in Bamako and on later finding herself in Dakar had discovered that the scene was even bigger there. Accra was but one stop in her itinerary as a young diplomat, and here, too, she had discovered a very lively salsa scene. She came practically every Wednesday with or without her Ghanaian boyfriend, who was himself a strict raw-food enthusiast and art photographer but had very little interest in any form of dancing, never mind salsa. He came mainly to sneak unobtrusive photographs about urban life for his well-received exhibitions in Ghana and abroad.[6]

Salsa as Cultural Meme

Accra's salsa scene cannot be separated from the international spread of the dance form all over the world. The general question we must ask is how this cultural meme (on analogy with phoneme and mytheme) has come to enjoy such widespread popularity in diverse places. Salsa congresses are held in a wide range of locations, including Dakar, Seoul, Hamburg, New York, Havana, London, and Bangalore among many others. It has even been suggested that a salsa congress takes place somewhere in the world practically every week (Borland 2009, 466). While Washburne (2008), Waxer (2002), Manuel (2006), and Borland herself have provided excellent explanations of the roots and spread of salsa, Ananya Kabir's summary of these in a paper she writes on the Berlin Congress of 2011 succinctly captures the various transnational vectors of the salsa phenomenon:

> Hybridity, dislocation and reformation underlie salsa, as suggested by its very name (Spanish for "sauce"). First used, reputedly, by a Venezuelan Disc Jockey, Phidias Danilo Escalona, to denote Latin dance music in the early 1960s, the term "salsa" had spread throughout Latin America by the 1970s. The dance-music complex's fluid label reflects its shifting, transnational character, but a deep history of migration subtends its transnational vectors. Salsa was created through the movement of people and rhythm cultures across Africa, the Caribbean, and the Americas. The fusion of European couple dances and lyrical styles with African rhythms and percussive traditions brought to the Caribbean through slavery created, in Cuba, the form of dance and music called "son." The son fed into the dance culture of New York from the 1930s onwards, giving rise to dance crazes: mambo, cha-cha-cha, and boogaloo. During the 1960s, these different traditions were re-developed by Puerto Rican immigrants to New York to create a more codified and stylized dance form which began to be called "salsa," after the new term for the music which was also rapidly getting slicker and more commercialized. By the 1990s, Pan-Latino migration to New York created "a second generation of salseros who co-opted the music of their parents, reinventing and transforming the salsa scene with sounds and expressions that better represented their

own experiences as Latino youth growing up in New York City." ([quoting Washburne 2008, 9], Kabir 2013)

The structuralist implication of the term "meme" proves to be highly suggestive, for on closer inspection we find that while the basic elements of salsa appear the same everywhere it is found, different cultural contexts come to inflect these elements in a variety of ways, such that important distinctions in the status of both technical elements and the social dimensions of individual salsa scenes come to be manifested.[7] Despite the changes that have taken place in the dance form through its many multiple itineraries from the slave plantations of Cuba to the overheated cultural hotbeds of New York and LA, salsa may be argued to have retained its African roots, revealed especially in the underlining percussion beats that are used to regulate the dance steps. Among Ghanaian salseros it is argued (and sometimes quite passionately) that the beat may be found in different genres of music, including even some well-known Ghanaian church songs. Thus they feel salsa is a return back home of something that was taken away from its source in the course of slavery. In reality, however, it is the new quality of attentiveness and listening that has been enhanced in salseros that should be remarked upon. As a rule all beginner salsa dancers are first instructed to "listen to and count the beat" in trying to master the main steps of the dance. In Accra this new form of attentiveness then migrates to the manner in which other music forms are heard, such that suddenly an underlying salsa matrix seems to be manifest in songs that were previously never identified as such. The return of salsa to Africa then cannot be said to be a return in any simple sense of the word. It is rather the installation of a fresh quality of attention to beat and rhythm that was originally forged in the crucible of diaspora. If there is a history of salsa soundscape to be written in accounting for its global popularity, then it must necessarily include the structure of listening that it enjoins upon its practitioners, something that allows the latent features of the soundscape to be detected in other domains. This is one of the lessons to be drawn from the Accra scene.

On the whole salseros identify three distinguishable styles of salsa dancing, each initiated on a different beat in the song. Cuban-style salsa and the so-called On-1 style (also called LA style) both involve movement on the first and fifth beats from an initial standing position. The On-2 variant, in contrast, initiates movement on the second and sixth beats. As it evolved mainly among New York dancers of Puerto Rican origin, On-2 is also variously referred to as "New York" or "Puerto Rican" style. The Cuban variant is further distinguished from the cross-body or linear movements that mark On-1 and On-2 variants of the dance. Hence aficionados consider Cuban salsa as not equal to, but actually separate from, all other On-1 variants, even though like them the dancers start on the first beat. The difference between Cuban and all other styles (both On-1 and On-2) is that in the Cuban version the partners circle each other while in all other cross-body styles you have to dance in a linear "slot" if you want to successfully fend off accusations of being a country bumpkin. The Cuban style of salsa may also incorporate a choreographed group "wheel" (La Rueda), in which the female partners always move on and are switched between male partners among a designated group. The effect of synchronicity in this dance routine comes from the fact that there are certain "calls" made by a male leader of the rueda, who is either self-appointed or designated as one by the group as the rueda assembles. Everyone in the rueda, especially the men, should know what the calls mean for smoothly prosecuting the dance moves.[8]

Many salsa instructors in Accra learned to hone their skills by watching YouTube videos of other salsa instructors. Even though the Cuban version is not entirely precluded, the shared English-language provenance of the YouTube videos and the fact that many of them come from New York or LA means that it is the Puerto Rican version that many of these salsa instructors were first introduced to. In practice, however, there is no strict division between Cuban and Puerto Rican styles for them, with many instructors starting out learning one variant but then gradually migrating to stick with another one or, as often happens, incorporating the two styles for different segments of a salsa event. Thus the two young couples we encountered earlier at Coconut Grove that had set up a mini-competition with the Mexican salsero were practicing a form of La Rueda, with dizzying switching of partners within their tight-knit group setting them out from all others. In answer to my curious questioning later, however, the young dancers informed me that they were comfortable with both On-1 and On-2 variants and could choose either depending on context. This was not unusual among the instructors either.[9] Among salseros in Accra, it is also not uncommon to find quite a bit of freestyling, with the really good Ghanaian female dancers imposing their personal signatures by way of hand and body gestures or the more common whining. While whining is mainly associated with Jamaican dancehall, it may also be described as a thoroughly Ga traditional dance form. Whining is very much to be seen at funeral or outdooring (child-naming) functions, where there is ample opportunity to dance to Ga songs with a great deal of competitive whining between women of all ages. Even though there is ample evidence that salsa was part of high-class Ghanaian culture from at least the mid-1950s, it is the set of people who were introduced to it in the late 1990s to whom the current configuration of the scene must be traced. By the 1960s Ghanaian highlife had synthesized jazz, church cantatas, vaudeville, ragtime, soul, Afro-Latin dance, and rock with established forms of storytelling and neo-traditional music and dance into a new whole. As Jesse Shipley puts it, highlife derived from "a pastiche of African, black diasporic, and European styles that reflected the movements of workers, sailors, preachers, and entertainers across the Atlantic, beginning in the late 19th century" (Shipley 2013, 34). Those who went ballroom dancing in the 1960s followed strict dress codes, and it was not unusual for such events to be arranged as part of the itinerary of foreign dignitaries touring the country or of Independence Day celebrations and such other national events. Live band music was de rigueur at such times, something that is not pertinent to the evolution of the salsa scene in today's Accra.[10] However, by the early 1980s the legendary C. K. Mann and his Carousel 7 were releasing songs that had an evident salsa percussive beat to them. Two of these, "Asafo Bessuon" and "Maa tu Aboa," are still popular on Accra's salsa scene today. The *Salsa con Gana* album released in 1996 features several old C. K. Mann tracks beyond the two just mentioned but set to explicit salsa rhythms. Though most of the reworked tunes on the album still bear the largely melancholic blues air for which C. K. Mann is justifiably famous, the underlining percussive beat follows the one familiar to salsa-music lovers the world over. At the same time the current salsa scene in Accra is firmly rooted in a form of Latinidad, but with a healthy dose of African and Caribbean music, which as noted already is most evident in the lineup segments to salsa dance events. But the heavy Latinidad flavor to the scene accords with the overall inflection of salsa in other parts of the world.

Conversion Narratives of the Salsa Kind

Despite the explosion of energy I witnessed at Coconut Grove in 2009 and the fact that this current iteration of the scene owes much to the platform provided by CitiFM from the end of 2004, today's salsa scene in Accra has to be traced to a tight-knit set of people who first fell in love with salsa, began dancing it and, as numbers and interest expanded, experienced it as providing a fulfilling lifestyle choice. Salsa was seen to entail a lifestyle commitment and involved the development of particular forms of personal narratives as a means of aligning oneself to a like-minded dance community.

Thus everyone I spoke to had a salsa conversion narrative to share. I call them conversion narratives because of the sharp before-and-after quality of the stories I was told. Before being introduced to salsa, these people ordinarily enjoyed the same leisure activities as everybody else, but after being introduced to the dance form, they repudiated all else and became obsessive about salsa, even taking on the role of salsa evangelists either through attempts to convert other friends to join in, actively organizing and/or participating in salsa shows and events, or themselves becoming dedicated salsa instructors. The mark of the before-and-after quality of these conversion narratives is that after being introduced to salsa the people I interviewed felt that their lives had changed irreversibly, to the degree that they could not contemplate their lives without salsa. Each conversion story that follows suggests a number of vectors, the most significant of which is that the point of conversion was also an articulation of transnational networks, either in terms of personal or familial trajectories or as an aspect of the dramatic encounter with expats and foreigners who were in the country for one reason or another. The transnational dimension to the conversion narratives was further consolidated via the Internet, partly as an aspect of YouTube videos of famous salsa instructors, and also in the tracking of stories from salsa congresses from all over the world and the sharing of pictures and information on salsa-related events via the ubiquitous Facebook (Kabir 2013).

Martina Odonkor is of mixed German and Ghanaian parentage. She spent her childhood in Accra but moved to England with her parents in 1982. She completed secondary school there, then went to Cambridge University to read French and Spanish for her undergraduate degree, and returned for an MPhil in Latin American Studies in 1991. In addition to fluency in English, Spanish, and French, Martina also has a good command of German. While her conversion experience is not as dramatic as the ones we are going to encounter later, it is no less serious for the commitment that followed from her introduction to salsa. Martina had always had a serious interest in dance and at Cambridge participated in ballroom and Latin dancing and even auditioned to join the university's dance team. She failed to get in, but this did not prevent her from following her passion and dancing whenever she could. She returned to Accra at the end of 1992 where she started working as a social-development consultant. She began a career in creative writing, a passion since her teenage years.[11] In July or August 1998, she was told about salsa classes taking place at Costa Rica Bar in the Ringway Hotel at Kokomlemle. There she found a buzzing salsa scene that she promptly joined. Martina has remained an avid salsa dancer despite her hectic schedule as a development consultant, a fiction writer, and the mother of two children. Like Marlin, whom we shall encounter shortly, she is not as active on the scene as she was before due to the demands of her work and family, but she makes sure to keep abreast of the goings-on in the salsa scene and goes out to dance and meet up with old friends as often as she can.

Josh Ansah is a dance instructor. As he tells it his eureka moment came sometime late in 1997 or early 1998, when he was invited to the Cuban embassy for a Cuba Day event. He was astounded to see everyone, even little children as young as five, dancing impeccably to salsa rhythms. He interpreted the scene as a remarkable example of communal harmony and was so moved by the experience that he immediately set his mind on taking lessons. A Cuban-trained Ghanaian doctor had been giving free salsa lessons from his home. Josh immediately joined up with him. But it was the effect that salsa had on his personal life that marked the encounter as a conversion experience. At the time of his first introduction to salsa, he had recently completed a diploma in accounting at the Institute of Professional Studies at Legon and had been working for a few months as an accountant at the Cocoa Marketing Board (CMB), a perfectly respectable and indeed much sought-after place of work and one that would guarantee him a secure, if somewhat slow, rise to wealth and comfort. But salsa changed all that. After a year of dancing salsa and becoming more convinced of the merits of taking it on full-time, he resigned his position at the CMB and enrolled for a degree at the School of Performing Arts at the University of Ghana. This caused a major rift between him and his family; some of them refused to speak to him ever again. Undaunted, Josh completed his degree and took up the job of salsa instructor full-time.

Marlin (not his real name) is currently a doctor at Korle Bu, Ghana's renowned teaching hospital. He had come to Accra on a UNESCO scholarship from a nearby African country and was enrolled in the medical school at the University of Ghana. The medical program at the university entails completing three years of residency on the Legon campus and being shuttled by bus daily to and from Korle Bu for premed classes. It is only after passing a strenuous examination at the end of the third year that medical students relocate permanently to Korle Bu, staying in student residence at the hospital and continuing their studies there. For many medical students the first few months at Korle Bu tend to be extremely difficult, as all friends from the previous three years at the Legon campus generally have very little appetite to make the trip to Korle Bu to visit. Marlin himself had been an avid partygoer while on campus and tells how when they returned to Legon from Korle Bu in the first three years he would immediately find something to eat then just go out and crash a party until the wee hours of the morning. The hard-partying lifestyle was no longer possible at Korle Bu, so he and Sammi, his best friend and also an avid partygoer, felt a major existential crisis. They were extremely bored. One day in June 1998 Sammi came to Marlin's room to say he had heard there was some interesting new dance called salsa being taught at the Costa Rica Bar. The two friends immediately determined to check it out. At the time the classes at Costa Rica were run exclusively on Tuesdays, so on the next Tuesday Marlin and Sammi went along to see things for themselves. They had no idea what to expect, but when they arrived Patsy Sterling (on whom more shortly) was giving a lesson on a variation of La Rueda, with couples in a large circle switching partners on cues from her during the music. The two friends stood agape at what they saw that night. They were well and truly hooked! As Marlin tells it, they became so passionate about salsa that even on days that there was no salsa available anywhere in town they would load up a CD player and loudspeakers, go to a spacious fuel station, set the equipment up on the bonnet of the car, and begin playing and dancing to salsa. Other friends would be called on the phone to come to the fuel station, and within a short time an open-air salsa party was in full swing. Marlin and Sammi were later to choreograph several salsa shows as part of larger offerings at the National Theatre and other venues. They also ran a fund-raiser for the National Cardiothoracic Unit at Korle Bu in 1999, which suggests that even in those early days salsa was a point of curiosity and interest even for non-salseros. The two friends also attempted to promote products as part of the salsa drive; a special alcoholic drink was launched to much fanfare but failed to take off in the end. Marlin and Sammi were also responsible for a dynamic change in Accra's salsa community, something we will come to in a moment.

Of all the salseros I had the opportunity to interview, Lumo Bortei-Doku was clearly the one that had thought most about the evolution of the scene. He had spent part of his childhood in Toronto, taking piano lessons to a high level of proficiency before relocating with his family back to Ghana as a teenager. Something of his musical training shows itself in his incredible memory for detail and his facility for discussing both music and dance with great confidence and acuity. Not only was Lumo conversant with the main personalities from the early days, he himself had established a dance company called Dancation (i.e., dance plus sensation) in 2000 and had busied himself teaching salsa, promoting shows, and generally keeping an eye on various business models that had emerged for organizing the scene. Lumo went to Achimota School (Motown), the famous secondary school that has produced many of the country's political and cultural elites. Along with students from mainly middle-class families, Motown also tends to attract children of Ghanaians living abroad and of expats in Accra. In this respect its student profile is similar to those of the American Lincoln School, the Ghana International School (GIS), Roman Ridge School, and the SOS School at Tema, all of which have diverse communities. The shared cultural demographic of these schools was to play a significant part in the expansion of salsa in Accra, with Lumo at the center of it. He attended the University of Ghana to study for a degree in agricultural science, but his entrepreneurial and cultural interests quickly outstripped those he had in agriculture. Toward the end of 1997, he began running an e-mail service at Legon, which was very handy for the many foreign students on campus. Having cultivated several American students as friends, he finally ended up dating an African-American dance major. It was she who dragged him one fateful Tuesday to Costa Rica so she could find out more about salsa. Lumo went somewhat reluctantly and was not immediately taken with it, but accompanied his girl-friend regularly after that in order not to cause offense. When it came time for her to head back to the United States, she got him to promise to learn salsa so he could become proficient by the time of their next meeting. He agreed but returned to Costa Rica mainly from nostalgia. It did not take him long to become completely converted, and by 2003 he had organized the first salsa dance competition at the Apollo Theatre to which at least five hundred people showed up.

Lumo has always been an avid cultural entrepreneur. Apart from Dancation, which was originally set up as part of his larger ambition to create entertainment shows for TV, he began teaching salsa at various high schools in Accra midway through 2002. Originally invited to prepare students at GIS for a variety show they were putting on at the end of the school year in May, he quickly came to be the agent for the spread of salsa among high school students at other elite schools. With just two weeks to go for the variety show the only students who bothered to show up for his salsa classes at GIS turned out also to be the coolest and hippest at the school. None of them knew how to salsa before meeting him, but the dance routines they put on at the variety show were met with loud applause. The following year the GIS dance club was completely oversubscribed, with everyone eager to learn salsa. From GIS Lumo got invitations to teach salsa at the Roman Ridge School and at Lincoln with visits to various other high schools in Accra following in quick succession. Before long a large cohort of middle-class youth had been converted to the dance form, and it was considered de rigueur as a mark of fresh cosmopolitan style. As noted earlier, along with Motown the various schools that Lumo ended up teaching at have a highly diverse and multicultural demographic, something that reflects the wider salsa scene in Accra in general.

People, Venues, and Salsa Evolution

Everyone I spoke to agreed that the current salsa scene must ultimately be traced to the energetic efforts of the British-Jamaican Patsy Sterling who first ran the salsa classes at Costa Rica in 1998.[12] At the time Patsy was working for the UK's Department for International Development (DFID) and was based in Accra as part of her stint. She had started salsa lessons for her friends in the living room of her house and as these grew in popularity decided it might be a good idea to find a bigger venue where things could be continued. An approach to the owners of the Ringway Hotel led to an agreement for her to use the Costa Rica Bar area for her salsa lessons. This was a clever business move by the management of the hotel, since the presence of salseros guaranteed a steady stream of customers, a substantial number of whom came just to watch people dance while lounging around the bar and buying drinks. The first batch of early salseros at Costa Rica was constituted mainly of expatriates, with only a smattering of Ghanaian men and even fewer Ghanaian women. Among this early crowd were Martina Odonkor, whom we have already encountered; Estelle Sowah, at the time working at Golden Tulip Hotel, later moving on to Busy Internet, and as of 2010 the director of Google Ghana; Sally Darko, whose family owned one of the first moving companies in the country; Tony Mattouk, whose family owns Paloma, a popular hotel on the Ring Road; and Marco Mancini, an entrepreneurial Italian-Ghanaian who happened to be Patsy's boyfriend at the time, along with various people from the diplomatic community in Accra. Patsy began to train salsa instructors, several of whom went on to become established names on the salsa circuit. As we can see from the names and occupations just listed, most of Accra's early salseros and salseras were drawn from the professional classes, and without exception had transnational and diasporic connections. This situation was held practically the same until toward the end of 2001, by which time the scene had expanded to include a younger generation, and with Ghanaian dancers outnumbering expats. However, despite the fact that with its increasing popularity the salsa demographic in Accra has changed from how it was in the late 1990s, it is still the case that the scene seems to predominantly serve the leisure interests of the educated middle classes with strong transnational or diasporic connections. The most lively places where salsa is to be found in Accra today speak to these transnational networks: Coconut Grove; the Golden Tulip Hotel not far from the airport; the Aviation Sports Club, also a short distance from the airport but from a different direction; and Bella Roma, a club on the side street to Frankie's and just off Oxford Street—all places where you are likely to meet a really diverse and multicultural crowd. The irony in this scenario is that while salsa may have originated in the Cuban slave plantations and subsequently become a means for people from Latin America to express their cultural dance preferences in New York and Los Angeles, its return to Africa has been via the circuits of the middle classes and their transnational cohorts.

In the early stages, that is between 1998 and roughly the end of 2001, salseros considered themselves a close-knit community and regularly shared concerns about one another's welfare along with information about salsa happenings. The steady process of the commercialization of salsa ultimately led to the fraying of this communal feeling. As a general rule the nature of salsa event handling in the early years dictated that salseros were heavily at the mercy of hotel and club managements, most of which saw salsa strictly in terms of how it might bring business onto their premises. It did not take long for both salseros and the operators of the early salsa venues to begin seeing business potential in salsa, except that their motivations for drawing benefit from it were markedly different. The rift between salseros and venue operators ultimately came to turn on the question of whether it was possible to charge gate fees for salseros as well as for ordinary clients who might be coming to the premises only to have a drink and to watch but not dance. In other words, the question of a split between spectators and participants and the profitability of either group increasingly became an issue. Patsy had refused to charge gate fees while running the classes at Costa Rica, and the understanding with the Ringway Hotel's management seemed to rest mainly on the number of punters her classes could draw onto the premises to buy drinks off the bar. The question of the relative standing of participants versus assumed spectators came to a head during Patsy's farewell party in August 2001. By that time difficulties with the management at Ringway Hotel had forced her to move the salsa classes to Afrikiko, a much more lively joint situated at Kanda, one of the upwardly mobile neighborhoods we encountered in previous chapters. While the Costa Rica Bar was a generally quiet affair except on the Tuesday nights of salsa, Afrikiko on the other hand had a long-established reputation as a restaurant and drinking spot well before the advent of salsa. For much of the 1990s, it was synonymous with the best entertainment and live music in town, and was so popular that a branch under the same name was opened in 1997 in Hackney in north London. The key difference between Costa Rica and Afrikiko was that the latter already had an extensive and dedicated clientele list so that salsa was perceived as but one addition to its popular menu of entertainments.

The no-gate-fee policy had already been put to the test with the increasing success of salsa shows that members of the early salsa community had put on either as a segment of larger shows or as stand-alone offerings. By 2001 salsa shows had featured prominently at the National Theatre, the Apollo Theatre, La Palm Beach, Alliance Française, the Golden Tulip, and the Lincoln International School prom among other venues. It had also become a regular offering at corporate events. Once the principle of charging fees for salsa shows at such venues was established, it began to seem odd not to charge gate fees for coming to dance at other venues such as Costa Rica and Afrikiko. Ad hoc and largely halfhearted arrangements were in play for a while, but it was at Patsy's farewell party that matters came to a head. As the story is told, a series of unfortunate events became focalized around the party, making it highly memorable but not for the right reasons.[13] The first and most controversial item was the question of how to distinguish between salseros and salseras who were to be charged gate fees to enter the venue, and regular Afrikiko customers, some of whom had no interest in salsa and were only coming to the place to enjoy their routine beer and food. But there was another problem, which could not have been anticipated by the organizers of Patsy's bash. Many members of the early salsa community who had actively supported its spread from the days of Costa Rica felt personally affronted to suddenly be asked to pay gate fees on arrival at Patsy's Afrikiko party. What is more, some salseros and salseras insisted that they had participated in or otherwise contributed to a number of recent successful shows at other venues without collecting fees so they felt strongly entitled to come into the Afrikiko party for free. To compound it all, the serving staff at Afrikiko began to sense that the arguments about fees among the salsa crowd at the gate were preventing regular Afrikiko customers from entering the premises uninhibited, thus potentially depriving them of substantial tips for the evening. One furious waiter marched abruptly to the gate to insist that everyone be allowed to enter the premises for free. A huge slanging match ensued: the police were hurriedly called in. By the time things returned back to normal something dramatic had shifted in the salsa community. The details of the epiphanic moment are not clear, but apparently one of the co-organizers of the party who was close to Patsy made the exasperated and ill-judged announcement that "salsa in Accra is going to be suspended until further notice." This astounding announcement was met with spluttering shock and anger from the other salseros and salseras present and proved to be the proverbial straw that broke the community's sense of cohesion.

Marlin and Sammi took the decision there and then to register a group called the Salsa Dance Company as a strictly salsa-oriented promotional organization. They got the management of the Aviation Sports Club to lend them their premises and began to run salsa classes there shortly after the Afrikiko fiasco. In the meantime and in an attempt to woo back the salsa crowd, Costa Rica had decided to invite Lumo to run its Tuesday salsa nights in place of the departing Patsy Sterling. This was on the strength of his already having run a fairly successful salsa night at Volta Hall in Legon several months previously. For reasons that are not entirely clear, the folks running things at Aviation decided to hold their salsa also on Tuesday nights, thus setting up a direct challenge to the operation at Costa Rica. This led to further splits within the already-fragile community. From this time on even the terms for describing going to dance salsa changed from the hitherto ubiquitous "I am going to salsa" to "I am going to this or that person's salsa." From the inception of the Aviation/Costa Rica split in 2002, Marlin and Sammi's arrangements seemed the more popular. They were seen to be generally the more interesting crowd and, being medical students, had managed to draw a large number of their fellow medics into the fold. Sammi was thought by most people to be especially charismatic, which also meant that women in particular were more attracted to the Aviation scene than to the Costa Rica one.[14] By 2004 the scheduling clashes between the two venues had largely been resolved, with more lively venues springing up to challenge these first two. And yet the residual effects of the original differences between Costa Rica and Aviation had had a decisive effect on the overall sense of community. No longer was it possible to think of a unified salsa community; rather it was now organized as a strictly commercial enterprise instead of something that people indulged in for fun and to hang out with like-minded friends. At both venues the question of gate fees was resolved in favor of charging a straight fee for entering the premises on the days on which salsa was being offered. Effectively this meant that the venues in question had been converted into salsa venues, as opposed to being drinking or multipurpose spots that merely happened to host salsa from time to time. One paid the gate fee, went in to take the dance class, then either joined the more experienced salseros and salseras on the dance floor or just entered to lounge at the bar and have a drink.

The business model just described was entirely dependent on obliterating the difference between participant and spectator and charging a flat gate fee for entry to the venue. But this also meant that the success of the model turned heavily on two not necessarily related factors, namely, the reputation of the venue for offering other services beyond salsa, and the attractiveness of salsa for drawing both salsa and non-salsa customers to the venue. The two were mutually interrelated and ultimately inseparable in the history of salsa in Accra. It is the possibility of joining salsa and non-salsa customers at the same location but with the dance as the main attraction that was later taken up by CitiFM / Coconut Grove and polished into a multifaceted and highly successful business model. CitiFM and the hotel completely dispensed with the gate-fee element and replaced it instead with corporate sponsorship to pay for the floor space at the venue. In other words, the gate fee was being paid, but not by those that came to the venue on salsa nights, irrespective of the reason why they were there. The reward for corporate sponsorship was first that the company's products were mentioned repeatedly during the course of the Wednesday *Salsa Mania* radio program, and second that the teeming crowds of salseros and salseras were exposed to insistent subliminal advertising about the particular product that was being privileged. Sponsors of the Coconut Grove salsa scene have included Coca-Cola, Close UP, and Baileys, among various others. To my question as to why Baileys was on this list since salseros are generally not known to be fans of alcohol, Lumo's answer was highly instructive: "You are making a big mistake, you know. The folk dancing salsa think that they are there just having fun, but in fact they are actually there to provide entertainment for the consumption of the non-salsa people sitting around the pool. All those portly men that come to Coconut Grove do not come to dance but to watch the young people wriggle their waists. They [the portly men] are the real targets of Baileys and the other corporate sponsors, not the salseras dancing away without a care in the world."

While this interpretation may sound cynical to other observers, the point to be noted is that Lumo himself has tried to replicate the no-gate-fee sponsorship model at Bella Roma where he runs a regular and very popular Thursday salsa session. The key problem with the model he describes, as he himself was quick to admit, is that Coconut Grove has the advantage of location (offering ample parking and being at a high-end and safe neighborhood, for instance), scale (a very spacious dance space with adequate room also for setting up the classes and the music equipment), and atmosphere (the magnificent swimming pool). What is more, because it is first and foremost a hotel, some of its clients take the Wednesday night salsa party as an attractive aspect of their stay there. Coconut Grove has become a much-fancied tourist destination in the city precisely because of the salsa on offer on Wednesday nights. Of the various venues offering salsa in Accra today, it would be extremely difficult to replicate the general advantages of Coconut Grove, making the link between large salsa crowds and thus corporate sponsorship anywhere else in town that much harder to replicate. The CitiFM / Coconut Grove business model is thus tied to a specific configuration of factors, all of which come to give the venue a special place in the history of salsa in Accra.

Space and the Education of Transnational Desire

The question of space as might be applied to the salsa scene in Accra requires a variegated and multitiered mode of analysis. In the first instance, the space of salsa in Accra's urban milieu was initially tied to the apparently banal issue of location. What venue would be the best to sustain a dance class and how would salsa also service the interest of profit making for the venue operators were the pressing questions in the early years. For the early salsa community, the specifically aesthetic character of the dance venues was not of primary concern. Community was more important than profit, at least for salseros and salseras. Both Costa Rica and Aviation had modest physical and aesthetic advantages as dance venues. (The Ringway Hotel and its Costa Rica Bar have since been torn down, but Aviation still remains a popular salsa location.) Yet the quarrel over profit making that ensued on the growing popularity of salsa also meant that locational questions came to take on added salience since they were now tied to the commercial viability of salsa for different interests. The first sign of salsa's decisive commercialization, and thus the alteration of the sense both of physical space and of community may be discerned at the moment when Marlin and Sammi set out to register an official limited liability company with a board of directors and the entire apparatus of business accountability after the ill-fated party at Afrikiko. The commercialization of salsa was in a sense inevitable, but the precise contours of the event and its outcome bear reflecting upon for the shift from a communal sensibility to a more commercial and thus capitalist one. Marlin and Sammi's company sought to operate salsa as a profit-making venture and not just for the entertainment of a community, no matter how close-knit that community may have been at the time. In this they moved beyond the expression of sentiment to honing astute business skills, something that the early venue operators had long desired yet could not achieve because they were effectively outsiders to the salsa scene itself. If it is true that the process of salsa's commercialization in Accra was well under way before Marlin and Sammi decided to form their company, it is also true that as well-regarded members of the early salsa community they helped to focalize the intersection between symbolic and economic capital in the production of a cultural product, in this case salsa. Marlin and Sammi converted the substantial *symbolic* capital of being well-known salseros into the economic capital of a salsa *business*.[15] Lumo had of course registered Dancation a couple of years earlier, but the original inspiration for his company was to develop programming primarily for television. Thus Marlin and Sammi are of historical importance for the specific articulation of salsa entrepreneurship by making salsa a successful business as opposed to just a leisure-dance activity. After them several salseros registered businesses to take advantage of the dance's popularity. By the time of the collaboration of CitiFM with Coconut Grove, however, the salsa scene's economic logic had been well and truly severed from its cultural logic. With the expansion of the salsa demographic, it was no longer necessary to carry the symbolic capital of being a salsero in order to make profit out of the salsa scene. Even though CitiFM hired a number of salsa instructors to teach at their Wednesday bash the DJs themselves are not required to know very much about the dance form. Salsa is just music to them, and they do not necessarily need to be dancers to be good DJs. To the radio station, salsa is purely a commercial enterprise.

The spatial question lends itself to another inflection. At the core of the early salsa community and in its subsequent iterations, people with transnational networks and connections heavily dominated the scene. Whether the salseros and salseras of the early years had been entirely formed within the local context of Accra, such as Josh, or had had stints elsewhere, such as Martina, Marlin, and Lumo, through salsa each of them ended up developing elaborate transnational networks. Lumo has even gone a step further to establish a research project on identity and diaspora, for which he actively interviews every foreigner he comes across for his or her sense of the relationship between Africa and its many elsewheres. His questions are elaborate and comprehensive and cover a wide range of conceivable topics under the general rubric of diaspora identity. The transnational demographic of the salsa scene ensures that it has a high saturation of stories of lives in other places, whether for leisure or for work. It is now commonplace for the salsa venue to be the preferred location for the mingling of diverse races and cultures, old and young people. A salsa venue such as Coconut Grove is thoroughly multicultural as opposed to being merely multiethnic, since different cultures must interact within the performative repertoires that undergird salsa worldwide, rather than those limited to an exclusively local dimension. This is despite the many re-inflections of the salsa memes we spoke of earlier. When people strike up friendships at salsa events, the material space provided by the venue is not really what inaugurates and sustains the friendship. Rather it is the fact that the salsa venue instantiates a transnational imaginary regulated by the recognizable parameters of a passionate dance whose roots/routes derive both from a diasporic African past and a now global Latinidad.

Fundamentally, however, salsa must be understood as part of the education of desire for urban youth in Accra. This derives in large part from what we have already noted to be its wide-ranging multicultural inflections. But beyond that it contrasts sharply with other modes of music and dance that may also be seen to divulge significant modalities of the transnational. As Shipley (2013) has adroitly shown, the roots of hiplife come from the determined entrepreneurial impulses of several returning diasporic Ghanaian youth from London, New York, Germany, and other places in the late 1980s and early 1990s who sought to reshape the culture of hip-hop they had been introduced to in the diaspora and provide it with a determinedly local flavor. Reggie Ossei, Obrafor, Obuor, Sarkodie, and the other hiplife stars Shipley attributes this process to essentially reconfigured hip-hop in Ghana by turning to local-language proverb forms and song motifs for rapping over old highlife samples. Thus hiplife was born as a hybrid amalgam of hip-hop with highlife and took the country by storm. However, its transnational imaginary is still heavily dominated by a hip-hop ethos and aesthetic, making some critics wonder whether it is nothing but the local addendum to African-American music culture, a desperate mimesis rather than the product of original creativity. The overall dress codes of hiplife artistes, their body language, the often expletive-filled language that they favor in personal interviews, and the heavily self-referencing codes that they make central to their songs speak to a strong African-American hip-hop ethos.

Contrastively, the transnational imaginary of salsa appears to be quite different. In the first place, the music does not aspire to being anything local: everyone is in tacit agreement that the best salsa music is sung in Spanish. Despite the leavening that is provided by the variant lineup music that we encountered earlier, it is still the case that Spanish-language music is what dominates the salsa scene in Accra, thus aligning it decisively with its overall transnational character reiterated in the various cities where it is found. Second, unlike hiplife, salsa is a partner dance that follows a strict dance form, with the On-1 and On-2 variations both instilling a disciplined manner of dancing that is not to be found in other local dance genres. Hiplife dancing alters with changing fashions, but salsa is first and last a disciplined set of steps upon which may be constructed a variety of routines and maneuvers in which both partners participate in full knowledge. In hiplife dancing there is no requirement to synchronize your dance steps with those of your partner; it is perfectly acceptable to dance to your own sense of rhythm and style with little reference to the person you happen to be dancing with. Third, the salsa scene is the only one in which a woman is considered to be primarily a dance partner and not a sexual object. It is only at salsa, as Lumo put it in our interview, that "you can lay your hand on a woman's waist and not get immediately slapped for it." Several salsa scholars have suggested that salsa allows for a particular disposition of freedom for female dancers. Sexual hints may be dropped during the course of a dance by an unknown man, but these can also be quickly assimilated into the dance and thus neutralized, allowing the woman to retain some choice as to whether she will allow a sexualized narrative to follow from the dance or not (Borland 2009). True, salsa is itself an extremely sensual dance and the best dancers can project themselves as incredibly hot and sexy, and yet their implied sensuality is always re-contained within the discrete form of the salsa dance unit itself.

Finally, the popularity of today's salsa is heavily a function of the social circuits generated by Facebook and other social platforms and sustained with image feeds and updates on salsa happenings both locally and from across the world. This means that the scene in Accra is necessarily also fed and energized by the same ego-loop that has become a hallmark of Facebook: everything you are involved in is subject to the immediate update, delivered in narrative form but also heavily augmented by images, both of which may then immediately get "liked" by many others who you are never likely to meet but who may also supply you with further words and images from a similar discursive context of experience. Salsa is a prime engine of such updates all over the world and in its local instantiation generates a sense of participation in a community of like-minded people that is not easily replicable for the hiplife scene.

In closing we are obliged to return to Vera. What does someone with her background tell us about the salsa scene in Accra? One thing for sure is that Vera's taste for salsa is part of her overall orientation toward gaining mastery of the many and variable discourses that circulate in Accra and that she hopes will give her a better way of navigating opportunities in the city. For her salsa provides one of a growing repertoire of practices for cosmopolitan self-fashioning. Though she is from a lower-middle-class background, she left home early and considers herself a self-made woman. For salsa to continue to retain its interest for Vera, it would have to provide something more than just entertainment. She has already expressed her desire to meet more people, to travel and see the world, and perhaps even to fall in love with someone exotic and charming. And for all these reasons, the transnational dimensions of salsa provide an excellent education of her desire.

CHAPTER 6

Pumping Irony: Gymming, the Kòbòlò, and
the Cultural Economy of Free Time

The gymming culture in Accra illustrates something quite different from
that of the salsa scene we encountered in the previous chapter. The term
"gymming" represents a range of activities centered on use of the gym, from
bodybuilding to aerobics and fitness exercise, yet also points to a particular
lifestyle choice centered on a certain working-class dimension to gym culture. Thus when someone says "so and so has been gymming," in contrast
to simply "going to the gym," it means more than simply suggesting that
he or she goes regularly to the gym for exercise. Gymming represents an
entire ethos and way of life grounded in different aspects of urban culture.
The discursive repertoires by which the predominantly male gymmers style
their masculinity make for a sharp set of contrasts between the gymming
and salsa scenes. Here the interpellation of masculinity within the gymming
scene derives from a different relationship between local and transnational.
While gymmers in Accra sculpt their bodies with the aim of increasing their
physical appeal in a manner not different from their counterparts in other
parts of the world, they simultaneously have to struggle against the stereotypes of violence and criminality with which they are often viewed within
Ghanaian society. Moreover, as chubbiness is still firmly linked to power and
success in much of Africa, the appeal of the sculpted body comes to lie more
in what practical uses it can be put to than as an object exclusively for aesthetic appreciation. Thus apart from the few who frequent gyms for fitness
purposes, as a general rule gymmers in Accra want to put their sculpted bodies forward for hire, either as the bodyguards of politicians (a position that is
heightened in significance during election-cycle years), as bouncers at various events, or for walk-on roles in the expansive Gollywood movie industry.
Almost without fail, however, all the gymmers I interviewed had it in mind
to one day end up either in Hollywood or somewhere else in the West as

personal trainers for the rich and famous. This dream was so ubiquitous as to form the default aspiration for gymmers. It is this aspiration that provides an important preliminary contrast to the salsa scene. Whereas salsa in Accra took shape under the influence of various protagonists with broadly transnational and middle-class backgrounds in the late 1990s, the gymming scene is a largely working-class one. Its relationship to transnationalism is shaped more by the highly influential imagescapes of muscular masculinity that were made prominent by the Hollywood action movies of the 1980s. And in contrast to the salsa scene, expats and transnational travelers have had very little to do with the shaping of the gymming scene and its discursive repertoires. To follow the relation between gymmers and the social category of the kòbòlò, typically defined as an unemployed and good-for-nothing lounger, is also to see how gymming is predominantly related to the social difficulties that male migrants from other parts of the country often face in adjusting to the economic vagaries of Accra life. Furthermore, tracing the history of gymming in today's Accra to that of the warrior-soldier from the precolonial period will help to highlight various ironies and contradictions that have become embedded in the image of the masculine mascularity in urban society. The discursive repertoires by which masculinity is shaped in the gymming context will also be aligned to the larger urban scripts of transition signaled in tro-tro inscriptions and vehicle slogans that we encountered in chapter 4.

The material for this chapter is drawn mainly from interviews and focus group discussions in six gyms in the Legon-Madina area and from one-on-one interviews conducted each summer between 2009 and 2011. Samuel Ntewusu, my local research assistant, and I regularly visited and took active membership in two fitness gyms at Madina, with additional visits to another four that we attended less frequently. Sixty gymmers drawn from three different gyms were involved in the focus group discussions, with eight in-depth one-on-one interviews also undertaken to demarcate threshold moments within the gymming cycle for individual participants. While the personal interviews were more structured and tended to be used for highlighting life-course events, focus group discussions were informal and pursued as the opportunity presented itself, for example early on Saturday mornings when there was a good mixture of people at the relevant gyms we visited. There were also visits to the beach with members of one gym group and a focus group discussion after a soccer match that a second gym had organized to publicize its activities to the local community. Follow-up interviews and video taping of various gym activities were also undertaken, along with the taking of scores of photographs.[1] Much of the focus of this chapter will be on the White Chapel Gym at Madina Zongo, with contrasts being drawn between it and the First Fitness Gym at Madina New Road. As a rule, gyms in Madina are heavily neighborhood oriented and, unlike some high-class gyms we shall be referring to shortly, tend to pride themselves on having an organic relationship to their immediate social environments. This was especially evident with the White Chapel Gym, where most of the gymmers came from the same northern migrant communities as those of their immediate neighborhood. The focus on White Chapel Gym and on its leader Tanko allows us also to historicize the status of the northern migrant community in Accra and the relation of its youth to the category of the kòbòlò, not as good-for-nothing lounger, but as part of the transitional phase of adjustment to city life.

As already pointed out, the main contrast between gymming and salsa lies in the different social fractions that participate in the two scenes. In general it is the middle classes and their transnational cohorts that tend to dominate the salsa scene, while the gymming scene is heavily oriented toward the under- or unemployed. The main exemplification of this contrast, however, is not the well-equipped gyms that have now sprung up all over the city and whose format replicates what may be encountered in large cities elsewhere in the world. The gyms at Pippa's, the Golden Tulip, or the Royal Richester Hotel that we visited have some of the most sophisticated equipment available. They also have extraordinarily high membership fees ranging from GHC 100–GHC 150 ($80–$130) per month, with drop-in fees of GHC 15–GHC 20 ($10–$15) per visit. As a rule these high-end gyms also have dedicated in-house instructors that charge a fee separate from membership fees to provide personalized attention to their customers; they also frequently run aerobics classes. The high-end gyms are fully air-conditioned and in many instances also have swimming pools attached to them. Given the exorbitant fees, the high-end gyms are evidently designed for the exclusive pleasure of the rich and famous. It was not unusual, for example, to meet the legendary Ghanaian soccer star Abedi Pele at Pippa's gym; and I was told that Pippa's was a popular meeting place for members of the Ghana Black Stars team. Both Michael Essien (of Chelsea and Real Madrid fame) and Sulley Muntari (of Portsmouth, Inter Milan, Sunderland, and more recently of AC Milan fame) have been known to visit Pippa's when in town. To top all that, Marcel Desailly, the Ghanaian-born ex-captain of the France soccer team has resettled in the country and opened Lizzy's Sports complex, a magnificent sports outfit at East Legon not far from Pippa's, replete with two full-scale soccer pitches, a swimming pool, and all the best sports equipment that can be dreamed of. It is currently the buzz of sports enthusiasts and has attracted attention from several African teams, some of which have used Desailly's sports complex's training facilities to prepare for tournaments. All the high-end gyms in Accra are located in environments that also provide drinking and other pleasant distractions, so that it is also not unusual for people "going to the gym" to break off for a bottle of beer or some other beverage on their way out. All the high-end gyms mentioned here are situated in such environments, with Pippa's perhaps being exemplary in this respect because of its location in the A and C Shopping Mall complex, with a full complement of shops, coffee bars, restaurants, accessible children's play areas, and handy car parking. A similar observation may be made with regard to the Tesano Sports Club, one of the oldest in the country and whose gym is part of a complex set up comprising tennis and squash courts, a large swimming pool, and a well-stocked bar and restaurant, all contained within the same premises. Going to the Tesano Sports Club has always been associated in the popular urban imagination with mixing with high-class people and having lots of fun. Pippa's and Tesano Sports Club are located at East Legon and at Tesano, respectively—both much sought-after upper-middle-class neighborhoods.

Different idiomatic expressions help distinguish high-end and working-class gym cultures. As a rule, someone going to do regular keep-fit exercises at a high-end gym will announce that he or she is simply "going to the gym." Participants in the high-end gym culture tend to have busy lifestyles and visit the gym as the opportunity presents itself, and sometimes to network, meet friends, and socialize after gym work. They are not strictly speaking gymmers as such. For the gymming scene, the preferred expression would be the pidgin "I dey go gym." The phrase "I dey go" in Ghanaian pidgin when followed by a noun or a verb means either "I am going to a place" or "I am going to perform an action," depending on the context. The word "gym" in the sentence just cited is often used as a verb, allowing the sentence to mean either "I am going to the gym" (on analogy with, say, going to the market), or as the performative action of gymming (on analogy with, say, running). The "doing" of gym is also conveyed in other formulations, such as "so-and-so dey gym hard these days" or "today we for gym at least two hours flat before we go home." One sharp contrast between going to the gym and doing gym is also to be seen in the difference between just keeping fit and becoming "macho" (i.e., becoming generally muscular and well built from bodybuilding). A further contrast in the two exercise cultures is to be seen in the differences between keep-fit clubs that may or may not have gyms attached to them and stand-alone gyms that are not part of a keep-fit club or some other such outfit. Several keep-fit clubs mushroomed in Accra in the 1980s, perhaps the most popular being Achimota Keep Fit Club. Keep-fit clubs are communal enterprises that often organize group outings in the form of marathons, fitness walking, and cycling for their members. Such clubs may also double up as welfare organizations, often arranging contributions on the bereavement of one of their number, or generally extending small loans when a member falls into one or other financial difficulty. It is not uncommon for keep-fit clubs to also organize neighborhood cleanup campaigns, thus placing an explicit social inflection to the question of keeping fit. (This was particularly common during Rawlings's accession to power in the 1980s.)

To complicate matters further, the Achimota Keep Fit Club in fact evolved from the Achimota Golf Club, which has traditionally drawn a large elite clientele from both Ghana and abroad. And it is also closely associated with Achimota Secondary School (Motown), which was opened by the colonial administration in 1927 and has, along with Mfantsipim (Kwabotwe) in Cape Coast, historically been the breeding ground for the country's political and cultural elites. In line with the link between the Achimota Keep Fit Club and the Achimota Golf Club, the keep-fit club model is in general often adopted by youth in a neighborhood as a vehicle for organizing sporting activities (typically soccer). Thus it is not unusual for the term "keep-fit club" to act as a synonym for sports club, something that became quickly evident when I first started researching the gymming phenomenon. Without exception the keep-fit clubs I visited at different locations had almost no interest in gymming as such, but mainly in organizing soccer matches or group jogs on the weekend for their members. Keeping fit is important for such clubs, but it is the collective social dimension of performing exercises together that essentially defines them. The gymming scene, on the other hand, is dominated by ideas of bodybuilding and body sculpting. As we shall see presently, the White Chapel Gym is very unusual in having a fully worked-out social vision, which derives predominantly from the organic relationship it has with its largely northern migrant neighborhood at Madina. The distinctions between keep-fit clubs and gymming cultures must also be attributed to generational differences. Older people tend to join keep-fit clubs while the younger generations tend toward gymming. There are also more married women in the keep-fit scene than there are in the gymming scene, generally making the former more family oriented than the latter.

Without exception the equipment at the working-class gyms we studied was a stunning testament to innovative forms of recycling. The equipment at the gyms was on the whole completely modest, with a heavy preponderance toward free weights rather than cardiovascular equipment. Everything had been put together from recycled car parts and materials. At the White Chapel Gym all their equipment had been assembled from Hyundai and Toyota car parts, while at First Fitness Gym the equipment was mainly from discarded army vehicles. The different sources of equipment had to do with the peculiar informal networks that the founders of the gyms had had with used Korean and Japanese car salesmen and retired army personnel, respectively. With the help of enterprising welders and automobile repairers, the gyms had customized all their own equipment from free weights to benches to the free-motion strength circuits (incredible designs!) to the weight bars and other equipment. As a rule aerobic equipment such as treadmills and bicycles was minimally present, and even when present their use was highly restricted because of concerns with electricity costs; early morning group jogs were undertaken to cover cardiovascular exercises at such gyms. All the working-class gyms were also much smaller in floor space than the high-end gyms we encountered earlier, with core memberships of twenty-five to forty regulars paying an average of between GHC 15–GHC 20 ($10–$15) per month. Due to unemployment the payment of membership dues was often done on an ad hoc basis, and it was not unusual for some members to pledge to pay up after they stumbled into good fortune or their economic circumstances changed for the better. Another marked contrast between these working-class gyms and the larger, high-end ones lay in the varying degrees of camaraderie and silence that could be found in the different settings. There was always light banter, the telling of all manner of personal and urban stories, lots of laughter, and mutual encouragement from members of the working-class gyms during their workouts, while in the high-end gyms clients conducted their exercises in almost complete silence unless they happened to have come along to the gym together. The giving and taking of unsolicited advice on appropriate diets and bodybuilding routines was also standard in the working-class gyms, with their gym organizers or leaders conventionally doubling up as free fitness instructors, something that was used to increase the attraction of the gym to potential members. There was clearly a sense of brotherhood in the working-class gyms that was completely absent from the high-end ones. This may also be due to the generally smaller size of the working-class gyms, so that on busy days it was practically impossible to get access to certain pieces of equipment without coming to an informal verbal agreement on who was next in line to use this or that dumbbell or weight. The waiting time was filled with chitchat and light banter. Contrastively the generally well-equipped nature of the high-end gyms meant that interaction was never a necessity, thus making it less likely that people would talk to one another.

Membership of the working-class gyms was also heavily gendered in favor of men, yet it was also clear that they felt highly flattered when women joined their number. A fair bit of subtle and not-so-subtle competitive preening took place among the male gymmers, since a central objective of gymming was sexual attractiveness to the opposite sex. The preening took place whether or not there were women around, and there were lots of stories (some quite ribald) told by the gymmers about encounters that they had had with women because of their fitness and physical appeal. It was not unusual to hear that some gymmers had met with foreign women and been able to "cut out" (i.e., go abroad), something that was evidently of interest to all the gymmers I spoke to. Anecdotal evidence suggests that some gymmers took bodybuilding steroids at least for a while during the gymming cycle of their lives. Among serious gymmers, however, those who had taken steroids are looked down upon. They were considered as not being good enough to "push" weights by their own strength and were often openly mocked for relying on help from drugs. Some gymmers also had quite detailed information on the history of bodybuilding in the West, with the names of Eugen Sandow, Attila the Strong, Arnold Schwarzenegger, and a few others featuring prominently in discussions. There did not seem to be matching knowledge of the activities of the Ghana Bodybuilding and Fitness Association (GBFA), an accredited organization of the National Sports Council. Admittedly, the GBFA was only accredited in 2006. It managed to run the tenth Mr. Africa Bodybuilding Championship in Accra in February 2011, in which bodybuilders from fifteen African countries participated in various categories.[2] However, none of the several gymmers I spoke to seemed to have much knowledge of the championship. This may be because it was pitched mainly at accredited bodybuilding professionals, which would immediately have ruled out the standard gymmers.

"Adwoa aaaay, Plenty Money Dey Soldier Line . . .":
Interpellations of Masculinity and the Scene of Gymming

At one point in *Aké: The Years of Childhood*, Wole Soyinka recounts the antics of a local lunatic who vows to face Hitler and his men squarely if they ever attempt to set foot on Aké soil.[3] This is in the midst of World War II, but because

Soyinka is writing his memoirs from the perspective of childhood, all the events of the war as they were felt in his hometown are covered with a patina of deflationary humor. Paa Adatan, the lunatic, uses his self-proclaimed bravery to get favors of food and money from the market women of Aké. When he is handed a few pennies by Wole's mother, he draws a straight line in front of her shop and declares: "Dat na in case they come while I dey chop eba for buka. If they try cross this line, guns go turn to broom for dem hand. Dem go begin dey sweeping dis very ground till I come back. Make dem try am make I see" (1981, 110–111). Later on the redoubtable Paa Adatan has to prove his mettle against some soldiers who come to purchase items at Wole's mother's shop, but after a brave struggle he is overpowered and tied up. The point of this short-lived but memorable character in Aké is to parody the war and to show how little it meant at the level of local existence in spite of its world-historical significance. For Soyinka the war does not invoke in the imagination the grand values of fortitude, courage, or resourcefulness. Rather, it is figured in the text as somewhat laughable and, in the context of Aké, largely insignificant.

The parodic representation of the war in Soyinka's text is in direct contrast to the historic impact that soldiers and the military have had on many African societies. The soldier returning from war attracted immense interest because of the stories about different parts of the world he had been to. He was also the focal point of a variety of political and communal interests. As many African political historians of the period have noted, soldiers demobilized after World War II provided a ready pool of disaffected and restless young men (they were all exclusively men) that helped to intensify the decolonization struggle. The fateful events that took place in Accra on February 28, 1948—when war veterans marching to Christiansborg Castle were fired upon and three of them were killed—was but the tip of the iceberg of social disaffection that had been festering since the start of the war. However, the image of the soldier also made an impact on quite a different domain of significance, namely, on the aesthetic appeal of muscular masculinity. To understand this impact, we will have to look at the status of the warrior-soldier in the precolonial and colonial periods, the formation of the army and police under colonialism, and the overall impact that the image of the well-built soldier was to have on the social imaginary under J. J. Rawlings throughout the 1980s and 1990s.

Even though warfaring ethnic groups such as the Ashanti, the Akwamu, the Gonja, and the Dagomba had well-known and much-feared standing armies, these did not displace smaller private militia groups among them. And in the coastal areas, wealthy merchants took the title of *obrempon* (big man; Ga *oblempon*) and raised private militias as part of their retinue. In addition to this, merchant warlords also raised their own private armies to fend off European political and economic domination (recall Okaija in the 1720s, whom we encountered in chapter 3). Military historian Festus Aboagye points to an important exception to these private armies: "A singular departure would be the Zabrama army of Babatu in the 1890s, which was bidding, through the weight of intervention wars and campaigns, to carve out a Zabrama 'mercenary' state from among the Grunshi, and perhaps among the Bassari, Gonja and Dagbon states as well. Thus, the Zabrama army of Babatu was initially a private army, which through political and military machinations evolved into a quasi-national army" (Aboagye 2010, 193). As we shall see shortly, the process Aboagye describes here of an initially private army providing the seeds for a national force would come to be replicated in the hands of the colonial administration itself, but on a larger and more multiethnic scale.

Drawing upon European accounts of Ga military organization, John Kwadwo Osei-Tutu also notes two categories of warriors that could be found in the colony from the seventeenth to the nineteenth centuries. First were "soldier-retainers or bodyguards as well as . . . mercenaries and professional soldiers (including their slaves)" who were employed by Ga chiefs and wealthy merchants (Osei-Tutu 2002, 20). Among these soldiers were also numbered Dutch mercenaries and sailors, who were retained at an exorbitant cost to local chiefs (Osei-Tutu 2002). The second category comprised socio-military groups (*csafoi*, sing. *asafo*), formed from free citizens that subsequently evolved into autonomous organizations through which the influence of the youth could be exerted on the chiefly and political elites of each town (Osei-Tutu 2002, 21; also Aboagye 2010, chapter 4). Testament to the influence of the asafo groups on Accra's political and cultural landscape is still marked by street names, such as Asafoatse Nettey Road, which lies in front of the Bank of Ghana in the Central Business District.[4] The title of *asafoatse* (father of the asafo) was conferred upon the leader of this quasi-military organization and often implied someone who had had experience in war. In Ga culture the asafoatse is very highly regarded and has historically been known to have been an active participant in chieftaincy disputes. European merchants on the coast also organized local militia to protect the commercial routes leading to and from the European forts and castles.[5]

Beyond the Ga, various ethnic communities in the Gold Coast Colony also had their own militias (in contrast to standing armies or those drawn from compulsory conscription during times of war), the most prominent of these being the militias among the Fantis and the Ashantis. Upon being made governor at Cape Coast in 1830, Captain George Maclean took over the command and organization of the militiamen attached to European merchants on the coast. However, increasing disputes with the Ashanti kingdom meant that the informally trained militias were no longer adequate to the task of protecting European interests. The Ashanti War of 1873–1874 was to prove a turning point in the reconfiguration of local militias. In the 1860s Captain John Glover had recruited several hundred Hausa and Yoruba mercenaries in northern Nigeria for the formation of a militia force to protect the colony of Lagos. A large number of these mercenaries were runaway slaves. Seven hundred of Glover's Hausa Constabulary, as they were then called, were sent to the Gold Coast to be deployed in the Anglo-Ashanti War. They were augmented by discharged British soldiers from Sierra Leone and the Gambia, along with the Fanti Force, the local militia at Cape Coast. By the time this enlarged militia invaded Ashanti in 1873, they numbered eighteen hundred men and this led in no small part to the defeat of the Ashantis. In 1876 their name of Gold Coast Hausa Constabulary was changed to the Gold Coast Constabulary. The Police Ordinance of 1894 encouraged the recruitment of four hundred members of the Gold Coast Hausa Constabulary for the formation of an embryonic police force, but while they were now to provide civil duties, military training was still maintained to accommodate emerging crises and security exigencies within the colony. In 1901 this group was further split into the Gold Coast Constabulary and the Gold Coast Regiment, which was later itself integrated into the Royal West African Frontier Force. However, the separation of police and military functions remained more rhetorical than real, such that despite the creation in 1921 of separate escort, mines, and railway units, the police remained essentially an armed force "directed at the paramilitary protection of political and, especially, economic interests of the colonial powers" (Deflem 1994, 52).

As Anthony Clayton and David Killingray note, the performance of Hausas and of men drawn from other northern tribes in the Anglo-Ashanti wars had a major impact on peacetime recruitment into the colonial forces throughout the period. Colonial recruitment into the early police/army was based on the notion of a "martial race." From the earliest incarnation of Glover's Hausa Constabulary onward, recruitment had been heavily from among northerners, both in Nigeria and in the Gold Coast. In the Gold Coast, there was thus a heavy preponderance of men from the Northern Territories, most of who were Muslim and spoke Hausa. They were treated as though they were from the same tribal grouping, which meant essentially the imposition of a homogenizing colonial rubric upon a disparate cluster of ethnicities. Colonial thinking assumed that northerners were more manly and dedicated, and able to traverse long stretches of land on foot without getting tired or indeed complaining. Behind this notion of manliness, however, was also the idea that northerners were less contaminated by the European and Christian ways of the south. Colonial administrators in Nigeria, for example, opined that Ibos were wily and never to be trusted, mainly because of the negative effect Christianity had had in softening their character and making them overly bold and demanding (Clayton and Killingray 1989, 175–192). But it must also be remembered that in relation to the Ashanti wars colonial recruitment practices fell in line with the divide-and-rule tactics they came to deploy consistently throughout the colonial period. As will be recalled from Aboagye's observation, Babatu set up a private army whose ultimate objective was the forging of a Zabrama state. This was not his only objective. He was also keen to protect his people from Gonja slave raids, undertaken at the time to satisfy the requirement to pay annual tribute to the Ashanti kingdom.

During the period of the slave trade, the vast geographical region that later came to be designated by the colonial administration as the Northern Territories had already had a long and fraught interaction with the Ashanti. Ashanti invaded Dagomba in 1744–1745 and when the Dagombas sued for peace and protection, they were required to render an annual tribute of five hundred slaves, two hundred cattle, four hundred sheep, four hundred cotton cloths, and two hundred cotton and silk cloths to the Ashanti king. Ashanti power also extended to the Gonja, where Salaga had became a major slave entrepôt by the end of the eighteenth century. Periodic rebellion by the Dagomba and Gonja issued in punitive Ashanti expeditions.[6] The assimilation of men from the northern tribes into the expeditionary force that would come to defeat the Ashanti was then pitting old enemies against each other under the aegis of a new colonial military apparatus. Furthermore, because Ashanti did not fully fall under the control of the British until its occupation in 1896, the Emancipation Ordinance of 1874 debarring slavery was not observed there. Several slaves escaped from Ashanti to settle in villages in the Accra plains as well as within the town itself. Most ex-slaves in villages such as Abokobi and Apenkwa were Dagombas and Grunshies that "appear to have escaped captivity in Ashanti . . . by way of the Fanti states" (Miers and Roberts 1988, 89).[7] Recruitment into colonial expeditionary forces and subsequently into the police and army may also have been an instrument of colonial intervention into post-slavery conditions in the colony and elsewhere. The colonial recruitment policy was later to have a major impact on patterns of migration and settlement in southern towns, including Kumasi and Accra. Upon demobilization many northern soldiers who had been deployed as part of the Gold Coast Constabulary or the army in these towns settled in zongos or stranger quarters.[8]

During the colonial period the preference for recruitment from the north was applied predominantly to the non-commissioned officer (NCO) class, while the officer class remained staffed by British men and only much later by suitably educated Africans, and mainly from the South. In Ghana the northern policy of recruitment into the NCO class in both the police and the army was to continue practically undiluted until the 1980s, when the accession of J. J. Rawlings to power finally put paid to the idea that only northerners could make good security personnel. His regime introduced a broad quota system for entry into the army so no single ethnic group could remain dominant. And yet the idea of a "martial race" remains a firm part of popular lore in Ghana to this day. It is not unusual to hear people say that northerners are the bravest, most honest, and also most dependable members of the police and army and that they make loyal private security officers.

Another aspect of militias in Ghana's history came with the emergence of Neighborhood Watch Committees for the purpose of community self-protection that developed as an explicit dimension of security policy during the Rawlings era. These NWCs developed as offshoots of the Committees for the Defence of the Revolution (CDRs) that had been established in December 1984 to replace the disbanded People's Defence Committees introduced into the political system from January 1982. The CDRs were established in every neighborhood in the country in a stratified system that incorporated the district, regional, and finally the national versions at the top of which perched the ruling junta itself: the People's National Defence Council (PNDC). In addition to the new political structure inspired in the main by governance models in Cuba and Libya, Rawlings was also to send several youths to Cuba for military training. On their return these youths were drafted into a People's Militia and were referred to by the simple moniker of "militia" for short. Many of these young men (and a few women) had been taken away in their late teens to early twenties and on their return became significant instruments of social intervention. The regime's original objective had been for the militias to be reintegrated into their various NWCs and to help with local security affairs, but it did not take long for them to be seen as exclusively loyal to the regime and to Rawlings himself. Sleek and always smartly dressed in military fatigues, the militias remained a constant source of revulsion, awe, and wonder for the rest of the population. The combination of NWCs, militias, and the CDRs was an unconscious reprisal of the long history of militias that had evolved from the precolonial European mercantile period, as we have already noted.

The alteration of the exclusive and official association of northerners with special martial character in Rawling's 1980s went side by side with the spread of an image of the well-built soldier as a desirable figure of emulation, at least in his or her physical form. This shift to what might be considered a purely aesthetic function for the martial body must be understood as part of a wider discursive shift in the image of muscular masculinity that was inaugurated under Rawlings. From his second coming at the end of 1981, soldiers were no longer secluded in their barracks but were instead given a ubiquitous (and some would say baneful) social presence among civilians, often performing functions previously undertaken by the police: directing traffic, making civil arrests, and guarding various public installations. It was also not unknown for soldiers and the militias to be deployed as agents of political and oftentimes even personal vendettas, giving both groups an unsavory reputation among the population. The structural adjustment programs instigated by the IMF from the mid to late 1980s referred to in chapter 4 were also to trigger major social dislocations, with vast numbers of unemployed youths turned out onto the streets to fend for themselves. The period also marked the second substantial wave of migration out of the country, with the first, a mere trickle in comparison, having taken place just after independence in the 1960s and mainly tied to the quest for educational opportunities abroad.[9] The waves of Ghanaians to Nigeria had been ongoing since the economy started seriously wobbling in the late 1970s, but the early 1980s marked the real big surge of emigration, first to Libya, and after the mid-1980s to various parts of Europe. Those youth who were unfortunate enough to remain behind were exposed to a constant image feed of the well-built and attractive military figure, with Rawlings at the core of this discursive imagescape. He has always been a highly charismatic figure, and upon his emergence onto the political scene made it plain that he was much interested in keeping fit and maintaining a tough image of masculinity. For a while in the early years of his reign, he bore the nickname of "Junior Jesus" (from his initials J. J.—Jerry John), and many young men were inspired to behave like him. His signature aviator sunglasses, worn at all times of day and night, were a fundamental part of the persona of the revolutionary air force pilot, giving them an immediate veneer of fashionableness. While Ghana's

Fourth Republican democratic dispensation has been in place since January 1993 and coincides with Rawlings's conversion from military leader to civilian statesman, this did not necessarily mean a complete attenuation of the image of the military man or indeed of his visibility in the public sphere. That was to come only eight years later with the election victory of the more civilian-minded National Patriotic Party in 2000. Much muscling around of people (both literally and metaphorically) along with a machismo culture of impunity was in evidence throughout the nineteen years of Rawlings's rule. As things turned out, many unemployed men and women attempted to get into the army during the period and when they failed, as most of them invariably did, they were attracted to gymming and to the overall economy of bodybuilding. As a good example, Emmanuel (Emma), an instructor at the First Fitness Gym, was first converted to gymming by a soldier who had opened a gym in his neighborhood in the early 1990s. The soldier took Emma and his friends through rigorous military-style exercises and barked rapid commands as if he was training them for the army. This early training was to have a major impact on Emma's sense of being a gymmer, and he was not the only one I interviewed who had been inspired by the image of muscular military masculinity.

The attractions of muscular masculinity that came into prominence during the long Rawlings era must, however, be placed in the context of other cultural discourses that helped to compound the repertoire of male image making in the country. The eighteen-month dusk-to-dawn curfew introduced by Rawlings between 1982 and 1984 served to completely alter the leisure industry. One of its offshoots was the death of all the famous movie theatres such as Orion, Opera, Odeon, Palladium, and so forth that had previously specialized in showing Bollywood and Chinese films. The kung fu films of the 1970s were especially popular with boys, who did not fail to try all kinds of kung fu and karate moves on the playground. The demise of these movie theatres coincided with the use of the VCR in the immensely popular daytime video parlors that sprang up all over the city to cater to the movie-loving populace. But as the Bollywood and Chinese movie industries lagged behind in formatting their movies for the VCR, this in turn meant the flooding of Ghana's market with movies from Hollywood. The VCR became a prime and perhaps the most important instrument for altering leisure values and thoroughly Americanizing them among the populace. Within a short time, all Bollywood and kung fu movies had been quickly replaced by Hollywood action movies, with the Arnold Schwarzenegger and Jean-Claude Van Damme series of blockbusters coming to completely dominate the imagination of many Ghanaian youth that flocked to the now-ubiquitous VCR parlors. Coinciding as it did with the already-strong military-inflected masculinity put into circulation by Rawlings, these Hollywood blockbusters ensured that the image of the muscular action hero came to compound the already-existing discourses of muscular masculinity that were in circulation at the time.

Two further complications we ought to note regarding aggressive muscularity are that (a) most forms of muscularity were at least until the change in qualifications required for entry into the noncommissioned officer class associated almost exclusively with the military, the police, and by a curious transposition, with illiteracy; and (b) muscularity was, and to a certain degree still is, associated with either violent or criminal tendencies. The strenuous physical training that is universally enjoined for the military and other security services also ensures that the sculpting of the body is inextricably linked to the regimes of formality that the security apparatus invokes. The sanctioned forms of physical training tied to the formal domains of the police and army may be interpreted as representing the larger framework of instrumentalism that inheres in these two domains, with the body thus the correlative of such instrumentalism. Since bodybuilding competitions have not historically provided a viable forum for the explicit display of the sculpted body as an object of pure aesthetic contemplation, it is the largely instrumentalist appeal put into circulation by the Western-style security apparatus that has remained dominant in Ghana. The combination of these two factors—the grafting of physical training to militarized institutional spheres and the absence of a platform for contemplating the sculpted body's aesthetic appeal as such—has ensured that bodybuilding and gymming have developed under the sign of a profound contradiction. Gymmers have been left to draw mainly on the athletic/aggressive muscularity put in in the public sphere by figures of military men such as Rawlings. This has in turn been amplified through the imagescapes of aggressive muscularity that abound in Hollywood that also came to dominate popular culture in Ghana and much of Africa from the 1980s. If the harshness of the stereotypes attaching to muscularity has been attenuated with time, it is still the case that a "macho" man falling on the wrong side of the law is normally assumed to confirm the idea that the entire bodybuilding/gymming scene is given to aggression and bears an inherent moral deficit.[10] All macho men are implicated in the bad fate of any one of their number, something that the gymmers I interviewed were at pains to criticize and distance themselves from at all cost.[11] Given the general perception that they are potentially violent and criminal, gymmers take extraordinary pains to at least be *seen* as law-abiding. Thus they exert immense effort to make themselves directly relevant to society, predominantly by helping to quell trouble wherever they happen to find themselves. Countless stories are told of a macho man voluntarily stepping forward to put down trouble at venues he happens to be present at or, as is often also the case, to resolve conflicts inside of his own community.

Notwithstanding the image of aggressive muscularity described thus far, another discourse that appears to be its negation and that is also well rooted within the Ghanaian social imaginary and that has to be read in dialectical relationship to it is the discourse of desirable chubbiness. Chubbiness here covers a broad spectrum of body types, stretching from carrying a few extra pounds to being moderately overweight. Obesity itself is the subject of considerable concern and not thought to be incredibly attractive among Ghanaians, especially with the growing awareness of the links between obesity and various chronic diseases. In the Ghanaian traditional culture that also tips decisively into the cosmopolitan domain, a chubby body is conventionally considered the source of potential largesse and a sign of success, power, and definitely a good degree of sexual attractiveness.[12] It is not uncommon for Ghanaians to comment on how well a person looks by saying, "ei, you have put on ooh," meaning "you have gained a bit of weight," which is considered a very good thing. This applies to both men and women. For most people in Ghana, the lean or overly slim adult body is associated with poverty, lack, or downright meanness. Hence as a general rule impoverished people who might be quite lean and have good muscular definition quickly strive to gain weight as soon as they shift into a higher income bracket. This is well illustrated in the pictures that people send upon going for long sojourns abroad. Almost without fail the unstated objective is to show that the traveler has not done too badly; the shorthand signature for this is the display of some form of weight gain. This is not to suggest that a lean and fit body is not admired in Ghanaian society, but that it is definitely not the hegemonic norm within the social imaginary. Attractive masculinity is defined in terms of power, influence, and financial wherewithal, and a well-fed body is taken as a correlative of such elements. We shall return to the contradictions between the discourses of muscularity and chubbiness a bit later, for now only noting that what passes for physical attractiveness in Ghana is far from homogeneous and carries different and sometimes even conflicting contextual inflections.

Because most gymmers are poor and it is their un- or underemployment that gives them the free time to take to gymming, the ones I spoke to without exception said they wanted to be able to "cut out." The desire to leave the country to seek out better economic possibilities is not unusual among Ghanaian youth, but the repeated ideal of life in Hollywood seems to be most strongly articulated among members of the gymming community. Gymming is thus an aspect of the negotiation of urban free time at the interface of a complex imaginary, partly driven by images of aggressive masculinity generated from within the country, but also heavily inflected by the imagescapes of the discourse of aggressive muscularity popularized by Hollywood. In this gymmers occupy a similar position to the category of the kòbòlò, for whom free time is a burden that must be replaced by employment in the tedious cycle of urban life. Like gymmers, the kòbòlò's time spent waiting for better opportunities is also filled with epic dreaming of an economic kind.

The Kòbòlò and the Problematic of Free Time

The Ga word "kòbòlò" (pl. kòbèlòi) is defined primarily as a good-for-nothing street lounger. However, it turns out on closer inspection to be a much more complex sociological category that encapsulates a transitional state of urban existence at the intersecting vectors of space, time, and longing. While there are female kòbòlòi (more on this group later), the term normally designates a masculine sphere of urban crisis.

If economists describe the kòbòlò in terms tied predominantly to the informal economy, it should also be noted that the term ultimately transcends any inert economic categorization. Akin to the area boy in Lagos popular lore, the term "kòbòlò" also has resonance with the Dakarois *fakhman*, a term that designates a good-for-nothing street loiterer and potential criminal.[13] Like the area boy and the fakhman, the kòbòlò combines the meanings of good-for-nothing rascal and mischief maker, and sometimes incorporates features of the petty criminal. The kòbòlò is at once all and none of these and has to be defined via a number of specific sociocultural features alongside the economic one. There is a certain edginess to being a kòbòlò in Accra, displayed first and foremost by the attachment to street life, but also in the preferred speech forms (typically pidgin English), dress codes, and overall cheeky swagger that marks the kòbòlò's overall demeanor: one may even be accused of "walking like a kòbòlò." Even though the social category of kòbòlò extends from street kids to young adults, the pertinent sociological detail is not age but the fact that kòbòlòi are in a *structural transition between socially acceptable age-related activities*. Thus with respect to children, for example, the kòbòlò is the street kid who is not in school, either by choice or parental neglect. The first adult reaction on seeing a child in uniform on a school day out on the streets of Accra is to ask whether he or she is doing kòbòlò things (to bò ko is an intransitive verb which means being kòbòlò, i.e., doing such things that kòbòlòi are presumed to do). The young-adult kòbòlò, on the other hand, is seen to be between life phases, looking for a job, or as often happens in an age of travel, for a way out of the country. It is also not unusual for the kòbòlò to be between short-term, low paying jobs in the informal economy, the defining condition here being not the jobs themselves but the existential condition of impermanence that they generate by being both low-paying and transitory. The young-adult kòbòlò is never perceived as a tramp or beggar as that is a distinct social category altogether; if he lacks a place to return home to he may spend the night on the street, but this is not a feature that the kòbòlò is predominantly defined by. The most important vector of the kòbòlò's identity is street life, for the young-adult kòbòlò does not become so by choice; he is always on a quest to escape the vagaries of such existence. The period of transition of the kòbòlò may be short or long, but the crucial detail is that the kòbòlò has only attenuated social and familial obligations during the relevant phase of transition; the exit from this phase is immediately marked by the taking seriously of such obligations if they exist, or by adopting them if they don't. Settling down to marriage, children, and a responsible job are all signs of moving out of the kòbòlò phase.

As noted in previous chapters, the street is both a spatial vector and the producer of cultural logics by virtue of the social interactions that it enables and instantiates. The kòbòlò is not the only category from street life that might be deployed for understanding the relationship between social interaction, labor dispositions, and the urban street. Thus while food vendors in Accra are mostly women, kòbòlòi tend to be men. This does not mean that there is a strict gender demarcation between the two categories, but that the predominance of one or other gender within a particular intersection of vectors (spatial, labor, etc.) has to be taken into account in explaining the gendered socioeconomic relationships that each category implies. For example, a focus on the social category of the kayayoo (female head porter), which is also common at lorry parks and markets all over the city, would produce a different understanding of social relationships than that of the kòbòlò.[14] Another inflection might be produced by looking at the category of street children, whose transitional economic status is much more problematic and fraught than that of either the kayayoo or the kòbòlò.

The problem of the kòbòlò's transitional adjustment to urban life is also typically a feature of rural-urban migration, where new migrants to the city have no immediate ties to the urban economic nexus and yet must be integrated into the labor market as a necessary aspect of their survival. The vast expansion in urban populations along with the dramatic dislocations in urban life since the oil crises of the 1970s has spelled an ineffectual integration of the increasingly large numbers of rural poor who find themselves in urban conurbations across the continent. This has also greatly expanded the informal economy of African cities. It was Keith Hart who first conceived the term "informal economy" in the 1970s to describe Ghana's vast yet at the time grossly misunderstood nonwage labor sector.[15] His original study of the variegations of the economic sector has remained definitive for understanding the informal economy in Africa and other parts of the developing world. In general terms the formal sector refers to wage employment that is documented and registered by the state, while the informal sector refers to nonwage labor that lacks the predictability and economic security of formal sector work.[16] As a general rule, the informal sector is marked by fantastic entrepreneurial aspiration, something that is especially highlighted by Esther de Bruijn in her study of the Ghanaian market literature industry (2013). Hart's observations on the fantastic aspirations that are born out of the informal sector are still true in Accra today and are also the product of the disjunctures produced by global capitalism. As he puts it, "Petty capitalism . . . offers itself as a means of salvation. If only the right chance came, urban workers could break out of the nexus of high living costs and low wages which is their lot."[17] Seeing that approximately 85 percent of the active Ghanaian workforce is in the informal sector and that this includes at least 60 percent of the residents of Accra, some of whom are formally employed and yet work part-time in the informal sector, the informal economy defines the lives and livelihoods of most of the city's residents.[18] Workers in this grouping include the likes of tailors, hairdressers, shoe repairers, vulcanizers, tro-tro drivers and their assistants (called "mate" in Ghana), head porters, hawkers of various kinds of goods, sellers in markets and at roadside stalls, artisans, and many others often misrecognized as unemployed.[19] Their ranks are also joined by the confidence trickster who makes his living by preying upon the misplaced aspirations of urban dwellers for the get-rich-quick scheme or the ability to get a visa to go abroad. The current crop of evangelical pastors that have sprung up all over the city may be added to this lot. The kòbòlò may occupy one of these enumerated roles, or as is often the case, may take up several of them either simultaneously or in sequence as the opportunity presents itself. And because legitimacy "is derived essentially from Ghana's laws and presumably coincides with the morality of 'respectable' Ghanaians," the informal sector is assumed by most economic observers to lie firmly within the domain of illegality, a perception that, however, lacks nuance and complexity.[20] As Carolyn Nordstrom (2007) has shown, the informal sector, as distinct from the private sector, is an essential part of all economies worldwide, even in the advanced economies of the West. For African economies the distinction derives from the relative size of the informal economy and the degree of shading between that and the formal sector. The forever-expanding phase of "waiting for a job" has thus gradually been filled by new social forms as well as existential modes of negotiating the economic lacunae of such a condition. Thus the question of the kòbòlò must ultimately be understood as a question of dislocated urban life in an uncertain economic world. As we shall see presently, the Madina Zongo neighborhood provides us with a good example of migrant dwellers in the city who may become kòbòlòi as part of the negotiation of urban life.

Given the kòbòlò's position within the structure of urban transition, the most salient feature of this sociological category is not whether they are law-abiding or not but rather the degree to which they are burdened by free time. Put formulaically, the poor have free time while the rich have leisure. For the kòbòlò free time is a function of un- or underemloyment and the effort to trade free time for labor time or wages is a critical impulse of the condition. Free time in this respect is then an aspect of the kòbòlò's potential assimilability to the dominant yet fragile economic system that is sustained by the interface between formality and informality, which the kòbòlò often bitterly critiques but of which he wishes to be a part precisely as a means of escaping the brutal vagaries of free time. It would, however, be a cardinal error to romanticize the individual kòbòlò's attachment to street life: he is no flâneur or one for solitude. His wanderings are driven by the desire toward self-improvement, and his engagement with the urban is a conduit for augmenting the skills required to "make it" or die trying. Finally, while most kòbòlòi tend to have only basic education, with the increase of unemployment in the country their ranks have been swollen in the last decade with graduates from various tertiary institutions.

From the standpoint of the kòbòlòi's attitude to urban space, it is also evident that they do not represent a homogeneous spatial category. A correlative of their impulse toward mobility and self-improvement is that they tend to cluster around certain economically active hubs both on and off the street. These vary according to the dynamics of spatial and turf constraints, but it is not unusual to find a heavy concentration of kòbòlòi at lorry parks, markets, filling stations, and generally at places that represent an explicit concentration of *people on the move*. The distribution of kòbòlòi on Oxford

Street also shows that apart from clustering around the several banks, forex bureaus, restaurants, and filling stations, they also tend to congregate around specifically youth-oriented locations such as nightclubs and fast-food joints. We may thus productively break down this sociological category further in relation to the spatial locations or hangouts they may be found at in order of priority: car and passenger-mobility concentration sites (lorry parks, filling stations, where there are immediate opportunities for making some money); a combination of both carpooled and people-concentrated sites, such as at the famous Makola Market in the Central Business District of Accra where the Rawlings Park combines with the famous market to provide a broad range of opportunities; or much less commonly at heavily people-concentrated sites (restaurants, shops, the Accra Mall, etc.), where the kòbòlòi also tend to provide a variety of services, such as valet parking and security for parked vehicles, assistance with carrying of shopping bags, and so on. Exercise gyms provide another location for the kòbòlòi; these are distinctive from the other sites just noted because of the direct and intensely competitive focus on body image and self-sculpting that emerges here as an essential aspect of negotiating the burdens of free time. Kòbòlòi spatial orientations are by no means mutually exclusive. Indeed a kòbòlò may have different cluster points and may weave between them as mood or opportunity dictates.

"If You Want to Survive in the World, Chale, Weight Is the Answer"

The opinion above was proffered by a gymmer at a focus group discussion meeting Samuel Ntewusu and I organized with members of the White Chapel Gym in August 2010. It was a view warmly shared by other members of the group and one that was expressed subsequently in a variety of ways at other gyms. However, in the particular context of the Madina Zongo where White Chapel is located, this opinion bears wider implications about the status of northern migrants in today's Accra.

The Hausa word "zongo" means simply "stranger quarters" and is normally used in Ghana to designate the communities occupied predominantly by people from the north of the country.[21] The zongos in Accra include Tudu, Sabon Zongo, Nima, Mallam, Accra New Town, Sodom and Gomorrah, and Madina Zongo. Stranger communities date from the trans-Saharan slave trade, an important feature of which was the creation of special migrant quarters in various towns along the commercial routes that were traversed by the caravans that plied them bearing goods and often also human beings for sale from North Africa and beyond. In the nineteenth century, one of the most famous of these stranger quarters was the slave market at Salaga in today's Northern Region of Ghana. Many zongos also developed in coastal towns to take advantage of trade with Europeans, with the period of British rule also seeing a systematic consolidation of such migrant quarters for people from the Northern Territories.[22] As we noted earlier, the opportunities to work in the Gold Coast Constabulary and in the army also enticed many northern men to move south. The reasons for the migration of northerners to the south of the country may have varied over time, but they include the effects of the slave trade, greater opportunities for work in the South, and the structure of the colonial tax system and the land policies that made it difficult for northerners to subsist on agricultural production. The various wars and ethnic conflicts that took place in the late 1980s and early 1990s in northern Ghana also led to major population displacements to the south. Thus Madina Zongo, along with the other zongos in Accra, has always been a concentration point for migrants from the north among whom has solidified a sense of cultural differentiation from their surrounding communities of southerners. This and the fact that all northerners were banded together under a single ethnic label by the colonial government and subsequently by many southerners have also served to consolidate a sense of collective identity for them that is both chosen by the community and imposed by others. On closer inspection, however, every zongo has a distinct demographic constitution. Ntewusu points out in his study of Madina that currently the largest northern ethnic group of the township is the Kotokolis, with the Nawuris being the smallest. However, the very early settlers at Madina were mainly Zabrama and Gao, and first arrived between 1959 and 1966 while Ewes, Akans, and some Muslim Gas joined their number between 1968 and 1973 (Ntewusu 2005).[23] Madina Zongo was founded by Alhaji Seidu Kardo in 1959 after an initial dispute regarding his right and that of his followers to settle at Shiashie (today's West Legon), some seven miles from Accra and close to the University of Ghana at Legon. Alhaji Kardo and his followers had been asked to vacate the Shiashie land because of government plans to expand the airport and the motorway leading from it following the urban expansions that took place after World War II. (Neither of these in the end came anywhere close to the site of the original Shiashie settlement.) In compensation Kardo and his followers were offered land three miles farther north from Shiashie at the present-day Madina Zongo. Kardo suggested that the site be called Madina after its namesake in Mecca, and it was only several years later when Madina had attracted many other ethnicities and become a bustling township that the name zongo was attached to the original neighborhood where Seidu and his followers had initially settled. The designation of Madina Zongo as a zongo after the fact, and when it was actually not a stranger quarter but the founding settlement of a larger township, may have been due to the labeling that was conventionally used to help migrants from the north to easily identify the Muslim and largely Hausa-speaking quarters in any township they arrived at down south. In 1964 a second wave of northern migrants came to join Seidu and his followers. Dagadu, who had initially been given a piece of land by the La mantse Nii Anyetei Kwakwaranya II to establish a settlement at Botor, led this second wave. This second group asked to move from the Botor land because it had been designated by Nkrumah's government for the building of a trade-fair site earlier in the same year. Some of the people at Botor decided to move to other zongos such as Nima, Tudu, and Cow Lane that were closer to their original location, but several others went with Dagadu to the new land assigned to them by the La mantse at Madina. In both the Kardo and Dagadu migrations to Madina, the shared trigger was their displacement from original locations in other parts of the city due to government urban-development plans.[24] The pattern of such internal urban displacements seems to have mainly affected migrants from the North, something that distinguishes them sharply from, say, the people at Ga Mashie who have robustly resisted being moved from their original locations to make way for any form of development project or, indeed, rehabilitation schemes. The nature of such internal displacements also illustrates the tenuous relationship that northern migrants have historically had to urban lands—a fact that further consolidates their identification as sojourners and thus "from the north," despite some northerners having been resident in the city for several generations after the Anglo-Ashanti wars of the 1870s.

What made White Chapel Gym the most distinctive among the ones Ntewusu and I visited was the explicit and sophisticated understanding of the roles they had to play as an integral part of the Madina Zongo community. The life itineraries of Tanko and a few others at the gym confirm the essential lineaments of northern migrants' life cycles and their integration into zongo communities in the south. Tanko is thirty-two and comes from Zabrama parents. His father and grandfather originally came from Niger and were among the early cattle traders in Accra in the 1940s and 1950s. Later his father branched out into selling jute bags. These occupations fall in line with the general occupations of many northern migrants to Accra after independence, as noted by Ntewusu in his study from 2005. Trade in kola nut or cattle was often the first point of entry for those who styled themselves primarily as traders, and the sale of jute bags was an aspect of urban livelihood diversification for northerners in Accra as many of them found themselves having to provide bagging services for maize, cassava, and other agricultural products from other parts of the country at Accra's large markets. Contrastively thirty-year-old Abdulai Salia's family hails from Sisala in the Tumu district of the Upper West Region. He came to settle in Madina after his university education. His father is a driver and his mother a trader, and the entire family live in Kumasi where Abdulai himself was born. After senior secondary school there, Abdulai was admitted to Legon to read English and sociology, and after completing his degree decided to remain at Madina Zongo. He started gymming at the White Chapel while looking for a permanent job. Having been out of university since he was twenty-three, he found the wait long and boring, and gymming helped him to cope. Happily, after some five years and through his gymming and participation in the various security-related activities with other members of the White Chapel Gym, he was recruited into the Ghana Fire Service and was lucky enough to be posted again to Madina after his training. He still comes to White Chapel whenever the opportunity presents itself. A third gym member, Abdul Razak Adam, is thirty-one and of Wangara descent. His father works as a driver for the Ghana Cocoa Marketing Board, and his mother is a trader in Madina. Razak is currently a land agent and sells land around Madina, Abokobi, and surrounding places. This is a job firmly located within the informal economic sector and thus open to all the vagaries and inventiveness that Keith Hart spoke of in his study. Collectively Tanko, Abdulai, and Razak represent the different trajectories that northerners have followed in migrating and settling in southern cities in Ghana. Fundamentally, however, it is the zongo communities such as that at Madina that provide them with a safe social haven out of which they navigate their life cycles through the city.

Tanko and the other members of the White Chapel Gym we interviewed agreed that a strong group solidarity exists in the zongo because they all feel they are essentially foreigners in Accra and marginalized socially, economically, and politically. To quote Tanko on this subject: "This sense of marginalization has created a sense of belongingness to the extent that each defends the other. Usually the police are attacked any time they want to arrest anybody within the community. As a result the Madina Police Commander has to depend on members of the gym who mostly are members of the Neighbourhood Watch Committee to make arrests on his behalf." Tanko and his friends prided themselves on their Neighborhood Watch Committee and a White Chapel Welfare Association that had also helped extend their activities well beyond the immediate concern with bodybuilding. Haatso, Adenta, and the wider Madina township, along with Legon, are all places they scour at night to prevent criminal activities. Even though their claims to be a steady arm of policing in the wider Madina township may have been somewhat exaggerated, members of the gym asserted with pride that they had completely wiped out petty theft and robbery within the zongo area itself.

Yet it is not just the consciousness of providing security that occupied the minds of the members of the White Chapel Gym. They were also quite keen to project weightlifting as a valuable sport and leisure activity that is safe and to be practiced by very respectable people such as themselves. One of the ways they achieved this objective of respectability was to organize regular public social events at which they set up demonstrations and informal lectures on weightlifting. At one football (soccer) match we recorded between members of the gym and the general public at the local park, gym equipment was moved onto the pitch and a competition was set up to help select players for each side. Anyone wanting to play on either team had to lift weights starting at seventy pounds before they were allowed on the teams. It turns out that this was a clever ploy designed to eliminate any professional football player who might come to play so that the gymmers could avoid embarrassment. Tanko stated as much at the interview:

First of all we want to advertise ourselves. Every one passing by the park will know that today is a day for macho men. Also anytime that we play football you know we are not football professionals so it is a game for nonprofessionals. But we need to also display our specialization which is weightlifting as a way of balancing the game. It makes everything complete. If people will get bored with the football just because we may not play well they will definitely be happy about the weightlifting, which is our specialization. Secondly, last year some professional footballers came and played though they were not weightlifters. That act did not reflect the real identity of us since some groups felt cheated and besides because such people are professionals they are able to run faster with the ball and in an attempt to follow them at such a pace we either fall or get completely tired. Some of us felt pains the next day because we kept turning at angles that we should not have. Finally, we brought in the weights so that we can identify the real macho men. We are putting weights of an average of about seventy pounds so if you are able to lift it then you are qualified to play the ball but if you are not able to lift it then you are disqualified. We realized that some people came and could not lift so we have to disqualify them.

In the event the lifting of weights ended up becoming a competition between members of the White Chapel Gym and those from other gyms in the area that had come for the opportunity to show off their strength. As things progressed the screening for the soccer match settled into a spontaneous weightlifting match between members of the White Chapel and Van Damme Gyms, with much cajoling and laughter from the gathered crowd for the competitors on either side. Several non-gymmers who had not been able to lift the required starting weights were allowed to join the teams in the end.

What passes for a gym at White Chapel is really the narrow space behind the building where Tanko rents a room. It measures forty-seven feet by six feet and looks more like an alleyway rather than a proper gym space. A makeshift canopy covers the space to protect the equipment from inclement weather. The makeshift quality of the gym is, however, deceptive. Strict rules are applied to all gymmers who use it. Weights and dumbbells are lined up against the back wall, and no one is allowed to go out of turn on any equipment. The counting of repetitions of exercises is done with the aid of pebbles collected in several differently sized calabashes or empty milk cans, depending on the number of pebbles. Because of the small size of the gym there is no electronic equipment of any kind. Of the seventy-strong membership of the gym, some twenty-five are regular attendees. Out of these only four claimed to be in regular employment, mainly as mechanics or drivers' assistants on passenger lorries. In 2009–2010 White Chapel charged a one-off membership fee of GHC 20 ($15), with no subsequent monthly fees. This was in recognition of the fact that most members were unemployed and thus that it may have proved difficult to have them pay regular monthly dues for continuing membership. White Chapel's membership fee structure was highly unusual for the gyms we visited. However, its members were often encouraged to make contributions for the purchase or replacement of equipment. As many of the gym members were mechanics they also acted as an important source of discarded car parts that were key to the replenishment of the gym equipment. The educational background of the gymmers varied from no school at all to some time at college, with two or three being university graduates. Most of the members were drawn from the immediate White Chapel vicinity itself and were thus Muslim Hausa-speaking migrants from the northern parts of the country. There were no women enrolled in this particular gym, although talk of them was rampant. The inherent educational, linguistic, and cultural homogeneity of White Chapel Gym was not replicated in the other gyms we visited, where the ethnic and educational backgrounds seemed to be more varied. In all the gyms that we visited, including Tanko's, pidgin English was used as the lingua franca, with other indigenous languages such as Hausa, Twi, or Ga used in a highly creative mode of code-switching between pidgin and the other languages. None of the regular members of White Chapel Gym were married, even though there was a lot of talk about how to improve their standing with women. Members' ages ranged from eighteen to thirty-five, with seniority determined not by age but by how much one could "push iron" and how many years they had consistently spent at it. Though just thirty-two years of age, Tanko has been pushing iron consistently for at least ten years and is unanimously acknowledged to be the leader of the gym.

Several reasons were given for becoming members of the gym, the most common being as a means of escaping the boredom of unemployment. The burden of free time for gymmers appeared to be no different from that for the kòbòlòi we encountered earlier. Despite the stereotype of criminality and violence that normally attaches to gymmers, many of them suggested that gymming gained them a certain acceptability in society that had not been available to them hitherto. They are frequently given free admission to concerts, music premieres, and major beach events, with the expectation that if any trouble arises they will actively help to quell it. Making themselves attractive to the opposite sex was also universally cited as a reason for coming to the gym, as was the fact that other men tended to envy their well-built bodies. All the gymmers expressed a sense of superiority over chubby-looking men, and especially those in the political classes whom they felt were nothing but corrupt gluttons.

At a focus group discussion at First Fitness Gym in the summer of 2010, the conversation once turned to the general image cultivated by politicians in Ghana. The overall consensus of gym members was that the popular phrase "chop make I chop" had a particular salience for the political class, given how fat most of them became upon gaining positions of power. The conversation in this instance was triggered when Isaac, who was not a gymmer but frequently came to hang out at the gym, got the bright idea to start a Mr. Ghana Weightlifting Competition and came by to share his frustration about the insensitive responses he had been receiving from the various offices he went canvassing for financial support. Isaac had designed a sophisticated poster and some fancy publicity material that he had been touting at various offices in town in an effort to gain sponsorship for the competition. All his exertions had ended in failure so he returned to the gym to complain about the "big man's mentality" in Ghana. The consensus was that the big man wanted to chop but did not have any interest in letting the small man "chop small." There was a fair degree of irony in the fact that Isaac was indeed a very slim man and that he might well have benefited from an augmentation to his diet not in a metaphorical but in a literal sense. Everyone sided with him in his lament, and there was a long series of stories the others told about the insensitivity of people once they acceded to power. The discursive evocation of corruption that the gymmers expressed—as being encapsulated in the body of the chubby politician—brought to mind what Achille Mbembe describes in relation to the representations of bodily excess in Cameroun's political cartoons (2000). Except, perhaps, for one small yet quite significant difference: the gymmers' critique was not born out of any clear ideological understanding of the coupling of corruption and the body politic, here embodied in the chubby politician. On the contrary, there was a satiric derision on the one hand that was also tied to a strong desire to attain to the position of those in power on the other. It is this contradiction that, for example, allows gymmers to disdain chubby politicians before elections and yet agree to work for them and brag about it to their fellow gymmers.

As it became increasingly clear that these gym enthusiasts were kòbòlòi in the strictly structural transitional sense of the concept, I came to see the earlier answers they gave me regarding reasons for gymming as ultimately an orientation toward change and self-transformation as an obligatory aspect of the enforced waiting of urban life. If the discursive repertoires of the gymmers were contradictorily woven out of ideas of a muscular masculinity culled from Hollywood action films on the one hand, and (at least for those at White Chapel Gym) from traditional notions of care for the community of fellow migrants on the other, there was also an ethical sensibility that derived not so much from anything to do with bodybuilding but from the discursive urban scripts with which they were thoroughly familiar. This ethical sensibility must be tied to their shared status as kòbòlòi, attempting to move between life phases but constrained to remain in a state of expectant waiting because of the vagaries of economic conditions in the city. Like the kòbòlòi the gymmers were burdened by free time and used to drawing broad insights from the vehicular inscriptions on tro-tros that we encountered in chapter 4. Thus the heated debate about "chop-make-I-chop" politicians" was part of a larger awareness drawn from rumors about happenings about town, urban stories about those who were "making it," and the general information about political and social events extracted from the various lively FM stations in Accra. All these are sources for vehicular slogans that create a shared sense of popular wisdom.

In their attitudes to urban scripts they seamlessly invoked proverbs and other such rhetorical devices that were evidently shared with tro-tro slogans. These invocations were typically used to establish the overall discursive tenor of their discussions. Whereas at White Chapel the "No Pain, No Gain" slogan printed underneath the painting of a muscular bodybuilder at the entrance to their gym asserted the specific moral economy to bodybuilding itself, that slogan was just one of a vast array of entextualizations that frequently popped up in the often animated arguments that broke out on various topics. For example, in another heated argument at First Fitness Gym about how some ruling NDC politicians had begun enriching themselves during their term in office, the gymmers quickly split into ruling party and opposition supporters, with both sides peppering their arguments with proverbs and wise sayings evidently taken from vehicle slogans: "Ebi Ti Yie, Na Ebi Nti Yie Koraa, Why?" (Some Are Living Well, but Others Are Not Living Well at All, Why?), "Wan Hwe ne Yie a, Won Hu ni Yie" (If You Don't Look Well, You Will Not See It Well), "The Day Shall Come" (this slogan normally refers to Christian apocalypse, but in this instance was used with reference to the next cycle of national elections that was to be held in December 2012). The almost constant invocation of proverbs in modulating their arguments was a sign of the degree to which gymmers' ethical discourse is heavily informed not exclusively by any specific indigenous language traditions, but by the vast array of ready-made wisdom in the tro-tro slogans. The recourse to the implicit discursive ethos encapsulated in vehicular slogans sets up a peculiar contrast with the sensibility of the more educated classes. In the scores of arguments that I had while at boarding school and university in Ghana from the mid-1970s to the late 1980s, it was extremely rare to find people who could consistently invoke colorful proverbs or wise sayings of any sort. The Western-style pedagogy we had been exposed to succeeded in drilling such facility out of us, such that in the rare instances where tro-tro slogans were referenced in conversation they were the object of humor and fun rather than of any serious recognition. The few people among us who commanded traditional proverbial idioms were the objects of an ambivalent attraction. Given that English was the language of formal instruction at all levels of the educational system and of government business, perhaps at the heart of the ambivalence was the question of whether such people were ultimately "bush." The same issue plays out in a different way in the perceived differences in the quality and character of program offerings between Accra's exclusively English-language FM stations and those either of exclusively Akan- or Ga-language usage. It is not uncommon to hear complaints that the exclusively local-language FM stations wallow in sensationalism and overall poor news coverage, while the English-language ones are typically styled as more sophisticated and open-minded. The extreme version of either position is of course completely false, but there is something to be said for the fact that as a general rule the proverbial facility that the gymmers exhibit is not commonly to be found among those who have had heavy Western-style education, or even if it is, that educated people tend to demonstrate this facility only when they are speaking their own indigenous languages and in particular contexts. In a manner of speaking then, for the gymmer as for the kòbòlò, the proliferation of vehicular slogans across Accra's urbanscape must be understood as granting them simultaneous access to the moral economy of proverbial rhetoric and to the cosmopolitan sensibilities of the *vehicular* language as such.

To specifically posit the kòbòlò and the gymmer as particular types of interpreter of the urbanscape is not to say that these scripts are the only things they read. Rather, it is to note the specificity of their mode of reading, which, as we have seen previously, is imbued with the sense of the transitional dimensions of urban life, and of which the vehicle slogans are themselves an articulation. The gymmer, like the kòbòlò, is a material sociological instantiation of the entextualized *vehicular* logic of the tro-tro slogans, as well as an actor who deploys these slogans as a means of demarcating the ambit of his social understanding. The coupling of discursive repertoires from Western sources of robust athletic masculinity with versions of such ideas that have historically circulated in Ghana, along with invocations of thoroughly Ghanaian multilingual urban scripts, positions gymmers and kòbòlòi at the intersection of tradition and modernity, of the local social imaginary and the transnational imagescape. They are also at the very conjuncture of the difficult processes of self making that are enforced upon them by the overabundance of free time. In these various intersections, gymmers and kòbòlòi allow us also to see the various spatial and discursive overlaps that we encountered in the salsa scene in the previous chapter and, beyond that, in the nature of youth cultures in early twenty-first-century Accra.

CHAPTER 7

The Lettered City: Literary Representations of Accra

The spatial dynamics of Accra's evolution and its current status as a place of fertile exchanges between the local and the global provide a productive setting for exploring the literary writings of and about the city. As Edward Said points out: "Every act of criticism is always literally tied to a set of social and historical circumstances; the problem is in specifying or characterizing the relationship, not merely in asserting that it exists; then the critic goes on to choose between competing social tendencies" (2000, 177). The question of context raises acute problems for interpreting the relation between literature and urban society, whether for Accra or for any other African and Third World cities like it. For despite all appearances to the contrary, literary context retains an unsettling elusiveness as an object of commentary. Sometimes the task of contextualization appears to be merely that of providing historical background to the literary text in question. A second question, which appears to be a variant of the first and is especially pertinent to the study of African literature, is the degree to which such literature is to be taken as a form of sociohistorical chronicle and thus able to yield direct insights into discrete sociological formations. In partial answer to this long-standing question in African literary criticism, we might counter that the social world itself is the product of referential relays that are encapsulated in discursive ensembles in which different fragments "speak" to each other across a nexus of knowledge, ideology, and power. For the study of African literature, this ensemble has always to be understood as involving both literary and nonliterary discourses: government policies and documents, media representations, opinions from everyday life, the colonial and historical archive, as well as the many discourses of orality that articulate both social realities and the epistemological orientations to such realities. Finally, contextualization may also involve not just historical details but the tracing of themes and thematic clusters that appear purely intrinsic to the larger literary history of which the particular text is a small part and that may only tangentially relate to social history as such. The task in this instance is to understand the asymmetrical nature of the relationship between variant histories that may or may not intersect with the literary domain.

It is this interdisciplinary and multidimensional way of making sense of texts that I want to adopt in exploring the literary representations of Accra in this chapter. In line with the focus on spatial logics that has guided *Oxford Street* thus far, the discussion here will be focused on novelistic narrations of urban space. As a general rule, narrated space within the novel is tied to genre conventions: the space within a realist text is quite different from that to be found in a surrealist or magical realist one. Furthermore, narrated space is a product of language, such that the linguistic devices that are used to express the sense of space produce specific inflections to the space that is represented. Hence we find that the spatial character of Amma Darko's almost journalese realist novel *Faceless* (2003) is quite different from Kofi Awoonor's *This Earth, My Brother . . .* (1972). The alternation between stream of consciousness and realist sections in *This Earth* allow us to discern how the proximity of different representational registers within the novel produces a feverish image cycle suggestive of a charged and ultimately unsatisfactory eschatology. And the eschatology is as much a function of history as it is of spatiality in this novel. Like the modernist texts from which it takes inspiration, the spatial logic of Awoonor's novel is highly suggestive of deep mythological resources of both classical and indigenous vintage. At the same time, as we shall see, the proximity between realism and symbolism (as in Awoonor's novel) or realism and the registers of the esoteric (such as we find to a degree in Darko) also reveal that the space of the city is of permeable phenomenological boundaries, the consequence of which is the problematization of causality, space, and the social relations that these concepts demarcate.

To allow us a simple heuristic opening for exploring the nature of narrated space in these urban novels of Accra, I propose to look at them primarily in terms of spatial traversal, that is to say, of the characters' movement from one spatial location to another. In the long realist tradition of the novel, the traversal of space is quite often a way of rendering it an inert sociological and historical backdrop to the vicissitudes of characterization. In such instances space is often foreshortened or abbreviated and thus appears only relevant as the demarcation of the time spent in departure from and arrival at vaguely realized locations. Here space is just setting, while character is of primary interest. Space then rarely "comes into its own" unless it is somehow percolated through the consciousness of a character, either as a sudden impingement, such as in the spatial epiphanies as we find in Tayib Saleh's *Season of Migration to the North*, or Joseph Conrad's *Heart of Darkness* to which Saleh's novel is thematically related, or as a means by which the character him/herself registers the passage of spacetime, as in Ezeulu and Obika's long walk to Okperi in Chinua Achebe's *Arrow of God*. In the novels we shall be exploring here, space is not so readily effaced in the course of its traversal. Rather, in all the instances mentioned earlier, the traversal from one location to another also registers the movement between different ethical domains. This is most tellingly the case when the middle-class protagonists of *Faceless* and *This Earth* are forced either by circumstance or choice to visit a seedier or more decrepit part of town than they are accustomed to. The simple narrative expedient of making them enter a slum is without fail the trigger for the exposure of an ethical impasse that raises implications either for the protagonist's sense of identity or about their hitherto unexamined understanding of the basis of social order and organization. This aligns Darko and Awoonor to, say, Dickens and Joyce, respectively, except that in the case of the Ghanaian writers the switch between spaces is also a switch between different notions of the relationship between the real and the esoteric, or between forms of causality that are not entirely reducible to human expediency or even understanding.

Crucially, though, in the urban novels of Accra that interest us here, spatial traversal is ultimately tied to the revelation of sentiment. Sentiment is, however, not to be interpreted as ordinary feeling or emotion, but as the means by which an ethical sensibility evolves, is registered as a mode of being-in-the-world, and, by force of circumstance, either reaffirmed, qualified, or even abandoned by the protagonist.[1] Sentimental heroes and heroines essentially imagine that their goodness and sense of judgment can have a transformative impact on the world around them. The form of the bildungsroman is traditionally devoted to exposing the impediments standing in the way of a sentimental education for the growing protagonist, such that the evolution and disclosure of ethical sentiment is attained at a cost: sometimes of alienation, sometimes of despair, and even of the loss of sanity in the more extreme cases. Mikhail Bakhtin, in his essay on the significance of the bildungsroman in the history of realism (1986), notes that as a narrative form the bildungsroman represents a fundamental shift in modern thought as contrasted to that to be found in "premodern" narratives such as those dedicated to adventure, romance, trial, ordeal, and so forth. Whereas premodern narratives encapsulated in myths and legends situate the protagonist as an unchanging and static entity, a constant around which other aspects of the narrative take the role of "variables," the bildungsroman presents the hero as a dynamic center of narrative gravity such that plot changes are linked to the changes taking place within the protagonist himself or herself. Bakhtin's insight turns on seeing the bildungsroman as representing a fundamental way of conceptualizing the relationship between time and space. If premodern narratives present the protagonist as static and unchanging with variables in plot occurring as variables in episodic space, in the bildungsroman both space and time are represented as aspects of the protagonist's unfolding consciousness. For Franco Moretti (1987), on the other hand, the protagonist's inner restlessness and thus elective mobility as depicted in the bildungsroman are inherently tied to a future orientation, a break from the generational or historical past as a necessary instrument of self-discovery and maturation. The protagonist's interiority and how it is represented thus become critical aspects of novelistic discourse.

The trajectory of spatial traversal tied not merely to movement from one location to another but as a challenge to sentimental interiority is best seen in Awoonor's This Earth. From a quite different direction we also find this trajectory in operation in Martin Egblewogbe's "Mr. Happy and the Hammer of God" (2010), a text published almost five decades after Awoonor's novel yet concerned with the same question of sentimental education conducted primarily through the restless traversal of space. While we are encouraged to identify with the protagonist of Egblewogbe's fascinating short story, we are also obliged to take his quasi-philosophical observations on different aspects of the city he is traversing with some measure of doubt, primarily because of the tinge of insanity with which his character is drawn up for us. In the end we find that there is not much distance between Awoonor's Amamu and Egblewogbe's Dervi. They are both deeply alienated characters bearing within themselves a whiff of morose pride that tips over into an intractable solitude. The major difference between the two characters, however, is that Amamu's alienation is due to his bearing the world-weariness of a hypersensitive lawyer and member of the cultural elite, while Dervi slides from a great job at a reputable bank in the city via a nervous breakdown to join the precarious dregs of the unemployed. In both instances we never know whether to attribute the fervent interpretations of the cityscape to their possession of superior insights that have been mercifully freed from the constraining hegemonic logic with which reality is organized, or whether they merely represent the embittered commentary of social anchorites. Such a reading would be somewhat reductive, since it focuses entirely on character without paying attention to the other narrative variables by which such fictional protagonists take shape. As we shall see presently, Amamu is a much more complex character; the comparison to Dervi is meant to indicate the persistence with which the trope of traversal has been tied to the problematization of sentimental education in the Ghanaian novel.[2]

The urban texts we will be looking at also represent space as the correlative of social relations. These are grounded in the ethnography of the domestic sphere in Darko and in the acute discontinuities of the sociopolitical domain in Awoonor. Social relations have also been represented in the form of material objects in other novels of the city, where the circulation of material objects expresses the reification and distortion of social relations as such. For Accra, like many other cities in Africa and elsewhere, must also be perceived as a "social space [that] contains a great diversity of objects, both natural and social, including the networks and pathways which facilitate the exchange of material things and information. Such 'objects' are thus not merely things but also relations. As objects they possess discernible peculiarities, contour and form" (Lefebvre 1992, 77). The most sustained and excoriating literary representation of the reduction of social relations to the materialism of objects in all of African literature must be Ayi Kwei Armah's *Fragments* (1969). The thematic of that critically acclaimed novel has now become almost normative in much of the Gollywood movies set in the city, but sadly evacuated of the critical force with which Armah infused the theme. Gollywood places materialism on the altar of a shallow cosmopolitan self-fashioning abetted by the vociferous prosperity discourses of evangelical Christianity, thus preventing us from seeing the objects as the collective distortion of social relations.

Ethnographies of the Domestic Sphere: Kanda
versus Sodom and Gomorrah

On first reading Amma Darko's *Faceless*, one might be forgiven for thinking that it falls into a simple journalistic realism devoted to the depiction of life in two distinct class settings, the first being the home of middle-class Kabria and her family at Kanda and the second that of Fofo and her friends in the slum district of Sodom and Gomorrah. Indeed, journalism is a significant motif in the unfolding of events in the novel. This is primarily conveyed through the figure of Sylv Po and his highly popular *Good Morning Ghana*, a current affairs and investigative show broadcast on the fictional Harvest FM.

The essentially journalistic character of the narrative is also conveyed in the detailed descriptions that Darko provides of the two main settings between which the narrative account oscillates, along with that of a third space that we find is none other than Ga Mashie, a neighborhood we have encountered several times earlier in this study. In keeping with its largely journalistic narrative orientation, the novel conveys the sense of being relentlessly issue-driven, focusing primarily on the ways in which Kabria and her coworkers at MUTE working in collaboration with Sylv Po attempt to raise awareness about the precarious lives of street children. (MUTE is a non-governmental organization glossed by the narrator as "just that: Mute. As in silence. Not an acronym." But their interests are in women and children.)

And yet the initial impression of journalistic verisimilitude that might be reinforced by a comparison with the many Accra newspaper reports on the same social phenomena is slowly dissipated when we discern certain rhythmic and repeated patterns that undergird the spatial character of the text. The descriptions of the apparently mundane and repetitive cycles of Kabria's family life provide the first signals of these patterns. There are three things that Kabria constantly worries about and to which her mind keeps returning at different times of day: the daily school run for her three children, her paltry monthly salary and thus her concerns with the nature of her workplace, and the vagaries and misdemeanors of Creamy, her old and beat-up VW Beetle. However, far from being nebulous and indeed random, there appears to be a strict system to her ruminations. Whereas her concern with the children looms large in her mind primarily during the morning and late-afternoon school runs, her concern with Creamy is almost constant. Her concern with Creamy provides a steady mental soundtrack to her exhausting days. Creamy is no ordinary old and beat-up car, either: it is her friend and confidant as well as her most irritating companion. Kabria talks about and to Creamy almost incessantly, thus making of the car a distinct character in its own right. We are told early on, for example, that "after one of Creamy's many plastic surgeries," it was left "so tattooed that it required urgent re-spraying" (39). This triggers the sudden and unpleasant recognition in Kabria's mind that her paltry pay packet would have to be augmented by something eked out of her husband. She undertakes an enterprising and humor-laden campaign of harassment to persuade Adade, her husband, to help her yet again to restore the car to a semblance of decency. This involves her driving the "tu-tu-tu-tu-tu-tu" Creamy to his office one fine afternoon, pretending to be innocently coming to inquire how his day is going. The threat of further embarrassment before his colleagues at work is enough to make Adade agree that same evening to surrender the money she needs for Creamy. At another point Kabria has a serious internal debate with herself as to whether Creamy can be said to have a soul (175). This proves inconclusive, but we are given to suspect that she thinks so anyway. Her husband, the children, and all her friends have learned to accommodate the significant personal role Creamy plays in her life and proceed to give her pieces of advice, both solicited and unsolicited, about how to pamper the car in hopes of guaranteeing its continuing cooperation. What appears at first to be the mere motif of eccentric personification of an inanimate object turns out to be a highly significant aspect of Kabria's own characterization and of her traversals of urban space. For Creamy is not just an objective expression of Kabria's instincts of caregiving, of which we get ample evidence from the way she manages her household, but is itself the exemplary metronome around which various interruptions to her daily rhythms are structured. In other words, the various car failures that we see her attempting to negotiate as she traverses Accra's urban space are the interruptive occasions for reflections about the makeup of the city and the vicissitudes of the life of a middle-class, overworked, and underpaid woman within it. The insults that rain upon her from other irate road users frustrated by her sluggish and frankly decrepit vehicle are only one form of the city's intrusions into her persistent reveries about family and work.

Furthermore, it is Creamy that foregrounds the essential precariousness of the intersection between class and gender in the novel, for the car provides the constant reminder that her passage from one point to another across the cityscape is also the interweaving of the distinctive yet overlapping roles of mother, wife, and worker. More crucially, the transitions between roles at all times of the day are never entirely smooth, nor is their success entirely guaranteed; the transitions are utterly exhausting at a mental and physical level and are always subject to frustrations because of Creamy's unpredictable performance. Her husband, on the other hand, observing regular office hours (and with the added bonus of a drink with his mates after work) suffers no such travails regarding familial roles and spatial traversals. Nevertheless, the near impossibility of Kabria's balancing act, expressed through the existential status given to Creamy in her life and mind, is essentially obscured for us by the fact that the narrative provides her another conduit for articulating her identity that lies beyond the domain of family and labor, namely that of being a crusader for the rights of street children. Without this outlet, which is really a way of transcending the apparent limitations of the daily options available to her, Kabria's life would have been merely an illustration of the near-impossible conditions surrounding a twenty-first-century middle-class career woman's life choices in a partly dysfunctional city.

C. L. R. James famously comments on this impossibility in a letter written in 1944 to his American girlfriend, Constance Webb:

> With the increasing opportunities that modern production (and the development of ideas based upon it) gives to women, a new type of woman arises. She is called a career woman. The name is stupid but very revealing. A man is never a career man. That is his privilege. He can have his career, and the finest fruit of his successful career is wife and children. But the woman is called career woman because her "career" in modern society demands she place herself in a subordinate position or even renounce normal life. The social dice are loaded against her; and the plain fact of the matter is that they are loaded, not only in the economic opportunities, but in the minds of men.[3]

The loading of the dice "in the minds of men" that James refers to here is amply illustrated in Adade's expectation that his wife will always be at home to take his briefcase from him at the front door when he arrives from work. When later in the novel she has to stay out late in pursuit of a lead relating to Fofo, he is thrown into abject confusion to find himself obliged for once to act as primary caregiver to his own children. He pretends to be asleep when his wife returns home later that evening, but is clearly sulking quietly behind his eyes wide shut. Kabria is not fooled (134–135).

The specifically ethnographic texture of the representation of Kabria's household is also conveyed through the regular reiterations of their daily domestic routines. These are reiterations with subtle differences designed to foreground the dynamic nature of the domestic sphere as a distinctive space for shaping familial relations. Several times we are offered detailed descriptions of cooking (what is being cooked, how, and by whom) as well as of family mealtimes at breakfast or dinner. And different members of the household are characterized in relation to what they do or do not do at the dining table. One morning Ottu, Kabria's seven-year-old son, materializes at the breakfast table nonchalantly holding up a sock in his hand. The scene that unfolds is especially funny and ought to be read in full:

> "Why are you standing there with one sock?" Kabria asked him.
> "I don't know." He replied coolly with a shrug.
> Adade who was finishing his breakfast was still engrossed in his papers.

"You don't know why you are standing there and holding one sock?"

Ottu sensed the growing irritation in Kabria's tone. "I know," he replied; but continued to stand there anyway, with the one sock, not in the least perturbed by Kabria's crossness.

Kabria dipped quickly into her reserves to top up her patience and succeeded in asking with the calmness of a saint. "Since you know, would you mind telling me?"

"What?"

Kabria sighed in exasperation. "Why you are holding one sock?"

"Because I can't find the other."

Kabria had to top up her patience very quickly again. Then she asked, "Where did you find this one?"

"Inside my shoe," Ottu mumbled.

"And was the other sock not inside the other shoe?"

"I didn't find the other shoe. Have you seen it?"

Kabria's patience became depleted. "No, I haven't!" in a tone that spoke volumes. "Do I wear it with you?" (57)

On another morning, Obea, Kabria's sixteen-year-old daughter and eldest child, decides to set the table for breakfast with her toothbrush still sticking out of her mouth from the bathroom. Her mother wonders to herself what must have gotten into this child, but decides to avoid a battle that might only disrupt her already-pressured morning routines. The twelve-year-old Essie's simmering sibling rivalry with her younger brother, on the other hand, makes for great friction but also fine comedy; whatever she is asked to do for Ottu ends up in a squabble of words into which their mother must intervene not for their sakes but to protect her own sanity from their endless bickering. Adade's irritating habit of hiding behind the newspaper at breakfast, a ruse that allows him to disavow any participation in the domestic mini-crises of the breakfast table, alongside the variant personal ticks and foibles of the three kids and their mother make for the exposition of a lively family environment. It is clear that the detailed descriptions of this domestic sphere, along with Kabria's reveries about how to anticipate and take care of different family needs, are designed to establish her household not only as the space of love and caregiving but also of predictability and ultimate security.

If the rhythms of Kabria's household provide us with an ethnography of the domestic sphere, they also pose the question of privacy and how this category is to be understood as part of a spatial logic. The question is expressed primarily with respect to Obea's sex education, a subject that is inadvertently forced upon Kabria's consciousness one morning when she finds her daughter surreptitiously reading some material before breakfast that she hurriedly shoves under her pillow on seeing her mother enter the room. Kabria sneaks back to take a peek at the reading material before dropping the children off at school. She finds to her absolute shock and horror that they are sex and HIV education pamphlets from the Planned Parenthood Association of Ghana (PPAG). This triggers a rush of questions in her mind, all centered on whether her daughter has already become sexually active and how, as a responsible mother, she might gently get her talking about it. Her fears turn out to be completely unfounded, as the pamphlets had been freely circulating at school as part of a new public health awareness drive. But Darko's point in raising the question of Obea's sexual knowledge in this safe middle-class domestic environment is to provide a counterpoint to the endangered sexual lives of Fofo, Baby T, their mother Maa Tsuru, and the other females that we see at Sodom and Gomorrah and at Ga Mashie. We find then that the principles by which the character of Kabria's household is established are rhythmic in the quotidian sense of reiterated routines (morning chaos, then breakfast, then the school run, then the reverse trajectory at close of day) and that these demarcate a familial social space of nurture, love, care, and privacy. Creamy, operating as a trigger for Kabria's reveries about how to fulfill her several roles, provides the link between different spatial orders in the text (which are at the same time expressive of different social relationships), thus placing the parameters of distinctive social arrangements alongside the one we are accustomed to seeing unfolding in Kabria's household.

Fundamentally, then, the overall significance of Kabria's domestic space derives from the way in which it is used to establish a sharp contrast to that of Sodom and Gomorrah, and then tangentially, to Ga Mashie. The contrast between the three locations is conveyed not through details of geographic specificity but rather in the contrast between a detailed ethnography of middle-class domesticity and its unstated codes of security and privacy and the absence of such representational density for the slum districts. Strictly speaking, what domesticity we have for slum dwellers is conveyed not through the descriptions of Sodom and Gomorrah itself but rather through those of Ga Mashie, where Fofo's mother lives in a compound house. But even here the descriptions of Ga Mashie relate the essential absence of daily domestic routines: both of Maa Tsuru's two sons leave home to work at the seashore never to return again by the time they are ten and eleven; Baby T, her older daughter, is sexually abused first by her stepfather and then by a hitherto kindly neighbor and then subsequently sold into prostitution by age twelve. Fofo, her second daughter, runs away from home shortly thereafter to avoid a similar dastardly fate. Even though both Fofo and her older sister find themselves in Sodom and Gomorrah, Baby T's subjection to the control of a pimp and an older prostitute she is given to reside with prevents her from establishing any natural relationships with her family or friends. Her life is absolutely devoid of privacy, much less of the shared rituals that allow for the constitution of any forms of familiarity. In shifting the narrative to Sodom and Gomorrah and then Ga Mashie, the text abjures the depiction of domestic/familial affiliation and sentiment and instead focuses on the sharp contrast produced by their absence.

Whereas the novel lays out distinctive spaces of domesticity and (non) privacy, reading it strictly in narratological terms we are obliged to place Darko's Ga Mashie halfway between Kabria's household and the epic moral aridity of Sodom and Gomorrah. As we noted a moment ago, it is in Ga Mashie that we are presented with familial relations in which love, affection, and the notion of privacy are distorted to the point of nonexistence, while at Sodom and Gomorrah both familial relations and the question of privacy are comprehensively disavowed in the primary instance. At the same time, one thing that is shared in both domains is that much of the lifestyle described in both Ga Mashie and Sodom and Gomorrah is depicted as taking place out of doors and under the full gaze of the public. The putative "public sphere" we find in these instances must be understood as the product of interlinked domains of surveillance. These domains manifest themselves at various levels, including the circulation of rumors regarding the curse that has been imposed upon Maa Tsuru and her progeny, at the level of street sense by which Fofo and her friend Odarley are able to ascertain where their enemies might be lying in wait for them, and finally with regard to the sources of information by which the FM station attempts to piece together the facts about Baby T's death and mutilation. At the final and most dispersed level of signification is what is mediated specifically through the collaboration between MUTE and Sylv Po's morning radio show. At each domain of public scrutiny, the "eye" of the public is situated either as an aspect of a character or cluster of characters that bear elusive witness to events or, as in the case of the radio station, in the collective urban public's display of concern about the goings-on about town as encapsulated in the phone-ins to the radio station. Thus for Ga Mashie, an all-knowing eye is vested in the octogenarian Naa Yomo, who never leaves her chair in the courtyard of Maa Tsuru's compound house; for Sodom and Gomorrah a similar role is fulfilled by the women working at the blue hair braiding kiosk, who function as a deeply problematic Greek chorus: all-knowing yet highly reluctant to disclose what they know about the mutilated body that was found just behind their kiosk. It is only much later that we discover the reason for this chorus's reluctance: rumors have been carefully spread that Poison, the brutal lord of this underworld, is mightily interested in what kind of account is being circulated about Baby T's death and that anyone known to be putting out a version not approved by him might attract an unwelcome visit.

Rumors clearly perform a disciplinary function at Sodom and Gomorrah. In the case of Naa Yomo and the Ga Mashie household, on the other hand, the old woman is the purveyor of stories of all kinds, including the private and personal histories of people such as Maa Tsuru, the history of the earthquake of 1939 that decimated the district (as we saw in chapter 2), as well as stories about the British colonial presence. What prevents Naa Yomo from performing the function of a griot is that her all-knowingness and the stories she spins out seem at once garrulous and evasive; this is how they appear to Kabria when she pays Naa Yomo an investigative visit with another of her coworkers. The eye of the radio station, on the other hand, might be taken as a sanitized version of the chorus function that we have seen invested first in the women of the blue kiosk and then in Naa Yomo. What prevents us from interpreting the radio show as anything other than a switchboard for the circulation of urban gossip, however, is that, as in most talk shows with phone-in components, there is no way of predicting what kind of intervention will be made via the phone lines. Thus the radio show allows for a more dialogical structure of debate and discussion that requires the specific mediation of the radio-show host for its unfolding. The apparent superiority this suggests in contrast to the other two domains of the public gaze is not devoid of problems, for even the radio show is liable to being hijacked by fabricated opinion, as we see when an anonymous caller insists that the body of the mutilated girl was not that of Baby T but of a kayayoo, a female head porter. The shift of register to a kayayoo implies that the dead girl may have been punished for contravening group dictates and ethnically sanctioned behavioral stipulations, the punishment for which was death. The potential red herring is only discovered to be such much later in the narrative, since the anonymous caller was none other than Baby T's madam, prompted to the ruse by Poison.

Faceless provides us with two divergent and ultimately irreconcilable approaches to the question of agency: these are the forensic and the esoteric. The first is encapsulated in the mystery-thriller dimension of the largely journalistic mode of representation, while the second is adduced as an explanation for the horrific events that have afflicted Maa Tsuru and her daughters. In essence these two represent diametrically opposed framings of agency and ultimately relate to the sense of incommensurability produced by the intractable problems of the city. As we shall see presently, each of the texts we are discussing thematizes this incommensurability with reference to different forms of esoteric causality. *Faceless* meditates on what is involved in protecting women's privacy (read sexuality) as an aspect of the veridical forensic procedures of the mystery thriller. Hence the news of Baby T's badly mutilated body enters the narrative first in a roundabout way by Maa Tsuru herself when Fofo pays her a reluctant visit to complain about Poison's unwanted sexual attentions (47–49), and then, more substantially for the direction of the narrative, by Sylv Po on his morning show. This also serves to insert an interpretative process of delayed decoding that is definitive of the mystery thriller. But the delayed decoding in *Faceless* operates on multiple dimensions at once. As soon as Kabria and her colleagues at MUTE take Fofo off the streets and adopt her as their primary concern, they find themselves also bound by the elusive process of discovering her family background in order to determine how they might initiate her rehabilitation. But the concern with discovering Fofo's family is inextricably tied to the possible interpretations of the meaning of her sister's mutilated body.

The link between charity and mystery quests is thus established upon Kabria's very first encounter with Fofo at the Agbogbloshie Market. Disguised as a boy, Fofo steals Kabria's bag and is saved from being lynched on the spot by Kabria's quick-witted declaration that the child is her long-lost nephew. That Fofo is reluctant until much later in the novel to divulge any useful information about her background might have led to a stalling of the MUTE women's interest in her, but for the fact that when they were driving away from the market she had blurted out to Kabria that the dead body found at Sodom and Gomorrah was that of her sister. Since Sylv Po had already made street children a tantalizing topic of his show and in fact had specifically mentioned the mystery surrounding the dead girl's body a few days back, Fofo's statement attracts immediate attention. The MUTE women are thus placed under obligation to get to the root of the murder, which the police had long abandoned as a pointless investigative cul-de-sac. To understand Fofo's background the women at MUTE are also obliged to solve the mystery of the abandoned body. Thus the forensic template foregrounds rational human veridical procedures for the resolution of riddles of urban existence. This level of the text bespeaks an understanding of causal agency quite different from what is discursively implied in ideas pertaining to esoteric causality.

If the absence of privacy for Fofo and her family is to be expected as a consequence of their broken relationships and the fraught nature of existence within a slum neighborhood, the novel introduces a peculiar causal explanation for this condition by depicting Maa Tsuru as the victim of a curse placed on her at birth that extends generationally to her daughters. The curse is not only experienced in terms of a miserable biography but also signifies as a form of negative magnetism and contamination. Not only do Maa Tsuru and her daughters attract the interest of preying and destructive men, but their curse contaminates the fates of these men as witnessed by the collapse and suicide of Onko as an ostensible punishment for his rape of Baby T. Fate is invoked explicitly when Kabria is first introduced at the start of chapter 2: "Fate's machinery got into motion elsewhere that same Monday dawn and placed on a string, two destinies joined carefully at their seams by an unclear thread. Like a shadow crossing paths at the bidding of death's uncanny ways, Kabria, in the comfort of her modest home in a middle class suburb of Accra, remembered that her regular garden eggs and tomato vendors at the Agbogbloshie market would be expecting her." By turning to the curse as the explanatory machinery to account for the evil that befalls these unhappy women, *Faceless* also produces an intersection between the esoteric and forensic logics that make up this mystery thriller, for Kabria and her colleagues come to be posited as a collective deus ex machina that is meant to resolve both the mystery and the unfortunate accursed lives of Fofo and her family. The larger and much more complex social problem deriving from urban decay and the improper assimilation of parts of the city's urban population is in this way discursively scaled down to a struggle between the esoteric (in the form of curse, fate, and ill luck) on the one hand and the forensic (in the form of charitable human agency) on the other.

What might be read in *Faceless* as a retreat from social critique or even a concession to superstition must, however, be interpreted in terms of the representation of the intractable epistemological character of the city itself. The city's intractableness is an aspect of its socio-geography. In Accra it is not always that things are what they seem, especially when considering the often surprising shifts from poverty to wealth and vice versa that abound in rumor as well as in media reports. (One recalls the vehicular slogan "All the World Is a Stage" that we encountered in chapter 4.) The unpredictability of changes in fortune may sometimes be seen as the function of urban space itself, something that can be illustrated in the history of Sodom and Gomorrah. Currently with an estimated population of eighty thousand people pressed into 3.1 square kilometers and bordered to the south by the Korle Lagoon, to the west by Sabon Zongo, and to the east by Agbogbloshie Market, the slum of Sodom and Gomorrah has the highest population density of Accra's twenty-five slums.[4] Originally the area now called Agbogbloshie went by the name of Fadama, so designated by the earliest settlers from the north who arrived there in different waves in the 1960s and 1970s. Fadama is Hausa for "swampy" and was an appropriate designation for the area, originally a wetland on the banks of the Korle Lagoon. A major flood during the late 1960s led to the government's relocation of the northern squatters to New Fadama in the Abeka district of Accra. As a parallel and not necessarily unrelated process, the government acquired the vast expanse of Fadama/Agbogbloshie in the 1970s to be developed as the South Industrial Area for the location of various light industries, but in the event the plan was only partially realized. The choice of the area for the siting of industries was not entirely accidental, for it was coextensive with the area called Galloway, a few miles farther east of Agbogbloshie, and so named after the headquarters of Thomson, Moir and Galloway, important contributors to colonial development projects during the governorship of Gordon Guggisberg in the 1920s.[5] Indeed, the original influx of northern immigrants may well have been due to the promise of construction jobs that the industrial zone was to provide. Today this industrial zone is populated by large firms such as KIA Motors, Mercedes-Benz, Toyota, and Rana Motors, respectively, along with the semi-industrial paints manufacturers Azar Paints and the very well-known Graphic Corporation. Given that the Fadama area had long been a destination for northerners, many of whom were also yam and cattle traders, the industrial land that remained unused quickly got converted into the site of an unofficial market.

After the bombing of Makola in June 1979, the pressure to decongest the CBD and to find an alternative food market led to the designation of Agbogbloshie as the city's official yam market and thus also the destination for all foodstuffs that came from the northern parts of the country. Stalls for the Agbogbloshie Market were constructed in the 1980s on the old site of Fadama, and the market quickly grew into a lively fresh produce alternative to Makola. The area's abiding links with the north took a more traumatic turn during the interethnic conflicts that exploded sporadically between the Nanumba and the Kokomba between 1994 and 2000.[6] Thousands of refugees fleeing the war came to settle in Accra on the only available stretch of unoccupied land that had long been the unofficial location for northern traders outside the traditional squatter quarters of Sabon Zongo, Tudu, and Nima. It is not clear how the slum got its biblical designation, but this was likely attributed to it by concerned denizens of nearby neighborhoods at Korle Bu who saw in the slum, not without some justification, the preservation of the worst urban social vices. Before 2000, the image that had come to dominate media reports of life at Sodom and Gomorrah was that of the garbage that choked the Korle Lagoon, a failed object of dredging efforts for every government since the colonial period. After 2000, another image was added: that of the near-permanent fires of e-waste disposal mounds that were deposited on the unused strip of land to the immediate west of the slum by cynical local operators in collusion with Western industrialized firms. A walking visit I paid to the slum in the summer of 2012 confirmed some of the worst stories that had been reported about it. Even though many of its denizens are hard-working migrants who commute on a daily basis to work in different parts of the city, the slum location itself reflects many of the elements to be found in Darko's novel as well as in the newspaper reports concerning it. Droves of flies descend on anything that remains immobile for longer than a few seconds, children defecate in the full glare of the noonday sun, narrow al-leyways are crowded with prostitutes of different ages and demeanors, and rows upon rows of ramshackle habitations made of every imaginable mate-rial from wood and concrete to the more flimsy cardboard boxes and even plastic bags clog the tight space. And yet it is instructive that the slum has been named Sodom and Gomorrah, for while it invokes the terrible fate of the biblical town of iniquity, what it really signifies is the inexplicability of urban transformations that can produce such a slum right in the core of the capital city itself. For, unlike the earlier Tudu (est. 1911–1915), Sabon Zongo (in the same period as Tudu), and Nima (from 1931), Sodom and Gomor-rah is not located on the outer boundaries of the township and thus does not demarcate the threshold of a no-man's-land that is primarily settled by strangers. Rather, growing as it did in the 1990s on the only sizable piece of wasteland between already-constituted and well-established neighbor-hoods, the slum speaks to the constant threat of the inversion of planned urban spatial hierarchies into chaos. Because the earlier slum districts lay at different times on the distant outskirts of the growing Accra township, this oscillatory opposition between the planned and the chaotic remained largely concealed as a material fact that defined the city. Finally, one of the greatest ironies of Sodom and Gomorrah is that it sits right alongside the Korle Lagoon, the abode of Korle, the Ga titular water deity reputed to have aided in the founding of all of Accra lands.

Thus, behind Amma Darko's representation of variant causalities in *Faceless* also lies the larger and more intractable historical dimensions of the city. For it is not entirely clear to anyone whether the accretions to the city proceed systematically or merely in response to various contingencies. As we have noted in previous chapters, in certain cases the evolution of built space was triggered specifically by epidemics and natural disasters, with mainly the whites-only neighborhoods originally benefiting from central planning. The population explosion that has affected the city since at least the early 1980s has seen demography confound city planners at every turn. But with time it has also been assimilated to the "anything can happen" attitude by which denizens of the city conduct their lives. Since anything can happen at both spatial (accretions) and personal (rich today, poor tomorrow) dimensions of Accra's urban space, it is no wonder that esoteric causalities get an almost equal showing with other forms of representation in the urban literature of the city.

Nausea and the Underworld: Kofi Awoonor's This Earth, My Brother . . .

Whereas in *Faceless* the space of the slum is established as a counterpoint to that of middle-class domesticity, it remains strictly coded within the boundaries of a scrupulous journalistic realism. In accordance with the dictates of the genre of mystery thriller that is overlaid by a discourse of charity and rehabilitation, Darko's novel retains a distinct air of practicality about it. Its purpose is ultimately to raise awareness about a specific set of social issues. However, despite the fact that the middle-class Kabria and her friends at MUTE undertake a journey into the sordid milieu of the slum, their social world remains intact for there is no real danger of the disruption of boundaries or the intrusion of the moral aridity of the slum district into the lives of the middle-class protagonists. *Faceless* does not do the work of the bildungsroman as suggested by Bakhtin. This is not just because the focal point of the narrative is primarily that of the adult Kabria, but that the recognition of moral disorder that is enjoined for her and her friends is not correlated to any sense of existential crisis and thus to the necessity of making fundamental life changes. In sharp contrast, in Awoonor's novel the entrance of Amamu into Nima is designed not to answer any direct questions regarding the social malaise represented by slum life but to produce a terrifying existential crisis for the protagonist, the ultimate outcome of which is insanity. To put this theme in context, we must recall that *This Earth* was published in

1972 and was quickly identified as providing an excellent example of modernist experimentation. All the elements of high modernism that are normally associated with the Western novel are to be seen in Awoonor's first novelistic offering. Derek Wright provides a superb synopsis of the main elements of This Earth in his discussion of the variant forms of eschatology and apocalypse that merge into a fervid Africanist modernism:

> In Awoonor's novel, however, the oppositions are of a different order. Here, the scatological presentation of the visible, historical world is countered and, to some extent, overridden by eschatological considerations of the life of the spirit in another, unseen one. The naturalistic prose chapters carry Amamu forward through the vignettes of a representative colonial childhood and adolescence, in the course of which the debris of colonial history and its legacy in postcolonial Ghana is accumulated and stored in the novel's collective consciousness. But in contradistinction with this linear movement, the book's poetic interludes carry Amamu back in a circle to a visionary rediscovery of his lost childhood cousin Dede who, in his personal subconscious, is identified with figures from a pre-European African mythology—notably Mammy Water, the mermaid or Woman of the Sea with magical, supernatural powers—which has survived the depredations of a century of colonialism. The Westernized linear time of the prose narrative is, in Gerald Moore's words, "only a measure of the intervals between moments of vision." This cycle of return to a reborn childhood is, moreover, complicated by being tied to a parallel eschatological cycle: the visionary liberation achieved by what Amamu refers to as the assumption of the "body" of Dede's death can be purchased only by his own passage through madness and bodily death, and this death is presented as a process through which Amamu is reborn into the spirit world from which he arrives in the village of Deme in the first chapter.[7]

We may reorder the main elements of Wright's account in this passage and further on in his essay for our own purposes: historical elements conveyed in scatological terms yet subtend an eschatological matrix of utopian projection. The eschatological matrix opens itself up to the circulation of various supplementary images, including those of Mammy Watta, the legendary mermaid common to West African folklore, along with the other pregnant private symbols of butterfly, dunghill, and regenerative chrysalis that ebb and flow through the mind of the protagonist. At the same time, the inherent cyclicality of these images is set alongside a more linear teleology that is mimetic of the bildungsroman, and whose ultimate objective is the fusion with the childhood love of Dede, the achievement of which requires a form of psychological dismemberment and the disavowal of the self. This in turn speaks to a form of Christological symbolization for Amamu and the implication that he is fated to be a sacrificial carrier, a *pharmakos* in the idiom of classical Greek theatre.[8]

From the perspective of spatial logics, the most important element of This *Earth* is the peculiar and often unsettling sense of modularity by which the city is experienced. Amamu's regular traversals of the city are conveyed essentially as alienating experiences that produce repetitive hermeneutical crises in his own mind. His passage through the urbanscape discloses a space that is marked by an inherent discontinuity and which itself signifies the stubborn failure of social transformation. As a general rule Amamu traverses Accra as if it were a space of incomprehensibility, with different aspects of the city steadfastly persuading him of his out-of-placedness. He also feels thoroughly damned to being persistently misunderstood both by members of his own class fraction and by the many women in whom he seeks solace. The novel suggests that the spatial discontinuities he feels in his mind also derive in part from historical problems in colonial and postcolonial history. Amamu's cultivated solitude suggests an immediate and sharp contrast to the characters in *Faceless*, for in Darko's novel the women at MUTE act as a collective in all things, sharing stories about their woes and tribulations, supporting each other in negotiating the bewilderments of city life, and, most importantly, acting as a detective collective when it comes to solving the mystery of Baby T's death. Despite the fact that Kabria is our focal point to the middle-class life demarcated by her household, she is not allowed to be the exclusive center of agential choice and action within the narrative. All major decisions that she takes in solving the mystery are taken in consultation with the women at MUTE acting as a collective. And even when, as happens from time to time, Kabria takes decisive actions on the basis of instinctual interpretations of immediate contextual cues, she returns to her MUTE colleagues to report and systematically justify her initial instincts. Contrastively, in Awoonor's novel Amamu's crisis is of an interpretative and existential kind that is strictly individualized. His trajectory is closer to the form of the bildungsroman we noted earlier, with different dimensions of space and time correlated to his own unfolding crises of consciousness.

As has been noted by most commentators on *This Earth*, the novel's highly unusual narrative structure makes it distinctive within African writing. This is because of the bold modernist experiments Awoonor undertakes with narrative form. Chapters of third-person realist narration (1, 2, 3, etc.) that unveil Amamu's biography and aspects of the country's history alternate with chapters of interiorized stream of consciousness (1a, 2a, 3a, etc.) in which the purpose is to track an effervescent set of images driven by his experiences of nostalgia, anxiety, fear, and sometimes even speculative utopian desire. But these largely symbol-laden chapters also cannibalize references to Ghanaian history in such a way as to render them a serious interpretative problematic for the protagonist. Furthermore, the interiorized chapters also fuse a series of subtle Christological and religious references that have Amamu at their center. In this way Amamu is styled *in his own mind* at once as a loner, as the product of a deeply problematic colonial and postcolonial history, as a privileged if unsettled interpreter of past and future, and as a potential sacrificial character. And even though the stream of consciousness chapters seem to take off from particular events introduced within the realist ones, the fit between the alternating realist and nonrealist chapters is far from secure, such that the interiorized chapters may sometimes be read autonomously from the realist ones and vice versa. From chapter 13, however, the alternating sequence is abrogated in favor of exclusive focalization through the prism of realism, except that this is a realism heavily laden with the elusive motifs that we have become accustomed to in their incremental repetition in previous interiorized chapters. There is good reason for this apparent abrogation, for in fact by this point Amamu has suffered a nervous breakdown that undermines his capacity to establish distinctions between reality and the domain of his fraught interiority. The epiphanic moment of collapse comes in the visit he makes to Nima in search of Yaro, his long-serving houseboy. Yaro's nephew Ibrahim and some friends have been arrested by the police for stealing some sheep and poultry from a house in the adjacent neighborhood of Kanda. Ibrahim has suffered severe beatings from the police, and Yaro's terrifying task is to try to rescue his nephew from the Nima police station. But the police insist on someone that "sabe book" to sign the documents that would be used to grant Ibrahim bail. Hand-wringing anguish for Yaro: enter Amamu.

The description provided of Nima in chapter 12 is vividly scatological in a way that gives the slum a much more disturbing spatial realization than Darko's Sodom and Gomorrah. For whereas Sodom and Gomorrah was frightening because of the violent characters that maraud its streets, Nima on the other hand is shown in Awoonor's novel to be the ultimate encapsulation of decrepitude and decay. The slum is described as symbolically skirting the west central part of the city "like a vulture" and is strung around various "dunghills" that have been conveniently misnamed in the view of the narrator as garbage dumps (151). More important, contrasts and contradictions are established between Nima and other Accra neighborhoods to mark it off as an urban wasteland. As the narrator has it, Nima developed parasitically on the emergence of the American army base at Cantonments during World War II, thus attracting squatters from all across the country, but especially from the north. (By tying the formation of the township to World War II, Awoonor provides us a foreshortened and in fact anachronistic historical account; as we saw in chapter 2 Nima was first settled in 1931 by Alhaji Amadu Futa and his followers and was the subject of intense litigation well into the 1950s. The war was important for its evolution but was by no means the exclusive trigger of the slum's formation.) Nima is typified by the narrator as a place of temporary sojourners whose transitional nature nevertheless extends into a condition of permanent precariousness. The narrator opines that it "always needs a Moses to move any captive race of squatters," but that Nima had no such Moses. The idea of a salvational Moses immediately inscribes Nima into a history of captivity and victim diasporas, thus tying it to the repeated Christian religious motifs that have been discursively associated with Amamu up to this point in the novel. The narrator further suggests that Nima is also the product of the class hierarchies that have governed the spatial formation of the city. The slum's location at the then outskirts of the town and the fact that all real job opportunities lie at a spatial remove from the slum ensure that it evolves from the 1940s into a veritable dormitory neighborhood servicing the more affluent districts of Kaneshie, Ridge, and Kanda. The terms of class hierarchies are established by the narrator with reference to the distant hills of Legon, where professors launch elaborate disquisitions on Fabianism without reference to the oppression in their own Ghanaian society. The hierarchies also relate to the oppressive violence of the police and other security agents, and to the heartless bureaucracy of the city council and its various agencies that treat the denizens of Nima as a worthless drain on municipal resources. That Nima is also the location of prostitutes that service "Lebanese merchants from Beirut, Italian builders working on the Volta, Japanese sailors from the port of Tema [coming] upon the city for short squinted dusky diversions" (154) means that the slum is also located on a transnational circuitry of leisure and cheap thrills. Like the Sodom and Gomorrah of the 1990s that becomes the dumping ground for computer parts, the Nima of the 1960s depicted in This Earth is already imagined as spatially and economically affected by the brutal vagaries of transnational capitalism that place it firmly at the bottom of the pile. While

Nima supplies laborers and sexual workers to denizens of the rest of the city, the effects of its collective disavowal by municipal authorities and the elite classes mean that it comes to be associated only with filth, disease, decay, and death in the social imaginary of people such as Amamu.

When Amamu walks into Yaro's neighborhood, then, the scenes that he encounters in his spatial traversal have accumulated all the elements necessary to the invocation of existential nausea:

> Amamu picked his way carefully that sullen afternoon through faeces human or canine, you cannot tell which, rotten food and puddles of urine, all sending into the hot rising air a chorus of pungent smells and odours. On the first alley behind the mosque, he felt he was near Yaro's house. The air smelled of frying plantain, fish and spices. Along the edges of this leaning alley, four women were frying tatale and plantain, shouting themselves hoarse at urchins in tatters hell bent on theft. He paused to ask one of the urchins who volunteered to lead him there for a fee.
>
> Yaro's house was on the edge of a big gully. Like all the other gullies, it was carved by many rains. Just before the alley swings and bends among the houses, the gully runs on into the depths below with sharp intent. It was a mud house. The gate was made of planks from key-soap packing cases. It was half open. There were in the compound four mud houses menacingly facing each other. An old Moslem was crouching by the side of a short wattle fence washing his testicles with water from a green kettle. The little boy said something to him in Hausa. He turned round slowly, still clutching his invisible testicles, and pointed to one of the mud houses. As if uninterrupted he proceeded with his ablution with a faraway look.
>
> He knocked on the door on which there were charcoal lines recalling to his mind the sign of the Passover. A grunt replied from inside. A little red-eyed boy in the early grips of malaria opened the door. He was naked and clean shaven, dried mango juice on both corners of his mouth. (155)

The sharp assault on all his senses (shit, which was indecipherable as human or canine) and the smell of frying plantain, along with the peculiar animation attributed to various objects (the leaning alley, the alley that swings and bends among the houses and the mud houses that face each other with repressed menace) come together to define Amamu's journey as a sudden epiphany. For the first mark of an epiphanic experience is the intensification of the perspectival sensorium. This also insinuates a sense of representational porosity between the world of objective details and that of the inner workings of the protagonist's mind. Because much of the porosity of these two domains has already been fully explored in the interiorized "a" sections of the novel, and despite the fact that the description in chapter 12 is controlled and dedicated to the elaboration of the external perspective, we know that all the details are being intimately translated into a register of turmoil in Amamu's own mind. However, the purpose of this particular epiphany (and there are several that we might point to in the course of the remainder of the novel) is not to produce a sense of integration or wholeness, as epiphanic moments in literature are often assumed to do, but to generate disjuncture and fragmentation. It is thus a negative epiphany.[9]

Amamu's epiphanic journey into Nima unfolds along two different representational axes simultaneously. The first pertains to the discontinuous spatial character of Accra itself and the second relates to the more nebulous classical invocation of the descent into the underworld. Here, we must pause to recall the only epigraph to the novel, which is culled from Canto I of Dante's *Inferno*: "In the middle of the journey of our life I came myself within a dark wood where the straight way was lost. Ah, how hard a thing it is to tell of that wood, savage and harsh and dense, the thought of which renews my fear! So bitter is it that death is hardly more." This famous and much-quoted opening to *The Divine Comedy* is an appropriate allegory for Amamu's journey into the urban hell that is Nima. The dark wood where the straight way was lost of the epigraph not only proleptically invokes the Nima slum, it also suggests that the protagonist is a quest hero in search of answers to deep spiritual and existential questions. What is referred to in Dante as worse than death is literalized in *This Earth*, for in the next installment of the narrative from chapter 13 onward we find that Amamu has abandoned his home and all attendant responsibilities and simply become a denizen of the streets. He sets out on the same evening of the visit to the Nima police station on a lengthy itinerary that takes him from his home in Kanda to the Kwame Nkrumah Circle then up along the Ring Road through the Airport Residential Area and then on and on and on beyond the city limits until he arrives at the beach in Keta where he sits under the symbolic Indian almond tree of his nostalgic reveries that we saw in the interiorized sections of the novel. While the place markers in this long itinerary may all be read for symbolic cues, especially in relation to the times and contexts in which they have appeared within the earlier interiorized sections of the novel, the real point of the toponyms is to demarcate a *via dolorosa* of pain, fatigue, and suffering as he progressively sheds his clothing and thus all signifiers of secure identity. (We are obliged to note in passing that the itinerary described by the narrator for Amamu is supposed to be read as a series of emotional rather than specifically geographical markers. This is because strictly speaking to go from Kanda to Kwame Nkrumah Circle and then to the Airport Residential Area along the Ring Road is to go backward from a starting point and then forward to another point then sideways before retracing one's steps to follow a straight line along the coast to Keta, a well-known coastal town to the far east of Accra. The three locations that Amamu traverses before heading off to Keta serially demarcate monuments to decolonization and to two of the most salubrious middle-class neighborhoods in the city. It is almost as if Amamu's itinerary is a series of goodbyes to an elliptical historically temporality made up of the impulses of decolonization on the one hand and the narrow interests of his own class fraction on the other, as if in a forlorn quest for a possible resolution to his existential crisis.)

Amamu is discovered several days later at Keta. In his mind he has finally embraced his "woman of the sea":

> Then slowly he saw her, the woman of the sea, his cousin love of those years long, long ago rising from the sea. She rose slowly, head first, adorned in sapphires, corals and all the ancient beads her mother left for her pubertal rites. She rose slowly from a dream sea. The sea was real: the sun was beating down hard and cruel. It was like a scene in that waking dream of fever. It seemed suddenly that the centuries and the years of pain of which he was the inheritor, and the woes for which he was singled out to be the carrier and the sacrifice, were being rolled away, were being faded in that emergence. Here at last, he realized with a certain boyish joy, was the hour of his salvation. (179)

Derek Wright is correct to note in his essay cited earlier that the reiterated "dunghill and butterfly, night soil dump and regenerative chrysalis, are antithetical, not complementary images" (25). As he notes further, "Awoonor's sombre prose places more emphasis on an antiquity of unalleviated suffering, the sheer oppressive weight of past pollutions, and forebodings of some final apocalypse than on regenerative deliverance in the present. . . . 'Sacrifice' and 'salvation' look to religious and supernatural alternatives, and the "emergence" takes place on a personal rather than a public level" (25). It is clear that the multitiered scatological (physical decay) and eschatological levels (saturated symbols) out of which his environment and his consciousness are woven in tandem frustrate any form of epic action, so that his madness is ultimately the retreat into an exclusive private sphere of interiority in which the quest for salvation is disconnected from any of the sociopolitical and cultural contradictions that lie outside of his mind and within the urban landscape. Thus, despite the appearances of a salvational ending, the ultimate point of rest for Amamu must not be interpreted as one of integration but rather of discontinuity. For to achieve what appears to be a form of spiritual coherence, he has had to shed the middle-class pretensions of the sensitive lawyer and come to terms with the ridiculous pointlessness of his vocation in the face of the gargantuan social abjection that is Nima. The Nima that confronts him is a challenge and counterpoint to all the middle-class haunts (the senior civil servants' clubhouse, the university campus, the courts) around which his identity as a privileged city lawyer has been shaped. The places that he shares with his class fraction are also markers of an elite cosmopolitanism, places that suspend the messiness of colonial and postcolonial history for the apparently dispassionate pursuit of the quasi-revolutionary discourse already hinted at by the professors at Legon. How much these elite landmarks are themselves the disguises of insurmountable sociopolitical contradictions becomes visible to Amamu only when he enters Nima, their direct counterpoint and negation. The traversal from one class-coded space of urban society to another equally class-coded domain then triggers a frightful emotional collapse, implying simultaneously that the hierarchical structuring of urban society has been a necessary precondition for the semblance of ordered discourse that has sustained the social formation of his class fraction in the first place. At a personal level, the colonial and postcolonial ciphers of social crisis that manifest themselves in the discontinuous urban spaces enjoin a measure of elective solitude for the middle-class protagonist as long as these different spaces retain their strict features of incommensurability in his mind. Once he is forced to admit that the incommensurability is no mere function of spatial form, but the essential dialectical structure of urban society as such, he is confronted by the inescapably corrupt contaminations of his own class position. This requires him to distance himself from mere contemplation and to pursue a form of decisive action, that is, revolution. This, however, is something that Amamu is incapable of. Thus, despite the fact that This Earth is more beautifully written than Faceless, the essential agency that Kabria and her friends ascribe to themselves for intervening in the social domain appears ultimately more attractive to an observer than Amamu's assimilation into a longed-for world of eschatological forms.

The two novels we have looked at by no means exhaust the representational character of the urban space of Accra. A fuller account would have to deal with the phenomenologically complex novels of Kojo Laing, in which space takes shape on the border between surrealism and magical realism. Thus both *Search Sweet Country* and *Woman of the Aeroplanes* conceive of urban space as an externalized kaleidoscope of multiple phenomenologies that leak and bump into each other. This kaleidoscopic leakage comes to affect characterization as well, such that at various points Laing's characters seem to take on the emotional hue of the spaces they traverse and vice versa. Thus in Laing's novels space is essentially anamorphic and constitutes in itself a potent intervention into the very structure of thinking that makes up urban society.[10] Laing's novels are extremely recalcitrant to any sustained interpretation and defeat any easy conclusions with their protean and elusive metaphorical saturations. And yet what is commonly shared by Laing, Darko, Awoonor, and several other Ghanaian writers who have attempted to represent the space of the city is the persistent urge to understand space as located on a continuum between the real and the esoteric. It becomes a means for grasping the incommensurable nature of changes in fortune that manifest themselves both at the social and characterological levels, and which the Western bildungsroman is ultimately not suited to fully exposing without some form of augmentation. The evolutionary split between "premodern" and modern forms of narration that Bakhtin spoke of in his essay is not so easily sustainanble for African literature because the resources of orality that writers usually draw from install an occult zone of polysemy between myth and realism in different configurations for narrative. This is as true for the realism of Achebe as it is for the magical realism of Ben Okri. The plethora of spatial viewpoints offered by the thriving Ghanaian film industry (Gollywood) that tends to dramatize the permeable boundary between the real and the esoteric in urban life ensures that the oscillations between the two becomes a central part of the social imaginary well beyond the scope of literary writing. And it is the direct impact that Gollywood is having on our understanding of urban space that poses the next challenge. An account of urban representation, the novels can only be taken as the preamble to such a task.

CONCLUSION

On Urban Free Time: Vladimir, Estragon, and Rem Koolhaas

The city . . . does not tell its past, but contains it like the lines of a hand, written in the corners of the streets, the gratings of the windows, the banisters of the steps . . . every segment marked in turn with scratches, indentations, scrolls. Cities are invisible stories and stories are invisible cities.

—Italo Calvino, *Invisible Cities*

If Italo Calvino's *Invisible Cities* evokes a cartography of desires, hopes, and vague ideas, it is because it couples a strong sense of place with that of ephemeralness. Each city Marco Polo arrives at is both scrupulously material and yet peculiarly evanescent. Read in a certain light, *Invisible Cities* becomes a way of reading all cities we come to, for who would deny that a city is as a much a place of emotional investments as it is the domain of brute geographies? And so, we find, it is for the urban critic.

In *Theory from the South* the Comaroffs put forward a definition of Afromodernity that is pertinent to what we might extrapolate from *Oxford Street* for application elsewhere. As they note, Afromodernity demands to be seen not as a derivate copy or counterfeit of the "real thing" of Euromodernity, but in its own right as "a hydra-headed, polymorphous, mutating ensemble of signs and practices in terms of which people across the continent have made their lives" (2010, 7). Afromodernity "is a vernacular—just as Euromodernity is a vernacular—wrought in an ongoing, geopolitically situated engagement with the unfolding history of the present" (9).[1] They suggest then that the global South, and Africa within it, affords privileged insights into the workings of the world at large. The Comaroffs provide a number of examples to illustrate this proposition, including Brazil's seizing of the initiative in the innovation of the biofuel economy, the extension of India's auto industry into Britain, and the impact of the Hong Kong banking sector on the development of new species of financial market, among various others. Or, in another register, the emergence of South Africa, a major force in the international mineral economy, as the America of Africa, an African America eager to experiment with constitutional law, populist politics, and, even if hesitatingly, post-neoliberal forms of redistribution. Or, in yet a third register, the rise of new forms of urbanism, as in Lagos, where many of the trends of canonical modernity are displayed, where "Western cities can be seen in hyperbolic guise" (14).[2]

Both their views of Afromodernity and the urban hyperbole that they point to with respect to Lagos have been a regular thematic in discussions of urban Africa. Thus for Rem Koolhaas, Lagos exemplifies lessons to be learned for "the city yet to come," to echo the felicitous title of AbdouMaliq Simone's book on African cities (2004). If the proposition that African cities foretell the life of world cities in general gives us pause due to evidence of dire decay and outright chaos that marks many of them, it is not because Africa does not provide salutary lessons for the global elsewhere, but that the lessons to be derived from the continent are mired in apparently intractable paradoxes and contradictions, making the process by which we extract the lessons as important as the lessons themselves. And if, as I propose to show presently, Lagos does instigate insights about urban form for a global elsewhere, it is not necessarily in the terms in which these have been couched by the Comaroffs, Koolhaas, and other commentators on that energetic yet bewildering city. This is not just because their models are afflicted by a measure of romanticism regarding the inventiveness of African urban dwellers, but because in many instances their conclusions do not derive from an understanding of the relationship between ephemera, process, and structure in the formation of the African urban. As I see it, ephemera (or the ephemeral) is a placeholder for variant cognates such as the unsayable, the elusive, the ineffable, and the transitional. And yet it is important to note that what might pass for the ephemeral in all the multifarious inflections I am trying to impose upon it is also the direct product of structure and is what lends structure its formal particularity in the final instance. Since in all commentaries on urban Africa there is an oscillation between descriptions of structural morphologies and the relationships that people establish with these, the ephemeral or ineffable is set aside for the sake of detailing what is visible and thus objective. In other words, the contradiction between African urban architectural, transportational, or built environment and the ephemeral human interactions that people establish with these is always (I use this adverb advisedly) resolved in favor of ever more proliferating descriptions of the physical and material forms themselves. Neither affect theory nor phenomenology, for example, is a part of urban studies, whether of the African or the Western variety. Thus one of the central challenges to be faced for extrapolating from African cities derives from the difficulty entailed in distinguishing between what has immediately concrete implications for describing the urban and that which appears on preliminary encounter to be merely ephemeral. The distinction soon reveals itself to be defective, for any immersive ethnographic account of African cities will show that all that appears ephemeral contains consequences for understanding the social relationships that undergird urban society. Thus instead of an all-that-is-solid-melts-into-air attitude with regard to ephemera, we might underscore the direct opposite for the African city: nothing is ephemeral or concrete, but framing makes it so. The role of rumors and urban myths in the shaping of attitudes toward the bureaucratic state and municipal apparatus in Africa, for example, provides telling evidence of the place of ephemera for understanding African cities. For rumors and urban myths are the transactional glue that hold African urban societies together. As I have noted elsewhere, the interactions with officialdom that circulate freely in African cities often entail the translation of the bureaucratic apparatus into the domain of gift exchange, with all the concomitant expectations of reciprocity that this involves. Bribery and corruption are what government ministers indulge in with their girlfriends, but for the proverbial man on the street making a gift to an official at say the passport office is a means not just of getting things done in good time but also of accruing symbolic capital that may later be called back either for one's own use or for the massaging of one's social networks. Thus is a system of patronage constructed for the ordinary African and a separation installed between the perceived corruption of state officials and the "something small" that changes hands between ordinary folk and the little and not-so-little gatekeepers of bureaucratic authority.[3] The ultimate challenge in describing the African city then is methodological and among other things entails the fundamental question of the means by which we integrate the study of assumed ephemera into our interpretations of material conditions and how we read the two domains for insights into processes and structure. Here Accra provides a handy preface to Lagos not in the form of straightforward homology (the cities are starkly different in their histories, their current configurations, and the relationships they have with the nation-states of which they are a key part) but with respect to the relationships between apparent urban ephemera, processes, and the social and material forms that appear salient for extrapolation to urban theory in general.

Rem Koolhaas's work on Lagos has become justifiably famous for the degree of hopeful affirmation that he expresses with regard to that city's material form. Both his essays in Okwui Enwezor's *Under Siege* (2002) and in the collective statements in the *Mutations* collection (2000) proffered by the Harvard Project on the City that he directs pose Lagos as an example of a new reality, a reality that has to be accounted for in its specificity and from which object lessons are to be drawn for understanding urban forms elsewhere. For Koolhaas and his collaborators, Lagos offers not the standard image of urban blight, the collapse of social services, and overpopulation but rather the realities of heady urban inventiveness that resolves itself into the constant recycling of both objects and space. Of the thirty-three megapolises projected to be in place by 2015, twenty-seven will be found in the developing world, with the population of Lagos at anything between eighteen and twenty-three million estimated to be among the largest. Furthermore, there is an expressed impulse in the Harvard Project to properly describe how this African city works, both as a prototype of the African urban and as a projection of cities elsewhere in the world. Like other scholars of urban realities in the developing world that we noted in the introduction, Koolhaas laments the substantial failure of standard Eurocentric discourses. Thus: "This work is not inspired by the need to discover ever more exotic, violent, extreme urban thrills, but by the realization that the engrained vocabulary and values of architectural discourse are painfully inadequate to describe the current production of urban subsistence. They perpetuate an image of the city that is essentially Western, and subconsciously insist that all cities, wherever they are, be interpreted in that image; they systematically find wanting any urban form that does not conform. Our words cannot describe our cities with any precision or pleasure" (Koolhaas 2002, 175).

Note that in this brief essay, Koolhaas, a world-renowned urban architect, is predominantly interested in urban architectural forms and their relation to subsistence. This interest carries into the ways in which he and the Harvard Project describe Lagos and what they perceive to exist between denizens of the city and its infrastructural environment. Every part of Lagos's decrepit stretches of superhighways, crumbling coverleaf intersections with their supporting frameworks and interstitial structures of road embankments, railway tracks, and extensive and multiple shorelines have been "colonized by a host of secondary industries and services: cement block factories, vulcanizers, roadside mechanics, hairdressers, markets, and so on" (Koolhaas et al. 2000, 177). And at Jankara, Lagos's largest market, four coverleaf ramps have been taken over as a giant recycling exchange where every piece of debris is liable to be transformed from one state to another. The recycling is not geared to the domestic sphere as such but insistently toward insertion into the circuits of market consumption. Lagos's famous go-slows (traffic jams) also provide market opportunities in which everything is bought and sold from ice-cold water to food to foreign magazines, much like what we see on Oxford Street and in other parts of Accra. Finally, its roads "are not plan lines between points, but perhaps its most elastic and variable spaces, made more enabling by local modifications which deny the road's insistent linearity—guardrails are removed, jersey barriers put aside. At all bottlenecks, the road is converted to allow movement in a maximum of directions" (Koolhaas et al. 2000, 686).

And yet it is precisely at Koolhaas's suggestion of the template of Lagos's vast recycling culture that we ought to pause. Since primary household units, the walls between them, and the larger external environment of highways and coverleaf ramps are all subject to some form of recycling that was unanticipated by their original use, it would be a mistake to interpret recycling only as what takes place with respect to objects and their transformations. Rather, the recycling of objects in Lagos must be read as a material correlative of *wider practices of the recycling of urban life forms and of space* that take place within the domain of the informal economy. Unlike the criticisms that have been made of Koolhaas's observations about Lagosians' inventiveness by various commentators, I extend his largely literal use of the term "recycling" into a more metaphorical and thus more nuanced register. The accusation that Koolhaas's Lagos is overly romanticized and ahistorical and that the view from the presidential helicopter from which Koolhaas and his team draw their conclusions about the city are inorganic and false is pertinent to evaluating his observations. Yet Koolhaas and the collective Harvard Project on the City are remarkable for providing a thoroughly *spatial* sense of the city that starts from the lowest common denominator of the household unit and rises systematically to encompass the entire urban sphere.[4] Thus the understanding of Lagos's urban morphology is vividly spatial in a way that nimbly sidesteps the essentially ethno-political historical accounting by which many of his critics have evaluated his work.[5] As in the case of Accra, ethno-political histories rarely succeed in extracting the spatial implications of such realities. To be sure ethno-political histories do have their value, and indeed part 1 of *Oxford Street* explored several aspects of such histories for the evolution of Accra. But at all times the major challenge has been to produce a thoroughly spatial history of the city, with the ethno-political transformations that we found with respect to the Ga Mashie akutsei (Alata, Otublohum, etc.), the Afro-Brazilian Tabon, the Danish Euro-Africans of Osu, and the various northern zongos (Tudu, Nima, Madina) being read for spatial cues that might allow us to interpret today's Accra beyond the temporalities of ethno-history.

It is the terms by which Koolhaas frames the social relationalities of space for Lagosians that require revision and not the spatial descriptions themselves. Here is where a sense of the dialectical relations between ephemera, processes, and structure becomes relevant. What Koolhaas recognizes as the frenetic recycling of objects and space is not merely a feature of inventiveness but rather the product of urban free time produced by the vagaries of the informal economy. We have already encountered the concept of free time in relation to the kòbòlòi of Accra (chapter 6), but here I want to elaborate the concept in a different direction to take account of the phenomenology of free time as an integral aspect of the collocation of the social imaginary and of what Cornelius Castoriadis describes as "systematic delirium." We can largely agree with his assertion that "the institution of society is the institution of social doing and of social representing/saying" (1987, 36). Distinguishing between individual and social imaginaries, Castoriadis assimilates the category of socially meaningful signification to that of the social imaginary and argues for seeing social significations as efficacious in constituting societies. Signification, in his terms, does not refer solely to specific symbols but to various dimensions of representation on the basis of which other things are represented. Further, these representations have a practical efficacy since people perform actions on the basis of such representations. Thus, for example, the "economy" and the "economic" are central social imaginary significations which do not "refer" to something but on the basis of which a host of things are socially represented, reflected, acted upon, and made as economic (362). Following Castoriadis, we might think of the social imaginary as *a signifying chain or series, all the links of which are not necessarily visible or manifest at all times.* In other words, the chain of signification is often ephemeral, yet on the basis of which a range of social forms acquire meaningfulness. There is nothing pathological about the systematic delirium: it derives from a mode of abstraction that combines incoherence with rationality and grafts representation to larger categories such as society, economy, and politics. Even if ultimately servicing different objectives, the systematic delirium operates as much at the level of interpersonal social relations as it does at the level of urban form, especially for cities such as Accra and Lagos.

As we might recall with respect to our discussion of the social conditions of the kòbòlò, the poor have free time while the rich have leisure or, in another formulation suggested to me by Ackbar Abbas at the Johannesburg Workshop in Theory and Criticism in 2013, the poor have time while the rich have space. Strictly speaking, however, free time must be seen as the product of the informal economy, and thus of the incoherence brought on by the dysfunction of the postcolonial African state in general. Free time must also be recognized as an unbearable burden that the under- and unemployed attempt to exchange for labor or work time. From the original description of the concept of informal economy put forward by Keith Hart in his landmark study of the phenomenon in Accra's Nima in the 1970s, we must also recall that the informal economy is marked by fantastic entrepreneurial aspirations. What Hart describes as entrepreneurial aspirations are arguably as much a question of necessity as they are of choice. More importantly, for grasping the specific character of free time, the informal economy must be understood as enjoining, nay enforcing, a constant capacity for recycling of tasks and job roles via which grassroots entrepreneurship gets articulated: the same person may today be a vulcanizer, tomorrow a barber, and the third a porter carrying head loads at the bustling central market of Makola or Jankara. As a general rule, the most entrepreneurial actors within the African informal economy switch roles in a progressively upward spiral so as to transcend meniality and move into roles that entail participation in ever vaster and complex networks. All the workers mentioned in Koolhaas's description of Lagos fall firmly within the informal economy nexus. Among their number may also be counted the confidence trickster (visas to America or Europe, anyone?), as well as the large crop of earnest evangelical pastors that preach the prosperity gospel at various venues scattered across African cities, from makeshift churches to traffic intersections. The job roles just described and the fluidity of their transformations are to be found in Accra and Lagos as much as in Dakar, Nairobi, Duala, Johannesburg, and other cities like them across the continent. The central thing to note here, however, is the relationship between free time and the necessity for recycling or reinvention of the self that is an inescapable product of the informal economy.

Predominantly, while the informal economy may be understood as constituted by objective and even measurable economic vectors (the contraction of the state, lack of jobs, poor socioeconomic and educational infrastructures, or other forms of economic crises brought on by uncertainties in the processes of globalization at large), one of its primary consequences is a particular structuration of free time and its attendant phenomenology of waiting. The choice is not between work and rest, or work and boredom, but between active and inactive understandings of the agency that is required to survive the incoherences generated by economic informality. This view requires the interpretation of free time as at once a set of urban practices *and* a peculiar phenomenology that is experienced *as an obligation to do something* as a way of combating the vagaries of free time. Because survival is the ultimate question at issue, doing nothing is not really an option for participants of the informal economy. A handy way of grasping the phenomenology of free time I am trying to elaborate here is to imagine that *Waiting for Godot* had been written by a Lagosian with a full awareness of the vagaries of the informal economy. As is well known, in Beckett's play Vladimir and Estragon attempt to cope with the burden of free time they experience of waiting for the elusive Godot by way of inventing various games of language (not language games, a related but different concept). But because there is no clear end in sight language collapses under the insistence of meaninglessness produced by uncertainty. The games with language sometimes also entail empty gestures as providing signal proofs that despite everything the two tramps do exist. Thus, in one telling instance:

VLADIMIR: This is becoming really insignificant.
ESTRAGON: Not enough.
Silence
VLADIMIR: What about trying them.
ESTRAGON: I've tried everything.
VLADIMIR: No, I mean the boots.
ESTRAGON: Would that be a good thing?
VLADIMIR: It'd pass the time. (Estragon hesitates.) I assure you it'd be an occupation.
ESTRAGON: A relaxation.
VLADIMIR: A recreation.
ESTRAGON: A relaxation.
VLADIMIR: Try.
ESTRAGON: You'll help me?
VLADIMIR: I will of course.
ESTRAGON: We don't manage too badly, eh, Didi, between the two of us?
VLADIMIR: Yes, yes. Come on, we'll try the left first.
ESTRAGON: We always find something, eh Didi, to give us the impression we exist? (64)

The scenario of waiting and attempting to exercise proofs of their existence while they negotiate the burden of free time is central to the meaning of the dramatic action. Nevertheless, unlike what we might assume about the character of waiting for things to change for the better in places like Accra and Lagos, because *Waiting for Godot* is ultimately devoid of economic rationality, the games of language that Vladimir and Estragon play end up being utterly emptied of any vestiges of practicality. Had Beckett been a hypothetical Lagosian he could very well have had Vladimir and Estragon turning themselves into entrepreneurial artisans of waste, recycling not just language but any objects by which they might productively negotiate the vagaries of free time. In this respect their interaction with Lucky and Pozzo would have been conceived quite differently. From the perspective of a semi- or unemployed Lagosian, what a greater missed opportunity than that Vladimir and Estragon do *not* try to sell Estragon's recalcitrant boots to the evidently wealthy and self-involved Pozzo when he enters the action in Act I?[26]

From Wole Soyinka's distinctly Beckettian *The Road*, on the other hand, we get another form of waiting that is saturated with ritual import and thus partially disguised as pertaining to another mode of being. This is how the play opens:

> *Professor is a tall figure in Victorian outfit—tails, top-hat, etc., all thread-bare and shiny at the lapels from much ironing. He carries four enormous bundles of newspaper and a fifth of paper odds and ends impaled on a metal rod stuck in a wooden rest. A chair-stick hangs from one elbow, and the other arm clutches a road sign bearing a squiggle and the one word, "BEND."*

> PROF: [*he enters in a high state of excitement, muttering to himself*]: Almost a miracle . . . dawn provides the greatest miracles but this . . . in this dawn has exceeded its promise. In the strangest of places . . . God God God but there is a mystery in everything. A new discovery every hour—I am used to that, but that I should be led to where this was hidden, sprouted in secret for heaven knows how long . . . for there was no doubt about it, this word was growing, it was growing from earth until I plucked it. . . . (157)

Professor's extravagant motley Victorian outfit is a marker of his previous middle-class affiliations from which, by the start of the play, he has obviously dissociated himself. The whiff of anachronism suggested by his peculiar sartorial sense is not entirely misplaced, since his domineering character is also meant to recall a cross between a lord of the underworld and Fagan, the familiar villain of Dickens's *Oliver Twist*. Professor is in a vigorous quest for what he calls the Word, the spirit of which he tries to arrive at by assembling a range of quotidian scripts (the bundles of newspapers; paper odds and ends) and road signs, alongside the deployment of a hybrid interpretative mechanism that combines Yoruba semiotics with a quasi-Christian sensibility. He claims to have a pact with risks, dangers, and death, and the social periphery in which he undertakes his quest is populated by jobless lorry park touts and other characters that make their living from petty document forgery, the provision of "protection" for politicians, and epic daydreaming. While the jobless lorry park touts provide a good example of the enforced and burdensome waiting that is entailed in the informal economy, the strong religious quest motif provided by the eccentric Professor means that the action is ultimately geared toward a ritual catharsis. This is what we see at the very end, when in invoking the spirit of Ogun Professor triggers panic among the touts and is stabbed by Say Tokyo Kid. He thus becomes a *pharmakos*, the Greek sacrificial carrier that is taken to purge the community of its ritual contaminations.

In both the plays by Beckett and Soyinka we have just looked at waiting might be productively seen as an aspect of existential alienation that enforces the recycling of both space and language in a variety of ways. Yet even though both sets of characters pursue their existence on the peripheries of society, their alienation must not be misunderstood as merely that of social separation. Rather alienation must be understood as what is generated by the impossibility of providing a coherent account of oneself because of the contamination of the tools and instruments by which that account might be launched. In the urban contexts of Lagos, Accra, and elsewhere in Africa, the poor and unemployed wait while cobbling together the means of such accounting. Free time is not the same as freedom, but the direct product of an incoherent economy.

If the informal economy is the product of economic conditions, then free time is its phenomenological dimension. It is this that leads to the impulse to recycling selves, objects, and space. If Lagos provides prefatory lessons for cities elsewhere it is not necessarily in the terms outlined by the Comaroffs, Rem Koolhaas, and others. For as all economic indices have shown, the global economic meltdown of 2008/9 on cities such as Athens, Rome, London, Lisbon, Stockholm, and in many parts of the United States spells an expansion of free time the degree of which has not been visible in the global North for several decades. The cycles of capitalist accumulation and crises that have been starkly evident since at least the end of World War II now produce completely different responses from the economically oppressed because of the level of sophistication and the potential for immediate collective action engendered by today's social media. At issue in today's mass mobilizations is a new form of political and economic critique that appears on the surface to be ad hoc and thus transitory. From the urban protests in France of 2009, the Occupy Movements of 2010, the violent London protests of 2011, the Arab Spring of 2010–2011, and the protests in Istanbul, Stockholm, and Brazil in 2013, the last few years have been marked by mass political actions triggered by what appears on the surface to be simple quotidian events, yet that have masked long histories of disgruntlement. While these protests do not seem to have clearly set agendas for seizing power and altering the structures that impoverish, disempower, and confuse the masses and seem to peter out to concede to reform instead of revolution, they cannot be underestimated for what they reveal about the burdens of free time that have been generated from the disjunctures in the global economy.[7] As I am arguing it here, if what we see in the West today is the articulation of the political dimension of free time, then we ought to be prepared to contemplate that the systematic delirium that has been most starkly evident in African cities has incubated reiterable forms of action that are now being generated from the burden of free time in the West. And in that case the lessons that cities like Accra, Lagos, and others provide for the rest of the world derives not from the interaction of people with frayed and crumbling infrastructure, as crucial as that is, but rather with the modalities by which endangered urban dwellers are forced to do something or die trying. Today, the something to be done may simply involve recycling space and objects, tomorrow the ad hoc mobilization of political sentiment, but the day after that this may call for the ultimate revolution.

APPENDIX

Tro-tro Inscriptions

1. ODO GRACE
2. YOU TOO CAN TRY
3. GOLD NEVER RUST
4. STILL BIG JOE
5. SIMPLEMAN
6. NYAME NA AYE
7. OKYESO NYAME
8. GOD FIRST
9. ANGELS ON GUARD KEEP OFF
10. GRACE AND MERCY
11. APUU TOO
12. SENIOR
13. HAVE U SAID IT TODAY (IN FRONT) THANK U JESUS (BACK)
14. JESUS TUMI WURA
15. WHAT HAVE I DONE?
16. BLESSING (3X) IE ON 3 VEHICLES
17. JOE RINGO
18. PROV. 26:21
19. ATAMFO BEBEREE
20. AWURADE NE ME HANN
21. AWURADE KASA
22. FATHER FORGIVE THEM
23. CHRIST IN YOU THE HOPE OF GLORY
24. TOLOBA
25. NYAME YE ODO
26. ALLAHU AI BAR
27. MEKA SE YESU YE
28. ENYE EASY
29. SMALL BOY
30. DROMO NAA
31. GOLD NEVER RUST
32. EMMANUEL (4X)
33. UNITY
34. SUPER
35. MORNING STAR
36. STOP THAT
37. POYOMAN
38. ABRABO YE BOKOO
39. NYAME BEYE
40. STILL AGOSU
41. FEAR A PERSON
42. STILL OFIE
43. ISHIA ALLAHU (2X)
44. YESU MO
45. PRAYER IS THE KEY
46. YEHOWA
47. NYAME NE MEDIMAFO
48. WITH GOD
49. BLESSED HANDS
50. NEW MAN

51. PATIENCE
52. JESUS LOVES YOU
53. STILL THE LIVING GOD
54. ASASE WURA
55. NOT BY POWER
56. ASK GOD
57. MEDIMAFO TE ASE
58. NEVER SAY DIE
59. MAN OF GOD
60. ONLY ONE NAME JESUS
61. ADOM ARA KWA
62. ANOINTING
63. KABAAKA
64. STILL THE LIVING GOD
65. PRESS ON
66. KRAMO
67. AGYA NIE
68. GLORY BE TO ALLAH
69. ZION BOY
70. CRY YOUR OWN CRY
71. RELAX
72. SUFFER TO GAIN
73. NYAME BA
74. MARANATHA AWURADE BRA
75. GOOD BROTHER
76. ALL FOR GOD
77. MPAEBO
78. KING DAVID
79. SURO NIPA
80. RESPECT
81. EYE ADOM
82. GOD'S PROPERTY
83. KABASHU
84. WONDERFUL JESUS
85. NO FOOD FOR THE LAZY MAN
86. ABRANTIE
87. ADOM OOOO
88. GOLDEN BOY
89. DESTINY

90. YESU TUMI WURA
91. YEHOWA
92. KEEP ON PRAYING
93. 16+10=26
94. JEHOVAH ROHI
95. ELUM
96. NYAME NE HENE
97. ALL FOR GOD
98. HE WILL MAKE IT
99. NOTHING LATE
100. ENVY NOT
101. WINNERS
102. HAVE FAITH IN GOD
103. IT IS THE LORD
104. FEAR NOT
105. EHO
106. HAPPY YOURSELF
107. EYE MMERE
108. PRAYER IS THE KEY
109. ELSHADDAI
110. WHO JAH BLESS
111. GREAT PROVIDER
112. STAFF
113. YESU MO
114. THINK TWICE
115. ALL SHALL PASS
116. WHAT IS WRITTEN IS
    WRITTEN
117. OKYESO
118. SWEET MOTHER
119. PASTOR EYE JESUS
120. TRUST ME
121. IF GOD IS YOUR CO PILOT
    SWITCH SEATS
122. AS IF
123. BY HIS GRACE
124. ELAH EBAL MUSAL
125. GOD IS ABLE
126. FUTURE

127. NHYIRA
128. BISA WO HO
129. PAPAYE
130. DO WO NUA
131. BOAFO PAPA
132. ENSO NYAME YE
133. GREAT GOD OF WONDER
134. BY HIS GRACE
135. JESUS
136. GOD IS ABLE
137. HOW LONG OH LORD
138. OUR FATHER
139. THE MISSIONARY
140. ONE STEP
141. JOB 16:7
142. ENTE SAA
143. OUTSIDER
144. OLD FOLKS
145. DON'T TRUST THEM
146. KONEKT
147. PAPA CLINTON
148. PRESS ON
149. ANIGYE NKOAA
150. NYAME BEKYERE
151. STAR
152. GOD'S TIME
153. DON'T GO THERE
154. ENERGY OF ALMIGHTY
155. OUR FATHER
156. EVERYTHING BY GOD
157. SO THEY ARE
158. ENSO NYAME YE
159. ONE DAY
160. FRENCHMAN
161. WATCH AND PRAY
162. YOU TOO
163. MY SAVIOR
164. ALL THE DAYS ARE EVIL SO
    WATCH AND PRAY

165. MMOGYA BI AKASA
166. REMEMBER THE JUDGMENT
    DAY
167. NAGODE
168. JAH LIVES
169. GOD FIRST
170. GHANAMAN
171. GOD IS FAITHFUL
172. TRUST IN GOD
173. DADA SONY
174. OUR REDEEMER LIVES
175. MESSIAH
176. THE SAME PEOPLE
177. LOVELY
178. KANKAMA
179. ONE DAY
180. HWE DEE AWURADE AYE
181. THE FAVOR OF GOD
182. BUT WHY?
183. FRENCH MAN
184. KRAMO
185. ENSURO
186. HOLY GHOST FIRE
187. NYAME WO HO
188. ONYAME NHYIRA
189. STILL HOLY FIRE
190. GOOD MASTER
191. WODEE WO MU A. . . . .
192. EYE NYAME
193. STAY BLESS
194. JESUS IS MY LIFE
195. DON'T GIVE THEM GABA
196. TAKE A STEP
197. NYAME NTI
198. NE MU NA NKWA WO
199. ZION
200. BLACK MAN
201. ME WURA
202. NYAME AKWAN

203. GOD IS GOOD
204. ENGO SRA NO NTI
205. ROCKY
206. OH SOME FRIENDS
207. PSALM 23
208. JAH GUIDE
209. GLORY BE TO GOD
210. BY GOD'S GRACE
211. SOLDIER
212. DO GOOD
213. DWEN ADWEN PA
214. MEDA NYAME ASE
215. WHO'S FREE?
216. NO WEAPON
217. STILL OLD SCHOOL
218. WHAT HAVE I DONE?
219. GOD' GIFT
220. COOL
221. DEFENDER
222. HOPE
223. HEAVEN
224. ONYAME TE ASE
225. CRUCIFY HIM

226. FAITH IS THE POWER
227. ISAIAH 61:10
228. KRONKRON
229. OLD JOE
230. WITH GOD
231. ABANDENDEN
232. LIVING GOD
233. THAT DAY
234. WITH GOD COOL
235. MPAEBO TIEFO
236. HOLY
237. DI WO FIE ASEM
238. RESPECT THE POLICE
239. YOUR BEST FRIEND CAN BE YOUR ENEMY
240. ABISIBAY
241. ALL POWERS BELONG TO GOD
242. TRIBE 12
243. COMMANDO
244. DON'T FORCE
245. MURPHY
246. NO ONE IS PERFECT

NOTES

Introduction

1. http://www.nytimes.com/interactive/2013/01/10/travel/2013-places-to-go.html?
_r=0, last accessed May 15, 2013.

2. Cohen (1997, 74).

3. Massey (1994).

4. Debates on these questions have been ongoing for decades but gained a new
lease of urgency through the work of UrbanAfrica (see, for example, their "Whose City
Is It Anyway" initiative: http://urbanafrica.net/news/2012/09/14/whose-city-it-anyway)
and also the Accra Millennium City Project that was launched in 2009 with the support
of the World Bank.

5. Roy (2005).

6. The interdisciplinary perspectives include insights from postcolonial studies,
philosophy, literary theory and criticism, and social theory in general. See Mbembe
and Nuttall (2008), Simone (2004), De Boeck and Plissart (2011). Myers (2011) provides
a comprehensive and lively account and critique of the work of the scholars listed above
in the introduction to his own book, while his final chapter proffers a fascinating
analysis of Somalia through a reading of the novels of Nuruddin Farah.

7. However, for discussion of the funding of government-built housing stock in
Accra, see the fine study by Samuel Osei Kwami and Francis Antwi, "The Impact of
Land Delivery and Finance in the Supply of Residential Accommodation in the Urban
Centres of Ghana: The Case Study of Accra, Tema and Kumasi," MSc thesis, Royal
Institute of Technology, Stockholm, 2004.

8. Even though Accra has not known a large or even substantial Chinese population
this has not prevented the establishment of quite popular Chinese restaurants, some
of which date from the late 1960s and early 1970s. The Chinese restaurants in the area
include Chikin' Likin', Tsing Tao, Noble Chinese Restaurant, Peking Restaurant, and
Dynasty, perhaps the most well known of them all.

9. Massey (1994), Harvey (1989).

10. Maxwell et al. (2000).

11. My views on the archeological method are heavily informed by Johnson (2010).
Kyvig and Marty (2010) also proved highly instructive, especially in framing operational

questions about how to research the apparently quotidian and thus easy-to-overlook features of everyday life.

12. On expressive totality, see especially Kellner (1989).

13. Indeed, I have provided a preliminary set of reflections on the Comaroffs' book in Quayson (2012).

Chapter 1: Ga Akutso Formation and the Question of Hybridity

1. The girls' names and other details have been changed to protect their identities. Conversation relayed to me by Ama in an interview in January 2012.

2. An ample description of the Abonse Market is to be found in chapter 2 of Odotei (1972).

3. Irene Odotei, personal communication, May 2012.

4. The account of the dynamics of Ga settlement patterns draws mainly on Odotei (1972, 1989, and 1991). She is the preeminent authority on early Ga historiography.

5. Stanley (1874, 76–77). Stanley's account is but one of several such travel narratives that were highly popular in the period. Others that pertain to Accra, but which, like Stanley's, typically start out from Elmina include Cruickshank (1834), Carnes (1852), Huntley (1850), and Gordon (1874). Along with the narratives of Ludewig Ferdinand Rmer Wisnes (2000), the diaries of Edward Castesen, and the countless letters that were written by the local merchant establishments to their factors in Europe, a fairly detailed if sometimes quirky image of the Gold Coast is produced and sustained over a long period of European contact with people in the region.

6. Stanley's mention of a desire for coolness and the procurement of unpolluted air attributed to the commandant's house obviously derives from ex post facto observations after landing, but which here have been incorporated into the first view of the city described from the arriving ship. This dual positioning of the description as though occurring prior to full knowledge of the township but effectively the product of a review of already-existing impressions perhaps shared or at least confirmed by other European denizens of the town would be of great interest from a postcolonial literary perspective, but should not detain us here. The inherent strangeness of the landscape, here marked especially by what is described as the "jabbering" of the locals and the onset of nausea felt by the Christian (read civilized) sensibility, replicates a discourse of colonial encounter the variants of which are to be seen in texts as diverse as H. Rider Haggard's *King Solomon's Mines* (1885), Conrad's *Heart of Darkness* (1897), E. M. Forster's *A Passage to India* (1924), Jean Rhys's *Wide Sargasso Sea* (1966), and Assia Djebar's much later reprisal of the same trope in the opening to her *Fantasia: An Algerian Cavalcade* (1993). The point here is not so much the accuracy or otherwise of Stanley's description, as the fact that he is writing about the town through an established template that couples the picturesque (the framing device of the reference to the terrace) with the sense of nausea that emerges from the encounter with the incomprehensible Other. See Carter (2010).

7. Evidence of European support of local warring factions in exchange for land and other privileges emerges most strongly from the eighteenth century, when part of the concern was also to gain advantage over rival Europeans. The case of Wilhelm Lutterodt is recounted in the Kokomlemle Consolidated Lands of 1940–1951. He was said to have

supported the Gas in some war in exchange for which he was given a large tract of land at today's Kokomlemle. Wilhelm Lutterodt's father was Georg August Lutterodt, who came from Denmark to act as governor of the Christiansborg Castle in 1801. His son Wilhelm became a well-established merchant prince and lived in Jamestown among the Gas (personal communication, Professor Clement Lutterodt, May 12, 2012). Another Dane, Conrad Svaneaker (forefather of today's Swaniker family), also married a Ga princess and was given extensive lands at what are today's Abelemkpe and Kwabenya (interview with Susanna Swaniker, January 18, 2012). Abelemkpe is currently a highly urbanized and a much-sought-after location within the city, while Kwabenya lies further outside the city but is also undergoing major processes of urbanization, especially following the spillover of housing for University of Ghana students and personnel after its expansion from six thousand students in 1991 to twenty-eight thousand by 2010.

8. Irene Odotei, personal communication, May 2012. But on this see also Quarcoopome (1992) and Sackeyfio (2008).

9. Sackeyfio (2008), Firmin-Sellers (1996), Osei-Tutu (2000).

10. The main exception to this general rule is the work of Richard Brand (1971, 1972). But in Brand's case, since his interest was mainly in the European influence on the town, his understanding of the spatial expansion of the city had no interest in Ga politics or akutso formation. My encounter with Richard Brand's work on Accra was instrumental in helping me to understand the significance of the specifically *spatial* organization of the city. Brand is of course not the only one who has written about such urban spatial arrangements (see Larbi 1996 and Grant 2008, for other insightful instances), but Brand's overall sensitivity to the relationships between space, demographic aggregates, social forces and urban planning is perhaps unparalleled in the scholarly writing on the city thus far.

11. For a comprehensive account of the links among various slaving sites on the Slave Coast, see especially Law (2004).

12. Parker (2000a, 14–15). Parker was himself inspired by Odotei (1972) and Quarcoopome (1993) before him, but I turn to his description here because he suggestively brings together in the same passage the various threads that would later prove decisive for Accra's urban form.

13. Robin Law's *The Horse in West African History* (1980) provides a fascinating account of the place of horses in the changing military and political terrain of Nigerian and West African history. From the 1860s freed Muslim slaves were to be brought together to form Glover's Hausa Constabulary, which again was based on their facility in horse riding. They later came to form the foundation of the Nigerian police and army. Glover's Constabulary also had an impact on the formation of the police and army in the Gold Coast/Ghana, but for a fuller account of this we will have to wait until chapter 6.

14. Verger ([1968] 1976), Matory (2005), Reis (1995, 97–99).

15. On the Yoruba tribes and their dialects, see Ajayi-Crowther (1998, chapter 26).

16. S. O. Akiwumi's story is to be found in Macmillan's *The Red Book of West Africa* ([1920] 1968, 208). This book, though written in an obviously racist and patronizing way, is remarkable for the diligence with which the author assembled information about the various commercial enterprises in the various West African colonies. His portraits of various businesses and personalities, both African and European, are packed with idiosyncratic descriptions and details, thus providing a lively and invaluable

resource for reconstructing the social and cultural life of the period. The only counterpart to *The Red Book* I can think of is Charles Francis Hutchison's *Pen-Pictures of Modern Africans and African Celebrities*, another extraordinary offering that was reissued in a new edition with an introduction by Michel Doortmont in 2005. The material on Justice Akiwumi was gathered from several online sources and from personal communication with Dorothy Afiriyie-Ansah, chief state attorney at the Ministry of Justice and Attorney General's Department in Accra.

17. Matory (2005, 53).

18. When the Gold Coast was fully taken over by the British government in 1821, it was first placed under the control of the government of Sierra Leone. After a hiatus from 1828 to 1843, when a committee of London merchants ran the administration of the two colonies, Sierra Leone resumed control again until 1850. The two colonies were then separated until 1866 when they were again put under the control of Sierra Leone. However, in 1874 the Gold Coast and Lagos were joined together to become the Gold Coast Colony, with Lagos gaining full autonomy some twenty years later.

19. Schaumloeffel (2009), Amos and Ayesu (2003).

20. Schaumloeffel (2009, 26).

21. Herman von Hesse points out that the acquisition of lands for agricultural cultivation by the Tabon was really a measure to solve a looming crisis that threatened the early returnees. Though some such as Aruna Nelson were content to stay at Otublohum, others, such as Mama Nassu, had originally been farmers in Bahia and were keen to enter into agricultural production. While the acquisition of lands was performed on behalf of all the Tabon as a collective, it was only a section of them that ended up cultivating the lands they were given. By the beginning of the twentieth century and with the increasing urbanization of Accra lands, the outlying areas of Asylum Down, Kokomlemle, and Adabraka where they had procured their lands began to generate strong interest from non-Tabon. This in its turn led to disagreements among the Tabon community itself about who could properly be allowed to sell these lands. Several cases were brought by Gas against the Tabon and among the Tabon themselves. See Von Hesse (2011); also Schaumloeffel (2009) and Quarcoopome (1993).

22. See especially Strickrodt (2003, 2008) and also Amos (2001).

23. Strickrodt (2008, 54–55).

24. Lokko (n.d.).

25. Lokko (n.d., 33).

26. Lokko (n.d., 58–62).

27. Schweizer (2000, 85).

28. Schaumloeffel (2009, 28–29).

29. Reis (1993, 160).

30. The Accra Water Rate Bill of 1925, revised several times subsequently, draws some very strong criticism from residents of Accra, including the chiefs. Some of the lively arguments are captured on the pages of the *Gold Coast Spectator*, November 29, 1930.

31. On the mentality and peculiar cosmology of company slaves brought on by their circumstances, see Kea (2005).

32. Samuel Ntewusu provides an exhaustive and fascinating account of the contribution of the Yoruba and northern merchant communities of Tudu to Accra's urban formation. See Ntewusu (2011). The argument about shifts in food dependency

for Accra and other urban centers in the Gold Coast in the *longue durée* is put forward persuasively by Ray Kea (1982). There is also speculation that the name Tudu may itself have been of Brazilian origin. The Tabon had opened shops around the area, and on being asked what they had on offer often replied "tudoo," meaning everything; this word was later used by the locals to designate the entire area. No other explanation has thus far been provided for this unusual place name, which does not seem to derive from Ga or any other local language. Thus its Brazilian provenance seems as likely as any.

33. See Huber (1999, 30–34), Feinberg (1989, 29–30), and Sebba (1997).

34. Amos and Ayesu (2003, 41).

35. Matory (2005, 65).

36. For example, the story of the Jews of Senegal is rarely told. In the early seventeenth century, Portuguese Sephardic traders settled on Senegal's Petit Côte, living as Jews under the guidance of a rabbi dispatched to them from Amsterdam. For a full account of this community and the trading links they established across West Africa, see Mark and Horta (2011). On the Syro-Lebanese of West Africa, see Malki (2008) and on the South Asians of East and South Africa, see Freund (1995), Ghai and Ghai (1970), and Bhachu (1985).

37. On hybridity in Mauritius, see especially Prabhu (2007), Verges (1999), and Lionnet (2012).

38. On the debates on citizenship for the Lebanese in Ghana, see Akyeampong (2004, 2006).

39. http://khanya.wordpress.com/2008/05/23/makwerekwere/, last accessed May 21, 2013. See also Matsinhe (2011).

40. There is of course a long-standing debate on multiethnicity in Africa, some positions of which I referenced earlier in this chapter. The general point about the fundamental relation between multiethnicity and historical societies is articulated in John Armstrong's now classic "Mobilized and Proletarian Diasporas" (1976). The main flaw in Armstrong's model is in his attempt to distinguish between archetypal and nonarchetypal diasporas; his general definitions of these categories lead him to privilege the Jewish diaspora, thus limiting the applicability of his insights to those that might be said to not fall under the archetypal/nonarchetypal binary. In his account, there is an ebb and flow to the recognition of the mobilized diasporas that depends on their instrumental usefulness or otherwise to the cultural and political elites of their host societies. But historically, multiethnicity has carried no guarantees for the protection of minority interests. Thus the point Armstrong makes about the necessity of multiethnicity to modernizing societies is one that would be more recognizable under the rubric of today's multiculturalism.

41. The best example of this misunderstanding is to be found in Hartman (2008) where she feels absolutely insulted to have been referred to as an obroni during her stay in Ghana as a Fulbright scholar researching the slave trade.

42. Schaumloeffel (2009, 81).

43. An example of such a land dispute, which almost caused irreparable damage to the Tabon community, was that brought in 1938 by J. E. Maslieno against J. A. Nelson, representing two established Tabon families. See Schaumloeffel (2009, 35–36) and also Quarcoopome (1992).

44. See Von Hesse (2011, 12, 14, 32–34).

Chapter 2: The Spatial Fix

1. Harvey first outlined the main terms of his account of the spatial fix by trying to answer a question regarding frontier accumulation in the writings of Hegel, Von Thünen and Marx ([1981] 2005) then more fully in The Limits to Capital ([1982] 2006). For further elaborations of the concept of spatial fix both engaging with Harvey, see also Arrighi (1994) and Baucom (2005).

2. This is a crude rendition of Immanuel Wallerstein's world systems theory, which despite robust critique still remains a persuasive model for thinking about the structure of the global economy. See his The Modern World-System II (2011) for a broader recapitulation of the classic formula he first proposed in 1974 that is most pertinent to postcolonial Africa in the era of empire.

3. co96/751/11, "Exclusion of Africans from European Residential Areas" (National Archives, UK).

4. Acquah (1958, 16).

5. See Roberts (2003) for a comprehensive and lively account of the dramatis personae of the events surrounding the bubonic plague. My own account draws mainly on Roberts, but augmented with material from documents in the National Archives in Accra.

6. See Simpson's Report on Plague in the Gold Coast in 1908 (1909), which became a handbook for dealing with the plague in its immediate context.

7. The dates for Ga-Adangme migration and the founding of their manjii (townships) are extremely difficult to ascertain, but Irene Odotei's account (1972) drawing on Reindorf, Romer, and various scholars is taken to be standard in the field. Asere and Sempe priority among the Ga akutsei is taken as common knowledge and was confirmed for me in an interview with her in May 2012.

8. Asere Mantse to Governor on Kaneshie, CS011/14/126/1951/30 vols. 1 and 2, Public Records and Archives Administration Department (National Archives, Accra).

9. The large and influential Bannerman family, of whom we shall have more to say in chapter 3, was a significant player in the politics of land acquisition in Accra. Charles, John, James, and Edmund Bannerman have ample mention in Parker (2000b) as well as in Kimble (1963) and also feature severally in Charles Francis Hutchison's The Pen-Pictures of Modern Africans and African Celebrities, first published in the 1920s.

10. One of these activists was the prominent Ga lawyer Amarkai Amarteifio, who organized rigorous resistance to Akyeampong's regime from his home at Kaneshie, and especially against the ill-fated Unigov referendum that sought the people's acquiescence to abolish multiparty democracy and in its place establish a "union government" of soldiers, chiefs, and other groups. Mr. Amarteifio is now the consul general of Sweden in Accra, a position he has held from the early 1990s. Through several interviews and conversations at various points throughout the life span of this project, he has regaled me with many fascinating stories about the social character of the Kaneshie resistance to Akyeampong, and also its relationship to the Ga Mashie area where he still has his ancestral family home.

11. Brand (1972, 335–338). But see also Amoah (1964) for another useful account of the period.

12. The point about who controls businesses in Accra sidesteps a much more important question, namely, where are the capitalist sources of funding for such busi-

nesses? A cursory look suggests that the largest businesses in Accra today are ̣
nantly run by foreign capital. Of the top twenty companies alphabetically listed
Ghana Stock Exchange on December 4, 2012, at least sixteen are wholly or predc
nantly owned by foreign capital. These include AngloGold Ashanti Limited, Afric
Champion Industries Limited, Aluworks Limited, Benso Oil Palm Plantation Lim ̲,
CAL Bank Limited, Ecobank Ghana Limited, Enterprise Group Limited, Ecobank
Transnational Corporation, Fan Milk Limited, Guinness Ghana Breweries Limited, and
Golden Star Resources Limited.

13. Dickson (1965, 104).

14. Dickson (1965, 108–109). Ivory was strictly speaking always a prized export even
during the slave trade. Yet now it was the entire group of export commodities that had
changed, with ivory now being part of a large cluster of export goods that included
more crops than gold and ivory, the dominant non-slave exports before abolition.

15. Interview with Jurgen Heinel in Hamburg, March 26, 2012. Mr. Heinel was sent
to Accra as the agent for Jos Hansen and Sons, a Germany company, in 1959. He was
just twenty-three but so loved the city on arrival that he ended up marrying a local
woman and remaining in Ghana until the late 1980s, when he fell foul of Rawlings's
regime and had to go back to Germany. He returned after the restoration of democracy
in 1992 but by that time the business environment had completely changed. Heinel
now splits his time between his homes in Accra and Hamburg.

16. The names of these and other merchants are provided in Macmillan ([1920] 1968,
203–214); the book contains helpful photographs of all the gentlemen in question.

17. Diversion of the kola trade through Accra was a key plank of the colonial administration's attempt at undermining Ashanti control of not just the northern trade but
also of their vassals in the Northern Territories. For a comprehensive account of the
political economy of kola, see Abaka (2005).

18. The account that follows draws heavily on Samuel Ntewusu's superb socioeconomic history of northern migrants to Accra (2011, 18–24).

19. The wealthier northern migrants owned and herded cattle, while the term
"zongo" is the Hausa word for "strangers' quarters" and is typically used to designate
the places that northerners live in various towns in Ghana.

20. Sir Arnold Hodson to Sir Malcolm MacDonald, October, 13, 1939; CO
96/762/31391/1939/1.

21. Nathan to Ronald Ross, November 30, 1901, Ross Archives, Cabinet A, Drawer
II, File 13, quoted in Dumett (1968, 170).

22. The term "administrative function" is inspired by Richard Brand (1971). However, he deploys the term mainly descriptively to capture the administrative logic that
undergirded the impluse behind residential segregation. While I acknowledge his
proposition that the colonial administrative and residential functions operated symbiot-
ically it is important also to understand the term more broadly as encompassing a wider
ensemble of practices that went well beyond just residential segregation to include rules
against white and native sexual relations as well as hierarchies of race within the colonial establishment itself. Hence, for purposes of determining salaries and privileges,
mixed-race personnel who had been posted to the Gold Coast were classified as black
and thus assumed to be better able to cope with living among the native populations.
However, their blackness did not extend to giving them permission to cohabit with

native women. Several such cases were brought against West Indian officers under Governor John Rodger's anti-concubinage edict of 1907. For more on this, see Ray (2013).

23. While racially integrated residential quarters in the Ga Mashie area were decisively discontinued from the 1890s, amalgamated commercial/warehouse/recreational land use was to continue until at least the 1930s. A good example of such amalgamated land is to be found in the description of "J. J. Fischer and Co. Limited, General Merchants, High Street" provided by Macmillan. The company specialized in textiles and also had a side interest in coca purchases. Thus, of their premises, "most of the entire space has a floor of concrete cement, which was made for the purpose of drying coca, and which in the evening is utilized for tennis." Their premises were laid out across an acre of land stretching from High Street to a promontory called Ju Ju Rock, cliffs overlooking the beach where merchandise was landed by surfboats. As Macmillan goes on to note: "The locality is certainly eloquent of the past and its suggestions in that connections are increased by the secret passage, now walled up, that led from the distant living quarters over the firm's stores fronting High Street to the beetling cliffs, down which there was a path to the surf-boats on the beach" (Macmillan[1920] 1968, 196–197). The racialized residential segregation that was fully evident in Accra by the 1930s accorded with general colonial practices elsewhere. See especially King (1976).

24. This is a point first made by Brand (1971, 41–44).

25. Lokko, nd, 33. In the nineteenth century the port at warri made it a center for the palm nut trade and also an attractive hub fro migrant workers.

26. Sir Arnold Hodson to Sir Malcolm MacDonald, Colonial Secretary, July 5, 1939. Earthquake: Restoration of Accra [and] Rehousing, CO 96/762/31391/1939/1. See also Kaneshie Layout Plan, CS011/14/126/1951/30 vol. 1 and CS011/14/127/1951/30 vol. 2.

27. See North et al. (1975), one of the earliest UN-commissioned policy documents to tell about the role of women in the country.

28. Letter from O. G. R Williams, Assistant Secretary and Head of the Waste Department, to Sir Arnold Hodson, July 12, 1939. Earthquake: Restoration of Accra [and] Rehousing, CO 96/762/31391/1939/1.

29. Larbi (1996, 197fn8).

30. The hole beside Ridge Hospital is vividly recalled by Kwaku Sakyi-Addo, renowned Ghanaian journalist and now CEO of the Ghana Chamber of Telecommunications. But the story about the ravine was told to me by Nat Nunu Amarteifio, mayor of Accra from 1994 to 1998. As he tells it, different parts of the ravine were used for dumping garbage. The site of the erstwhile ravine to the left of the University of Ghana's Accra campus (formerly Workers' College), where his own office is currently located, was a garbage tip until at least the end of the 1970s.

31. See Quarcoopome (1991).

32. A brief survey of where these gated enclaves are located in Accra bears out the point about the rehearsal of a particular form of middle-class cosmopolitan anxiety. They are as follows:

Second Circular Road (Cantonments):
—The Hamptons
—Cantonments Gardens
—Kaiser Cantonments Villas

—Meridian
Sixth Circular Road (Cantonments):
—Bordeaux
Firth Circular Road (Cantonments):
—Crystal Homes
Roman Ridge (Sir Arku Korsah Road):
—Cassa Bella
Airport Residential Area (on the same street as the Best Western Hotel):
—Kuku's Court
—Holi Flats
Airport Residential Area:
—Palm Court
—Earl's Court
Overlooking the Polo Grounds and right next to the airport:
—Polo Court

At a rough count, then, we have twelve new gated community developments that have sprung up since the early 1990s. The only other gated community of note in Accra is at Trasacco Valley in the Adjiringanor area close to East Legon, last accessed December 1, 2013.

33. Amaknwah (1989, 73).

34. "Earthquake: Restoration of Accra [and] Rehousing," CO 96/762/31391/1939/ vols. 1 and 2.

35. Interview with Nat Nuno-Amarteifio, June 2009. On the difficulties this has posed for evacuating and rehabilitating the area, see Bremer (2002), Razzu (2005), and UNESCO (2000).

36. John Parker (2000a) provides a fascinating and multilayered discussion of Ga intramural sepulchral practice which he adroitly connects to their complex cosmology.

37. The Manbii Party (town people's party, i.e., commoners) was formed in 1921 under the leadership of Kojo Thompson initially to contest Ga elites' attempts at controlling the Ga Mantse's stool, but later expanded its opposition to various colonial government ordinances. It folded in 1944 following the arrest of their leader but by that time had registered a major impact on Ga politics. Other political organizations of note were the Ga Shifimo Kpee (Ga Steadfast Association), which was instrumental in protesting Kwame Nkrumah's land policies for Accra. Also significant in the cultural politics of land acquisition and tenure were the various asafo (quasi-military) groups that came to channel vociferous youth interests from the 1920s to the 1950s. For more on these, see Firmin-Sellers (1996, 45–55), Sackeyfio (2008), especially chapter 3, and Quarcoopome (1992).

38. The description of the Ga land-tenure system that follows draws heavily on the account provided by Firmin-Sellers (1996). But Odotei (1972), Quarcoopome (1991, 1992, 1993), and Sackeyfio (2008) all provide ample confirmation from different directions of the same essential principles.

39. See Pogucki (1954, 18–20).

40. See Brand (1972) and Bobo (1974).

41. Kokomlemle/Akwandor Lands Case, SCT/2/6/28, Public Records and Archives Administration Department (the National Archives). A list of all the claimants to the

case is provided on the very first page of the proceedings, but a more succinct list of the main protagonists is to be found on p. 44 of the document.

42. SCT/2/6/28, Public Records and Archives Administration Department, p. 10.

43. SCT/2/6/28, Public Records and Archives Administration Department, p. 12, 15. See also Firmin-Sellers (1996, 40–41).

44. Personal interview, May 8, 2012. But Odotei has also written widely about Ga akutso formation both in her dissertation of 1972 and in the various articles already cited.

45. On this, see especially Quarcoopome (1992, 41) and the introduction to Odotei (1972). Korle is styled as a female deity and resides in the lagoon that lies to the west of Jamestown. There are two related Sakumo deities worshipped by the Ga: *sakumo fio* (small sakumo) lives in a small lagoon that borders Ga Mashie to the west and *sakumo onukpa* (big or elder sakumo) is the god of the people of Tema and lives in a lagoon between Nungua and Tema. Nai, on the other hand, is the head pantheon of all Ga townships and his priest, the Nai wulomo, is considered the high priest of the Ga Mashie state.

46. Kokomlemle/Akwandor Consolidated Lands Case, SCT/2/6/28, Public Records and Archives Administration Department, pp. 33–34. Confirmation of these principles are also provided in Pogucki (1954), as well as in Sarbah (1904). Firmin-Sellers's summary of the Ga land-tenure system also serves to illustrate the same principles, except that in her account lineage takes precedence over stool, thus preparing the way for the progressive assertion of individual family property rights as illustrated by Dr. Carl Reindorf and the claims of the Onomrokor We.

47. SCT/2/6/28, Public Records and Archives Administration Department, p. 40.

48. SCT/2/6/28, Public Records and Archives Administration Department, pp. 46–57.

Chapter 3: Osu borla no, sardine chensii soo

1. See Bacchus (1974, 21–25, 144–184). Also Dumett (1981) for a careful application of the concept with respect to the decision-making process that led to a shift in British policy from one of minimum intervention to full-scale colonialism during the Victorian era.

2. The impact of the European presence on Elmina in particular has been the subject of an especially fine study by Feinberg (1989).

3. Christiansborg Castle has had a potted history, starting out as a Swedish lodge in 1657, then a Danish fort in 1661, and experiencing a hiatus between 1679 and 1683 when it was owned by the Portuguese, who first garrisoned it and constructed a Catholic chapel inside of the then fort. Sold back to the Danes in 1683, it was famously taken over in 1693 by Asameni, an Akwamu and former cook in the employ of the Danes. He flew a blue flag with the image of an African warrior brandishing a dagger on it and invited English and Dutch trading ships to do business with him. Asameni returned the castle to the Danes in 1694 but took with him the keys to the castle back to Akwamu, where they have been retained as part of stool property. After passing into British possession in 1850, it was made residence of the British governors from 1876 to 1890, when abandoned until 1891, serving in the interim in turns as a constabulary mess and lunatic

asylum. The year 1902 saw it revert back to its official status as seat of government, a function that it retains to this day. For more on the history of the castle, see Dantzig (1980), Anquandah (1999), and Lawrence (1963).

4. For a direct account of the Danish positions with regard to various political maneuverings on the coast, see Hernæs (2003).

5. Much of the account of the spatial configuration of Osu up to the late nineteenth century will draw on Nii-Adziri Wellington's *Stones Tell Stories at Osu* (2011), a fascinating fictionalized history of the area. Wellington is a retired professor of architecture who had spent several decades at the Kwame Nkrumah University of Science and Technology (KNUST). I should like to say a special thanks to "Prof," as he is fondly called, for generously submitting himself to my countless questions on a trip that a group of us undertook to visit the Danish plantation settlement at Dakobi, at the bottom of the Akwapim hills in January 2012. Martina Odonkor (who features prominently in chapter 4) was the one responsible for organizing that magnificent trip; to her, special thanks are also due for introducing me to Prof, Mr Jurgen Heinel, Mae-Ling Lokko, and Kofi Adomako, all of whom I learned immensely from on that trip and in subsequent conversations and interviews.

6. These include the Reverend Carl Christian Reindorf, the redoubtable historian of the Gas and the Ashantis; Sir Emmanuel Charles Quist, the first speaker of the Legislative Council; Justice Nii Amaa Ollennu, a Supreme Court judge and one-time speaker of parliament; Professor C. O. Easmon, first dean of the University of Ghana Medical School; and Mr. Harry Sawyer, minister of transport during the Hilla Limann regime. The list is extensive and highly impressive, but even a cursory look at the names the Salem school has listed on their website shows a strong indication of the mixed-race heritage that made up Osu Salem well into the twentieth century. See Presbyterian Boys Boarding School, Osu Salem, http://www.osusalem.org/pages/ourhistory.php, last accessed August 12, 2012. A further history of the Osu Salem School school is provided by Wellington (2011, 264–276).

7. The stories of the establishment of various Osu akutsei is amply retold by Wellington (2011, 22–34). But see also Odotei [Quaye] (1972), for a more scholarly account.

8. See especially Odotei [Quaye] (1972, 16–20).

9. On the date by which Noete Doku was king of the Osus, see Kea (2000, 165). Several references to monthly payments being made to caboceers are to be found in Justesen (2005). For a general history of the Osus as an aspect of the larger history of Accra, see especially Odotei [Quaye] (1972) as well as Reindorf (1895).

10. Justesen (2005, 535, 541–542, 544).

11. Indeed, Okaija had a much more significant role in Ga history than the Danes grant him in their records. Parker points out that Okaija's success in consolidating power in the late 1730s is reflected in the ritual concentration of his akutso, where "tradition has it that the shrines of Nai, Sakumo and Kole were all removed from the Asere akutso to neighboring Gbese" (Parker 2000a, 210). The rest of Parker's account has to be quoted in full:

> On the death of Okaija a serious dispute arose over the mode of his burial. The Ga, it was held, had traditionally buried their dead wrapped in a woven mat,

although following the advent of Europeans on the coast the use of wooden coffins became increasingly common. Despite this innovation, *mantsemei* ("chiefs") and *wulomei* ("priests") continued to be buried in mats. Some of Okaija's sons, however, had been educated by the Dutch and—perhaps influenced by Christian instruction—insisted that their father be interred in a coffin. Traditionalists within the family were outraged, and a violent struggle for the possession of the body ensued between a "mat party" and a "coffin party," the latter supported by the soldiers of Kinka's Dutch garrison. A number of protagonists were killed before the coffin party succeeded in interring the remains within the Dutch fort. Memory of the incident is enshrined in Gbese's official oath, uttered to enforce judicial obedience by evoking the specter of the loss of life in past military conflict: "*Okaija adeka*"—Okaija's coffin. (Parker 2000a, 210)

12. The final, yet ultimately unsuccessful, onslaught of the Dutch on Danish Osu occurred in 1777. According to Wellington, this battle is commemorated in the naming of the neighborhood of Kinkawe (i.e., the house of the Kinka people), which signaled the place where the soldiers from Kinka in Dutch Accra set up their camp during the war with Danish Osu. On being victorious, the Osu royal family decided to move its household to Kinkawe to indicate the permanent conquest of their enemies (Wellington 2011, 24–25). See also Hernæs (2003) for several accounts of armed conflicts between African and European traders in eighteenth-century Gold Coast.

13. For a more thorough treatment of the same proposition, see Kea (1982), especially chapters 5–7, and Daaku (1970).

14. Some of the items listed here are taken from the lists put together from the ship *Fredensborg*, which sunk off the coast of Denmark in 1745. The ship was retrieved from the seabed off the coast of Tromøy in Norway. It had been sailing from the Gold Coast to Copenhagen when it sank, carrying Ludewig Ferdinand Rømer, who subsequently returned to West Africa and wrote a famous travelogue of his adventures there. Three items retrieved from the ship were put on display at the Norwegian Maritime Museum in Stockholm. See Svalesen (2000, 173–186). And on Rømer's narrative, see Winsnes (2000a). In the letters to the company in Copenhagen, there is also a frequent listing of the kinds of goods that must be sent down on the ships coming from Europe. Sometimes items such as brandy, gunpowder, and calico cloth are glossed for how popular or unpopular they are with the Africans and the reasons for this. For just two examples of such goods lists with brief glosses as to their desirability or otherwise, see Justesen (2005, 223–224, 330–333).

15. For an excellent account of gold mining and colonial capitalism in the Gold Coast during the nineteenth century, see Dumett (1999).

16. On the history of money and the banking system in the Gold Coast and West Africa, see Fry (1976) and Ayensu (2007).

17. The vowel sound in mɔn is the same for that in the word "kong"; mɔn is pronounced with a mild nasalized "g" at the end, which does not appear when it is written down. Special thanks to Ayebia Clarke for reminding me of the spelling of the Ga word for prison, and for taking me through the idiomatic expressions in the language that relate to imprisonment.

18. For an extensive account of Heinrich Richter's trading prowess, and the sociopolitical environment in which he made his wealth, see Justesen (2003).

19. It is hard to ascertain the veracity of this tale. Ole Justesen's extensive essay on Heinrich Richter makes no mention of the tunnel, even though he provides ample evidence that Richter was at least an active owner of domestic slaves. The period in which his business flourished most (1800–1849) also coincided with the abolition of slavery, even though the residual trade was to continue well into the nineteenth century. However, the story of the tunnel is so strongly asserted by the people in and around Tolo Mɔn that one suspects it must contain a grain of truth.

20. See also Ipsen (2008, 97, 93).

21. Selena Winsnes provides a fascinating description of the house and of some aspects of Wulff's life there in "There Is a House on Castle Drive: The Story of Wulff Joseph Wulff" (2000b). She confirms among other things that those Europeans living on the coast had a shared life of "pain, both physical and mental" (44). The emotional onslaught included illness and the threat of illness, deaths and the constant reminders of death posed by the auction of dead men's items, and a constant and grinding homesickness. For a fuller picture of Wulff, with a translation of his rich correspondence from the period, see also Winsnes (2004).

22. See Ipsen (2008, 64–65). A typical debit ledger for one Peder Østrup is also to be found in Justesen (2005, 1:291).

23. On Dutch piracy during the period, see Postma (2008).

24. For a case of gross disrespect shown by a merchant ship captain to a highly regarded caboceer, called Qvansang (Quansah), see Ipsen (2008, 190–193).

25. Ipsen (2008, 69–70).

26. Ipsen points out, however, that a letter written by Bishop Worm in Copenhagen (in response to a query sent by Governor von Suhm) was completely misread as providing justification for interracial marriages. This interpretation was read against the intent of the letter, which generally sought to declare the marriages between the Danish men and their African consorts as falling outside the pale of Christianity. For her extensive contextualization and account of Bishop Worm's letter and its subsequent strategic misinterpretation, see Ipsen (2008, 113–127) and for Suhm's letter, see Justesen (2005, 1:345–347).

27. On the Ga family system, see Field (1940), Azu (1974), Kilson (1974), and Robertson (1984).

28. The specific discourse of salvation from heathenism in Chaplain Svane's letter must be placed within the larger framework of the perceived lack of historical coevalness between Europe and its others. This discourse was to take a variety of forms, with the template of Christianity providing just one of the more prominent variants. For an elaboration of this idea, see Johannes Fabian's classic *Time and the Other: How Anthropology Makes Its Object* ([1983] 2002).

29. This point is also elaborated in a different register by Ipsen (2008, 127–139). She prefers the term "culture" to that of "ideology."

30. See also Ipsen (2008, 110–112).

31. Ipsen (2008, 131–134).

32. See Justesen (2003).

33. William St. Clair provides a detailed account of such practices and how they impacted upon the society at Cape Coast. See especially chapter 8 of his *The Door of No Return* (2006).

34. A distinction must of course be drawn between the domestic slave system and that of the transatlantic trade. For the most salient differences, see especially Perbi (2004).

35. Much good work has been done detailing the change in fortunes of the African community on the Gold Coast in addition to Kaplow (1977), the precise dating of the different phases is sometimes different for each commentator. See especially Reynolds (1974a) and Dumett (1983). On the economic history of colonialism during the Victorian period on the Gold Coast and elsewhere, see Hopkins (1973) and Peter J. Cain and Anthony G. Hopkins's magisterial *British Imperialism: 1688–2000* (2002).

36. Reynolds (1974a, 109).

37. Reynolds (1974a, 107–111); but also Kaplow (1977) and Dumett (1983).

38. See also Kimble (1963, 66–70) for a more detailed account of the rise of racism as a segment of imperialist ideology on the Gold Coast. A speech made by Arnold Hodson at the close of the first meeting of the 1939 session of the Legislative Council provided specific justification for not hiring Africans into what he called "technical positions," on the simple reasoning that there were none qualified for such posts. All the evidence of the steady rise in the number of educated Africans since the mid-nineteenth century was of course ignored by him. He requested further information from the various government departments on the appointment of Africans, their suitability, and what might be done to address the issue first put to him by members of the Legislative Council. See his speech and also the Colonial Secretary's letter to department heads of May 9, 1938, in "African Civil Service," co96/75759/7 (National Archives, UK).

39. Reverend Carl Reindorf gives an account of the complex causes of the resistance to the British poll tax and the subsequent bombardment in his *History of the Gold Coast and Asante* (1895, 329–341). One of the more fascinating features of Reindorf's *History* is the range of Ga songs and proverbs that he incorporates into his account. This is very similar to what Reverend Samuel Johnson does in *History of the Yorubas* (1921). For a discussion of the historiographical implications of incorporating oral materials into Samuel Johnson's account, see Quayson (1997, 20–43). And on Reindorf's ethnopolitics, see Parker (1998).

40. For a full account of this, see Ray (2013).

41. Kimble (1963, chapters 12 and 13). The different status accorded to chiefs and educated elites remained a bone of contention into the 1950s, to the point that at independence Kwame Nkrumah was even quoted as saying that he would chase the chiefs out of all legislative authority and that they would run and leave their sandals behind. (The chief's sandals are considered a symbol of his regal authority; the destoolment of a chief often involves the seizing of his sandals so that he is forced to tread barefoot on the ground. This is considered a real anathema, especially in Akan society.)

42. Hutchison/Doortmont (2005, 261–265).

43. Hutchison/Doortmont (2005, 245–248).

44. Hutchison/Doortmont (2005, 148–152).

45. Hutchison/Doortmont (2005, 347).

46. Hutchison/Doortmont (2005, 424–428).

47. Hutchison/Doortmont (2005, 394–396).

48. Hutchison/Doortmont (2005, 389–390).

49. See especially Asante (1936); also Jones-Quartey (1974).

50. Nii Kwabena Bonne III organized the boycott of European goods in protest of exorbitant pricing and the control of the AWAM (Association of West African Merchants) cartel on trade. The riots that ensued were to intersect with the march of World War II veterans with a petition to the castle and their being shot at on February 28, 1948. It has to be borne in mind, however, that these figures were not tied exclusively to Osu and were also as likely to be involved in affairs at Ga Mashie—through marriages and business networks—as they were with those at Osu. An instructive case is provided by Reindorf family history. Whereas Reverend Carl Reindorf seems to have made his home primarily in the Ashinte Blohum akutso of Osu, the wider family had links much further afield. Thus, as Firmin-Sellers reports, Charles Reindorf was very active in Ga Mashie chieftaincy politics, at one period acting as the *daatsetse* (kingmaker) and having a significant impact on the assertion of private rights to land as against the more collective claims put forward by stools and lineages. See Firmin-Sellers (1996, 53–56).

51. It is beyond the ken of this book to delve into the presence and evolution of the Lebanese community in Accra, but for a good sense of it, see especially Malki (2008).

Chapter 4: "The Beautyful Ones"

1. The term "vital immediacy" is Abiola Irele's in "Orality, Literacy and African Literature" (2001).

2. On obituary notices, see McCaskie (2006); on popular literary and performance texts that draw on oral traditions, Fagunwa (1968), Tutuola (1952), Cole (2001); and on concert party and film posters, Barber (2000) and Wolfe III (2000).

3. On the social imaginary in Accra and its connection to urban mythology, see Quayson (2003).

4. For a brief account of the introduction of motorized transport into the Gold Coast, see Heap (1990). A broader survey of developments on the entire continent is provided by the very useful collection edited by Gewald, Luning, and van Walraven (2009).

5. Reynolds (2008).

6. Lewis (1998) provides a useful typology of such sayings. One disagreement with his categories is in the separation between sayings pertaining to "Pain and Trials of This World" and "Appeals to God or Heaven." In reality the two segue easily into each other such that for analytical purposes they should really be seen as a single category. The only other failing of Lewis's admittedly preliminary and brief investigation is that he does not list sayings in any local language. This would have forced him to alter the relative percentages he assigned to several of his categories. See also Thompson (1996),

7. This translation draws largely on the one provided in Van der Geest (2009). I have made some emendations of my own where necessary to accord more closely with my knowledge of the local languages.

8. On this and the amazing history of the genre of hiplife music in Ghana, see Shipley (2013). In an uncanny reversal of the process just described, the slogan "All Die Be Die," which is to be found on a variety of expressive surfaces, was adopted

as the political rallying cry by Nana Akufo-Addo, the NPP's losing candidate for the presidential elections of 2012. Many political commentators were alarmed that he had wrenched a common and innocent saying, which in popular parlance is taken to mean that everyone is equal in death and thus you must not "Boast Yourself" (another popular slogan), and turned it into a barely concealed ethnic call to arms against supporters of the National Democratic Party (NDC), whose founder was from the minority Ewes.

9. See also Date-Bah (1980), Lawuji (1988), and Guseh (2008) for an illustration of the various kinds of typologies that have been generated to account for the variety in vehicle slogans. I have to admit to succumbing to the same impulse earlier. In my first attempt at understanding the lorry slogans, the first thing I did after assembling the long list of over three hundred items was to try and divide them into categories. What the categorization does is to immediately foreground a particular form of scientific rationality, when in fact that form of rationality is precisely what is repeatedly confounded by the mixed provenance of the slogans and their apparently endless capacity for proliferation and variation. Nothing short of a narratology of urban inscriptions that would account for the deep generative cultural grammar that inspires them would be able to do justice to their polysemic variety. On my own preliminary typologizing effort, see Quayson (2010).

10. It has to be noted, however, that adinkra cloths are amenable to a much wider variety of expressiveness than asafo flags, which as a rule are firmly tied to social militias with particular histories that are commemorated in their flags. Outside of funeral conventions, adinkra cloths can be used to express a range of sentiments, though admittedly not as wide as what we find on tro-tros and passenger lorries.

11. De Bruijn elaborates the concept of semiotic stacking in her chapter titled "Cultivating 'Vital Immediacy' in Ghana's Market Fiction" in de Bruijn (2013).

12. "All the World" was married to an aunt of mine we called Sister Abena in whose home at Nsawam I spent many pleasant vacations while at secondary school in the late 1970s and early 1980s. I never found out All the World's real name.

13. Market share statistics as of September 2012 posted by the National Communications Authority, http://www.nca.org.gh/40/105/Market-Share-Statistics.html, last accessed December 16, 2012. See also the somewhat celebratory "Mobile Penetration Hits 98% in Ghana," JoyOnline.com, http://business.myjoyonline.com/pages/news /201210/95084.php, last accessed December 1, 2013.

14. After a great deal of controversy, Vodafone bought a controlling stake in One-Touch, the government's cell phone operation. See "Vodaphone in Ghanaian Mobile Deal," BBC News, July 3, 2008, http://news.bbc.co.uk/2/hi/business/7487821.stm, last accessed January 28, 2009.

15. Interview with Syl Kowornu, director of ADS Services Limited in July 2007, which was in charge of all of TIGO's local advertising for the previous seven years until 2008 when, after a period of sharing tasks, it lost the advertising contract completely to Creative Eye.

16. See their website www.ceafrica.com, last accessed June 21, 2013. Creative Eye's advert campaigns have varied in content, the subsequent Be a Fan campaign focusing on popular sports in the country (boxing, soccer, basketball, etc.). The Express Yourself campaign has also thematized itself around various forms of creative expressiveness (music, painting, singing, etc.), and the models have varied between a transna-

tionally "placeless" black youth and those with a more recognizably local ethnicity. However, even here the emphasis is securely on a transnational imaginary, the overall artistic background to the pictures providing a decidedly nonlocal flavor to the adverts. For example, none of the adverts include musical instruments such as djembe drums or wooden xylophones, the preference being for acoustic guitars, drums, and other such instruments easily recognizable by a Western audience.

17. For more on this question, see Quayson (2013).

18. See, for example, De Boeck (2003) and Simone (2004).

19. See the appendix. I wish to say special thanks to Emma Pimpong, the research assistant who spent hours at various lorry parks collating the slogans.

20. For a highly nuanced discussion of the complex historical process in which this discursive translation took place, see Meyer (1999).

21. See Ghana Trades Union Congress policy discussion paper on incomes in Ghana, https://www.google.ca/search?q=Ghana+Trades+Union+Congress+policy+ discussion+paper+on+incomes+in+Ghana&oq=Ghana+Trades+Union+Congress+ policy+discussion+paper+on+incomes+in+Ghana&aqs=chrome. .69i57j69i64.1405joj4& sourceid=chrome&espv=210&es_sm=91&ie=UTF-8, last accessed February 3, 2009. For a broader discussion of the impact of the ERP on the country, see Hutchful (2002).

22. See Gifford (2004, 113–140).

23. http://www.TIGO.com.gh/, last accessed December 1, 2013.

24. Roughly ten U.S. cents at the time of writing. Apparently, these campaigns are so popular that they net anything between $70,000 to $100,000 a fortnight nationwide for the cell phone company. Interview with Charles Ampaw, host of the "Your Guess Is Right" game show on GTV, August 2009.

Chapter 5: "Este loco, loco"

1. See her work on www.facebook.com/AduAmaniKlodin, last accessed June 23, 2013.

2. The term "party" is not entirely accurate since this was a regular event that followed the same fairly strict format. However, I use party just to convey the sense of fun and sheer excitement that the event exuded. This sense was confirmed in several subsequent visits.

3. For the Azonto dance, see "Azonto Dance in Senior High Schools: Song by Sarkodie's—U Go Kill Me O" on http://www.youtube.com/watch?v=5HNWlnKhPDE, uploaded June 21, 2011, last accessed November 28, 2013. Another very popular song in 2009 was "Azonto Antenna" by UK-based Ghanaian hiplife artist FDG. However, it is not only at salsa that choreographed group dances were to be found. A flash mob took place in Accra on December 2, 2010, to launch Google Trader in the country. Five separate locations, including Oxford Street, Makola, and Kaneshie Market among them, were the sites of groups of people in colorful T-shirts dancing to music recorded by a Nigerian music artist. For more on this, see Bejamin Cole, In Motion: Tales of an Explorer, Technologist, and Adventurer, http://blog.benscole.com/2010/12/launching -google-trader-in-ghana.html, uploaded December 7, 2010; and http://www.youtube .com/watch?v=uUtsguaGjbY, uploaded December 9, 2010; both accessed on December 24, 2012.

4. See CitiFm Online, "CitiFm's Salsa Mania Is Back," June, 2011, http://citifmonline .com/mobile/index.php?id=1.435579, last accessed January 11, 2012.

5. Josh Ansah, Lumo Bortei-Doku, and Robert Klah, another interviewee who was also an instructor, all confirmed that salsa had taken them well beyond the shores of Ghana. In the case of Josh, he said he had been invited to help teach salsa across several cities in Nigeria. Typically he and other instructors would be put up in a hotel and would run intensive salsa dance classes in each city before moving on to another destination. Robert Klah also credited himself with choreographing several of the lineup dances. Other names that came up as having been highly inventive lineup choreographers were Patty and Sammy Gyapong, both of whom were very active in nurturing the early salsa scene in Accra. However, the notion of a single inspiration behind the lineups is some-what challenged by Marlin, who insisted in his interview with me that most of the line-ups were collaboratively choreographed so that to assign them to one individual is to somehow distort what was really a highly complicated process of collective cocreation.

6. Indeed, Nii Provençal took scores of pictures of Osu, Madina, Kaneshie, and Tudu for me as part of my research for the book. I want to say a special thanks to him and to Sara, his salsera girlfriend.

7. In Belfast, for example, the dance scene can still be used to differentiate between Protestants and Catholics, while in Dakar it bears the burden challenging dominant forms of the hierarchy of male/female interactions established within a largely Muslim society.

8. I want to say a special thanks to Ananya Kabir for giving me a proper description of the two variants of salsa. Kabir has been awarded 2.2 million euros by the European Research Council for a five-year project titled "Modern Moves: Kinetic Transnational-ism and Afro-Diasporic Rhythm Cultures" that started in April 2013.

9. Interview with a group of four salsa instructors at the Aviation Social Centre, July 2010, revealed that they all danced the On-2 variant, while Lumo Bortei-Doku states that he started out with On-2 but moved on to On-1 because it was easier to teach. The interview with Bortei-Doku was conducted in January 2012.

10. A few words on the dramatic shift from live music to recorded music that took place in Accra in the early 1980s: Until Rawlings's second coup at the end of 1981, live band music was a common source of entertainment in Ghana. Some, such as Uppers International, C. K. Mann and his Carousel 7, and the Classique Handels became legendary. A "Pop Chain" competition was also organized annually at which second-ary schools in the country could showcase the talents of their homebred bands. The competition involved rearranging and playing a specified Ghanaian song and playing one of the band's own compositions. The Pop Chain phenomenon was used for talent hunting, and many of the best players ended up on the live-band circuit. All this was to change dramatically on Rawlings's second coming on December 31, 1981. One of his first decisions was to impose a dawn-to-dusk curfew, with serious repercussions for anyone who contravened it. The curfew was in place for eighteen months, and one of its effects was to utterly change the leisure culture in the country. Since live band music was normally played and enjoyed at night, the curfew spelled its almost immediate demise. Most players migrated into churches, which became the only safe haven where they could still play instruments and entertain an audience. A boom in religious music followed. Also significant in this period was the demise of the large movie theatres

such as Opera, Orion, Palladium, Rex, and so forth. Almost all of these were taken over by church organizations and within a short time became decrepit and fell out of use. The demise of movie theatres also meant the rise of the technology of the VCR player, which was already becoming popular by the time of the coup. But with the home video machine also came the falling away of the early Bollywood and Chinese films that had dominated Ghanaian movie screens until then. Rather, the VCR technology walked hand in hand with Hollywood movies, most of which had been rapidly transferred to VCR tapes and were distributed accordingly. The Hollywoodization of Ghanaian film tastes and the later emergence of handheld video technology was to provide the seeds for the phenomenon of the Nigerian Nollywood and its Ghanaian counterpart, Gollywood. By the time of salsa's (and also hiplife's) emergence on the Ghanaian scene in the 1990s, an entire generation of youth had grown up without any knowledge of live band music whatsoever. The Internet along with computer mixers have ensured that salsa has gained ground purely on the basis of the new information technologies.

11. Martina Odonkor was the first-prize winner of the 2011 Burt Award for Children's Literature for her story "The Kaya-Girl."

12. Much of the account that follows is derived from interviews I had with Martina Odonkor and Lumo Bortei-Doku in January 2012. Prior to that I had interviewed Josh Ansah in August 2010, along with Thomas Darko, the DJ responsible for the Salsa Mania program on CitiFM that was broadcast simultaneously from Coconut Grove. I wish to thank all these people for their kindness and generosity, as well as Paa Kofi Manor, managing director of Ideal Concept Media, for agreeing at short notice to film four different salsa clubs and run interviews with some of the participants.

13. This is largely Lumo's version of events, which was corroborated in its essential details by Marlin, who was also at Afrikiko on that fraught August night.

14. This was both Lumo's and Martina's view of the differences between Aviation and Costa Rica. They stated their views completely independently of each other and at different moments in their interview cycles with me.

15. On the relation between symbolic and economic capital in the production of cultural goods, see Bourdieu (1986, 1987).

Chapter 6: Pumping Irony

1. I want to say a very special thanks to Samuel Ntewusu, my dedicated and enterprising research assistant who has worked with me since 2005, for setting up interviews with various gymmers in 2009–2010 and also arranging to have some of their activities taped and transcribed. Ntewusu completed his PhD from the University of Leiden in 2011 and is now research fellow at the Institute of African Studies at the University of Ghana, Legon.

2. See National Sports Authority, http://www.sportscouncil.com.gh/maincat_select_discipline.cfm?disciplineID=31, last accessed November 29, 2013.

3. The line in the section header is from a well-known marching song sung by soldiers that also became popular among high school students. It invites Adwoa to "go soldier line," that is, fall in love with a soldier, because soldiers have money and other things pleasing to women.

4. Others include Asafoatse Adama Street, Asafoatse Omani Street, Asafoatse Mensah, and the Asafoatse Ashie Street, all of which lie around the Kaneshie Market complex.

5. See Clayton and Killingray (1989).

6. See Wilks (1961, 14–20). It must be noted, however, that the relationship between Ashanti and its northern neighbors was more complicated than conveyed in this image of Dagomba and Gonja vassalage. Through a variety of instruments, including the resettlement of entire conquered populations, many parts of Ashanti came to have Muslim settlements, with some Muslims rising to become important persons in the court of the Asantehene. For more on these complex relations, see also Wilks (1989).

7. The village of Abokobi was set up by Zimmerman and the Basel Mission (later Presbyterian) in the 1870s to accommodate freed slaves and to provide them training for their transition to freedom. Johannes Zimmerman was also to translate the Bible from Hebrew into Ga and to compile the first Ga-English dictionary and made many astute observations about local customs. See N. A. Odoi (2004).

8. For a comprehensive account of this process of northern settlements in Accra, see Pellow (2002) and Ntewusu (2011).

9. See Manu (2006); also, Manu (2005).

10. In one reported instance during the presidential elections of 2012, some macho men were alleged to have stormed a polling station at Ablekuma North to burn some ballot papers. Further investigation showed that the news item had exaggerated the scene on all counts. See Isaac Essel, "Ablekuma North: Macho Men Burn Ballot Papers," MC: Modern Ghana, http://www.modernghana.com/news/434907/1/ablekuma -north-machomen-burn-ballot-papers.html, uploaded December 8, 2012, last accessed November 29, 2013. The Accra police commissioner also cited intelligence suggesting that macho men were unpacking arms at a house in Kokomlemle as an excuse to raid the headquarters of the NPP. Again, there was no evidence of either arms or macho men on their arrival. See "Police Raid NPP Research Office," Ghanaweb, http://www .ghanaweb.com/GhanaHomePage/NewsArchive/artikel.php?ID=259152, uploaded December 11, 2012, last accessed November 29, 2013.

11. The Daily Guide of Monday, August 3, 2009, provides a good example of this stereotypical response. Under the front-page banner of "Gym Instructor in Sex Scandal," the report goes on to suggest that the accused had been "loitering around the vicinity, and upon sighting the girl [whom he was apparently not acquainted with beforehand], allegedly held her hand at knife point and bundled her into a taxi and took her to a nearby washing bay" where he proceeded to sexually assault her. The entire article sought to establish a none-too-subtle link between the instincts of a wild predator and the fact that the accused was a macho man.

12. The picture galleries of Ghanaian celebrities in the arts, music, and politics to be found at http://photos.peacefmonline.com/gallery/photos/416/20458.php and at http:// ghanacelebrities.com, both last accessed March 28, 2012, give a sense of the full range of body types, with a preponderance toward chubbiness. Stars such as John Dumelo, Fiifi Banson, Bola Ray (Kwabena Anokye Adisi), Kwadwo Oppong-Nkrumah, and Kwame Sefa-Kayi are all media stars who may be considered chubby and yet are taken as among the sexiest male figures in town. They are all in their mid to late thirties and help to illustrate the change in body type that accompanies the switch in class. The issue of

chubbiness and its connection to sexiness is relevant in other parts of Africa, too. See, for example, Pascale Harter, "Mauritania's 'Wife-Fattening' Farm," BBC News, January 26, 2004, http://news.bbc.co.uk/2/hi/3429903.stm; "Fat Is Bad but Beautiful," *Economist*, December 17, 2011, http://www.economist.com/node/21541845; Ida Homer, "Big Is Beautiful in Africa, but Should Size Matter?" March 18, 2012, http://www.africaonthe blog.com/big-is-beautiful-in-africa-but-should-a-person%E2%80%99s-size-matter/. All sites accessed on December 1, 2013. A slight difference regarding the desirability of chubbiness is to be seen between Ghanaian women and men, which also appears to divide along class lines for particular phases of the life cycle. Among university female students, for example, the objective is certainly to be as slim and attractive as the women they see in magazines (read Western and non-Ghanaian). Their aspirations are no different from those of female university students in the Western world. However, the aspiration to slimness changes as soon as they cross the marital threshold. Then weight gain is a sign of having married well. With the onset of childbirth, the idea is firmly implanted that a woman ought to look "well" in the Ghanaian sense of the word. Women who have had children rarely feel guilty about gaining weight and have very little pressure put on them on account of it. Quite the opposite: the weight gain is used to distinguish themselves from slim women who have not proved their womanhood at the harsh altar of childbirth. This may sound odd or even retrogressive to Western feminists, but it actually serves to protect Ghanaian childbearing women from the unnecessary onset of existential guilt regarding the shape of their bodies after having children.

13. Literary texts provide the best examples of the kòbòlò as described here. Apart from Wole Soyinka's *The Road* and *The Beatification of Area Boy*, Ben Okri's short story collections set in the urban underworlds of Lagos are replete with them. Also noteworthy are Dambudzo Marechera's "House of Hunger," which presents a highly sophisticated intellectual kòbòlò in the person of the narrator; Athol Fugard's *Sizwe Bansi Is Dead*, featuring the kòbòlò as a cynical product of apartheid labor laws; Zakes Mda's *Ways of Dying*; and the South African film *Mapantsula* (dir. Oliver Schmitz, 1988). Each of these texts represents different aspects of the kòbòlò. The question as to why this social type is so popular in African literature is one we will have to set aside for another occasion.

14. On kayayei (pl.) in Accra, see Ntewusu (2011, 58–90). For a literary representation, see also Wolo (2012).

15. See Hart (1973) and (2006); also Obeng-Odoom (2011).

16. Hart (1973, 76), Obeng-Odoom (2011, 358–60). Obeng-Odoom also notes the relevance of wage-labor that falls below the minimum wage, thus further expanding the purview of the informal sector.

17. Hart (1973, 47).

18. Hart (1973, 66), Obeng-Odoom (2011, 360). The precariousness of the informal sector and the ways in which people are trying to negotiate this in Accra and other parts of urban Africa is now the subject of large private-sector-funded projects such as the Informal City Dialogues, which provides a forum for blogs, research papers, and ongoing interviews with slum dwellers. See http://nextcity.org/informalcity, last accessed June 25, 2013.

19. Hart (1973, 75).

20. Hart (1973, 64).

21. Northern Ghana itself comprises three administrative regions, namely, the Northern (capital Tamale), Upper East (capital Bolgatanga), and Upper West (capital Yendi) Regions.

22. See Schildkrout (1998), Pellow (2002), and Ntewusu (2005, 2011).

23. In his study of Madina Zongo, Samuel Ntewusu goes on to disaggregate the demographic constitution of the township as follows: "The ethnic composition of northern Ghanaians [at Madina] is: Dagomba, Mampruse, Nanumba, Gonja, Konkomba, Nawuri, Nchumburu, Vagla, Mo, Bassari, Chakosi (Anufu), Frafra (Nabdam), Kassena, Wala, Dargarti, Grunshi, Sisala and Bulsa. The ethnic composition of the groups from the Sahel, Nigeria and Francophone West Africa include Busanga, Fulani, Gao, Kotokoli, Losso, Mossi, Wangara and Zambrama" (2005, 14–15).

24. See Ntewusu (2005, 27–40) and also Quarcoo (1967).

Chapter 7: The Lettered City

1. On this point, see especially Margaret Cohen's fine study, The Sentimental Education of the Novel (1999).

2. The trope of traversal tied to a sentimental education is, strictly speaking, not exclusive to Ghanaian literature and can be seen in operation elsewhere. What is distinctive at least about the texts discussed here is the intrinsic relations established between spatial traversal and the boundary between realism and nonrealist explanatory apparatuses. Looked at in this way, the African literary texts that fall under the rubric become quite small and specialized, and include Soyinka's Death and the King's Horseman, Elechi Amadi's The Concubine, Syl Cheney-Coker's The Last Harmattan of Alusine Dunbar, and, of course, Ben Okri's superb picaresque and magical realist novel The Famished Road.

3. C. L. R. James, letter to Constance Webb, 1944, in James (1992, 144).

4. Darko provides a version of Sodom and Gomorrah's history in Faceless. See also the recent investigative program for Joy FM conducted by Anny Osabutey, "Squatters' Paradise: The Ins and Outs of Sodom and Gomorrah," http://edition.myjoyonline.com/pages/news/201109/72595.php, last accessed October 15, 2012. The slum has had a lot of media coverage, including: Babatunde Olatunji, "Sodom and Gomorrah: A Menace in Accra," Ghanaweb, http://www.ghanaweb.com/GhanaHomePage/blogs/blog.article.php?blog=937&ID=1000004179, last accessed October 15, 2012; "African Viewpoint: Sodom and Gomorrah Dilemma," http://www.bbc.co.uk/news/world-africa-15625427, last accessed October 15, 2012.

5. There is good reason to agree with Alistair Macmillan that the arrival of the Scottish-Canadian William Galloway in Accra had a major impact on its metamorphosis ([1920] 1968, 184). Galloway was born in 1875 in the town of Nepean in Ontario, which has since been amalgamated into the Ottawa-Carleton municipality. His family then moved with him back to Scotland in 1887. He spent five years from the age of seventeen in South Africa working in the building industry there, assisting in the construction of the Pretoria Law Courts and the Potchefstroom and Krugersdorp penitentiaries. He left South Africa just before the outbreak of the Boer War in 1898, enrolling in the architecture building degree program at Glasgow University. He was so

impressive that by twenty-six he was put in charge of expansion at the university while under the employ of Messrs. Alexander Muir and Sons. He moved to Nigeria in 1910 to participate in the Nigerian Railway survey. In Nigeria he was to meet and work closely with Sir Frederick Gordon Guggisberg, who was working on the same survey in the country. He moved to the Gold Coast in 1911, where he later joined the firm of Thompson and Moir as a partner. Guggisberg was appointed governor of the Gold Coast from 1919 to 1926 and is credited with some of the most significant development projects for the colony in the first half of the twentieth century. It was the firm of Thompson, Moir and Galloway that carried out most of the British administration's commissions, and it was credited with developing today's Ridge, the Kingsway Stores, the Bank of British West Africa (later Barclays bank, located on the High Street), Wesley Girls' High School in Cape Coast, Achimota College, as well as the Kumasi Post Office. Galloway's long experience working on civic buildings and public works in South Africa, Scotland, and Nigeria clearly stood him in good stead when he came to Accra. What is also interesting in Galloway's biography is the degree to which empire provided the platform for the shaping of illustrious careers. Typically the empire helped those of the political class, who traveled between different postings across the world, but it is obvious here that it also impacted the lives of other personnel. Significant also is the fact that this cohort of civil servants was thoroughly transnational, with Galloway's Scottish-Canadian background and his work experience in different countries proving the point. But it would not be awry for us also to see the cultivation of patronage when the opportunity presented itself. That happy circumstance of Guggisberg's governorship of the colony after he had already become acquainted with Galloway in Nigeria must have exerted a strong influence in the appointment of Thompson, Moir and Galloway as de facto architects and builders to the colonial government. For the life of William Galloway, see "Wullie Galloway Family History and Genealogy," http://www.otherwisewullie .ca/genealogy_William_Galloway.html, last accessed November 30, 2013.

6. For a discussion of the causes of the conflict, see Wiena (2009) and Bogner (2000).

7. Wright (1988).

8. On the concept of the pharmakos and how it relates to African literature, see Quayson (2007, 120–121).

9. On epiphanies in literature, see Bidney (1997). For a preliminary account of negative epiphanies, see Quayson, *Aesthetic Nervousness* (2007a, chapter 4).

10. On anamorphic space as a form of intervention in thought see, Beaumont (2009).

Conclusion

I want to say a very special thanks to Achille Mbembe and Sarah Nuttall for inviting me to present an early version of this chapter at the Johannesburg Workshop in Theory and Criticism in 2013. I had some quite amazing conversations with Achille and Sarah as well as with Ackbar Abbas, whose paper "Junk Space, 'Dogville' and Poor Theory" and his discussion of Rem Koolhaas prompted a complete shift in my thinking and thus in the focus of the chapter. I also want to seize this opportunity to thank Leigh-Ann Naidoo and her partner Kelly . . . for their quite incredible organizational acuity and overall generosity of spirit.

1. The Comaroffs' definition of Afromodernity does not expound on the place of the diaspora within it. But the fact that in 2005 the African Union declared the African diaspora the sixth region of the continent suggests that the conception of Afromodernity is being reworked and with more far-reaching implications. That Taiye Selasi's essay on Afropolitanism (2005) also ignited a lively discussion on Africa's re-inflection of cosmopolitanism also means that the concept of Afromodernity requires a much broader ambit than the Comaroffs provided it. But that will have to wait for another occasion. On Africa's many diasporas, see Quayson (2013).

2. For a wide-ranging evaluation of the arguments put forward in *Theory from the South*, see Quayson (2012) and the other essays published in *Cultural Anthropology* 27.1.

3. See Quayson (2003) and also Hashi (2013).

4. A very quick note on the Harvard Project's commentary on the primary unit of property being the Yoruba compound and how this has morphed into variant and heterogeneous morphology (Koolhaas et al. 2000, 661–663): we might add, first, that this is not dissimilar to what might be found among the Gas of Accra, and second, that both the organizing unit and its transformations have become so cross-cultural and ubiquitous that we must find its genealogy someplace else other than from within an ethnic source.

5. See especially Gandy (2005), Hecker (2010), and Fourchard (2010) for wide-ranging critiques of Koolhaas on Lagos.

6. It struck me while writing this section that Wole Soyinka's *The Road* appears to be more Beckettian than Lagosian, for though the play is resolutely set in Lagos and the characters are clearly operating under the impress of the informal economy, they do not recycle objects, much less space. What they do participate in is a cycle of epic dreaming, much of which involves imagining themselves driving powerful trucks across Nigeria. The only mode of recycling to be seen in the play is what we find with respect to Professor's gathering of signs of all kinds (newspapers, road signs, etc.). But even here it is in the service of his eccentric quest for the esoteric Word and not for the recycling of either objects or space.

7. We should also note the racialized dimension of some of the protests that I have listed. For the riots in London, Paris, and Stockholm all shared the common feature of being triggered by the callous police treatment of members of racial minorities. The history of immigration into Western cities has always been color coded, with failed projects of social and economic integration ensuring that there are large cohorts of deeply dissatisfied racial minorities in all these cities that suffer the vagaries of free time. Their anger and frustration is palpable, because unlike the generation of their parents they have grown up in these Western societies and have learned to call them home yet come to recognize the sharp contradictions between home and belonging that are the products of insensitive and racist policies.

REFERENCES

Archival Sources

Public Records and Archives Administration Department (National Archives, Ghana)
ADM 1/9/1–4 Original Correspondence. Letters from the Governor, Gold Coast, to local officials
ADM 1/10 Origianl Correspondence. Letters (Miscellaneous) from Officials etc. to the Governor, Gold Coast
ADM 5.2/1–17 Census Returns
CSO Papers (unclassified administrative papers from the 1930s)

National Archives, London, UK

C096 Gold Coast Original Correspondence
C097 Gold Coast Acts
C098 Gold Coast Sessional Papers
C099 Gold Coast Government Gazettes
C0100 Gold Coast Blue Books
Asere Mantse to Governor on Kaneshie, CS011/14/126/1951/30, vols. 1 and 2, Public Records and Archives Administration (National Archives, Accra), CS011/14/126/1951/30, vol. 1, Public Records and Archives Administration Department (National Archives, Ghana)
Exclusion of Africans from European Residential Areas, c096/751/11 (National Archives, UK)
Kaneshie Layout Plan, CS011/14/126/1951/30, vol. 1 and CS011/14/127/1951/30, vol. 2 (National Archives, Ghana)
Kokomlemle/Akwandor Lands Case, SCT/2/6/28, Public Records and Archives Administration (National Archives, Ghana)
Letter from O. G. R Williams, Assistant Secretary and Head of the West Department, to Sir Arnold Hodson, July 12, 1939. "Earthquake: Restoration of Accra [and] Rehousing," C096/762/31391/1939/1 (National Archives, Ghana)
Nathan to Ronald Ross, November 30, 1901, Ross Archives, Cabinet A, Drawer II, File 13 (National Archives, UK)

Sir Arnold Hodson speech to the Legislative Assembly, "African Civil Service," co96/75759/7 (National Archives, UK)

Sir Arnold Hodson to Sir Malcolm MacDonald, Colonial Secretary, July 5, 1939. "Earthquake: Restoration of Accra [and] Rehousing," CO 96/762/31391/1939/1 (National Archives, UK)

Sir Arnold Hodson to Sir Malcolm MacDonald, October, 13, 1939, CO 96/762/31391/1939/1

Electronic Sources

Ato Quayson, "Co-evalness, Recursivity, and the Feet of Lionel Messi." *Cultural Anthropology*, available at http://www.culanth.org/fieldsights/269-coevalness-recursivity-and-the-feet-of-lionel-messi, February 25, 2012, last accessed December 1, 2013.

CitiFM Online, "CitiFM's Salsa Mania Is Back," available at http://citifmonline.com/mobile/index.php?id=1.435579, June 11, 2011, last accessed December 1, 2013.

"Fat Is Bad but Beautiful," *Economist*, December 17, 2011, available at http://www.economist.com/node/21541845, last accessed December 2, 2013.

Ghana Policy Network, "Incomes in Ghana: Policy Discussion Paper," available at https://www.google.ca/search?q=Ghana+Trades+Union+Congress+policy+discussion+paper+on+incomes+in+Ghana&oq=Ghana+Trades+Union+Congress+policy+discussion+paper+on+incomes+in+Ghana&aqs=chrome.69i57j69i64.1405j0j4&sourceid=chrome&espv=210&es_sm=91&ie=UTF-8, May 19, 2004, last accessed December 1, 2013.

Ida Homer, "Big Is Beautiful in Africa, but Should Size Matter?" March 18, 2012, available at http://www.africaontheblog.com/big-is-beautiful-in-africa-but-should-a-person%E2%80%99s-size-matter/, last accessed December 2, 2013.

Isaac Essel, "Ablekuma North: Macho Men Burn Ballot Papers," MC: Modern Ghana, available at http://www.modernghana.com/news/434907/1/ablekuma-north-machomen-burn-ballot-papers.html, uploaded December 8, 2012, last accessed November 29, 2013.

Karen Leigh, "Accra, Ghana," *New York Times*, January 11, 2013, available at http://www.nytimes.com/interactive/2013/01/10/travel/2013-places-to-go.html?_r=0, last accessed May 15, 2013.

Khanya, available at http://khanya.wordpress.com/2008/05/23/makwerekwere/, May 28, 2008, last accessed December 1, 2013.

National Sports Authority, available at http://www.sportscouncil.com.gh/maincat_select_discipline.cfm?disciplineID=31, last accessed November 29, 2013.

Pascale Harter, "Mauritania's 'Wife-Fattening' Farm," BBC News, January 26, 2004, available at http://news.bbc.co.uk/2/hi/3429903.stm, last accessed December 2, 2013.

"Police Raid NPP Research Office," Ghanaweb, available at http://www.ghanaweb.com/GhanaHomePage/NewsArchive/artikel.php?ID=259152, December 11, 2012, last accessed November 29, 2013.

Samuel Nii Darko Dowuona, "Mobile Penetration Hits 98% in Ghana," JoyOnline.com, available at http://business.myjoyonline.com/pages/news/201210/95084.php, October 7, 2012, last accessed December 1, 2013.

Tigo Ghana, available at http://www.TIGO.com.gh/, last accessed December 1, 2013.
Trassaco Valley: Experience the Dream, available at http://www.trasaccovalley.com
/contact.php, last accessed December 1, 2013.
"Whose City Is It Anyway" initiative, available at http://urbanafrica.net/news/2012/09
/14/whose-city-it-anyway.

Reference Sources

Abaka, Edmund. 2005. *Kola Is God's Gift: Agricultural Production, Export Initiatives and the Kola Industry of Asante and the Gold Coast, 1820–1950.* Oxford, UK: James Currey.

Aboagye, Festus B. 2010. *Indigenous African Warfare: Its Concept and Art in the Gold Coast, Asante and the Northern Territories Up to the Early 1900s.* Pretoria: Ulinzi Africa Publishing.

Achebe, Chinua (1964). *Arrow of God.* London: Heinemann.

Acquah, Ione. 1958. *Accra Survey: A Social Survey of the Capital of Ghana.* London: University of London Press.

Addo N. O., and M. Peil. 1967. *Madina Survey: A Study of the Structure and Development of a Contemporary Sub-Urban Settlement.* Legon: Institute of African Studies, University of Ghana.

Ajayi-Crowther, Jacob. 1998. *General History of Africa: Africa in the Nineteenth Century until the 1880s.* Berkeley: University of California Press.

Akyeampong, Emmanuel. 1995. "Alcoholism in Ghana: A Socio-Political Exploration." *Culture, Medicine and Psychiatry* 19: 261–280.

Akyeampong, Emmanuel. 2004. "Memories of Place and Belonging: Identity, Citizenship, and the Lebanese in Ghana." *Ghana Studies* 7: 25–42.

Akyeampong, Emmanuel. 2006. "Race, Identity and Citizenship in Black Africa: The Case of the Lebanese in Ghana." *Africa* 76 (3): 297–323.

Amankwah, H. A. 1989. *The Legal Regime of Land Use in West Africa: Ghana and Nigeria.* Hobart, New Zealand: Pacific Law Press.

Amoah, Frank E. K. 1964. *Accra: A Study of the Development of a West African City.* Legon: Institute of African Studies, University of Ghana.

Amos, Alcione M. 2001. "Afro Brazilians in Togo: The Olympio Family, 1882–1945." *Cahiers d'Études Africaines* 162 (201): 293–314.

Amos, Alcione M., and Ebenezer Ayesu. 2003. "'I Am Brazilian': History of the Tabon, Afro-Brazilians in Accra, Ghana." *Transactions of the Historical Society of Ghana*, n.s., 35–58.

Anquandah, Kwesi J. 1999. *Castles and Forts of Ghana.* Paris: Atalante.

Appiah, Kwame Anthony. 1992. *In My Father's House: Africa in the Philosophy of Culture.* New York: Oxford University Press.

Appiah, Kwame Anthony. 2006. *Cosmopolitanism: Ethics in a World of Strangers.* New York: W. W. Norton.

Apusigah, Agnes Atia. 2004. "Gender Mainstreaming: The Ghana Poverty Reduction Strategy, or Is It?" *Women in Action.* http://isiswomen.org/wia/wia2–04/agnes.htm. Last accessed February 3, 2009.

Armah, Ayi Kwei. 1968. *The Beautyful Ones Are Not Yet Born.* Boston: Heinemann.

Armah, Ayi Kwei. 1969. *Fragments.* London: Heinemann.

Armstrong, John. 1976. "Mobilized and Proletarian Diasporas." *American Political Science Review* 70: 393–408.

Arrighi, Giovani. 1994. *The Long Twentieth Century: Money, Power, and the Origin of our Times*. London: Verso.

Asante, Clement, E. 1996. *The Press in Ghana: Problems and Prospects*. Lanham, MD: University Press of America.

Awoonor, Kofi. 1972. *This Earth, My Brother . . .* London: Heinemann.

Ayensu, Edward S. 2007. *Bank of Ghana: Commemoration of the Golden Jubilee*. Accra: Bank of Ghana.

Azu, Diana Gladys. 1974. *The Ga Family and Social Change*. Leiden, The Netherlands: Afrika-Studiecentrum.

Bacchus, William. 1974. *Foreign Policy and the Bureaucratic Process: The State Department's Country Director System*. Princeton, NJ: Princeton University Press.

Bakhtin, Mikhail. 1986. *Speech Genres and Other Late Essays*. Trans. Vern W. McGee. Austin: University of Texas Press.

Barber, Karin. 2000. *The Generation of Plays: Yoruba Popular Life in Theatre*. Bloomington: Indiana University Press.

Barber, Karin. 2006. *African Hidden Histories: Everyday Literacy and the Making of the Self*. Bloomington: Indiana University Press.

Barber, Karin. 2007. *The Anthropology of Texts, Persons and Publics: Oral and Written Culture in Africa and Beyond*. Cambridge: Cambridge University Press.

Baucom, Ian. 2005. *Specters of the Atlantic: Finance Capital, Slavery, and the Philosophy of History*. Durham, NC: Duke University Press.

Beaumont, Matthew. 2009. "The Anamorphic Estrangements of Science Fiction." In *Red Planets: Marxism and Science Fiction*, edited by Mark Bould and China Mieville, 29–47. London: Pluto.

Beckett, Samuel. 1986. *Waiting for Godot*. In *Samuel Beckett: The Complete Dramatic Works*. London: Faber and Faber.

Benjamin, Walter. (1986) 2002. *Moscow Diary*. Trans. Richard Sieburth. Cambridge, MA: Harvard University Press.

Bhachu, Parminder. 1985. *Twice Migrants: East African Sikh Settlers in Britain*. London: Tavistock.

Bidney, Martin. 1997. *Patterns of Epiphany: From Wordsworth to Tolstoy, Pater, and Browning*. Carbondale: Southern Illinois University Press.

Bobo, Benjamin F. 1974. "Economic Factors Influencing Migration, Urban Growth and Structure, Accra, Ghana." PhD diss., University of California.

Bogner, Artur. 2000. "The 1994 Civil War in Northern Ghana: The Genesis and Escalation of a 'Tribal' Conflict." In *Ethnicity in Ghana: The Limits of Invention*, edited by Carola Lentz and Stephen Nugent. London: Palgrave Macmillan.

Bordo, Susan. 2000. *The Male Body: A New Look at Men in Public and in Private*. New York: Farrar, Straus and Giroux.

Borland, Katherine. 2009. "Embracing Difference: Salsa Fever in New Jersey." *Journal of American Folklore* 122: 466–492.

Bourdieu, Pierre. 1986. "The Forms of Capital." In *Handbook of Theory and Research for the Sociology of Education*, edited by John G. Richardson, 241–258. New York: Greenwood Press.

Bourdieu, Pierre. 1987. *Distinction: A Social Critique of the Judgment of Taste*. Cambridge, MA: Harvard University Press.

Brand, Richard. 1971. "A Geographical Interpretation of the European Influence on Accra, Ghana Since 1877," PhD diss., University of Columbia.

Brand, Richard R. 1972. "The Spatial Organization of Residential Areas in Accra, Ghana, with Particular Reference to Aspects of Modernization." In "Spatial Structure and Processes in Tropical West Africa," *Economic Geography* 48 (3): 284–298.

Bremer, Alf. 2002. "Conflict Moderation and Participation: Prospects and Barriers for Urban Renewal in Ga Mashie." In *Visions for the City: Accra in the 21st Century*, edited by Ralph Mills Tettey and Korantima Adi-Dako, 106–116. Accra: Woeli Publishers.

Brooks, George E. 2003. *Euro-Africans in Western Africa: Commerce, Social Status, Gender, and Religious Observance from the Sixteenth to the Eighteenth Century*. Oxford, UK: James Currey.

Burrell, Jenna. 2012. *Invisible Users: Youth in the Internet Cafes of Urban Ghana*. Cambridge, MA: MIT Press.

Buser, Hans. 2010. *In Ghana at Independence: Stories of a Swiss Salesman*. Basel: Basler Afrique Bibliothèque.

Cain, Peter J., and Anthony G. Hopkins. 2002. *British Imperialism, 1688–2000*. London: Longman.

Carnes, Joshua A. 1852. *Journal of a Voyage from Boston to the West Coast of Africa: With a Full Description of the Manner of Trading with the Natives on the Coast*. Boston: J. P. Jewett.

Carter, Paul. 2010. *The Road to Botany Bay: An Exploration of Landscape and History*. Minneapolis: University of Minnesota Press.

Castesen, Edward. 2010. *Closing the Books: Governor Edward Castesen on Danish Guinea 1842–50*. Trans. Tove Storveen with an Introduction by Per Hernaes. Accra: Subsaharan.

Castoriadis, Cornelius. 1987. *The Imaginary Institution of Society*. Trans. Kathleen Blamey. Cambridge, UK: Polity Press.

Clayton, Anthony, and David Killingray. 1989. *Khaki and Blue: Military and Police in British Colonial Africa*. Athens: Ohio University Press.

Cohen, Margaret. 1999. *The Sentimental Education of the Novel*. Princeton, NJ: Princeton University Press.

Cohen, Phil. 1997. "Out of the Melting Pot into the Fire Next Time: Imagining the East End as City, Body, Text." In *Imagining Cities: Scripts, Signs, Memories*, edited by Sallie Westwood and John Williams, 71–84. London: Routledge.

Cole, M. Catherine. 2001. *Ghana's Concert Party Theatre*. Bloomington: Indiana University Press.

Collins, John. 1985. *Music Makers of West Africa*. Washington, DC: Three Continents Press.

Collins, John. 1992. *West African Roots of Pop*. Philadelphia: Temple University Press.

Comaroff, Jean, and John F. Comaroff. 2000. *Millennial Capitalism and the Culture of Neo-Liberalism*. Durham, NC: Duke University Press.

Comaroff, Jean, and John F. Comaroff. 2011. *Theory from the South*. Herndon, VA: Paradigm.

Cruickshank, Brodie. 1834. *Eighteen Years on the Gold Coast: Including an Account of the Native Tribes, and Their Intercourse with Europeans*. 2 vols. London: Cass.

Daaku, Kwame Yeboah. 1970. *Trade and Politics on the Gold Coast, 1600–1720: A Study of the African Reaction to the European Trade*. Oxford, UK: Clarendon Press.

Dantzig, Albert van. 1980. *Forts and Castles of Ghana*. Accra: Sedco.

Darko, Amma. 2003. *Faceless*. Accra: Sub-Saharan Publishers.

Date-Bah, E. 1980. "The Inscriptions on the Vehicles of Ghanaian Commercial Drivers: A Sociological Analysis." *Journal of Modern African History* 18 (3): 525–531.

De Boeck, Filip, and Margaret-Francoise Plissart. 2003. *Kinshasa: Tales of the Invisible City and the Second World*. Ghent, Belgium: Ludion.

de Bruijn, Esther. 2013. "Sensational Aesthetics of Ghanaian Market Fiction." PhD diss., University of Toronto.

Deflem, Mathieu. 1994. "Law Enforcement in British Colonial Africa: A Comparative Analysis of Imperial Policing in Nyasaland, the Gold Coast, and Kenya." *Police Studies* 17 (1): 45–68.

Deleuze, Gilles, and Félix Guattari. 1975. *Kafka: Toward a Theory of Mino Literature*. Minneapolis: University of Minnesota Press.

Dickson, K. B. 1965. "Evolution of Seaports in Ghana: 1880–1928." *Annals of the Association of American Geographers* 55 (1): 98–111.

Dumett, Raymond E. 1968. "The Campaign Against Malaria." *African Historical Studies* 1 (2): 153–197.

Dumett, Raymond E. 1981. "Pressure Groups, Bureaucracy, and the Decision-Making Process: The Case of Slavery Abolition and Colonial Expansion in the Gold Coast, 1874." *Journal of Imperial and Commonwealth History* 9 (2): 193–215.

Dumett, Raymond E. 1983. "African Merchants of the Gold Coast, 1860–1905: Dynamics of Indigenous Entrepreneurship." *Comparative Studies in Society and History* 25 (4): 661–693.

Dumett, Raymond E. 1999. *El Dorado in West Africa: The Gold Mining Frontier, African Labor, and Colonial Capitalism in the Gold Coast, 1875–1900*. Columbus: Ohio University Press.

Egblewogbe, Martin. 2010. *Mr. Happy and the Hammer of God and Other Stories*. Oxford, UK: Ayebia Publishers.

Fabian, Johannes. (1983) 2002. *Time and the Other: How Anthropology Makes Its Subject*. New York: Columbia University Press.

Fagunwa. 1968.

Feinberg, Harvey M. 1989. "Africans and Europeans in West Africa: Elminans and Dutchmen on the Gold Coast during the Eighteenth Century." *Transactions of the American Philosophical Society* 79 (7): 1–186.

Field, Margaret J. 1940. *Social Organization of the Ga People*. London: Crown Agents for the Colonies.

Firmin-Sellers, Kathryn. 1996. *The Transformation of Property Rights in the Gold Coast*. Cambridge: Cambridge University Press.

Fourchard, Laurent. 2010. "Lagos, Koolhaas, and the Partisan Politics in Nigeria." *International Journal of Urban and Regional Research* 35 (1): 40–56.

Freund, Bill. 1995. *Inside and Outsiders: The Indian Working Class of Durban 1910–1990*. Portsmouth, NH: Hieneman.

Fry, Richard. 1976. *Bankers in West Africa: The Story of the Bank of British West Africa Limited*. London: Hutchinson Benham.

Gandy, Matthew. 2005. "Learning from Lagos." *New Left Review* 33.

Gewald, Jan-Bart, Sabine Luning, and Klaas van Walraven. 2009. *The Speed of Change: Motor Vehicles and People in Africa, 1890–2000.* Leiden, The Netherlands: Brill.

Ghai, Dharam P., and Yash P Ghai, eds. 1970. *Portrait of a Minority: Asians in East Africa.* Nairobi: Oxford University Press.

Gifford, Paul. 2004. *Ghana's New Christianity: Pentecostalism in a Globalizing African Economy.* Bloomington: Indiana University Press.

Gordon, Charles Alexander. 1874. *Life on the Gold Coast.* London: Baillère, Tindall and Cox.

Grant, Richard. 2008. *Globalizing City: The Urban and Economic Transformation of Accra, Ghana.* Syracuse, NY: Syracuse University Press.

Grant, Richard, and Jan Nijman. 2002. "Globalization and the Corporate Geography of Cities in the Less-Developed World." *Annals of the Association of American Geographers* 92 (1): 320–340.

Guseh, James S. 2008. "Slogans and Mottos on Commercial Vehicles: A Reflection on Liberian Philosophy and Culture." *Journal of African Cultural Studies* 20 (2): 159–171.

Hart, Keith. 1973. "Informal Income Opportunities and Urban Employment in Ghana." *Journal of Modern African Studies* 11 (1): 61–89.

Hart, Keith. 2006. "Bureaucratic Form and the Informal Economy." In *Linking the Formal and Informal Economy: Concepts and Policies,* edited by Basudeb Guha-Khasnobis, Ravi Kanbur, and Elinor Ostrom. Oxford: Oxford University Press.

Hartman, Saidiya. 2008. *Lose Your Mother.* London: Macmillan.

Harvey, David. (1981) 2005. "The Spatial Fix: Hegel, Von Thünen, and Marx." *Antipode* 13 (3): 1–12.

Harvey, David. (1982) 2006. *The Limits to Capital.* London: Verso.

Harvey, David. 1989. *The Condition of Postmodernity: An Enquiry into the Origins of Cultural Change.* Oxford, UK: Blackwell.

Hashi, Fardowsa. 2013. "Bribery as a Form of Democracy." *Public Policy and Governance Review* 4 (2): 95–98.

Heap, Simon. 1990. "The Development of Motor Transport in the Gold Coast, 1900–1939." *Journal of Transport History* 11 (2): 19–37.

Hecker, Tim. 2010. "The Slum Pastoral: Helicopter Visuality and Koolhaas's Lagos," *Space and Culture* 13 (3): 256–269.

Hernæs, Per O. 1995. "European Fort Communities on the Gold Coast in the Era of the Slave Trade." In *International Conference on Shipping, Factories and Colonization,* edited by John Everaert and J. Parmentier, 167–181. Trondheim, Norway: Académie Royale des Sciences d'Outre-Mer—Koninklijke Academie voor Overzeese.

Hernæs, Per O. 2003. "African Power Struggle and European Opportunity: Danish Expansion on the Early 18th Century Gold Coast." *Transactions of the Historical Society of Ghana,* 7: 1–92.

Hesse, Hermann W. von (2011). "A Brief History of the Afro-Brazilian Community of Accra." BA thesis, University of Ghana.

Hill, Lawrence. 2001. *Black Berry, Sweet Juice: On Being Black and White in Canada.* Toronto: HarperPerennial.

Hill, Lawrence. 2007. *The Book of Negroes.* Toronto: HarperCollins.

Hopkins, Anthony G. 1973. *An Economic History of West Africa*. London: Longman.

Huber, Magnus. 1999. *Ghanaian Pidgin English in Its West African Context: A Sociohistorical and Structural Analysis*. Amsterdam: John Betjemans Publishing.

Huntley, Henry Vere. 1850. *Seven Years' Service on the Slave Coast of Western Africa*. 2 vols. London: T. C. Newby.

Hutchful, Eboe. 2000. *Ghana's Adjustment Experience: The Paradox of Reform*. New York: United Nations Research Institute for Social Development.

Hutchison, Charles Francis. 2005. *The Pen-Pictures of Modern Africans and African Celebrities*. Edited with an introduction by Michel R. Doortmont. Leiden, The Netherlands: Brill.

Ipsen, Pernille. 2008. *Kokó's Daughters: Danish Men Marrying Ga Women in an Atlantic Slave Trading Port in the Eighteenth Century*. PhD diss., University of Copenhagen.

Irele, Abiola. 2001. "Orality, Literacy, and African Literature." In *The African Imagination: Literature in African and the Black Diaspora*, 3–38. New York: Oxford University Press.

James, C. L. R. 1992. *The C.L.R. James Reader*. Ed. Anna Grimshaw. Oxford, UK: Blackwell.

Jameson, Fredric. 1981. *The Political Unconscious: Narrative as a Socially Symbolic Act*. Ithaca, NY: Cornell University Press.

Johnson, Matthew. 2010. *Archaeological Theory: An Introduction*. 2nd ed. London: Wiley-Blackwell.

Johnson, Samuel. 1921. *History of the Yorubas*. Lagos, Nigeria: CSS Bookshops.

Jones-Quartey, K. A. 1974. *A Summary of the Ghana Press, 1822–1960*. Accra: Ghana Information Services.

Justesen, Ole. 2003. "Heinrich Richter, 1785–1849: Trader and Politician in the Danish Trading Settlements on the Gold Coast." *Transactions of the Historical Society of Ghana*, n.s., 7: 93–192.

Justesen, Ole. 2005. *Danish Sources for the History of Accra, 1657–1754*. Vols. 1 and 2. Trans. James Manley. Copenhagen: Det Kongelige Danske Videnskabernes Selskab.

Kabir, Ananya. 2013. "The European Salsa Congress: Music and Dance in Transnational Circuits." In *The Blackwell Companion to Diaspora and Transnational Studies*, edited by Ato Quayson and Girish Daswani, 263–276. New York: Blackwell.

Kaplow, Susan B. 1977. "The Mudfish and the Crocodile: Underdevelopment of a West African Bourgeoisie." *Science and Society Quarterly* 41 (3): 317–333.

Kea, Ray. 1982. *Settlements, Trade, and Politics in the Seventeenth-Century Gold Coast*. Baltimore: Johns Hopkins University Press.

Kea, Ray. 2000. "'But I Know What I Shall Do': Agency, Belief and the Social Imaginary in Eighteenth-Century Gold Coast Towns." In *Africa's Urban Past*, edited by David M. Anderson and Richard Rathbone, 163–188. Oxford, UK: James Currey.

Kellner, Douglas. 1989. *Critical Theory, Marxism, and Modernity*. Cambridge, UK: Polity Press.

Kilson, Marion. 1974. *African Urban Kinsmen: The Ga of Central Accra*. London: C. Hurst.

Kimble, David. 1963. *A Political History of Ghana, 1850–1928*. Oxford: Oxford University Press.

King, Anthony, D. 1976. *Colonial Urban Development: Culture, Social Power and Environment*. London: Routledge.

Koolhaas, Rem. 2002. "Fragments of a Lecture on Lagos." In *Under Siege: Four African Cities: Freetown, Johannesburg, Kinshasa, Lagos* (Documenta 11, Platform 4), edited by Okwui Enwezor et al. Ostfildern-Ruit: Hatje Cantz Publishers.

Koolhaas, Rem, Stefano Boern, Sanford Kwinter, and Nadia Tazi. 2000. *Mutations*. New York: ACTAR.

Kyei, Kojo Gyinaye, and Hannah Schreckenbach. 1975. *No Time to Die*. Accra: Catholic Press.

Kymlicka, Will. 2007. *Multicultural Odysseys*. New York: Oxford University Press.

Kyvig, David E., and Myron A. Marty. 2010. *Nearby History: Exploring the Past around You*, 3rd ed. Lanham, MD: Altamira Press.

Laing, Kojo. 1986. *Search Sweet Country*. London: Heinemann.

Larbi, Wordsworth Odame. 1996. "Spatial Planning and Urban Fragmentation in Accra." *Third World Planning Review* 18 (2): 193–215.

Law, Robin. 1980. *The Horse in West African History: The Role of the Horse in the Societies of Pre-Colonial West Africa*. Oxford: Oxford University Press.

Law, Robin. 2004. *Ouidah: The Social History of a West African Slaving "Port," 1727–1892*. Oxford, UK: James Currey.

Lawrence, A. W. 1963. *Trade Castles and Forts of West Africa*. London: Jonathan Cape.

Lawuji, O. B. 1988. "Obituary and Ancestral Worship: Analysis of a Contemporary Cultural Form in Nigeria." *Sociological Analysis* 48 (4): 372–379.

Lefebvre, Henri. 1992. *The Production of Space*. Trans. Donald Nicholson-Smith. Oxford: Blackwell.

Lewis, George H. 1998. "The Philosophy of the Street in Ghana: Mammy Wagons and Their Mottos—A Research Note." *Journal of Popular Culture* 32 (1): 165–172.

Lionnet, Francois. 2012. *The Known and the Uncertain: Creole Cosmopolitanisms of the Indian Ocean*. Mauritius: L'Atelier d'écriture.

Lokko, Mae-ling. n.d. *The Brazil House*. Accra: Brazilian Embassy.

Macmillan, Alister. (1920) 1968. *The Red Book of West Africa: Historical and Descriptive Commercial and Industrial Facts, Figures and Resources*. London: Frank Cass.

Malki, Xerxes. 2008. "The Alienated Stranger: A Political and Economic History of the Lebanese in Ghana, 1925–1992." PhD diss., University of Oxford.

Mamdani, Mahmood. 2012. *Define and Rule: Native as Political Identity*. Cambridge, MA: Harvard University Press.

Manu, Takyiwaa, ed. 2005. *At Home in the World? International Migration and the Development of Contemporary Ghana and West Africa*. Accra: Sub-Saharan Publishers.

Manu, Takyiwaa. 2006. "An 11th Region of Ghana? Ghanaians Abroad." Inaugural lecture, Ghana Academy of Arts and Sciences. Accra: GAAS.

Manuel, Peter. 2006. *Caribbean Currents: Caribbean Music from Rumba to Reggae*. Philadelphia: Temple University Press.

Mark, Peter, and José Da Silva Horta. 2011. *The Forgotten Diaspora: Jewish Communities in West Africa and the Making of the Atlantic World*. Cambridge: Cambridge University Press.

Marshall, Ruth. 2009. *Political Spiritualities: The Pentecostal Revolution in Nigeria*. Chicago: University of Chicago Press.

Massey, Doreen. 1994. *Space, Place and Gender*. Minneapolis: University of Minnesota Press.

Massey, Doreen. 2005. *For Space*. London: Sage.

Matory, J. Lorand. 2005. *Black Atlantic Religion: Tradition, Transnationalism, and Matriarchy in the Afro-Brazilian Candomblé*. Princeton, NJ: Princeton University Press.

Matsinhe, Mario David. 2011. *Apartheid Vertigo: The Rise of Discrimination Against Africans in South Africa*. Farnham, Surrey: Ashgate.

Maxwell, D., Carol Levin, Margaret Armar-Klemesu, Marie Ruel, Saul Morris, and Clement Ahiadeke, eds. 2000. *Urban Livelihoods and Food and Nutrition Security in Greater Accra, Ghana*. Research Report No. 112. Washington, DC: International Food Policy Research Institute.

Mbembe, Achille. 2000. *On the Postcolony*. Berkeley: University of California Press.

Mbembe, Achille, and Sarah Nuttal. 2008. *Johannesburg: The Elusive Metropolis*. Durham, NC: Duke University Press.

McCaskie, T. C. 2006. "Writing, Reading, and Printing Death: Obituaries and Commeration in Asante." In *Africa's Hidden Histories: Everyday Literacy and Making the Self*, edited by Karin Barber, 341–384. Bloomington: Indiana University Press.

Meyer, Birgit. 1999. *Translating the Devil: Religion and Modernity Among the Ewe in Ghana*. Trenton, NJ: Africa World Press.

Miers, Suzanne, and Richard Roberts, eds. 2005. *The End of Slavery in Africa*. Madison: University of Wisconsin Press.

Moretti, Franco. 1987. *The Way of the World: The Bildungsroman in European Culture*. London: Verso.

Myers, Garth. 2011. *African Cities: Alternative Visions of Urban Theory and Practice*. London: Zed Books.

Nordstrom, Carolyn. 2007. *Global Outlaws: Crime, Money, and Power in the Contemporary World*. Berkeley: University of California Press.

North, Jeanne, Marian Fuchs-Carsch, Judy Bryson, and Sharna Blumenfeld. 1975. *Women in National Development in Ghana*. Accra: USAID.

Ntewusu, Samuel. 2005. "The Northern Factor in Accra: A Historical Study of Madina Zongo, 1957–2000," MA thesis, University of Ghana.

Ntewusu, Samuel. 2011. "Settling In and Holding On: A Socio-Economic History of Northern Traders and Transporters in Accra's Tudu: 1908–2008." PhD diss., University of Leiden.

Obeng-Odoom, Franklin. 2011. "The Informal Sector in Ghana under Siege." *Journal of Developing Societies* 27: 355–392.

Odoi, N. A. (2004). *A Brief History of Abokobi*. Accra: Presbyterian Press.

Odotei, Irene [née Quaye]. 1972. "The Ga and Their Neighbours, 1600–1742." PhD diss., University of Ghana.

Odotei, Irene. 1989. "What Is in a Name? The Social and Historical Significance of Ga Names." *IAS Research Review*, n.s., 5: 34–51.

Odotei, Irene. 1991. "External Influences on Ga Society and Culture." *IAS Research Review*, n.s., 7: 61–71.

Osei, Samuel Kwami, and Francis Antwi. 2004. "The Impact of Land Delivery and Finance in the Supply of Residential Accommodation in the Urban Centres of Ghana: The Case Study of Accra, Tema and Kumasi," MSc thesis, Royal Institute of Technology, Stockholm.

Osei-Tutu, John Kwadwo. 2000. *The Asafoi (Socio-Military) Groups in the History and Politics of Accra from the 17th to the Mid-20th Century*. Trondheim, Norway: Department of History, NTU, 2000.

Parker, John. 1998. "Mankraloi, Merchants and Mulattoes: Carl Reindorf and the Politics of "Race in Early Colonial Accra." In *The Recovery of the West African Past: African Pastors and African History in the Nineteenth Century*, edited by Paul Jenkins, 31–47. Basle: Basler Afrika Biblicgraphen.

Parker, John. 2000a. "Cultural Politics of Death in Early Colonial Accra." In *Africa's Urban Past*, edited by David M. Anderson and Richard Rathbone, 205–221. Oxford, UK: James Currey.

Parker, John. 2000b. *Making the Town: Ga State and Society in Early Colonial Accra*. Portsmouth, NH: Heinemann.

Patterson, Orlando. 1982. *Slavery and Social Death: A Comparative Perspective*. Cambridge, MA: Harvard University Press.

Pellow D. 2002. *Landlords and Lodgers: Socio-Spatial Organisation in an Accra Community*. New York: Praeger.

Perbi, Akosua Adoma. 2004. *A History of Indigenous Slavery in Ghana: From the 15th to the 19th Century*. Accra: Subsaharan.

Piot, Charles. 1999. *Remotely Global: Village Modernity in West Africa*. Chicago: Chicago University Press.

Pogucki, R. J. H. 1954. *Gold Coast Land Tenure*. Vol. 3, "Land Tenure in Ga Customary Law." Accra: Government printer.

Postma, Johannes. 2008. *The Dutch in the Atlantic Slave Trade, 1600–1815*. Cambridge: Cambridge University Press.

Prabhu, Anjali. 2007. *Hybridity: Limits, Transformations, Prospects*. New York: SUNY Press.

Quarcoo, A. K., N. O. Addo, and M. Peil. 1967. *Madina Survey: A Study of the Structure and Development of a Contemporary Sub-Urban Settlement*. Legon: Institute of African Studies, University of Ghana.

Quarcoopome, Samuel S. 1991. "The Politics and Nationalism of A. W. Kojo Thompson: 1924–1944." *Institute of African Studies Research Review*, n.s., 7 (1 and 2): 11–21.

Quarcoopome, Samuel S. 1992. "Urbanization, Land Alienation and Politics in Accra." *IAS Research Review*, n.s., 8 (1 and 2): 40–54.

Quarcoopome, Samuel S. 1993. "The Impact of Urbanization on the Socio-Political History of the Ga Mashie People of Accra: 1877–1957." PhD diss., Institute of African Studies, University of Ghana.

Quartey, K. A. B. 1974. *A Summary History of the Ghana Press, 1822–1960*. Accra: Ghana Information Services Department.

Quayson, Ato. 1997. *Strategic Transformations in Nigerian Writing: Rev Samuel Johnson, Amos Tutuola, Wole Soyinka and Ben Okri*. Oxford, UK: James Currey.

Quayson, Ato. 2003. "Social Imaginaries in Transition: Culture Heroism and the Genres of Everyday Life." In *Calibrations: Reading for the Social*, 30–55. Minneapolis: University of Minnesota Press.

Quayson, Ato. 2007a. *Aesthetic Nervousness: Disability and the Crisis of Representation*. New York: Columbia University Press.

Quayson, Ato. 2007b. "'I No Be Like You': Accra in Life and Literature." *PMLA* 122 (1): 252–255.

Quayson, Ato. 2010. "Signs of the Times: Discourse Ecologies and Street Life on Oxford St., Accra," *City and Society* 22 (1): 72–96.

Quayson, Ato. 2012. "Coevalness, Recursivity and the Feet of Lionel Messi." In "Special Forum on Jean and John Comaroff: Theory from the South." *Cultural Anthropology* 27 (1).

Quayson, Ato. 2013. "Africa's Diverse Diasporas: A Continental Longing for Form." In *The Oxford Handbook of Postcolonial Studies*, edited by Graham Huggan. Oxford: Oxford University Press.

Ray, Carina. 2013. "Interracial Sex and the Making of Empire." In *Blackwell Companion to Diaspora and Transnationalism Studies*, edited by Ato Quayson and Girish Daswani, 190–211. New York: Blackwell.

Razzu, Giovanni. 2005. "Urban Redevelopment, Cultural Heritage, Poverty and Redistribution: The Case of Old Accra and Adawso House." *Habitat International* 29: 399–419.

Reindorf, Carl Christian. 1895. *History of the Gold Coast and Asante, Based on the Traditions and Historical Facts: Comprising a Period of More than Three Centuries from 1500 to 1860*. London: Kegan Paul, Trench, Trubner.

Reis, João José. 1993. *Slave Rebellion in Brazil: The Muslim Uprising of 1835 in Bahia*. Trans. Arthur Brakel. Baltimore: Johns Hopkins University Press.

Report on the Census for Colony of the Gold Coast for the Year 1891. 1892.

Reynolds, Edward. 1974a. "The Rise and Fall of an African Merchant Class on the Gold Coast, 1830–1874." *Cahiers d'Études Africaines* 14 (54): 253–264.

Reynolds, Edward. 1974b. *Trade and Economic Change on the Gold Coast: 1807–1874*. London: Longman.

Reynolds, Jonathan T. 2008. "Social Mobility: Selling Transportation and Modernity in Independence-Era Ghana." *Working Papers in African Studies* no. 256, Boston University.

Roberts, Jonathan. 2003. "The Black Death in the Gold Coast: African and British Responses to the Bubonic Plague Epidemic of 1908." *Gateway* 3 (March): 1–53.

Robertson, Clare. 1984. *Sharing the Same Bowl: A Socio-Economic History of Women and Class in Accra*. Ann Arbor: University of Michigan Press.

Rothman, E. Natalie. 2011. *Brokering Empire: Trans-Imperial Subjects between Venice and Istanbul*. Ithaca, NY: Cornell University Press.

Roy, Ananya. 2005. "Urban Informality: Toward and Epistemology of Planning." *Journal of the American Planning Association* 71 (2): 147–158.

Sackeyfio, Naaborko. 2008. "The Stool Owns the City: Ga Chieftaincy and the Politics of Land in Colonial Accra, 1920–1950." PhD diss., University of Wisconsin, Madison.

Said, Edward. 2000. *Reflections on Exile and Other Essays*. Cambridge, MA: Harvard University Press.

Sarbah, Mensah John. 1904. *Fanti Customary Laws: A Brief Introduction to the Principles of the Native Laws and Customs of the Fanti and Akan Districts of the Gold Coast, with a Report of Some Cases Thereon Decided in the Law Courts*. London: William Clowes and Sons.

Schaumloeffel, Marco Aurelio. 2009. *Tabom: The Afro-Brazilian Community in Ghana*. Bridgetown, Barbados: Custom Books Publishing.

Schildkrout, Enid. 1978. *People of the Zongo: Transformation of the Ethnic Identities in Ghana*. Cambridge: Cambridge University Press.

Schweizer, Peter A. 2000. *Survivors on the Gold Coast: The Basel Missionaries in Colonial Ghana.* Accra: Smartline Publishers.

Sebba, Mark. 1997. *Contact Languages: Pidgins and Creoles.* New York: St. Martin's Press.

Selasi, Taiye. 2005. "Bye-bye Babar (Or: What Is an Afropolitan?)" LIP. http://thelip .robertsharp.co.uk/?p=76. Last accessed July 10, 2013.

Shipley, Jesse Weaver. 2013. *Living the Hiplife: Celebrity and Entrepreneurship in Ghanaian Popular Music.* Durham, NC: Duke University Press.

Simone, AbdouMaliq. 2004. *For the City Yet to Come: Changing African Life in Four Cities.* Durham, NC: Duke University Press.

Simone, AbdouMaliq. 2009. *City Life from Jakarta to Dakar: Movements at the Crossroads.* London: Routledge.

Simpson, William John Ritchie. 1905. *Treatise on Plague: Dealing with the Historical, Epidemiological, Clinical, Therapeutic and Preventive Aspects of the Disease.* Cambridge: Cambridge University Press

Simpson, William John Ritchie. 1909. *Report on Plague in the Gold Coast in 1908.* London: J and A Churchill.

Soyinka, Wole. 1981. *Aké: The Years of Childhood.* London: Rex Collings.

Stanley, Henry Morton. 1874. *Coomassie and Magdala: The Story of Two British Campaigns in Africa.* London: Sampson Low, Martin Low and Searle.

St. Clair, William. 2006. *The Door of No Return: The History of Cape Coast Castle and the Atlantic Slave Trade.* New York: BlueBridge.

Strickrodt, Silke. 2003. "'Afro-Brazilians' of the Western Slave Coast in the Nineteenth Century." In *Enslaving Connections: Western Africa and Brazil during the Era of the Slaver,* edited by J. C. Curto and P. E. Lovejoy, 213–224. Amherst, NY: Prometheus/ Humanity Books.

Strickrodt, Silke. 2008. "The Brazilian Diaspora to West Africa in the Nineteenth Century." In *AfricAmericas: Itineraries, Dialogues and Sounds,* edited by Ineke Phaf-Rheinberger and Tiago de Oliveira Pinto, 36–68. Madrid: Iberoamerica.

Svalesen, Lief. 2000. *The Slave Ship Fredensborg.* Bloomington: Indiana University Press.

Thompson, R. F. 1996. "Tap-tap, Fula-fula, Kia-kia: The Haitian Bus in Atlantic Perspective." *African Arts* 30: 36–45.

Trevallion, B. A. W., and Alan G. Hood. 1958. *Accra: A Plan for the Town.* Accra: Government printer.

Tutuola, Amos. 1952. *The Palm-Wine Drinkard.* London: Faber.

UNESCO. 2000. "The Old Accra Integrated Urban Development and Conservation Framework." Accra: UNESCO and the Ministry of Local Government.

Van der Geest, Sjaak. 2009. "'Anyway!': Lorry Inscriptions in Ghana." In Gewald et al., 253–293.

Verger, Pierre. (1968) 1976. *Trade Relations between the Bight of Benin and Bahia from the 17th to the 19th Century.* Trans. Evelyn Crawford. Ibadan, Nigeria: Ibadan University Press.

Verges, Francoise. 1999. *Monsters and Revolutionaries: Colonial Family Romance and Métissage.* Durham, NC: Duke University Press.

Wallerstein, Immanuel. 2011. *The Modern World System II: Mercantilism and the Consolidation of the European World-Economy, 1600–1750.* Berkeley: University of California Press.

Washburne, Christopher. 2008. *Sounding Salsa: Performing Latin Music in New York City.* Philadelphia: Temple University Press.

Waxer, Lise. 2002. *Situating Salsa: Global Markets and Local Meanings in Latin Popular Music.* New York: Routledge.

Wellington, H. Nii-Adziri. 2011. *Stones Tell Stories at Osu: Memories of a Host Community of the Danish Trans-Atlantic Slave Trade.* Accra: Sub-Saharan Publishers.

Wiena, M. 2009. *Ominous Calm. Autochtony and Sovereignty in Konkomba/Nanumba Violence and Peace, Ghana.* Leiden, The Netherlands: African Studies Centre.

Wilks, Ivor. 1961. *The Northern Factor in Ashanti History.* Legon: Institute of African Studies, University of Ghana.

Wilks, Ivor. 1989. *Asante in the Nineteenth Century: The Structure and Evolution of a Political Order.* Cambridge: Cambridge University Press.

Winsnes, Selena Axelrod. 2000a. *Ludwig Ferdinand Rømer's A Reliable Account of the Coast of Guinea, 1760.* Ann Arbor: University of Michigan Press.

Winsnes, Selena Axelrod. 2000b. "There Is a House on Castle Drive: The Story of Wulff Joseph Wulff." *History in Africa* 127: 443–448.

Wisnes, Selena Axelrod. 2004. *A Danish Jew in West Africa: Wulff Joseph Wulff, Biography and Letters 1836–1842.* Trondheim: Norwegian University of Science and Technology.

Wolfe, Ernie, III, ed. 2000. *Extreme Canvass: Hand-Painted Movie Posters from Ghana.* Los Angeles: Dilettante Press/Kesho Press.

Wolo, Mame [Martina Odonkor]. 2012. *Kaya-Girl.* Accra: Techmate Publishers.

Wright, Derek. 1988. "Scatology and Eschatology in Kofi Awoonor's This Earth, My Brother . . ." *International Fiction Review* 15 (1): 23–26.

INDEX

1891 Census, 38, 54, 78–79

Ababio, Kojo, 68
Abbas, Akbar, 245
Aboagye, Festus, 191, 193
Abonse Market, 38, 39, 255n2
Accra Mall, 28
Achebe, Chinua, 67, 215, 238
Achimota, 81, 172, 182, 187, 277n5
Acquah, Ione, 82–83, 260n4
Adabraka, 47, 49, 68–69, 81, 89, 90, 91, 258n21
Advertising (billboards), 11, 21, 31, 130, 134, 145, 147–53, 155, 156, 160, 177, 270nn15–16
Agbogbloshie, 225–27
Airport Residential Area (Airport), 10, 37, 66, 79, 80, 82, 235, 253n32
Akiwumi, Alfred Molade, 46
Akiwumi, S. O., 46, 73, 257n16
Akutso (pl. akutsei), 32, 38, 39, 69, 101, 106, 257n10, 265n11, 269n50; formation, 42–44, 264n 44
Akwamu(s), 33, 39, 44, 93, 103, 190, 264n3
Alata, 42–44, 45, 68, 69, 93, 244
Aliens Compliance Order, 57, 72
Allada, 43–44, 45, 106
Amoako, Salifu, 154
Amos, Alcione, and Ebenezer Ayesu, 52, 258n19, 259n34
Ampadu, Kwame Nana, 136, 138, 142, 144

Aneho, 101
Anglo-Danish Treaty, 30
Anglo-Dutch Treaty, 30
Ankra, Kwaku, 44, 46, 48, 52
Appiah, Kwame Anthony, 150
Armah, Ayi Kwei, 32, 143, 217
Armstrong, John, 55, 259n40
Asafo, 20, 27, 31, 32, 39, 43, 127, 129, 139, 141, 168, 176, 179, 191, 248n10, 251n37, 263n37, 270n10, 274n4
Asafoatse, 179, 262n4
Asare, Charles Agyin, 154
Ashanti(s), 37, 39, 42, 62, 72, 73, 74, 76, 79, 101, 103, 105, 106, 190, 192, 193, 205, 265n6, 274n6
Ashinte Blohum, 101
Awoonor, Kofi, 32, 214, 215, 216, 217, 229–38
Ayawaso, 33, 38, 39, 92, 93, 103

Bakhtin, Mikhail, 215, 216, 229, 238
Bannerman (family), 69, 100, 119, 120–21, 260n9
Barber, Karin, 137–38
Basel Mission (missionaries), 38, 88, 189, 100, 105, 262n7
Beckett, Samuel, 153, 246–48, 278n6
Benjamin, Walter, 14, 30
Bhachu, Parminder, 57, 259n36
Borland, 165, 181
Brand, Richard, 72, 78, 257nn9–10
Brazil House, 48–50

Brazil Lane, 48
British West Africa, 46–47
Brooks, George E., 115
Bubonic plague (1908), 33, 67, 68, 69,
    260n5
Burma Camp, 2, 82
Burrell, Jenna, 20
Busia, Kojo Abrefa, 34, 60

Caboceer, 102, 103, 108, 115, 265n9,
    267n24
Calvino, Italo, 239
Cantonments Road, 2, 3, 10, 11, 65,
    66, 70, 79, 82, 91, 102, 124, 154, 233,
    262–63n32
Casely-Hayford, J. E., 122
Central Business District (CBD), 10, 27,
    28, 65, 72, 73, 74, 76, 77, 79, 89, 90, 91,
    102, 154, 191, 203, 227
Chieftaincy, 32, 39, 43; and educated
    elites, 44, 50, 59, 61, 68, 69, 87, 88, 91,
    95, 102, 118, 121, 122, 123, 191, 258n30,
    260n10, 266n11, 268n41, 269n50
Chorkor, 80
Christiansborg Castle (Fort), 11, 33, 40,
    41, 50, 67, 91, 98–109, 113, 116, 117, 123,
    124, 190, 257, 264n3
Christiansborg Fort School, 21, 88, 89,
    96–103
Citational density, 143–44
Citational networks, 129
CitiFm, 163–64, 177, 178, 179
Cityness, 6–7, 31
Clayton, Anthony, and David Killingray,
    192, 193
Coconut Grove, 160–64, 168, 174, 177, 178,
    179, 180, 273n12
Cohen, Phil, 5
Colonial administration, 27, 32; admin-
    istrative function, 38; and census, 41,
    42–43; and chiefs, 51, 53–54, 70–92;
    and ethnicity, governmentality, 60, 66,
    68, 69; governmentality, 55, 57–59;
    interventions in the kola trade,
    262n23; and native rule, 50; and police,
    204, 261n17; and racial privilege, 121,

122, 123, 187, 191–93; and urban plan-
    ning, 100, 101, 105, 113, 115–19, 263n37,
    277n 5
Comaroff, Jean, and John Comaroff,
    33, 152–53, 239, 240, 248, 256n13,
    278n1
Conrad, Joseph, 215
Cosmopolitanism/cosmopolitan, 4, 53,
    82, 101, 113, 145–48, 153, 159, 163, 198,
    212, 217, 237, 262n32, 278n1
Crentsil, A. B., 25
Cybercafes (and comm centers), ix

Danish-Africans (Euro-Africans), 20, 21,
    42, 89, 103, 105, 106, 109, 110, 111–13
Dansoman Estates, 14, 70
Darko, Amma, 8, 32, 214, 215, 217–29,
    231, 232, 238, 276n4
De Boeck, Filip, and Margaret
    Plissart, 6
De Bruijn, Esther, 142, 201
Deflem, Mathieu, 192
Delueze, Gilles, and Félix Guattari,
    141–42, 145
Dickson, K. B., 72, 261nn13–14
Discourse ecologies, 129, 130, 132–33
Discursive environments, 129
Disease epidemics, 66, 68, 70, 71, 123
Doku, Noete, 102–3
Doortmont, Michel R., 119–23, 258n16,
    260n9
Dowuona, Frederick Noi, 123
Duncan-Williams, Nicholas, 154

Egblewogbe, Martin, 216
Enchantment, 20, 130, 150–53, 156, 159
Entextualization, 137–38, 139, 141, 143,
    144, 145, 151, 211
Enwezor, Okwui, 242
Expressive archive(s), 129, 130, 137
Expressive fragment, 21

Ferguson, Geroge Ekem, 119
Firmin-Sellers, Kathyrn, 87, 89, 257n9,
    263nn37–38, 264n43, 269n50
Fort Crévecoeur, 41, 44

Ga Mashie, 15, 19, 25, 26, 27, 31, 38, 42–43, 50, 53, 55, 57, 58, 60, 62, 64–65, 67, 69, 71–74, 76, 78, 81, 88, 89, 93, 95, 100–101, 103, 122–24, 205, 218, 222–24, 244, 260n10, 262n23, 264n45, 257n50, 264n45, 269n50

Glover, John (Captain), 192

Gordon Guggisberg (Sir), 71, 227, 277n5

Grant, Richard, and Jan Nijman, 67

Hart, Keith, 201, 206, 275

Harvey, David, 20, 64, 255n9, 250n1

Heward-Mills, Dag, 154

Hill, Lawrence, 150

Horizontal archaeologies, x, 30, 31, 155

Hutchison, Charles Francis, 119–23, 258n16, 260n9

Hutton-Mills, Thomas, 122

Hybridity (hybrid), 27, 31, 32, 38, 39, 43, 44, 47, 48, 52, 53, 62, 63, 64, 99, 101, 150, 165, 169, 180, 248, 259n37

Imagescape, 129, 130

IMF, 4, 66, 67, 152–55, 156, 195

Indirect Rule, 40, 53, 54, 55, 57 59, 87, 88, 117, 122

Influenza epidemic (1918), 67

Ipsen, Pernille, 108, 109, 112, 113, 114, 267

Irele, Abiola, 269n1

James Fort, 41, 48, 49, 106

James, C. L. R, 220, 276n3

Jameson, Frederic, 86, 152

Jamestown, 29, 30, 32, 36, 39, 52, 66, 60, 73, 76, 88, 112, 245n7, 251n45

Jamestown Harbor, 36, 60–61, 62, 63, 64, 65, 66, 67, 73

John Rodger (governor), 118

Justesen, Ole, 110, 111, 265nn9–10, 266n14

Kabir, Ananya, 165, 169

Kanda, 2, 10, 66, 90, 91, 174, 217, 232, 233, 235, 236

Kaneshie, 2, 65, 69–70, 77, 80, 91, 233, 260n8, 262n26, 271n3, 272n6, 274n4

Kaplow, Susan, 116, 117, 118

Kardo, Seidu (Alhaji), 204

Kimble, David, 121

Kinka, 41, 42, 44, 103, 109, 118, 266n11

Kinkawe, 101

Kòbòlò, 184, 185, 199–203, 209, 210, 212, 244, 245, 275n13

Kokomlemle, 2, 47, 49, 90–92, 94, 97

Kokomlemle Consolidated Lands Case, 86, 87–92, 94–95, 256n7, 258n21, 263n41, 264n46, 274n10

Koolhaas, Rem, 33, 240, 242–45, 248, 277, 278n4

Korle Bu, 170, 171

Korle Gonno, 67, 68–70, 80, 89

Kyei, Kojo Gyinaye, and Hannah Schreckenbach, 151

Kymlicka, Will, 56–57

Labone, 10, 66

Lagos, 7, 46, 47, 48, 52, 53, 76, 199, 240–49, 249n18, 275n13, 278n5

Lagos Colony, 192, 258

Lagos Town, 90

Laing, Kojo, 32, 237, 238

Larbi, Wordsworth, Odame, 81

Lefebvre, Henri, 19–20; rhythmanalysis, 217; spatial practice, 23, 28–30

Legon, 81, 95, 170, 172, 176, 184, 185, 186, 204, 206, 207, 233, 237, 263, 273n1

Lokko, Mae-Ling, 48, 265n5

Maclean, George (captain), 192

Madina, 78, 184, 185, 187, 202–4, 205, 244, 272n6, 276n23

Madina Zongo, 185, 202, 214, 205, 276n23

Makelaar, 44, 47, 52

Makola, 10, 14, 27–28; founding, 33, 37, 45, 76, 79, 81, 89, 90, 102, 154, 203, 227, 245, 271n3

Makwerekwere, 58, 259n39

Mamdani, Mahmood, 53–54

Mamprobi, 80

Man (manjii), 38, 68, 260n7

Mann, C. K., 168

Massey, Doreen, 5, 6, 20, 255n9

Matory, Lorand, J., 45, 46–47, 52, 60, 257n14, 258n17, 259n35
Mbembe, Achille, xi, 6, 210, 277
Miers, Suzanne, and Richard Roberts, 193
Ministries, 2, 10, 79
Moretti, Franco, 216
Motorized transport, 131–32
Multiculturalism, 38, 54–59, 63, 149, 162, 173, 174, 180, 259n40
Multiethnicity (multiethnic), 38, 53, 55–56, 59, 180, 191, 259n40
Myers, Garth, 6, 255n6

Nagôs (Anago), 45
Narika-Bruce, F. V., 122
National Congress of British West Africa (NCBWA), 120, 122
New York Times, 1–2, 4
Nima, 2, 65–66, 90–91, 96, 138, 203, 205, 228, 229, 232–34, 235, 237, 244, 245
Nkrumah, Kwame, 27, 37, 66, 70, 71, 82, 85, 138, 148, 235, 263n37, 268n41
Nleshie, 41, 42, 67, 109, 118
Nordstrom Carolyn, 202
Northern Territories, 27, 42, 51, 74, 119, 193, 204, 261n17
North Ridge, 47
Ntewusu, Samuel, 76, 124, 184, 203, 204, 205, 258n32, 261n18, 273n1, 274n8, 275n14, 276nn22–23
Nyaniba, 10, 66, 123

Oblempon, 31, 32, 179
Okaija, 103, 191, 265–66n11
Osei-Tutu John Kwadwo, 191
Osu, 1; as tourist destination, 2, 3, 4, 6, 10, 12, 31, 32, 33, 35, 38, 41, 54, 65, 66, 67, 71, 81, 85, 88, 89, 91, 92, 95, 96, 98, 99, 100, 101–25, 154, 244, 264n5, 264n7, 264n8, 266n12, 269n50, 272n6
Osu Alata, 101, 106
Osu Salem School, 100–101, 265n5
Otabil, Mensa, 154
Otublohum, 33, 42–45, 47, 50, 93, 244, 258n21

Oxford Street, 4; as archive, 132, 134, 145–50, 174, 239, 243; billboard advertising, 33, 41, 67, 98, 99, 100, 101, 102, 124, 125, 129, 130; cell phone advertising, 151–152; and enchantment, 153, 154, 155, 157; as high street, 10–16, 28; and Lagos, 271n3; shops/shopping, 23, 26, 27, 30; walking on, 20, 21

Parker, John, xi, 44–47, 85, 120, 257n12, 260n9, 263n36, 265–66n11, 268n 39
Patterson, Orlando, 114
Piot, Charles, 130
Prabhu, Anjali, 259n37
Price, Richard, and Sidney Mintz, 60

Quaque, Philip, 100
Quartey-Papafio (family), 119–20
Quartey-Papafio, A. B., 122
Quist, Emmanuel Charles, 122, 123

Rawlings, Jerry John, 27, 28, 81, 102, 106, 187, 190, 194–97, 203, 261n15, 272n10
Reindorf, Carl Christian (reverend), 123, 260n7, 262n46, 265n6, 268n39, 269n50
Reindorf, Charles, 89, 264n46
Richter, Emmanuel Johann, 112–13
Richter, Ernest, 123
Richter, Heinrich, 106, 112–13, 267n12
Richter, Philip Christian, 123
Ridge, 2, 10, 65, 66, 67, 68, 70, 79, 80, 81, 82, 118, 123, 124, 233, 277n5
Ringway Estates, 3, 10
Rothman, Natalie E., 56
Roy, Ananya, 5

Sabon Zongo, 77, 203, 227, 228
Salaga Market, 65, 74, 76
Saleh, Tayib, 215
Sawyer, A., 122
Scissors House, 50
Scriptural economy, 130, 134, 137, 139, 145
Sekyi, Kobina, 119, 122
Semiotic stacking, 142
Shipley, Jesse, 168, 180
Sidney (hip life musician), 138

Sill, Ulrike, 100
Simone, AbdouMaliq, 6–8, 20, 33, 240, 255n1, 271n18
Simpson, W. J. R., Sir, 68, 260n6
Slums, 4–7, 66, 90, 215, 217, 222, 227–28, 229, 232, 233, 235, 238, 275, 276
Small, Edward Francis, 122
Social imaginary, 130, 139–40, 142, 152–53, 190, 198, 199, 212, 234, 238, 244, 269n3
Sodom and Gomorrah, 203, 222–28, 232, 233, 276n4
Soyinka, Wole, 189–90, 247–48
Space: aggregations, 70; anamorphism, 257n10, 277n10; as kaleidoscope, 238; recycling, 244, 245, 248–49, 278n6; representational, 215, 216, 217; salsa, 149, 153, 178, 180; sociocultural, 64; urban, 4–6, 7, 8, 19–20, 22, 28, 29, 30, 32, 33, 66, 67, 78, 83–85, 97, 199, 202, 214, 219, 226, 229, 231, 232, 236, 237; urban recycling, 242–43
Spatial: analogues, 149, 152; deterritorialization, 91, 98, 99, 100, 104, 122, 124, 141–42; ecologies, 4, 39, 40, 42, 43, 48, 52, 71, 73, 77, 78, 81, 82, 83, 84, 86, 87; logics, 17; logics, traversal, 179, 200, 202, 203, 212, 213, 214; peripheries, 5, 6, 7; practice, 19–21, 22, 23–24; precepts, traversal, 30–32; spatial logic, 222; spatial logics, traversal, 228, 229, 231; temporalities, 29; traversal, 215–17, 219, 232, 233, 234, 235, 237, 238, 243, 244, 257n10, 265n5, 276n2; urban patterns, 8
Spatial aggregations, 31
Spatial fix, 64–67, 71–73, 97, 123, 260n1
Spatial logics, 17, 32, 200, 214, 231
Spatial practice(s), 24
Spatiality, 6, 17, 244
Svane, Elias (chaplain), 110–13

Tabon: Afro-Brazilians, 31, 37–38; arrival, 47; on becoming Ga, 43, 44–46, 64, 86, 91, 95, 244, 258n21, 259n32; names, 46–48; Portuguese trade language, 54, 60, 61–63; transnational trading links,

49, 50–51; urban skills diversification, 51–52
Taylor, Theodore (Nii Kwabena Bonne III), 124
Tesano, 2, 81, 186
Tigo, 3, 11, 12, 15, 123, 134, 145, 146, 148, 149, 150, 152, 156–57, 270n15, 271n23
Transnationalism, 4, 12, 32, 32, 33, 46, 52, 60, 66, 81, 99, 124, 130, 132, 134, 146, 148, 149, 150, 152, 153, 156, 160, 164, 165, 169, 173, 174, 179, 180, 181, 183, 184, 185, 212, 233, 271n16, 277n5
Trevallion, B. A. W., and Alan Hood, 70, 82–86
Tro-tro, 18, 19, 21, 23, 31, 32, 33, 135–36, 138, 142–45; scriptural economy, 151, 152, 154, 155, 184, 201, 210, 211, 212, 270n10
Tudu, 2, 45, 51, 65, 66, 76, 77, 81 89, 90, 124, 140, 203, 205, 228, 224, 258n32, 272n6

Urban transcripts, 130, 135

Van der Geest, Sjaak, 136, 139
Van Hein, H., 122
Vehicular language, 141–42, 144
Verger, Pierre, 45, 257n14
Verges, Francois, 259n37
Victoriaborg, 67, 70, 79, 82, 118, 123

Washburne, 165
Waxer, 165
Weku shia, 85
Wellington, Nii-Adziri, 107, 123, 124, 265n6, 266n12
West Legon (Shiashe), 204
Wetse Kojo, 44, 71
Wright, Derek, 230, 236
Wulff, Josef Wulff, 100, 107, 267n21

Yellow fever epidemic (1911), 67, 68

Zeleza, Paul, 52
Zongo(s), 40, 65, 76, 77, 90, 194, 203, 206, 207, 244, 261n19